Psychology in the Courts

Psychology in the Courts

INTERNATIONAL ADVANCES IN KNOWLEDGE

Edited by
Ronald Roesch
Raymond R. Corrado
and
Rebecca Dempster
Simon Fraser University, Burnady, Canada

Routledge
Taylor & Francis Group
LONDON AND NEW YORK

First published by Routledge

This edition published 2013 by Psychology Press

Published 2022 by Routledge
4 Park Square, Milton Park, Abingdon, Oxon OX14 4RN
605 Third Avenue, New York, NY 10017

Routledge is an imprint of the Taylor & Francis Group, an informa business

Typeset by Expo Holdings, Malaysia

Publisher's Note

The publisher has gone to great lengths to ensure the quality of this reprint but points out that some imperfections in the original copies may be apparent.

British Library Cataloguing in Publication Data

A catalogue record for this book is available from the British Library

ISBN 978-0-415-26892-9 (hbk)
ISBN 978-0-415-65400-5 (pbk)

Contents

Part 3: Civil and Criminal Court

Part 4: Eyewitness Evidence and Testimony

Preface

This is an exciting time for the field of psychology and law. The last 20 years have witnessed a rapid expansion, with psychologists now engaged in a wide range of roles in both the civil and criminal justice systems. Graduate programs specifically in psychology and law have proliferated, and there are now a number of joint degree programs in which graduates receive both a law degree and a doctoral degree in psychology.

The primary organizations representing psychology and law in North America—the American Psychology-Law Society (Division 41 of the American Psychological Association)—and Europe—the European Association of Psychology and Law—have held separate conferences for many years. At the EAPL annual conference in Siena, Italy in 1996, David Carson suggested that the two groups should jointly sponsor an international conference. This dinner table suggestion was quickly embraced by both APLS and EAPL, and the conference was held at Trinity College in Dublin, Ireland from July 6–9, 1999. The co-chairs of the conference were David Carson, a law professor at the University of Southampton, England, who represented EAPL, and one of the editors of this volume, Ronald Roesch, a professor of psychology at Simon Fraser University, who represented APLS. The conference was a huge success, attended by over 600 delegates from 27 countries. Virtually all the key professional groups were represented, including psychologists, lawyers, judges, psychiatrists, nurses, and social workers.

The conference was opened by a welcoming address by the President of Ireland, Mary McAleese, who got the conference off to a great start by focusing on the two disciplines of psychology and law. She drew on the 'Building Bridges' theme from her own presidency to discuss the importance of greater interaction between the two disciplines of psychology and law, to truly become a more interdisciplinary and international field. As President McAleese so aptly put it, "We should be open to drawing in new ideas, new applications, to consider fresh directions, to refuse arbitrary limits on intellectual exploration, to explore the fresh fields that an inter-disciplinary and cross-cultural outlook can offer us." We are honoured to include her address in this volume.

The organizers of the conference agreed that two books should be published based on selected papers presented at the conference. This volume focuses on psychology in the courts while the other volume, edited by David Farrington, Clive Hollin, and Mary McMurran, focuses on violent and sexual offenders. There were over 60 papers submitted for this volume, and unfortunately we had space to accept only about one-third of them. The selected chapters are grouped into five major sections: Adolescents, Juries, Civil and Criminal Court, Eyewitness Evidence and Testimony, and Victims of Crime. We are also pleased to include an invited address given by our colleague, James Ogloff.

We want to thank David Carson who did the bulk of the work in selecting a wonderful site for the conference at Trinity College and a masterful job of organizing a stimulating program for the conference. Jill Elliott was a pleasure to work with and she made sure the registration and scheduling went off without a hitch. Thanks also to Harwood Academic Publishers, for their suggestions for the organization of the two books and support for the book series.

The Dublin conference was clearly a success and it is our hope that this volume will give readers a sense of the intellectual energy and excitement that the conference participants experienced. The success of this conference led to an agreement that APLS and EAPL will co-sponsor a conference every four years, so we are already looking forward to the next one in 2003.

Ronald Roesch
Raymond R. Corrado
Rebecca Dempster

Contributors

Akintunde A. Akinkunmi (MBBS, LLM, MRCPsych) is Consultant Forensic Psychiatrist & Clinical Director, North London Forensic Service, Camlet Lodge Regional Secure Unit, Chase Farm Hospital Site, The Ridgeway, Enfield, Middlesex, EN2 8JL (Tunde.Akinkunmi@enfieldcc-tr.nthames.nhs.uk).

Peter B. Ainsworth is Senior Lecturer in the Department of Applied Social Science, University of Manchester, U.K. and is also Director of the Henry Fielding Centre for Police Studies and Crime Risk Management. His main research interests are in the fields of applied and forensic psychology, and in particular the application of psychology to policing. Correspondence: Henry Fielding Centre, 4th Floor Williamson Building, University of Manchester, Manchester M13 9PL (Peter. B. Ainsworth@man.ac.uk).

Michael Antonio received his Master's degree in Criminology from the Department of Sociology and Criminal Justice at the University of Delaware in 1999. He is currently working as an Associate Research Scientist in the Criminal Justice Research program at Northeastern University. Correspondence: Northeastern University, College of Criminal Justice, 716 Columbus Ave., Boston MA 02115 (miantoni@strauss.udel.edu).

Ramón Arce (Ph. D. 1989, University of Santiago de Compostela) is professor of Judicial Psychology at the University of Santiago de Compostela (Spain). His main research focus is jury decision making and judge decision making. Other research topics are eyewitness testimony and detection of faking behavior. He has published many articles, books-research, handbooks, and chapters in these areas in Spanish, French, English and Portuguese languages.

Michele Peterson-Badali is a registered psychologist and assistant professor in the Department of Human Development and Applied Psychology at the Ontario Institute for Studies in Education of the University of Toronto. For the past 15 years her research has focused on the youth justice system and children's rights issues, with a view to informing policy development in these areas.

Scott R. Beach is Director of the Survey Research Program at the University Center for Social and Urban Research at the University of Pittsburgh. He is also an Assistant Professor at The Graduate School of Public Health. He received his Ph.D. in social psychology from the University of Pittsburgh in 1993. His research interests include reactions to criminal victimization, the health effects of chronic stress, and the processes underlying self-reports of health behavior.

Angela Birt, received her Master's degree in Cognitive Psychology at the University of British Columbia in 1997. She is currently working on her Ph.D. at UBC and is conducting dissertation research at Dalhousie University in Halifax, Nova Scotia, Canada. Her research interests lie primarily within the domain of human memory, including such areas as recovered memory, "false" memories, trauma and memory, implicit and explicit memory, prospective memory, and the effects of aging and dementia on memory.

Eric Blaauw is senior lecturer at the Vrije Universiteit Amsterdam (VUA). He is the director of the Forensic Psychology Program, a program that focuses on risk assessment (for violence, suicide and other incidents) and guidance programs in jails and prisons and on the behavioral analysis of violent crimes. Blaauw received his Ph.D. at Leiden University. He is also the coordinator for the VUA of the exchange programs with Simon Fraser University and the University of Portsmouth. He is a board member of the Dutch Forensic Medical Association and editor of *MODUS, Journal of Criminal Investigations and Forensic Sciences*. Address: VUA-Clinical Psychology, Van der Boechorststraat 1, 1081 BT Amsterdam, The Netherlands (e.blaauw@psy.vu.nl).

Robert Blizard, FRSS, Medical Statistician, Department of Psychiatry and Behavioural Sciences, Royal Free and University College Medical School, Royal Free Campus, Rowland Hill Street, London, NW3 2PF.

Elizabeth Charman is Senior Lecturer in Psychology at London Guildhall University. Her most recent research concerns the competency of jurors in highly publicized cases, and the way in which they seek to understand and process trial evidence. Correspondence: Department of Psychology, Guildhall University, Calcutta House, Old Castle Street, London E1 7NT UK (Charman@lgu.ac.uk).

Irwin Cohen received a Master's degree in Criminology from the University of Toronto and a Master's of Applied Criminology from University of Ottawa. He is currently working on his Ph.D. in the School of Criminology at Simon Fraser University and conducting research on serious and violent young offenders. He has published in the areas of mental health, young offenders, youth justice, and terrorism/torture.

Raymond R. Corrado is a professor of Criminology at Simon Fraser University. He received his Ph.D. in Political Science at Northwestern University. He is well known for his research on the juvenile justice system in Canada, and he has also conducted research on terrorism. He recently organized a NATO Advanced Research Workshop on youth violence. Correspondence: School of Criminology, Simon Fraser University; Burnaby, BC, Canada; V5A 1S6 (corrado@sfu.ca).

Louise A. Cumbley, BSc. (Hons.), MSs. (Foren) is Assistant Psychologist, North London Forensic Service, Camlet Lodge Regional Secure Unit, Chase Farm Hospital Site, The Ridgeway, Enfield, Middlesex, EN2 8JL.

Francis C. Dane, Ph.D. is the William Heard Kilpatrick Professor at Mercer University (Macon, GA, USA). His primary position is in the Department of Psychology in the College of Liberal Arts, and also serves as Adjunct Professor of Research in the Department of Internal Medicine at the Mercer University School of Medicine. After earning a Ph.D. from the Social Psychology Program at the University of Kansas in 1979, Dane held academic positions at SUNY College at Oswego and Clemson University. He has published in the areas of research methods and ethics, social psychology, jury decision processes, prejudice and stereotypes, and in-hospital cardiopulmonary resuscitation. He is the Editor of *Contemporary Social Psychology.*

Rebecca Dempster is a doctoral student in the Clinical-Forensic program in the Department of Psychology at Simon Fraser University. She is currently completing a pre-doctoral internship at the Centre for Addiction and Mental Health in Toronto, Ontario. Her research interests include the study of violence risk assessment, sexual offenders, and psychopathy.

Francisca Farina (Ph.D. 1990, University of Santiago de Compostela) is professor of Basic Psychology at the University of Vigo (Spain). Her areas of research are family custody evaluations, eyewitnesses testimony, and judicial decision making.

Ian Freckelton is a barrister in full time practice in Melbourne, Australia. He is also Professor of Forensic Psychology and Honorary Associate Professor of Forensic Medicine at Monash University, Melbourne and Adjunct Professor of Law and Legal Studies at La Trobe University, Melbourne. He is the Editor-in-Chief of *Psychiatry, Psychology and Law* and the Editor of the *Journal of Law and Medicine*. Contact: c/o Barristers' Clerk Howells, Owen Dixon Chambers, 205 William Street, Melbourne, 3000, Victoria, Australia (I. Freckelton@latrobe.edu.au).

Jonathan Freedman obtained his B.A. from Harvard, and completed his Ph.D. in Psychology at Yale. He has taught at Stanford and Columbia, and now teaches at the University of Toronto. His research interests have included social influence, the effects of crowding, television violence, and more recently, legal issues.

Carrie Fried is a graduate student in community and developmental psychology at the University of Virginia. Her research focuses on adolescent criminal decision making and criminal culpability. Other research interests include the development of aggression and violence and the prevention of child abuse and neglect.

Eugenio Garrido (Ph.D. 1975, University of Salamanca) is full professor of Social Psychology in the Department of Social Psychology and Anthropology at the University of Salamanca. He is the coordinator of the Criminology Degree of the University of Salamanca, where he teaches psychology and law. His research interests are social cognitive theory, eyewitness testimony, police research, victimology and the detection of deception. Correspondence: Catedrático de Psicología Social, Facultad de Psicología, AVDA. de la Merced, 39005SALAMANCA (garrido@gugu.usal.es).

Gayla Goodman, BA (Hons.) Assistant Psychologist, North London Forensic Service, Camlet Lodge Regional Secure Unit, Chase Farm Hospital Site, The Ridgeway, Enfield, Middlesex, EN2 8JL.

Pär Anders Granhag, Assistant Professor, Department of Psychology, Göteborg University, Sweden. Current research focus: investigative interviews, eyewitness memory/meta-memory, and different psycholegal aspects of deception. Correspondence: Gothenburg University, Department of Psychology, P.O. Box 500, SE-405 30 Gothenburg, Sweden (pag@psy.gu.se).

Martin S. Greenberg is a Professor of Psychology and Chair of the Social Psychology Program at the University of Pittsburgh. He received his Ph.D. from the University of Houston and has taught at the University of Michigan and Washington University. He is co-author of *After the crime: Victim decision making*, and *Social psychology of the criminal justice system*. Correspondence: Department of Psychology, University of Pittsburgh, Pittsburgh, PA 15260 (Greenber@pitt.edu).

Valerie P. Hans is Professor of Sociology and Criminal Justice and Professor of Psychology at the University of Delaware, where she teaches courses on psychology and law, jury decision making, and other topics. She received her Ph.D. in Social Psychology from the University of Toronto. She is coauthor (with Neil Vidmar) of *Judging the Jury* (Plenum, 1986) and author of *Business on Trial* (Yale University Press, 2000), which examines how the public treats business and corporate wrongdoing.

Terry Honess is Reader in Psychology at City University, London. In addition to juror processing of trial evidence he researches family dynamics and their implications for adolescent adjustment.

Michael Hough is a Professor at the South Bank University in London. His recent publications include *Probation Round the World*. He is Director of the Social Policy Unit at the South Bank University.

Michael Levi is Professor of Criminology at Cardiff School of Social Sciences, Cardiff University, Wales. Most of his work has been on fraud and organised crime, and his most recent book, *White-Collar Crime and its Victims*, is published by Oxford University Press.

Jaume Masip is in the Department of Social Psychology and Anthropology at the University of Salamanca. He teaches social psychology of crime to criminology students, and is doing his Ph.D. on the nonverbal detection of deception. His research interests are nonverbal behavior, verbal and nonverbal detection of deceit, and the role of facial appearance on social judgments. He has given some courses on detection of deception to police officers and undergraduates.

Mary McAleese has served as the President of Ireland since 1997. After graduating from Queen's University Belfast, Mary McAleese was called to the Northern Ireland Bar and practiced mainly in criminal and family law. In 1975 she was appointed Reid Professor of Criminal Law, Criminology and Penology in Trinity College Dublin, a position she held until 1979 when she joined RTÉ as a journalist and presenter. She returned to the Reid Professorship at Trinity in 1981, while still continuing part-time with RTÉ. In 1987, Mary McAleese was appointed Director of the Institute of Professional Legal Studies which trains barristers and solicitors for the legal profession in Northern Ireland. In 1994, she was appointed a Pro-Vice Chancellor of Queen's University Belfast.

Mercedes Novo and **Dolores Seijo** have Ph.D. degrees in psychology and serve as experts in psychology in Spanish courts. Both conduct research on judicial decision making.

Candice Odgers is a Master's Student in the School of Criminology at Simon Fraser University. She is currently conducting research with female youth in conflict with the law, specifically with young women serving custodial sentences. She has published and presented in areas relating to the treatment of females by the youth justice system, female youth violence and homicide, risk assessment and female young offenders, as well as mental health and gender issues relating to juvenile justice.

James R. P. Ogloff is trained as both a lawyer and psychologist. He is an Endowed Professor of Law and Forensic Psychology at Simon Fraser University. He is also Director of Mental Health Services for British Columbia Corrections. He gave the 2000 Kenneth G. Gray Lecture to the Canadian Psychiatric Association (Prize for distinguished contributions to law and psychiatry) and received the 1995–1996 Award for Excellence in Professional Training from the Canadian Council of Professional Psychology Programs.

Stephen Porter received his doctorate from the Forensic Psychology program at the University of British Columbia in 1998. He is currently an Assistant Professor and Chair of the Forensic Psychology area at Dalhousie University in Halifax, Nova Scotia, Canada. His research interests include eyewitness and recovered memory, deception detection, trauma, and violent crime. He received a President's New Researcher Award from the Canadian Psychological Association. Correspondence: Dalhousie University, Department of Psychology, Halifax, N.S., B3K 4J1, CANADA (sbporter@is.dal.ca).

Joseph M. Price has been a trial lawyer with the 300-lawyer, Minneapolis-based, international law firm of Faegre & Benson LLP (Minneapolis, Denver, Des Moines, Frankfurt, London) since 1972. His practice focuses almost exclusively in the area of products liability defense, specializing in litigation involving medical devices and pharmaceuticals, toxic torts, and mass tort litigation. His experience includes litigation involving intra-uterine devices, mammary and orthopedic prostheses, urologic implants, cardiovascular devices, and a variety of prescription and over-the-counter drugs. He is a 1969 graduate of the University of Minnesota and graduated from the University of Minnesota Law School in 1972.

N. Dickon Reppucci has been a Professor of Psychology at the University of Virginia since 1976. He received his Ph.D. from Harvard University in 1968 and was an Assistant and Associate Professor at Yale University from 1968-1976. He is an author, co-author or editor of more than 120 professional books, chapters, and articles. His major research interests include children, families and the law, especially juvenile justice and adolescent development, and the prevention of child abuse and neglect.

Julian V. Roberts is a Professor of Criminology at the University of Ottawa and Editor of the *Canadian Journal of Criminology*. His recent publications include "Public Opinion, Crime and Criminal Justice" (with Loretta Stalans) and "Making Sense of Sentencing" (with David Cole). Address: Department of Criminology, University of Ottawa, P.O. Box 450, Station A, Ottawa, Ontario Canada K1N 6N5 (jroberts@uottawa.ca).

Ronald Roesch is Professor of Psychology and Director of the Mental Health, Law, and Policy Institute at Simon Fraser University in British Columbia, Canada. Professor Roesch received his Ph.D. in clinical and community psychology from the University of Illinois in 1977. His interests include research on forensic assessment and jail/prison mental health programs. He served as president of the American Psychology-Law Society and as editor of *Law and Human Behavior*. He is a fellow of the Canadian Psychological Association and the American Psychological Association. His most recent book, edited with Stephen Hart and James Ogloff, is *Psychology and law: The state of the discipline*. Correspondence: Department of Psychology; Simon Fraser University; Burnaby, BC, Canada V5A 1S6 (roesch@sfu.ca).

Joti Samra is a Ph.D. candidate in the Clinical-Forensic Psychology program at the Mental Health, Law, and Policy Institute at Simon Fraser University. Ms. Samra's research interests include response bias and malingering in personal injury contexts, consistency and biases in parole decision-making, and public attitudes toward the legal system. Correspondence: Department of Psychology; Simon Fraser University; Burnaby, BC, Canada V5A 1S6 (jsamra@sfu.ca).

Jerry I. Shaw is a Professor of Psychology at California State University, Northridge. He received his Ph.D. in social psychology from UCLA in 1969 and spent three years as a visiting professor at the University of Göteborg, Sweden, and one year as resident director of California State University's international programs in Sweden and Denmark. He has published frequently in the areas of attribution, social cognition, and psychology and law. His recent research has focused on defendant status effects and the effects of eyewitness testimony vs. physical evidence on jury decision making.

John Shaw is an assistant professor of psychology at Lafayette College in Easton, Pennsylvania. He received a B.A. in Latin and Economics from

Vanderbilt University in 1977. After graduating from Stanford Law School in 1980, he practiced criminal law as a prosecutor and a public defender in Los Angeles, California. John received his Ph.D. in social psychology from UCLA in 1994, and he taught at the University of Texas at El Paso for three years before joining the psychology department at Lafayette in 1997. His research interests include eyewitness memory, eyewitness confidence, and jury decision making. Correspondence: Department of Psychology, Lafayette College, Easton, PA 18042-1781 (e-mail: shawj@lafayette.edu).

Paul Skolnick is a professor of Psychology at California State University, Northridge. He received his Ph.D. in social psychology from Purdue University in 1969 and spent two years as a visiting professor at the University of Salzburg in Austria and the University of Malaya in Malaysia. His recent research focuses on empirical studies in jury decision making and the effects of defendant characteristics such as race and status on verdicts. Correspondence: Department of Psychology, California State University at Northridge, Northridge, CA 91330 (paul.skolnick@csun.edu).

Emma Spjut, M.Sc., Department of Psychology, Göteborg University, Sweden. Currently Emma is studying different aspects of the Cognitive Interview.

Merrie Jo Stallard, is managing partner at Litigation Insights, a litigation and communication consulting firm. She has provided litigation support, including research design, issue analysis, mock trials and focus groups, to a variety of clients, and has been instrumental in the development of thematic strategies for case presentation. Stallard earned her M.A. in Social Psychology and Ph.D. in Communication Studies at the University of Kansas. She continues to research jury decision making and reduction strategies for hindsight bias. Correspondence: Litigation Insights, 6400 W. 110th Street, Suite 203, Overland Park, KS 66211 (mjstallard@litigationinsights.com).

Aldert Vrij is Professor of Social Psychology at the University of Portsmouth (UK). His main research interests now lie in deception, both in nonverbal correlates of deception and verbal correlates of deception, the evidence of child witnesses, and police officers' shooting behaviour. He has published more than 200 articles and 5 books on the above topics. Correspondence: University of Portsmouth, Psychology Department, King Henry Building, King Henry 1 Street, Portsmouth, PO1 2DY, UK (aldert.vrij@port.ac.uk).

Diane Warling is a Ph.D. Candidate in the School and Child-Clinical Psychology program at the Ontario Institute for Studies in Education of the University of Toronto. Her research interests are in the area of juvenile justice policy and programs for young offenders. Diane also works for The Arson Prevention Program for Children at the Centre for Addiction and Mental Health, Clarke Division. Correspondence should be sent to Diane Warling, c/o TAPP-C, Centre for Addiction and Mental Health, Clarke Site, 250 College St., Toronto, Ontario, M5T 1R8 (diane_warling@camh.net).

Frans Willem Winkel is director of the Achmea Foundation Victim and Society (Stichting Achmea Slachtoffer en Samenleving) sponsored victimology program associated with the department of Clinical Psychology of Vrije Universiteit Amsterdam (VUA). He studied criminal law (MA-law) at Erasmus University Rotterdam, psychological methodology at the University of Amsterdam (MA-psych.), and earned a Ph.D. from the social psychology program at VUA. He is president of the European Association of Psychology and Law (EAPL), and serves on the Executive Board of the World Society of Victimology (WSV). Together with Aldert Vrij he is co-directing the Amsterdam-Portsmouth program on "Discrimination in Legal Contexts." Address: VUA-Clinical Psychology, Trans1/Bs1, NL-1081BT Amsterdam, The Netherlands (fw.winkel@psy.vu.nl).

Jennifer Woolard is an Assistant Professor of Criminology and Psychology at the University of Florida Center for Studies in Criminology and Law. She received her Ph.D. in community and developmental psychology at the University of Virginia. Jennifer's research focuses on adolescent development and the legal system, and violence against women. Jennifer is also a member of the MacArthur Network on Adolescent Development and Juvenile Justice with several projects focusing on juveniles.

Keith Woythaler and Tana Zerr are both undergraduate psychology majors at Lafayette College. Keith and Tana worked on this research as part of Lafayette's EXCEL Scholar program, and both plan on attending graduate school to pursue doctorate degrees in social or clinical psychology.

John Yuille is a Professor of Psychology and Chair of the Forensic Psychology program at the University of British Columbia. Dr. Yuille received his doctorate from the University of Western Ontario in 1967. He has published widely on eyewitness memory, child sexual abuse, and criminal investigation approaches.

Patricia Zapf is an Assistant Professor of Psychology in the Clinical Psychology-Law Concentration at the University of Alabama. She received her Ph.D. in Clinical-Forensic Psychology from Simon Fraser University in Canada. Dr. Zapf's research interests include conceptual models of competency (criminal and civil), the development and validation of forensic assessment instruments, forensic evaluation, and mental health law. Contact: Department of Psychology, University of Alabama, Box 870348, Tuscaloosa, AL, 35487-0348 (pzapf@bama.ua.edu).

Opening Address
President Mary McAleese

Céad míle fáilte romhaibh go léir. Tá áthas an domhain orm go bhfuil mé anseo libh inniu.

I am delighted to be here with you today to officially open this Conference and I would like to thank my old friend David Carson, Chair of the Organising Committee, for his very kind invitation. You are all most welcome to Dublin, and I hope that your stay here will be both productive and enjoyable.

Some of you may know that the theme for my Presidency is 'Building Bridges'. Little did I know, when I chose it, that it would include building bridges between the disciplines of psychology and law. Let alone on an international scale! However I am very pleased to do so. Particularly as you have chosen such an appropriate city as Dublin for your Conference.

The breadth and depth of topics to be considered at this Conference clearly demonstrates how the study of psychology and law has blossomed in recent years. The old stereotype, that it was all about eyewitnesses and memory—occasionally about juries—has been shown to be too limited for present day needs. Although we shouldn't perhaps, totally ignore its value in relation to juries, particularly if you go along with the view of Abraham Lincoln that: "A jury too frequently has at least one member more ready to hang the panel than to hang the traitor."

But I think recent studies have demonstrated that we should set our sights higher—that the scope for an inter-disciplinary approach is far broader than had previously been imagined. To continue my bridge analogy, if those old days were represented by the Ha'penny Bridge—which you may know is a narrow pedestrian bridge that crosses the River Liffey not far from this College—then the present state of psychology and law may be better represented by O'Connell Bridge, which also crosses the Liffey. The point to note about O'Connell Bridge is that it is wider than it is long. It therefore allows for a far more productive and varied level of exchange between one side and the other.

That can only be of benefit to both disciplines. And indeed the expansion of interest in pooling knowledge and ideas, exemplified by the numbers of papers and delegates at this Conference, must be applauded. If the full potential of that approach is to be realised, I suggest that a number of challenges lie ahead.

The first is Internationalism. Is the international character and potential of psychology and law being realised? While we must always be mindful of the significance of different cultures and goals, we should also acknowledge that different legal systems, laws, procedures and practices provide both lawyers and behavioural scientists with a rich and varied source of insight, experience and information from which to learn. We do not all need to use the same bridge to cross the river, especially at rush hour—and even more especially in Dublin. We should be open to drawing in new ideas, new applications, to consider fresh directions, to refuse arbitrary limits on intellectual exploration, to explore the fresh fields that an inter-disciplinary and cross-cultural outlook can offer us.

This Conference has representation from all five continents. Some countries are establishing their psychology and law associations. Hopefully we will all look for the wisdom that comes from insight and experience, whether negative or positive, outside as well as within, our own countries. We can always learn from others. I note, for example, that you have symposia on developments in restorative justice, whose origins have been traced to the Maoris of New Zealand. And many of you will, today, be debating the respective merits of investigatory and adversarial trial procedures.

Second, has the psychology-law bridge been designed for one or for two-way traffic? It is an inter-disciplinary subject. But this Conference, like comparable Conferences, is dominated by contributions from psychologists. The proportion of lawyers attending—and I am sure you are particularly gratified by the number of judges at this Conference—is growing. But more could and should be done to involve lawyers. As someone who has both practised and taught law, I know only too well how conservative and narrowly-focused that profession can be. Even those starting out on the career can quickly become caught up in 'how it has always been', or 'what is appropriate'. In professional practice both psychologists and lawyers must, quite rightly, work with the existing law and practices of their country. But law is also about finding better ways of investigating, deciding about and responding to crime, about better ways of examining witnesses, demonstrating proof, making judgments. Psychology can contribute much to this process. But we need to have two-way traffic, for both sides to engage fully in the debate. Can more be done to ensure this? I note that some of you will be discussing the potential for psychology to contribute to legislative law reform. That, surely, is an important way forward.

These, Ladies and Gentlemen, are a few of the challenges for psychology and law. I am sure there are many more. Where professional boundaries meet is often a place where walls are built—high walls which obscure the view each profession has of the other. The walls so often demarcate territory into which the other does not stray. It takes a certain professional humility to be willing to look over the wall. It takes a certain professional generosity to create pathways across the wall. That is what this Conference is engaged in—an open declaration of war on the professional vanity which impedes productive sharing—an exciting showcasing of the possibilities opened by professional humility and generosity.

I congratulate you on your openness. I hope you will leave this Conference refreshed, recommitted to your own vocation and with a wider understanding of the vocation of others, with many new friends made, many new shared memories—and much food for future thought and action. I trust you will have a good Conference and I am sure that you will find Dublin the most enjoyable of cities.

Go n-eiri go geal libh.

Invited address

JINGOISM, DOGMATISM AND OTHER EVILS IN LEGAL PSYCHOLOGY: LESSONS LEARNED IN THE 20TH CENTURY

James R. P. Ogloff

In the waning years of the last century, the influential American jurist Oliver Wendell Holmes rejected the mechanical view of the law commonly held in English Common Law and in early American and Canadian jurisprudence. The prevailing view was that to make a decision in a case, a judge need only review the facts of the case, identify the relevant principles from common law, and apply those principles to the facts with logic and due diligence. In one of his most famous quotations, Holmes wrote that

> The life of the law has not been logic: it has been experience. The felt necessities of the time, the prevalent moral and political theories, intuitions of public policy, avowed or unconscious, even the prejudices which judges share with their fellow-men, have had a good deal more to do than the syllogism in determining the rules by which men should be governed. (Holmes, 1881, p. 1)

As Holmes' quotation emphasizes, the law is influenced by the moral, political, public, and prejudicial influences that so pervade human society. As such, it seems only fitting that the discipline that studies human behavior and mental processes—psychology—should come to play a role in the law.

Just as the 20th century has seen a dramatic change in the way in which the law operates—at least in western countries, so too has it seen the emergence of the field of legal psychology. In this chapter, I will briefly review the birth and development of legal psychology in the United States. Although the field has seen strong development, particularly in the latter quarter of this century, the field must address and resolve a number of issues to ensure that the field develops to its potential—and gains international stature—as we enter the 21st century. Reflecting the title of this chapter, the issues to be addressed are fundamental and they permeate much of the work done in legal psychology. Rather than being fatalistic, the position taken here is that the field will benefit by recognizing and addressing these "evils." Before turning to those issues, though, it is important to trace briefly the roots and development of the legal psychology movement in the United States.

THE ROOTS AND DEVELOPMENT OF LAW AND PSYCHOLOGY IN THE TWENTIETH CENTURY

The development of the legal psychology movement has occurred more by chance than by planning. Indeed, as Melton (1990) has detailed elsewhere, the course of psycholegal studies (or whatever you want to call "it") has not been particularly well plotted. One would be hard pressed to find a common theme—let alone a common course—in the research and application of psychology to the legal system. The movement largely has been driven by psychologists, often with little knowledge of the law, conducting studies or practicing in areas of interest to them, based n their own disciplinary pedagogy. Freud himself, in 1906, in a speech to Austrian Judges, suggested that psychology has important applications for their field (Brigham, 1999).

Only recently have those in the area really begun to develop an integrated approach to the study of the law and legal systems. To a large extent, the success and impact of the legal psychology movement depends on the quality and diversity of our scholarship, and our ability to apply that knowledge to the legal system. Although the number of psychologists working in areas relevant to the law has grown, and the areas investigated have been expanded somewhat, the legal psychology movement still is relatively obscure, especially within the law.

As the quote by Holmes that appeared at the outset of this chapter alludes, the roots of the legal psychology movement can be traced back over 100 years to the period when legal scholars began to insist that to fully understand the law, we must examine and understand the social contexts from which the law was derived and that ultimately are influenced by the law (Friedman, 1985; Purcell, 1973). This perspective, which came to be known as sociological jurisprudence, "insisted ... [on] empirical observations of changing social conditions and [the replacement of] pseudologic with 'experience'" (White, 1976, p. 252). It was no longer enough to "know the law" by studying judicial opinions, the method that had become the cornerstone of legal systems in North America that were based on English common law. Indeed, Oliver Wendell Holmes (1897) himself wrote that "for the rational study of law ... the black-letter man may be the man of the present, but the man of the future is the man of statistics and the master of economics" (p. 469).

Following sociological jurisprudence, other movements evolved that also challenged the law to be aware of social and legal "realities" (see Purcell, 1973; Schlegel, 1979, 1980; Tomkins & Oursland, 1991; Twining, 1973; White, 1972). These groups, such as the legal realists, advocated drawing upon the social sciences for methodologies and perspectives from which to examine law, legal process, and legal decision-making (Kalman, 1986; Schlegel, 1979, 1980; Twining, 1973, 1985).

The first director of Harvard's Psychological Laboratory, Hugo Munsterberg, a student of Wilhelm Wundt at the University of Leipzig, is considered to be the "founder" of applied psychology (Boring, 1950; Hale, 1980; Moskowitz, 1977). Among other things, Munsterberg advocated applying psychology to the law, and criticized lawyers and judges for not embracing the research of psychologists that could be applied to law (Loh, 1981). In 1908, Munsterberg published *On the Witness Stand* (1908), a book in which he reviewed a number of "psychology and law topics." He ended his introduction by writing that "my only purpose is to turn the attention of serious men to an absurdly neglected field which demands the full attention of the social community" (p. 12). Happily, as we now know, psychologists have embraced the field of legal psychology in growing numbers. Were we to travel back some 90 years though, it would have seemed as though no rational lawyer would have given even a second thought to the potential that psychology could bring to the law.

Indeed, following the publication of Munsterberg's book, rather than embracing psychology and psychological research, lawyers and scholars chastised Munsterberg. In 1909, the renowned legal evidence scholar, John H. Wigmore (1909), criticized Munsterberg's work in a satire published in the *Illinois Law Review* (see also, Moore, 1907). Wigmore's criticism, reflecting the sentiment of many other legal scholars, was that Munsterberg's claims were exaggerated, and that psychology had not ascertained the data necessary to support Munsterberg's criticisms of the law. In his satire, Wigmore subjected Munsterberg's work to the scrutiny of cross-examination in a mock libel trial in which Munsterberg was accused of claiming more than his science could support or offer. Not surprisingly, Munsterberg was found guilty of exaggerating his claims (Ogloff, Tomkins, & Bersoff, 1996).

Despite Munsterberg's "trial," movements such as sociological jurisprudence and legal realism led to the integration of social science, including psychology, into the law school curriculum. At the same time, too, the importance of social realities was recognized by the United States Supreme Court in *Muller v. Oregon* (1908), a pivotal case that helped lead to the demise of the strictly "mechanical" view of the law. Curt Muller was a laundry owner who had been convicted of violating an Oregon statute that limited the workday of women who worked in factories or laundries to 10 hours. Muller argued that the statute was unconstitutional—a violation of the right to contract—and appealed his conviction to the U.S. Supreme Court. Arguing on behalf of the state of Oregon was Louis D. Brandeis, one of the nation's best-known lawyers, who was himself later to sit on the Court. As part of the case, Brandeis submitted an extensive brief.[1] Only a small part of the brief was devoted to legal arguments; the great majority of it contained non-legal materials relating the injurious effects of long workdays on women's health. It included empirical studies bearing on the topic of the effects of excessive work, especially on women; and reports of various commissions, conferences, both from the U.S. and in Europe. The Supreme Court upheld the constitutionality of the statute, and in his majority opinion, Justice Brewer made reference to the "very copious collection" of material that Brandeis had submitted. The term "Brandeis brief" soon became used to describe any collection of non-legal materials submitted in a court case, and the term remains in use today.

The original Brandeis brief remains the source of some controversy. For one thing, it is ironic that the liberal Brandeis compiled a brief that made reference to "the periodical semi-pathological state of women" and the existence of "general 'female weakness'" (quoted in Monahan & Loftus, 1982, p. 463); "this argument infringed on efforts, already underway, to secure equal treatment for women in other areas" (Monahan & Walker, 1994, p. 8). Brandeis believed this was necessary, however, because the Supreme Court had recently upheld a similar statute that applied to men in *Lochner v. N.Y.* (1905). The brief has also been criticized because of the low quality of the empirical evidence presented; it consisted primarily of "broad value-laden statements supported largely by casual observation and opinion" (Monahan & Walker, 1994, p. 8). But it must also be remembered that social science research was in a primitive state at this time.

Over the next few decades, criticisms of the "formalist" view, and suggestions to broaden the scope of legal thinking, culminated in what became known as the legal realist movement, which emerged in clear form about 1930 (White, 1972). The legal realist movement had a deep and lasting impact on legal thinking, scholarship, and practice. Melton (1990) has pointed to three important tenets of legal realism:

1. Law is the behavior of judges, whose decisions are necessarily affected by their personal experiences and biases.
2. Law is intended to promote social welfare.
3. To accomplish the ultimate goal of promotion of the common good, the legal system profits from systematic examination of social reality.

If these tenets are accepted, it is clear that psychology can provide assistance to the law in reaching its goals. It can help in examining the "personal experiences and biases" of judges, and, perhaps more important, can aid in the "systematic examination of social reality." Although legal realism as an identifiable movement had lost its force and vitality by the 1950s, many of its ideas have been incorporated into the fabric of contemporary legal thinking. It has become a cliche to say, "we are all realists now" (Finkelman & Grisso, 1994; Monahan & Walker, 1994).

The effects of the "realist revolution" can be seen in the famous Supreme Court school desegregation case, *Brown v. Board of Education* (1954). Over four decades later, the case is still "the best-known use of social science in any area of law" (Monahan & Walker, 1994, p. 148). Thirty-two social scientists—sociologists, anthropologists, psychologists, and psychiatrists—signed a "Brandeis brief" that was submitted on behalf of the plaintiffs. It described the damaging effects of segregated schools on the children who attended them. The Court ruled unanimously that segregated schools were unconstitutional. In its decision, the Court cited a number of the sources mentioned in the brief in its famous footnote 11, "the most controversial footnote in American constitutional law" (Rosen, 1980, p. 9).

The Court's decision was greeted by many as a sign that social science research had "come of age;" it had been taken seriously by the Supreme Court, and had a visible impact on the Court's decision. But the social science contribution was also the object of criticism. Some of the criticism came from those who opposed the decision. But even some of those who favored it expressed doubts. Cahn (1955), for example, worried about grounding constitutional rights on contemporary thinking in the social sciences. His concern was that while social psychologists of the day were liberal and egalitarian, the possibility existed that in the future it would be possible for racist or otherwise unpalatable notions to be presented as science. With such notions shrouded in science, the state of peoples' constitutional rights would be jeopardized.

From the 1920's until the 1940's, several eminent law schools included social science material into their law courses. Even more surprising, perhaps, is that psychologists and other social scientists were hired as part of law faculties beginning in the late 1920s (Kalman, 1986; Loh, 1981; Schlegel, 1979, 1980; Stevens, 1983). Interestingly, in the 1920s and 1930s, at least two books were published on the topic of "legal psychology"—a term for the field which has been resurrected by Small (1983) and Ogloff (in press). In 1926, M. Ralph Brown published a book called

Legal Psychology: Psychology Applied to the Trial of Cases, to Crime and its Treatment, and to Mental States and Processes. Then, in 1931, Harold E. Burtt published a book with the title *Legal Psychology*. The term "legal psychology" has appeared periodically from those early years until recent times (see, e.g., Parker, 1980).

For reasons that have not been entirely explained (see Ogloff, in press), the early legal psychology movement did not succeed. The movement was not rekindled until the 1960's; however, it has gained considerable momentum since that time (Ogloff et al., 1996). A significant milestone occurred along the way in 1976 when, for the first time, "psychology and the law" was reviewed in the *Annual Review of Psychology* (Tapp, 1976). Psychology has once again made its way into case books, and into the law school curriculum. Some law schools even have opened up more doors to social scientists, bringing them once again into law schools as faculty (Grisso, Sales, & Bayless, 1982; Melton, 1990; Melton, Monahan, & Saks, 1987; Ogloff et al., 1996; Tapp, 1976; Wexler, 1990). Furthermore, several graduate programs in legal psychology have been developed, including a few joint-degree programs that offer students both a law degree and doctoral degree in psychology (Ogloff et al., 1996). In addition, a multitude of journals and books in the area now exist—quite frankly, too many for anyone person to read.

Despite its long history, though, the legal psychology movement has had limited impact on law, and, until recently, it was focused primarily in North America. Support for the concerns I raise can be found in countless legal decisions, statutes, and legal policy decisions. In fact, we still are at the stage in legal psychology to celebrate those rare instances when the law does take heed of our work. For example, following an extensive review of the judiciary's use—or lack thereof—of child development research, Hafemeister and Melton (1987) concluded that:

> The use of social science is still controversial and rather uncommon, especially in state courts. Courts appear unsure of whether and how to use social science to examine the policy questions that they have been asked to decide in recent decades. As a result ... reliance on social science is still largely a "liberal" practice of judges who have an expansive view of the judiciary's role in shaping legal doctrine and protecting disenfranchised groups (p. 55).

In conclusion, the legal psychology movement has seen strong growth in the past thirty years. As the large number of attendants at this conference affirms, the field is beginning to develop internationally. As noted at the outset of this chapter, though, to take full advantage of the momentum we have gained, and to ensure that as the field develops, it does so in a manner that will be of maximum benefit to all. What follows, then, is a list of some observations I have made of some father obvious shortcomings in the field.

THE "EVILS" IN LEGAL PSYCHOLOGY

Jingoism

> -*n.* blatant or aggressive patriotism (applied to bellicose patriots after the use of *by Jingo!* in the refrain of a nineteenth century musical hall song).

As I begin to discuss some of the evils, shortcomings really,[2] of the legal psychology field, it seems appropriate that I begin with the concern that relates most directly to the very essence of the first international conference on legal psychology—jingoism. As noted above, jingoism pertains to being focused narrowly on one's own country. Unfortunately, much of the research and scholarly writing in the legal psychology literature focusses narrowly on one nation or another. Moreover, it is not even unusual that articles do not even go beyond jurisdictional boundaries within a nation.

Although much of the work in our field is specific to a particular nation or some select nations (e.g., death penalty research), the majority of the work we do is relevant across national borders. Particularly in large, insular, nations like the United States and to a lesser extent Great Britain, scholars in legal psychology sometimes ignore the differences in laws among nations. Such oversights are very limiting. As I have written elsewhere with colleagues, to develop and evaluate policy on matters such as mental health and criminal justice, considerable insight can be gained from the experiences gleaned in other nations (see Roesch, Ogloff, & Eaves, 1995).

To advance our understanding of principles in legal psychology we must consider the legal and social reality of other jurisdictions/nations for at least two reasons. First, as our field is evolving, we are beginning to articulate actual principles of behavior and we are gaining an understanding of the reality of law. As a result, we can test the validity of our work by assessing the extent to which our work is valid across political and national boundaries.

In addition, besides simply studying the influence, effect, and reality of laws on people, we in legal psychology strive, at least to some extent, to effect changes in society that help to improve our legal and social condition (Fox, 1999). By gaining some familiarity into the laws and legal traditions of other nations, we can surely benefit from gaining an insight into how matters are handled. Simply stated, we can learn from others' mistakes—and from their insights. By learning from what other nations do, we can enhance the scope and influence of our own work.

Dogmatism

> *n.* a statement or opinion forcibly asserted as if authoritative and unchallengeable, relating to a person prone to such statements, based on assumptions rather than empirical observations (Latin from Greek—opinion, belief, from *dukein* "to seem good").

As with all other areas of scholarship, dogmatism stifles creativity and progress within legal psychology. This is such a fundamental point, that to mention it here would seem supererogatory. Although discussion of this point does not require much space, it still is important enough to bear mentioning. By being dogmatic and adopting unyielding positions, one runs the very great risk of rejecting or ignoring important information that has the potential of enhancing our understanding of such matters. Furthermore, such behaviour is unethical (see Committee on Ethical Guidelines for Forensic Psychologists, 1991). Within legal psychology, researchers have occasionally adopted dogmatic positions, in spite of competing research findings.

Without identifying out particular authors or studies, it is apparent that the so-called "false" or "hidden memory" syndrome debate has resulted in some researchers taking hard-line positions (see Beyerstein & Ogloff, 1998). Given that the questions underlying this area of research are particularly complex, the adoption of rigid positions seems premature and particularly inappropriate. Moreover, given the implications for public policy, those taking such positions may be doing a disservice to the public. Beyond the concerns regarding the adoption of dogmatic positions in research and scholarship, practitioners in forensic psychology often take dogmatic positions on matters in dispute in particular cases. Rare is the case indeed when such positions ever would be warranted. Taking such positions brings our profession into disrepute. We all have heard too often about "whores in the courtroom" (American Judicature Society, 1993; Faust & Ziskin, 1988). Beyond such criticisms, though, lies the very real possibility that rather than furthering justice, our work may jeopardize it when practitioners adopt firm positions when not warranted.

It is perfectly appropriate for professionals to adopt differing opinions on some matters where reasonable people may disagree. Indeed, the "Specialty Guidelines for Forensic Psychologists" make reference to this by providing that the obligation to "present their findings, conclusions, evidence, or other professional products in a fair manner" "does not preclude forceful representation of the data and reasoning upon which a conclusion or professional product is based" (Guideline VII.D., Committee on Ethical Guidelines for Forensic Psychologists, 1991). The problem I am identifying here, though, occurs when positions are adopted either in ignorance of, or—even worse—in spite of, the research or other information available. Such strident behaviour is unethical and, again, does a disservice to the public and to the values of justice.

When psychologists are ignorant of current research and standard of practice in the profession, they run the risk of acting unethically. Relevant ethical guidelines mandate psychologists to obtain—and maintain—knowledge, skill, education, and experience in their areas of work (see Ogloff, 1999). For example, the "Specialty Guidelines for Forensic Psychologists" provide that "forensic psychologists have an obligation to maintain current knowledge of scientific, professional and legal developments within their area of claimed competence" (Guideline VI.A., Committee on Ethical Guidelines for Forensic Psychologists, 1991). Of greatest concern, of course, is when forensic psychologists adopt a position to support a position in spite of contradictory information. To this end, the "Specialty Guidelines" provide that forensic psychologists are precluded from "An attempt, whether active or passive, to engage in partisan distortion or misrepresentation. Forensic psychologists do not, by either commission or omission, participate in a misrepresentation of their evidence, nor do they participate in partisan attempts to avoid, deny, or subvert the presentation of evidence contrary to their position" (Guideline VII.D).

It is readily apparent that the difficulties discussed would be rectified if forensic psychologists would simply refrain from adopting dogmatic positions. Although simplistic, the message is clear. Continuing to adopt dogmatic positions without the appropriate empirical support and standards of practice, will not only stifle creativity and progress in the field, but also continue the unfortunate image of psychologists as whores in the courtroom.

Chauvinism

> *n.* smug irrational belief in the superiority of one's own race, sex, etc. (from French *chauvinisme*, after Nicolas *Chauvin*, legendary French soldier under Napoleon).

As the definition above indicates, chauvinism is a broad term. The concerns to be noted here pertain to sexism and ethnocentrism. For too long those in our field have ignored sex/ethnic/cultural differences and gender roles in the phenomena we study. Such glaring oversight in the selection of populations and questions we consider is nothing short of shameful. Moreover, while there are obvious exceptions, the field of legal psychology has had difficulty attracting women and members of visible minorities. During my years as a member of the Executive Committee of the American Psychology-Law Society, we have engaged in many discussions of the need to increase the membership of these key groups in the society and in the leadership of the organization. We have largely failed on both counts. Only a fraction of our members are visible minorities, and women are under-represented both in the society and on the Executive Committee.

To demonstrate how problematic the general concern about the lack of attention to some groups in legal psychology research, I will consider the issue of minorities and women in jails and prisons. In the United States, for example, African Americans are grossly over-represented in the criminal justice system (i.e., approximately 46.4% of those arrested for crimes are African American, while African Americans represent approximately 12.7% of the population of the U.S.; Department of Justice, 1994). By contrast, women are under-represented (i.e., approximately 24.2% of those arrested for crimes are women, while they represent approximately 52% of the population of the U.S.; Department of Justice, 1994). Although some attention has been devoted to these matters, the degree of work done is not commensurate with the apparent importance of the differences in representation. With respect to women in prisons, for example, they were largely considered "invisible" until very recently, and what was known about and done for male prisons was generally transferred to female prisoners (Rowe, Vazsonyi, & Flannery, 1995; Shaw, 1992, 1994).

Admittedly, more attention is being paid to ethnic minorities and women in legal psychology research. Nonetheless, much of the work that has been done is largely descriptive, identifying differences, rather than investigating the reason for differences, or ways of closing the gender and culture gaps—where appropriate. Beyond the need for a broadening the populations selected for research, there is a need in practice for forensic psychologists to be culturally sensitive and aware of the differences, including the different needs, of minorities and women.

Naïveté

n. artless or unsophisticated, lacking developed powers of analysis, reasoning, or criticism (from Latin *nasci* "to be born").

Perhaps as a result of our relative youth as a discipline, much of our work remains relatively naïve. Although it has improved, still too much of our work shows a lack of understanding and knowledge of relevant substantive law and procedural law. Moreover, the "psychology" in some of our work still demonstrates a lack of understanding and development of substantive research in psychology. In addition, most of our work still lacks any theoretical sophistication, forcing the work to be largely descriptive. As such, the findings of our studies often are often seem as mere examples of shortcomings in law rather than providing any sophisticated understanding of the phenomenon we are studying. Our naïveté regarding the law and our obsession with identifying shortcomings in the law—without suggesting and testing viable alternatives—reduces our credibility among lawyers, judges, and legislators.

Many people who work in the area of legal psychology lack sophisticated knowledge of the law. People have debated whether legal psychologists need to be trained formally in law (see Grisso, Sales, & Bayless, 1982; Hafemeister, Ogloff, & Small, 1990; Ogloff et al., 1996; Tomkins & Ogloff, 1990). This debate has culminated in consideration of the joint degree programs. Arguments against dual degree training have emphasized the costs of such training and the fact that most people who work in legal psychology focus on one or two specific areas of law. Those who support dual degree programs, by contrast, argue that while all legal psychologists do not require formal training in law, there are considerable advantages to pursuing formal training in legal psychology (Hafemeister et al., 1990). Foremost among these advantages is the ability of psychologists with law degrees to have a sophisticated understanding of the law. Indeed, many psychologists with little appreciation of law have "jumped into" legal psychology research only to produce work that is of questionable validity (see Hafemeister et al., 1990 for a discussion of this material; see also, Pfeifer, 1992).

While it may not be essential for every legal psychologist to have extensive training in law, it is important that psychologists who work in the legal psychology area to have an in-depth understanding of the law that pertains to their own areas of work. The most basic reason being that legal psychology research cannot be an effective catalyst in evaluating and changing the law if it lacks external validity and generalizability. Kone_ni and Ebbeson (1979) emphasized this point in their review of the external validity of simulated jury research. They wrote that "Research in applied disciplines must be concerned with issues of external validity and generalizability to an unusually high degree... What is surprising is the extent to which most studies in legal psychology have routinely ignored the external-validity problems, despite the obvious applied nature of legal psychology and the airing that the notion of external validity has received" (p. 40). Thus, having an appreciation of law and legal practice provides legal psychologists with the ability to examine the extent to which their research—and that done by others—may be externally valid.

A second reason for having a broad and in-depth understanding and appreciation of law is that it allows individuals the opportunity to identify interesting legal questions that are important for investigation by researchers in legal psychology.

A final reason for demanding that legal psychologists are knowledgeable about the law—especially that which is relevant to their own areas of work—is that such a requirement is ethically appropriate. Ethical Standard 1.04 (Boundaries of Competence) of the "Ethical Principles of Psychologists and Code of Conduct" (APA, 1992) states that "psychologists provide services, teach, and conduct research only within the boundaries of their competence, based on their education, training, supervised experience, or appropriate professional experience." To be "competent" in work as a legal psychologist, then, one would need some expertise in law.

Just as some legal psychology research can be criticized for lacking legal sophistication, so too can it be criticized for lacking any theoretical foundation, especially from a psychological perspective. For science—including social science and, in this case, legal psychology—to develop and advance knowledge, we must develop an understanding of "why" some phenomenon in law exists. Thus, it is not enough to know *what* types of pretrial publicity affect jurors, for example, but *why* they react the way they do and *how* the media affects their decision making. Only when we develop and test theories that provide these causal explanations can we begin to fully understand the phenomenon. Furthermore, once we understand the cause of the phenomenon, we can begin to learn how the law can be revised, when necessary, to better reflect the reality of human behavior. Unfortunately, the vast majority of the research that has been done, and continues to be done, by legal psychologists, only provides a description of "what" happens in the law, rather than providing any explanation of why or how the phenomenon exists. Unfortunately, very little of our work employs or develops psychological theories to explain the phenomena they study in the legal system (Small, 1993).

There is little doubt that the work of people in our field has provided us with considerable information about the law—and the validity of the assumptions the law makes regarding human behavior. However, future researchers would do well to move beyond describing the law and merely testing legal assumptions. Only by applying psychological theory to the law in an attempt to explain causal relationships between the law and human behavior will we be able to advocate valid legal reforms—and to finally have a meaningful impact on the law.

Myopia

n. inability to see distant objects clearly (from Greek – muein "to close" + ops "eyes").

My first book was titled "Law and Psychology: The Broadening of the Discipline" (Ogloff, 1992). It was my intention in that book to demonstrate the potential breadth of legal psychology. Although there has been some "broadening of the discipline," we are still focusing too much on relatively few, narrow, areas of psychology. Moreover, despite repeated warnings, topics covered by legal psychology remain narrow and obscure from a legal perspective. Two former editors of *Law and Human Behavior*, the official journal of the American Psychology Law Society, have joined with other scholars to express their concern about the relatively narrow range of articles submitted for publication in their journal (Roesch, 1990; Saks, 1986). Kagehiro and Laufer (1992), in the preface to their *Handbook of Psychology and Law* provided a content analysis of articles published between 1966 and 1990 (depending on availability) in the most prominent journals in legal psychology. The results showed that, despite repeated concerns such as those mentioned above, the vast majority of articles published were in the areas of criminal law and criminal procedure, evidence-related concerns, jury issues, and mental health law topics.

In addition to the work of Kagehiro and Laufer (1992), Small (1993) also analyzed the areas of research of articles published in *Law and Human Behavior* between 1986 and 1991. As Small's results confirm, despite repeated calls for "broadening the discipline," the majority of work in the field still fall into the areas of jury decision making and eyewitness testimony.

For psychology to meaningfully impact the law, psychologists in our field must continue to broaden the focus of their work in the law. There really is no limit to the scope of inquiry available to those who work in the field of legal psychology. Indeed, to the extent that *every* law has as its purpose the control or regulation of human behavior, every law is ripe for psychological study (see Ogloff, 1992). Perhaps as more psychologists now are more broadly knowledgeable about legal topics, and many have formal training in law, we can expect the areas of inquiry in legal psychology to more fully reflect the breadth of the law. In addition to criminal law, criminal procedure, evidence, and mental health law topics, legal psychologists would do well to broaden the scope of their work by considering the application of psychology to areas such as administrative law, antitrust, civil procedure, corporate law, environmental law, patent law, and family law. Such movement in the field would, again, further help ensure its continued success.

CONCLUSIONS

The legal psychology movement experienced considerable growth and success in the 20th century. Although it is impossible to recreate the excitement that permeated the "Dublin Conference," from which this book was spawned, the chapters reproduced in this volume and the accompanying one prepared by Professor David Farrington and his colleagues, attest to the breadth and excellence of work in our field. Despite our successes, which really culminated in the first joint meeting of the American Psychology-Law Society and the European Academy of Psychology and Law, in this chapter I have identified a number of concerns that must be addressed to ensure its continued development and maturation.

What made the Dublin Conference such a success, of course, was the fact that it brought together so many legal psychologists from so many countries. The concerns I raised in this chapter about the jingoism that has marked much of our scholarship surely will be addressed by a continued and ongoing awareness of the important work being done by people working in our field internationally. As we who attended the conference witnessed first-hand—we have a lot to learn from one another.

In addition to developing an awareness of the importance of the work being done internationally, and of different legal systems and policies, it is critical that legal psychologists do not adopt the adversarial nature that characterized the western legal systems. As a science, legal psychology cannot stand to be marred by plight of dogmatism that has already characterized some of the work that has been done. By its very nature, our work is very applied. Practitioners, therefore, share the obligation of ensuring that they maintain a balanced approach to their work.

Just as we must not ignore the work of others in the world, we must not ignore the important issues that relate to and emanate from a consideration of minorities and women. Moreover, our consideration of these populations must go beyond mere description. We must also continue to work toward bringing women and minorities into our discipline, and into the leadership of the field.

Beyond the matters to which dogmatism, jingoism, and chauvinism apply, it is critical that we overcome our naivete concerning the law and psychology. We must strive to ensure that the work is legally relevant and valid. To make meaningful changes to the law though, and to promote our understanding of such phenomena in psychology, psychologists must take their work to the next plane—that which involves a theoretical conceptualization that will help explain such things as causal relationships.

Finally, we must take our blinders off. No longer should we limit the focus of our work to areas that seem a "natural fit" for traditional psychology. For psychology to have a significant impact on the legal system, it is important that legal psychologists explore the rich questions that may be found across a broad spectrum of the law. By characterizing legal psychology questions as flowing from the law itself, rather than being a mere extension of some existing area of psychology, legal psychologists can help maximize the chance that their work will be relevant to the legal system, and may have some impact on it.

REFERENCES

American Judicature Society. (1993). The use and misuse of expert evidence in the courts. *Judicature, 77*, 68–76.

American Psychological Association. (1992). Ethical principles of psychologists and code of conduct. *American Psychologist, 47*, 1597–1611.

Beyerstein, B., & Ogloff, J. R. P. (1998). Introduction: Hidden memories: Fact or fancy? In R. A. Baker (Ed.), *Child sexual abuse and false memory syndrome* (pp. 15–28). Amherst, NY: Prometheus Books.

Boring, E. G. (1950). *A history of experimental psychology* (2nd ed.). New York: Appleton-Century-Crofts.

Brigham, J. (1999). What is forensic psychology anyway? *Law and Human Behavior, 23*, 273–298.

Burtt, H. E. (1931). *Legal psychology*. New York, NY: Prentice-Hall.

Brown, M. R. (1926). *Legal psychology: Psychology applied to the trial of cases, to crime and its treatment, and to mental states and processes*. Indianapolis, IN: Bobbs-Merrill.

Brown v. Board of Education, 375 US 483 (1954).

Cahn, E. (1955). Jurisprudence. *New York University Law Review, 30*, 150–169.

Committee on Ethical Guidelines for Forensic Psychologists. (1991). Specialty guidelines for forensic psychologists. *Law and Human Behavior, 15*, 655–665.

Department of Justice, Federal Bureau of Investigations. (1994). *Uniform crime reports for the United States*. Washington, DC: Author.

Faust, D., & Ziskin, J. (1988). The expert witness in psychology and psychiatry, *Science, 241*, 31–35.

Finkelman, D., & Grisso, T. (1994). Therapeutic jurisprudence: From idea to application. *New England Journal on Criminal and Civil Confinement, 20*, 243–257.

Fox, D. (1999). Psycholegal scholarship's contribution to false consciousness about injustice. *Law and Human Behavior, 23*, 9–30.

Friedman, L. M. (1985). *A history of American law* (2nd ed.). New York: Simon & Schuster.

Grisso, T., Sales, B. D., & Bayless, S. (1982). Law-related courses and programs in graduate psychology departments. *American Psychologist, 37*, 267–278.

Hafemeister, T., & Melton, G. B. (1987). The impact of social science research on the judiciary. In G. B. Melton (Ed.), *Reforming the law: Impact of child development research* (pp. 27–59). New York: Guilford.

Hafemeister, T., Ogloff, J. R. P., & Small, M. A. (1990). Training and careers in law and psychology: The perspectives of students and graduates of dual degree programs. *Behavioral Sciences and the Law, 8*, 263–283.

Hale, M. (1980). *Human science and social order: Hugo Munsterberg and origins of applied psychology*. Philadelphia: Temple University Press.

Holmes, O. W. (1897). The path of the law. *Harvard Law Review, 10*, 457–478.

Holmes. O. W. (1881). *The common law*. [New edition, edited by M. DeWolfe Howe, 1963]. Cambridge, MA: Harvard University Press.

Kagehiro, D. K., & Laufer, W. S. (1992). Preface. In D. K. Kagehiro & W. S. Laufer (Eds), *Handbook of psyhology and law* (pp. xi–xiii). NY: Springer-Verlag.

Kalman, L. (1986). *Legal realism at Yale, 1927–1960*. Chapel Hill, NC: University of North Carolina Press.

Konecni, V. J., & Ebbeson, E. B. (1979). External validity of research in legal psychology. *Law and Human Behavior, 3*, 39–70.

Lochner v. NY, 198 U. S. 45 (1905).

Loh, W. D. (1981). Perspectives on psychology and law. *Journal of Applied Social Psychology, 11*, 314–355.

Melton, G. B. (1990). Realism in psychology and humanism in law: Psycholegal studies at Nebraska. *Nebraska Law Review, 69*, 251–277.

Melton, G. B., Monahan, J., & Saks, M. J. (1987). Psychologists as law professors. *American Psychologist, 42*, 502–509.

Monahan, J., & Loftus, E. F. (1982). The psychology of law. *Annual Review of Psychology, 33*, 441–475.

Monahan, J., & Walker, L. (1994). *Social science in law: Cases and materials* (3rd ed.). Westbury, NY: Foundation Press.

Moore, C. (1907). Yellow psychology. *Law Notes, 11*, 125–127.

Moskowitz, M. J. (1977). Hugo Munsterberg: A study in the history of applied psychology. *American Psychologist, 32*, 824–842.

Muller v. Oregon, 208 U. S. 412 (1907).

Munsterberg, H. (1908). *On the witness stand: Essays on psychology and crime*. New York: Doubleday, Page.

Ogloff, J. R. P. (Ed.). (1992). *Law and psychology: The broadening of the discipline*. Durham, NC: Carolina Academic Press.

Ogloff, J. R. P. (1999). Ethical and legal contours of forensic psychology. In R. Roesch, S. Hart, & Ogloff, J. R. P. (Eds.), *Psychology and law: The state of the discipline* (pp. 403–422).

Ogloff, J. R. P. (in press). Two steps forward and one step backward: The law and psychology movement(s) in the 20th century. *Law and Human Behavior.*

Ogloff, J. R. P., Tomkins, A. J., & Bersoff, D. N. (1996). Education and training in psychology and law/criminal justice: Historical foundations, present structures, and future developments. *Criminal Justice and Behavior, 23*, 200–235.

Parker, L. C. (1980). *Legal psychology: Eyewitness testimony—jury behavior*. Springfield, IL: Thomas.

Pfeifer, J. E. (1992). Reviewing the empirical evidence on jury racism: Findings of discrimination or discriminatory findings? In J. R. P. Ogloff (Ed.), *Law and psychology: The broadening of the discipline* (pp. 331–351). Durham, NC: Carolina Academic Press.

Purcell, E. A., Jr. (1973). *The crisis of democratic theory: Scientific naturalism and the problem of value*. Louisville, KY: University Press of Kentucky.

Roesch, R. (1990). From the editor. *Law and Human Behavior, 14*, 1–3.

Roesch, R., Golding, S. L., Hans, V. P., & Reppucci, N. D. (1991). Social science and the courts: The role of amicus curiae briefs. *Law and Human Behavior*, *15*, 1–11.

Roesch, R., Ogloff, J. R. P., & Eaves, D. (1995). Mental health research in the criminal justice system: The need for common approaches and international perspectives. *International Journal of Law and Psychiatry*, *18*, 1–14.

Rosen, P. L. (1980). History and state of the art of applied social research in the courts. In M. J. Saks & C. H. Baron (Eds.), *The use/nonuse/misuse of applied social research in the courts* (pp. 9–15). Cambridge, MA: Abt.

Rowe, D. C., Vazsonyi, A. T., & Flannery, D. J. (1995). Sex differences in crime: Do means and within sex variation have similar causes? *Journal of Research in Crime and Delinquency*, *32*, 84–100.

Saks, M. (1986). The law does not live by eyewitness testimony alone. *Law and Human Behavior*, *10*, 279–280.

Schlegel, J. H. (1979). American legal realism and empirical social science: From the Yale experience. *Buffalo Law Review*, *28*, 459–586.

Schlegel, J. H. (1980). American legal realism and empirical social science: The singular case of Underhill Moore. *Buffalo Law Review*, *29*, 195–323.

Shaw, M. (1992). Issues of power and control: Women in prison and their defenders. *British Journal of Criminology*, *32*, 438–452.

Shaw, M. (1994). Women in prison: A literature review. *Forum on Corrections*, *6*, 13–18.

Small, M. A. (1993). Legal psychology and therapeutic jurisprudence. *Saint Louis University Law Journal*, *37*, 675–713.

Stevens, R. (1983). *Law school: Legal education in America from the 1850s to the 1890s*. Chapel Hill, NC: University of North Carolina Press.

Tapp, J. L. (1976). Psychology and the law: An overview. *Annual Review of Psychology*, *27*, 359–404.

Tomkins, A. J., & Ogloff, J. R. P. (1990). Training and career options in psychology and law. *Behavioral Sciences and the Law*, *8*, 205–216.

Tomkins, A. J., & Oursland, K. (1991). Social and social scientific perspectives in judicial interpretations of the Constitution: A historical view and an overview. *Law and Human Behavior*, *15*, 101–120.

Twining, W. (1973). *Karl Llewellyn and the realist movement*. London: Weidenfeld and Nicolson.

Twining, W. (1985). Talk about realism. *New York University Law Review*, *60*, 329–384.

Wexler, D. B. (1990). Training in law and behavioral sciences: Issues from a legal educator's perspective. *Behavioral Sciences and the Law*, *8*, 197–204.

White, G. E. (1972). From sociological jurisprudence to realism: Jurisprudence and social change in early twentieth-century America. *Virginia Law Review*, *58*, 999–1028.

White, G. E. (1976). *The American judicial tradition: Profiles of leading American judges*. New York: Oxford University Press.

Wigmore, J. H. (1909). Professor Munsterberg and the psychology of testimony: Being a report of the case of *Cokestone v. Munsterberg*. *Illinois Law Review*, *3*, 399–445.

Endnotes

1. Amicus curiae or "friend of the court" briefs to the courts are typically submitted by professional organizations or groups and summarize research relevant to a particular legal case, describing implications for legal issues before a court (Roesch, Golding, Hans, & Reppucci, 1991).
2. During the delivery of this address, I provided some specific examples of some of the shortcomings I believe exist in our field. In retrospect, though, the use of the examples detracted from my thesis. Following the address, during informal discussions with colleagues, rather than focussing on the particular message of my address, people instead debated whether the particular examples chosen fell into the categories I described. As a result, I have decided that in this chapter I would simply provide a brief description of the areas of concern I have identified.

PART 1

ADOLESCENTS

Chapter 1

TOWARD AN EXPANDED DEFINITION OF ADOLESCENT COMPETENCE IN LEGAL CONTEXTS

Jennifer L. Woolard, Carrie S. Fried and N. Dickon Reppucci

During the past decade, juvenile justice reform in the United States has been based on punishment and endorsed by the public as a means of protection from violent offenders. These reforms have included a lowering of the age at which juveniles can be transferred to the adult system—virtually every state has lowered its age to 14, but several have lowered it even further. For instance, the minimum age is 13 in North Carolina, 10 in Missouri, and 8 in Vermont and Wisconsin. Other states, such as Massachusetts, have made it possible to extend the length of sentencing well past the usual juvenile court jurisdiction age of 21 years. Still others have set the age of original jurisdiction for the adult system below the usual 18. For instance, the age in New York is 16, while North Carolina is at 17. Moreover, the process of judicial and legislative waivers have been supplemented in several states by an expansion of the possible crimes that can be invoked under legislative waiver and the addition of prosecutorial waiver. While this has led to an increased number of violent youth being transferred to adult court, the majority of youth transferred are accused of drug and property crimes (Snyder & Sickmund, 1996). If public safety is the goal, then these reforms are not working. Bishop, Frazier, Lanza-Kaduce, and Winner (1996) have reported that for Florida juveniles transferred to adult court, recidivism rates are worse for transfers than for comparable non-transfers in both short and long term follow-up studies. Moreover, given the fact that transfer to criminal court opens the door to the death penalty (Feld, 1999), the question, "Do children's crimes make them adults?", has taken on a new urgency for developmental/community psychologists to become involved in the juvenile justice arena.

This central psychological question requires an examination of developmental differences that may exist between children and adults. To approach this, we need to examine the related question, "What is the essential component of adulthood?". It is our contention that most of us would eventually agree that the concepts of maturity and judgment play a central role in any operational definition of adulthood, and that competence in decision making would be considered a critical element. Under the criminal law in most states, a competent adult is a person 18 or older who is a rational actor, autonomously choosing "to do the illegal act" on the basis of personal preferences and values (Bonnie, Coughlin, Jeffries, & Low, 1997). As a result, adults are responsible and accountable for their actions. Although it could be easily argued that there are many incompetent adults, our society has decided that individual autonomy is a critical element to our way of life and, therefore, the law cannot impinge on that autonomy except in cases of severe mental illness or mental retardation. However, for youth, the concept of immaturity and lack of judgment has often been the basis for not granting them equal rights with adults. Several Supreme Court decisions address this issue: *Parham v. J. R.* (1979), "Most children, even in adolescence, simply are not able to make sound judgments (p. 603)"; *Bellotti v. Baird* (1979), "minors often lack the experience, perspective, and judgment to recognize and avoid choices that could be detrimental to them (p. 635)"; and *Thompson v. Oklahoma* (1988), Adolescents under 16 "are less mature and responsible than adults (p. 834)."

Although one might expect clarity of definition regarding both theory and practice, psychologists have seldom studied the concept of maturity using matched adult and youth samples on any issue. The sparse existing research has usually defined maturity in terms of adolescents' ability to make decisions about their own actions and has focused on cognitive capacity, specifically the ability to reason, understand, and appreciate decisions as adults would. Researchers have used the legal standard of informed consent in medical decision making situations. Few differences have been found between adults and youth 15 years of age and older. Unfortunately, most investigations suffer from various methodological limitations, including small, unrepresentative, usually white, middle class samples of youth taking part in a simulated laboratory exercise (Scott, Reppucci, & Woolard, 1995). The major exceptions are Grisso's (1981) investigation of Miranda waivers that used delinquent adolescent and criminal adult samples, and Ambuel and Rappaport's (1992) study of abortion decision making by young women who have gone to a clinic to determine whether they are pregnant.

Only Grisso's (1981) research focused on legal decision making. His major finding was that adolescents 15 years and older of average intelligence were able to understand their Miranda rights as well as adults. However, he stressed that understanding these rights did not necessarily mean that adolescents were as capable as adults of asserting those rights. More recently, on a related topic, Peterson-Badali and Abramovitch (1993) found that younger adolescents think less strategically than older adolescents and adults about plea agreements.

A few years ago, Scott et al. (1995) proposed a judgment framework of adolescent competence and maturity that includes the standard cognitive factors of understanding, reasoning, and appreciation, but also several psychosocial factors that would be irrelevant or excluded under an informed consent legal framework. These factors, attitude toward and perception of risk, conformity and compliance in relation to peers and parents, and temporal perspective, are hypothesized to influence adolescent decision making and allow a comparison between subjective values that drive the choices of adolescents and adults. Steinberg and Cauffman (1996) expand this theory by reviewing the adolescent literature under the categories of responsibility, temperance, and perspective and concluded that "one could justify a distinction between individuals 16 and younger and those 17 and older (p. 268)." Even more recently, Lexcen and Reppucci (1998) summarize evidence that the adolescent brain has not reached biological maturity.

Each of these factors, influence of peers and/or parents, risk perception, and temporal perspective, has been linked to behavior and decision making, and each has been shown to change over the course of development (Scott et al., 1995; Steinberg & Cauffman, 1996; Redding, 1997). Moreover, each appears to be related to concepts of maturity and judgment. In addition, within the population of adolescents, factors such as socioeconomic status, race/ethnicity, and IQ may affect a variety of decision-making components, such as the meaning of risk and risky behavior, the number of opportunities to make decisions, the level of risk exposure, access to information, and degree of responsibility for decision-making consequences. How these factors combine with age and with the impact of social and cultural contexts to shape adolescent experience is unclear (Wilkinson & Fagan, 1996). For psychological researchers, a critical task is to analyze the components of decision making that are relevant in different legal contexts to provide policymakers with a more precise empirically-based understanding of the ways in which decision making of adolescents compares with that of adults. One way of doing this is to investigate the three developmental factors that Scott et al. (1995) delineate as being possible candidates for inclusion in an expanded definition of adolescent competence.

At least two types of competence, adjudicative and culpability, are significant in this current era of punishment reforms in which transferred youth are subject to adult penalties, and, even if retained in juvenile court, may receive longer sentences than previously. Adjudicative competence, or competence to stand trial, refers to a defendant having a degree of understanding to enable the defendant to consult with his or her lawyer, and both a factual and rational understanding of the proceedings against him (*Dusky v. U.S.*, 1960). In addition, the defendant must have the capacity to assist in preparing his or her defense (*Drope v. Missouri*, 1975). If an individual is found incompetent under either of these standards, the trial cannot continue. The only empirical studies (Cowden & McKee, 1995; Savitsky & Karras, 1984) to examine these standards used assessments of cognitive abilities developed for adults and ignored developmental psychosocial variables entirely.

Culpability refers to the degree to which individuals can be held accountable for their actions, and thus to what extent retributive punishment is appropriate. It also focuses on whether developmental immaturity should be a mitigating circumstance regarding any crime that occurs. Several scholars have argued that the developmental evidence supports a presumption of diminished responsibility for adolescent offenders, but not a complete absence of responsibility (Reppucci, 1999; Scott, 2000; Scott & Grisso, 1997; Zimring, 1998). Similarly, Feld (1999) argues that "Substantive justice requires a rationale for courts to sentence young offenders differently and *more leniently* than they sentence adult offenders and to recognize *youthfulness as a mitigating factor* (p. 16)." Cauffman and Steinberg (2000) suggest that youthful choices to offend may be based on an immature capacity to make decisions or be driven by transient developmental influences. If this is the case, then the presumptions of autonomy, free will, and rational choice on which adult criminal responsibility is based become weaker, and the criminal actions of juveniles are less blameworthy than similar acts of adults (Scott & Grisso, 1997). As such, youth should be subject to less punishment. In both adjudicative and culpability competence, we believe that a judgment framework rather than an informed consent framework should apply.

During the past five years, our research team has initiated several studies of these issues. We now turn to a discussion of preliminary findings from our studies of adjudicative competence and culpability. We believe that these data provide initial steps in developing a research agenda on these issues.

STUDY 1: COMPETENCE AND EFFECTIVE PARTICIPATION OF JUVENILE DEFENDANTS

The present study expands existing research to clarify the meaning of adolescent competence as a function of both adult competence factors and judgment factors by conceptualizing legally relevant decisions as a function of both judgment and cognitive competence factors with comparisons between adolescents and adults currently involved in the justice system. The analyses reported are guided by two primary questions: (1) Can adolescents perform as effectively as adults on measures of adjudicative competence? (2) Do the processes and outcomes of legally relevant decisions vary according to developmentally linked judgment factors?

METHOD

This report focuses on three sections of a larger interview protocol. Current intellectual functioning was assessed using the Kaufman Brief Intelligence Test (Kaufman & Kaufman, 1990), which comprises Vocabulary (V) and Matrices (M) subscales, representing verbal and nonverbal or performance abilities, respectively. The MacArthur Competence Assessment Tool—Criminal Adjudication (MacCAT-CA; Poythress et al., 1999) measured the understanding, reasoning, and appreciation components of competence to stand trial. Legally relevant decision making is measured using the Judgment Assessment Tool—Adolescents/Adults (JATA; Woolard, Reppucci, & Scott, 1996). Developed specifically for this study, the JATA is a three part interview which describes a male who has committed a robbery and faces a series of decisions: (1) talking with police; (2) consulting with an attorney; and (3) considering a plea bargain in the context of transfer to criminal court. Two categories of information are collected from respondents—a series of decision choices based on the information given, and the decision consequences that may follow from each choice.

Participants

Data were collected from 102 males aged 15 and younger, 103 males aged 16 and 17, and 115 males between 19 and 35 years old, all in secure confinement at a detention facility or jail awaiting trial. Approximately 43% were African American, 36% Caucasian, 10% Latino, 5% Asian, and 6% from other backgrounds. Approximately 59% scored in the average or above average percentile on the KBIT. About 25% of the sample was detained for offenses against persons, 25% for property crimes, 33% for court order violations such as probation violation, and the rest for various other offenses. Seventy percent of the group had previously been detained in the facility.

Analyses confirmed that the three age groups differed on some aspects of their demographic composition. Over half of the adult sample scored below average on the IQ test, compared to 33% of the young juveniles and 31% of the older juveniles, χ^2 (2, N = 315) = 9.90, $p < .01$. The samples also differed on the type of offense for which they were being held in detention, χ^2 (6, N = 305) = 51.01, $p < .001$. Inspection of the percentages indicates a larger proportion of both juvenile samples versus the adult sample were held for court order violations.

RESULTS

The first set of analyses used multivariate analysis of variance (MANOVA) techniques to test for differences in average MacCAT subscale scores across demographic, educational, and system experience variables. Because the age-based samples differed in the distribution of IQ scores, the first analysis examined age, race, and IQ variables together. Significant overall effects of Age, $F(6,584) = 2.5$, $p < .05$, Wilks = .95, and IQ, $F(3,292) = 8.62$, $p < .0001$, Wilks = .92, and an Age by IQ interaction, $F(6,584) = 2.15$, $p < .05$, Wilks = .96, were found. No main effect for Race or other interaction terms were significant. Univariate analyses on Age indicate that the main effect was significant for the Reasoning subscale, $F(2,294) = 6.84$, $p < .001$. Young adolescents (mean = 12.1) scored significantly lower than older adolescents (mean = 13.3), but were not significantly different from the adults (mean = 12.9). Participants with below average IQ scored significantly lower than those with average or above average IQ on Understanding, Reasoning, and Appreciation. The Age by IQ interaction was only significant for the Understanding subscale, $F(2,294) = 3.50$, $p < .05$ (See Figure 1).

We now focus on the first JATA vignette, which presented a scenario in which a juvenile was being questioned by police. Participants are asked to make decision choices at four points: what the vignette character should do after the initial story, immediately following the identification of options reviewed above; what the character's parents or peers would want him to do, depending on the instrument version; what the vignette character should do after hearing the parent/peer recommendation; and what the participant would do if he was in a similar situation. One-half of the respondents were asked about peers and one-half were asked about parents. The decision choices were coded as talking/admitting information, denying/lying about information, remaining silent/refusing plea bargain, or other. Because a proportion of the cells contained less than five respondents, Fisher's Exact Test was used instead of the standard chi-square test. Separate tests were

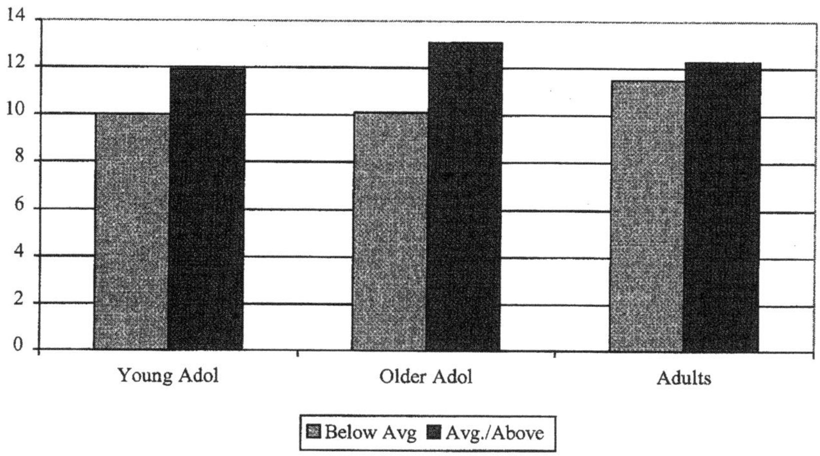

FIGURE 1: MACCAT UNDERSTANDING SUBSCALE SCORES BY AGE AND IQ

conducted for each of the four decision points and a significance level of $p < .01$ was used.

Table 1 provides the choices by decision point and age group. Significant differences in choices were found for the initial decision point and what the participant would do if in a similar situation. It is clear that the majority of respondents in each age group recommended and chose remaining silent for both decisions. However, for both these decision points, the percentage of respondents who chose ADMIT generally decreased with age and the percentage that chose REFUSE increased with age. Almost no adults chose the DENY option, but a percentage of both younger and older juveniles made that selection.

No effects were found for race, IQ, detention history, or type of offense. These findings suggest that the decision to talk to police or remain silent may vary with age, but not by other demographic or justice system involvement variables.

To check for age differences in the perception of what parents and peers may recommend, Fisher's exact test was used to examine the effect of protocol version, or asking for a parent's recommendation versus a peer's recommendation, on decision choice, while controlling for age. A significant effect for version was found for both sets of juveniles (Fisher's = .001) as well as the adults (Fisher's = .01). These results indicate that each sample reported a pattern of parent's recommendations, predominantly TALK, that differed from their pattern of peer's recommendations, which was predominantly to remain silent. Moreover, if the

Table 1: Number of Respondents Selecting Choices at Four Decision Points in Police Vignette by Age

	Young Juveniles N = 100	Older Juveniles N = 103	Adults N = 105	Chi Square
Joe should do				$p < .01$
Talk	12 (12.0%)	7 (6.8%)	9 (8.6%)	
Deny	17 (17.0%)	10 (9.7%)	2 (1.9%)	
Remain silent	70 (70.0%)	85 (82.5%)	90 (85.7%)	
Other	1 (1.0%)	1 (1.0%)	4 (3.8%)	
Parents would want				NS
Talk	39 (75.0%)	32 (61.5%)	23 (42.6%)	
Deny	0 (0.0%)	2 (3.9%)	1 (1.9%)	
Remain silent	10 (19.2%)	14 (26.9%)	24 (44.4%)	
Other	3 (5.8%)	4 (7.7%)	6 (11.1%)	
Peers would want				NS
Talk	4 (8.5%)	7 (13.7%)	7 (14.6%)	
Deny	7 (14.9%)	12 (23.5%)	6 (12.5%)	
Remain silent	35 (74.5%)	32 (62.8%)	31 (64.6%)	
Other	1 (2.1%)	0 (0.0%)	4 (8.3%)	
Joe should do (post parent/peer recommendation)				NS
Talk	27 (27.2%)	26 (25.5%)	24 (22.9%)	
Deny	0 (0.0%)	3 (3.0%)	0 (0.0%)	
Remain silent	72 (72.7%)	73 (71.6%)	80 (76.2%)	
Other	0 (0.0%)	0 (0.0%)	1 (1.0%)	
Participant would do				$p < .01$
Talk	28 (28.3%)	20 (19.6%)	17 (16.2%)	
Deny	12 (12.1%)	11 (10.9%)	2 (1.9%)	
Remain silent	56 (56.6%)	64 (62.8%)	72 (68.6%)	
Other	3 (3.0%)	7 (6.9%)	14 (13.3%)	

Note. Percentages within age categories in parentheses. Numbers for the parent and peer recommendation categories include half the sample.

categories are collapsed into ADMIT/OTHER, there is a significant effect of age on the parents vignette, χ^2 (2, N = 158) = 11.68, $p < .01$. Three-quarters of the young juveniles believed that parents would want the vignette character to admit, whereas less than half of the adult sample did. No differences were found for the peer vignette using this ADMIT/OTHER dichotomy.

Beyond the types of consequences associated with decision choices, the valence, or positivity and negativity, of the consequences can provide important information about the decision-making process. Within the judgment framework, the valence of consequences can be considered some indication of the costs and benefits associated with each decision option. Each of the consequences mentioned by respondents was coded as to whether it represented a positive or negative consequence for the individual. The consequences were summed across the three decision choices of ADMIT, DENY, REFUSE to create the total number of positive and negative consequences identified by demographic characteristics. Effects of age, $F(4,358) = 4.51$, $p < .001$, race, $F(2,173) = 4.44$, $p < .01$, and IQ, $F(2,180) = 5.86$, $p < .003$, were found. More total positive and negative consequences were mentioned by older juveniles than adults, and those with average or above IQ scores. Caucasians also mentioned more total negative consequences as compared with other racial groups.

The short or long-term nature of consequences provides information about a participant's temporal perspective when considering various decision choices. Each consequence mentioned by a participant was coded for whether it represented a short-term consequence, such as in the next few hours, or a long-term consequence, such as in the days or weeks ahead or longer. As with the analyses for valence, MANOVA was used to examine the total number of short and long-term consequences reported across decision options within each vignette. Significant effects for age, $F(2,352) = 5.08$, $p < .0005$, indicated that older adolescents mentioned more short-term consequences than adults did. The race analysis, $F(2,173) = 6.25$, $p < .002$, showed that Caucasians mentioned more short-term consequences than minorities. Those with above average IQ scores also reported significantly more short term consequences than those below average, $F(2,177) = 6.87$, $p < .001$. No differences in long term consequences were found for any demographic variable. When the proportion of long to short term consequences was used as the dependent variable, no significant effects of any demographic variables were found on the total proportion or the proportion within each decision choice.

DISCUSSION

This study presents preliminary results regarding judgment and decision making in legal contexts among adolescents and adults who were detained prior to their trials. Theories of judgment and psychosocial maturity hypothesize that a number of developmental factors may affect the decision-making process and outcomes for juveniles differently than adults. The central conclusion is that initial support for judgment theory (Scott et al., 1995; Steinberg & Cauffman, 1996) exists and age-based differences in judgment constructs relate to decision process and outcome in legally relevant contexts. As found in prior studies using a subsample of this dataset (Krause, 1998), IQ has a strong, consistent, positive relationship with MacCAT scores across subscales and across the age samples. Moreover, it appears that younger and older adolescents with below average IQ score lower than similarly situated adults on the Understanding subscale. This difference suggests that special attention must be paid to working with adolescent defendants who have below average cognitive skills as they may suffer from a double disadvantage.

The data also supported our hypotheses that decision options, outcomes, and judgment factors in legally relevant vignettes would change across age. Although the responses do not necessarily map onto actual behavior, the number of options generated and the choices made in the JATA do provide some information about decision-making capacities. These results indicate that age differences in decision choices do exist. Even though the majority of respondents recommended remaining silent in the wake of police questioning, the percentage of juvenile respondents recommending that the character admit to police, and that they themselves would admit to police, is higher than that of adults. It is possible that, under the stress of actual circumstances, juveniles could even perform worse, for instance, be less likely to assert their rights, than they do in hypothetical situations. The two juvenile samples were significantly different from adults on several context-specific measures of judgment, although the patterns varied depending on the specific factors considered. The analysis of the temporal perspective and valence of consequences mentioned in the vignette provides limited support for the notion that juveniles are considering different aspects of consequences than adults.

Our findings should be qualified by the cross-sectional self-report design and the limited sample sizes. The fact that significant age-based differences were found suggests that the measures and sample sizes were adequate to reveal existing relationships between measures, but because a cross-sectional design was used, we can only infer that age-based differences may represent developmental differences or changes over time in judgment and decision making. These limitations notwithstanding, it is clear that theories of judgment are important to the understanding of juvenile decision making in legal contexts. Measures of adjudicative competence developed for adults, while providing important information, did not capture several of the factors that differentiate adolescent decision making from that of adults.

STUDY 2: DEVELOPMENTAL INFLUENCES ON ADOLESCENT CULPABILITY AND DECISION MAKING IN CRIMINAL CONTEXTS

This study evaluates the influence of psychosocial factors in criminal decision making by asking adolescents to imagine that they are participants in a crime situation depicted in a five-minute clip from the movie *Sleepers*. In addition to answering questions about the decision making process based on the video, participants completed standardized measures of peer influence, temporal perspective, and risk perception (assessment of risk and risk preference). The study is guided by the following three research questions: 1) Is there an association between demographic characteristics, such as prior contact with the juvenile justice system, gender, and age, and standardized measures of the psychosocial factors or judgment in decision making in criminal contexts?; 2) Is there an association between the judgment factors that influence decision making in a criminal context and scores on standardized measures of the related psychosocial factors, or does the measure of decision making in criminal contexts adequately capture the psychosocial factors?; and 3) How do demographic characteristics, judgment in criminal contexts, and performance on standardized psychosocial measures relate to adolescents' assessments of culpability?

METHOD

Prior to participation, each adolescent was screened to determine whether he or she had seen the movie *Sleepers*. Those who had not seen the movie watched a scene in which four boys make a series of decisions beginning with a plan to steal hot dogs from a vendor and ultimately resulting in the presumed death of a man. The scene was edited into four segments. After each segment, the participants answered a series of questions in which they are asked to imagine themselves in the depicted situation. The questions in the first three sections focus on several aspects of decision making, including perceived risks and benefits, possible consequences, and the role of peer influence. The final section focuses on the punishment that the boys deserve and asks about the appropriateness of transfer to adult court. Adolescents who had already seen the movie were given two written vignettes describing similar crime situations and answered nearly identical questions. Then each participant completed standardized measures of peer influence (Berndt, 1979), future time perspective (Stanford Time Perspective Inventory; Zimbardo, 1990), and risk perception (Benthin, Slovic, & Severson, 1993).

Participants

The final sample included 119 adolescents (67.2% male; 32.8% female) between the ages of 12 and 18 (m = 15.57; sd = 1.52). Over half of the youths were in detention at the time of the interview (53.4%). Among the non-detained youths, 38.2% had had prior contact with the juvenile justice system, so that a total of 70.3% of the entire sample had some contact with the juvenile justice system. Approximately half of the sample was Caucasian

(48.7%) and nearly a third was African American (30.3%). The remaining 21.0% indicated they were either of Hispanic, Asian, or biracial descent. Minorities and males were over-represented among juveniles in detention. Non-Caucasians accounted for 71.4% of detainees, and 82.5% of detainees were males. Among non-detained youths, males (50.0%) and females (50.0%) were equally represented and Caucasians were over-represented (71.4%). There were no significant age differences based on gender or detention status. Of the 119 participants, 72 had not seen the movie Sleepers. Results in the next section are based on the data collected from all 119 participants, but results in the subsequent sections focus only on the Sleepers scenario and, therefore, only include data from the 72 adolescents who completed the Sleepers version of the study.

RESULTS

Relationship between demographic characteristics and standardized measures of psychosocial factors

An initial multivariate analysis (MANOVA) using gender, prior contact with the justice system, and age group was used to predict scores on standardized measures of the psychosocial factors. All of the psychosocial factors, such as resistance to peer influence, $F(7,105) = 2.51, p < .03$, future time perspective, $F(7,105) = 3.56, p < .003$, risk assessment, $F(7,105) = 2.30, p < .04$, and risk preference, $F(7,105) = 2.17, p < .05$—were significantly predicted by the combination of the demographic characteristics. However, while contact, $F(4,102) = 3.01, p < .03$, was a significant predictor in the MANOVA, neither age group, gender, nor any of the interactions among the three demographic variables were significant.

Univariate analyses (ANOVAs) were then used to identify which of the demographic characteristics were predicting each of the psychosocial factors. Resistance to peer influence, as measured by the Berndt vignettes, was predicted by the interaction between contact and gender, $F(1,106) = 5.09, p < .03$. Males with contact were less resistant to peer influence than males with no contact. However, females reported similar resistance to peer influence regardless of contact.

There were significant effects of gender, $F(1,109) = 4.05, p < .05$, the gender by age group interaction, $F(1,109) = 5.55, p < .03$, and the three way interaction between gender, age group, and contact, $F(1,109) = 12.47, p < .002$, in the prediction of future time perspective. Overall, females were more future oriented than were males, but this difference was most noticeable in the older age group. The three-way interaction is explained by the fact that among adolescents with no contact, gender and age contribute substantially to the prediction of future time orientation. However, among the adolescents with contact, there were minimal differences between older and younger youths and between males and females.

Risk assessment, as measured by six items from the Benthin, Slovic, and Severson Risk Perception Scale, was significantly predicted by age group, $F(1,109) = 5.84$, $p < .02$. Younger adolescents assessed activities as more risky than did older adolescents. Risk preference was also measured by six items from the Risk Perception Scale. The only significant predictor of risk preference was contact, $F(1,109) = 5.84$, $p < .02$. Not surprisingly, adolescents with contact were more likely to think the benefits of participation in risky activities outweighed the risks, as compared to adolescents with no contact.

Based on the lack of predictive value of including age group in the prediction of the psychosocial variables, we suspected that the rough grouping of adolescents into two age groups might be obscuring the effect of age on the psychosocial variables. As a result, an additional set of regression analyses used age as a continuous variable to predict performance on the psychosocial variables. These analyses confirmed that only risk assessment was linearly predicted by age, $F(1,116) = 9.57$, $p < .003$, Δ PRE = .08. However, when a quadratic component was added into the regression equation, age was also a significant predictor of resistance to peer influence, $F(2,112) = 7.10$, $p < .002$, Δ PRE = .09, and future time perspective, $F(2,115) = 3.31$, $p < .05$, Δ PRE = .05. In each case, the youngest adolescents appeared most similar to the oldest adolescents, with those in the middle of the age range (i.e. 15–16) indicating the lowest scores on resistance to peer influence and future time orientation.

Relationship between criminal decision making, background characteristics, and psychosocial factors

In order to measure the influence of peers in criminal contexts, a PEER REACTION composite (see Table 2) was created from four items from the Sleepers questionnaire. Scores on the Berndt measure of resistance to peer influence were used to predict scores on the PEER REACTION composite. Overall, youths who scored higher on the PEER REACTION composite, namely those who thought it was more likely that their friends would try and pressure them, also indicated more resistance to peer influence. Both the linear, $F(1,64) = 9.29$, $p < .004$, $R^2 = .13$, and quadratic, $F(2,63) = 8.59$, $p < .001$, $R^2 = .21$, effects of age were also predictive of PEER REACTION. Adolescents at the youngest end of the age range were most likely to think

Table 2: Peer Reaction Composite Items

How likely do you think it is that your friends would ... if you tried to walk away from the situation? (Measured on a 5-point scale)	Stop 1		Stop 2		Stop 3	
	M	*SD*	*M*	*SD*	*M*	*SD*
a. stop being friends with you	2.33	(1.52)	2.11	(1.34)	2.34	(1.45)
b. make fun of you or call you names	3.09	(1.47)	2.66	(1.42)	2.64	(1.43)
c. threaten to beat you up	2.07	(1.32)	1.86	(1.23)	2.09	(1.35)
d. actually beat you up	1.61	(1.05)	1.41	(.87)	1.71	(1.17)

their peers would try to pressure them. Again, we found a U-shaped effect, where adolescents in the middle of the age range suspected the least amount of pressure from friends and the oldest adolescents appeared more similar to the youngest adolescents. ANOVA analyses revealed that PEER REACTION was also associated with contact, $F(1,62) = 14.60$, $p < .002$, such that adolescents with contact were less likely to expect their peers would try to pressure them than adolescents with no contact.

In order to measure the influence of risk assessment in criminal contexts, the RISK ASSESSMENT composite (see Table 3) was created from five variables in the Sleepers questionnaire. Regression analyses revealed that the RISK ASSESSMENT composite was predicted by general risk assessment scores, $F(1,62) = 12.72$, $p < .002$, $R^2 = .17$. Youths who expected more negative outcomes in the Sleepers scenario also evaluated activities as more risky. There were no effects for any of the demographic characteristics in the prediction of the RISK ASSESSMENT composite.

Table 3: Risk Assessment Composite Items

How likely do you think it is that... (Measured on a 5-point scale)	Stop 1		Stop 2		Stop 3	
	M	(*SD*)	*M*	(*SD*)	*M*	(*SD*)
a. you and your friends will be caught by the police?	2.57	(1.30)	2.80	(1.20)	2.97	(1.24)
b. one of you will be badly hurt or killed?	1.81	(0.87)	2.07	(1.12)	2.36	(1.20)
c. someone else will be badly hurt or killed?	2.21	(1.08)	2.15	(1.18)	3.00	(1.26)
d. assuming you are caught, you and your friends will be found guilty of a crime?	3.49	(1.43)	3.93	(1.09)	3.97	(1.04)
e. you and your friends will spend time in detention or a correctional facility?	3.16	(1.44)	3.20	(1.34)	3.61	(1.24)

The total number of future consequences mentioned in the Sleepers questionnaire was used to predict standardized future time perspective scores. The number of future consequences did not significantly predict future time perspective. Of the demographic characteristics, the interaction of contact and gender predicted the number of future consequences mentioned, $F(1,67) = 5.62$, $p < .03$. Males with contact mentioned fewer future consequences, compared with males with no contact. However, for females the trend was reversed, such that females with contact mentioned more future consequences than those with no contact.

Contextual risk preference was measured as the proportion of benefits to risks mentioned in open-ended responses. The prediction of the benefit/risk proportion was not improved by including standardized risk preference scores in the regression model. Of the demographic characteristics, only gender was predictive of the benefit/risk proportion, $F(1,66) = 4.25$, $p < .05$. Not surprisingly, females thought of fewer benefits as a proportion of the total number of consequences mentioned than did their male counterparts.

Criminal responsibility and culpability

Whether or not an adolescent thought the youths should be transferred to adult criminal court (TRANSFER) and the worst expected punishment they would receive in both juvenile (JUVPUN) and adult criminal court (ADULTPUN) were the measures of culpability in the Sleepers questionnaire. Multiple regression and ANOVA were used to predict TRANSFER from demographic characteristics and scores on the standardized psychosocial measures. Chi-square and discriminate function analyses were used to determine the association between punishment categories (1 = *a year or less in jail or detention*; 2 = *unspecified amount of time in jail or detention*; 3 = *more than a year in jail or detention*) and demographic characteristics and psychosocial factors.

There was a significant linear effect of age on TRANSFER, $F(1,67) = 6.73$, $p < .02$, $R^2 = .09$, with the younger adolescents being more likely to say they should be transferred to adult criminal court. Contact was associated with JUVPUN, χ^2 $(2, N = 58) = 9.21$, $p < .02$, while gender, χ^2 $(2, N = 59) = 8.19$, $p < .02$, and age, $F(2,53) = 3.35$, $p < .05$, were associated with ADULTPUN. Youths with contact were more likely to think the juvenile court judge would sentence them to a year or less in detention or jail, while youths with no contact tended to be less specific with regards to the amount of time the judge would give. If the case was transferred to adult court, three quarters of males, but only a little over a third of females, thought they would be sentenced to over a year in jail or detention. Younger adolescents were also more likely to expect harsher punishment from the adult court judge. None of the psychosocial factors were associated with adolescents' assessments of culpability in the Sleepers scenario.

DISCUSSION

Drawing from the judgment theory of the development of adolescent competence, this study examined the decision making process in criminal situations in order to clarify the role that psychosocial development may play in criminal decision making. This is a necessary first step in moving towards an understanding of adolescent criminal responsibility and culpability. In summary, we found that there are reliable associations between several demographic characteristics, such as age, gender, and prior contact, and scores on standardized measures of the psychosocial factors. We also determined that the Sleepers measure of contextual decision making reliably related to several of the psychosocial factors, including peer influence and risk assessment. Unfortunately, the proportion of risks to benefits, and the total number of future consequences mentioned did not adequately capture the concepts of risk preference and temporal perspective. Contextual decision making was associated with demographic characteristics. Of note: (a) younger adolescents expected more pressure from friends, with a U-shaped effect, indicting middle adolescents expect the least pressure; (b) females thought of fewer benefits as a proportion of benefits to risks; and (c) males with juvenile justice contact thought of fewer long term consequences than males with no prior contact, but the reverse was true for females. Finally, adolescents' assessments of their own culpability indicated that: (a) younger adolescents were more likely to think they should be transferred, and to expect harsher punishment from the adult court judge; and (b) if the case was heard by a juvenile court judge, youths with contact expected more lenient sentences than youths with no contact.

This study is also limited by the cross-sectional design, which makes it impossible to make definitive conclusions regarding development. Longitudinal research could clarify some of the U-shaped age effects and could shed light on the differences in the developmental trajectories between youths with juvenile justice contact and those without. This would enable us to answer questions such as: Is consideration of others, both contextual and non-contextual, delayed for adolescents who have had juvenile justice contact, or do these adolescents continue to be less considerate of others even as they progress into adulthood? Another limitation of this study is the lack of an adult comparison group, which prohibits us from comparing the manner in which the psychosocial factors affect decision making in adolescence versus adulthood.

IMPLICATIONS AND FUTURE DIRECTIONS

Given the results of these preliminary studies, expanding the definition of competence in adolescence may make sense. Although the results are not clear cut, there were significant differences between youths and adults on several psychosocial variables in the study of competence to stand trial. Moreover, in the culpability study, several reliable associations were found between psychosocial measures and demographic factors, such as age and gender, and between these measures and contextual decision making. It is clear that the default extension of adult competence assessments to juveniles will not capture aspects of judgment that differentiate adolescent decision making from that of adults. Therefore, we believe that a judgment framework holds great promise for a developmentally sensitive understanding of juvenile competence.

Further research is needed on the specific aspects of adjudicative competence and on culpability per se before fundamental changes should be made to the current direction of juvenile justice reform in the United States. Generalizing to a system characterized by disproportionate minority confinement and an increasing female offender population requires continued research with larger and more racially and ethnically diverse samples of both male and female adolescents and adults facing legal decisions. Even so, these initial studies represent empirical attempts to clarify the assumptions about adolescent development that often remain unexplored and unchallenged in the political arena. The developmental differences found in this work emphasize that scientific evidence on judgment and competence can play a critical role in pushing the national debate on juvenile crime beyond rhetoric and anecdote.

REFERENCES

Ambuel, B. & Rappaport, J. (1992). Developmental trends in adolescents' psychological and legal competence to consent to abortion. *Law and Human Behavior, 16*, 129–154.

Bellotti v. Baird, 443 U. S. 622 (1979).

Benthin, A., Slovic, P., & Severson, H. (1993). A psychometric study of adolescent risk perception. *Journal of Adolescence, 16*, 153–168.

Berndt, T. J. (1979). Developmental changes in conformity to peers and parents. *Developmental Psychology, 15*, 608–616.

Bishop, D., Frazier, C., Lanza-Kaduce, L., & Winner, L. (1996). The transfer of juveniles to criminal court: Does it make a difference? *Crime and Delinquency, 35*, 179–201.

Bonnie, R., Coughlin, A., Jeffries, J., & Low, P. (1997). *Criminal law*. Westbury, N. Y.: The Foundation Press.

Cauffman, E., & Steinberg, L. (in press). Researching adolescent's decision making relevant to culpability. In T. Grisso and R. Schwartz (Eds.), *Youth on trial.* Chicago: University of Chicago Press.

Cowden, V. L., & McKee, G. R. (1995). Competency to stand trial in juvenile delinquency proceedings: Cognitive maturity and the attorney-client relationship. *University of Louisville Journal of Law, 33*, 629–651.

Drope v. Missouri, 420 U. S. 162 (1975).

Dusky v. United States, U. S. 402 (1960).

Feld, B. (1999). *Bad kids.* New York: Oxford University Press.

Grisso, T. (1981). *Juveniles' waiver of rights: Legal and psychological competence.* New York: Plenum.

Kaufman, A. S., & Kaufman, N. L. (1990). *Kaufman Brief Intelligence Test.* Circle Pines, MN: American Guidance Service, Inc.

Krause, M. (1998). Methodological and developmental issues in the assessment of adjudicative competence. Unpublished doctoral dissertation, University of Virginia.

Lexcen, F., & Reppucci, N. D. (1998). Effects of psychopathology on adolescent medical decision making, *University of Chicago Law School Roundtable, 5*, 63–106.

Parham v. J. R., 442 U.S. 584 (1979).

Peterson-Badali, M. & Abramovitch, R. (1993). Grade related changes in young people's reasoning about plea decisions. *Law and Human Behavior, 17*, 537–522.

Poythress, N. G., Nicholson, R., Otto, R. K., Edens, J. F., Bonnie, R. J., & Monahan, J, & Hoge, S. K. (1999). *The MacArthur Competence Assessment Tool—Criminal Adjudication: Professional manual.* Odessa, FL: Psychological Assessment Resources.

Redding, R. (1997), Juveniles transferred to criminal court: Legal reform proposals based on social science research. *Utah Law Review*, 711–763.

Reppucci, N. D. (1999). Adolescent development and juvenile justice. *American Journal of Community Psychology, 27*, 307–326.

Savitsky, J., & Karras, D. (1984). Competency to stand trial among adolescents. *Adolescence, 19*, 349–358.

Scott, E. (2000). Criminal responsibility in adolescence: Lessons from developmental psychology, In T. Grisso & R. Schwartz (Eds.), *Youth on trial.* Chicago: University of Chicago Press.

Scott, E., & Grisso, T. (1997). The evolution of adolescence: A developmental perspective on juvenile justice reform, *Journal of Criminal Law and Criminology, 88*, 137–189.

Scott, E. S., Reppucci, N. D., & Woolard, J. L. (1995). Evaluating adolescent decision making in legal contexts. *Law and Human Behavior, 19*, 221–244.

Snyder, H., & Sickmund, M. (1996). *Juvenile offenders and victims: A national report, 1996.* Washington, DC: US Department of Justice, Office of Juvenile Justice and Delinquency Prevention.

Steinberg, L., & Cauffman, E. (1996). Maturity of judgment in adolescence: Psychosocial factors in adolescent decision making. *Law and Human Behavior, 20*, 249–272.

Thompson v. Oklahoma, 487 U. S. 815 (1988).

Weinberger, D. A., & Schwartz, G. E. (1990). Distress and restraint as superordinate dimensions of self-reported adjustment: A typological perspective. *Journal of Personality, 58*, 381–417.

Wilkinson, D., & Fagan, J. (1996). The role of firearms in violence "scripts": The dynamics of gun events among adolescent males. *Law and Contemporary Problems, 59*, 55–89.

Woolard, J. L., Reppucci, N. D., & Scott, E. S. (1996). Judgment Assessment Tool—Adolescents. Unpublished manual.

Zimbardo, P. G. (1990). *The Stanford Time Perspective Inventory.* Stanford, CA: Stanford University.

Zimring, F. (1998). *American youth violence.* NY: Oxford University Press.

ACKNOWLEDGMENTS

These projects would not have been possible without the support and cooperation of a number of people. We thank the juveniles and adults who participated in the projects—their interest in and patience with our interview provided us valuable insight into their own experiences. Thanks also to the administrators and staff of the schools, jail and detention centers, particularly Dave Marsden, who allowed us to interrupt their daily routines without complaint. Graduate and undergraduate students too numerous to mention deserve recognition for faithfully serving as interviewers. Most importantly, Professor Elizabeth Scott of the University of Virginia Law School, was always available to discuss and clarify nuances of the law for instrument development and interpretation. Financial support was provided by the Virginia Department of Criminal Justice Services; Office of Juvenile Justice and Delinquency Prevention, U.S. Department of Justice; and the Virginia Center on Children, Families, and the Law.

Chapter 2

GIRLS IN JAIL: PUNISHMENT OR PROTECTION?

Raymond R. Corrado, Candice Odgers, and Irwin M. Cohen

In Canada, an increasing number of serious female offenders are coming into conflict with the law. Moreover, since the 1960s, the use of custody for female youth has been rising steadily and is expected to continue increasing given the crime control nature of many of the new youth justice statute proposals (Reitsma-Street, 1999). In addition, official police charge statistics suggest a marked increase in violent offending among female youth (Statistics Canada, 1998). Although it is clear that young women engage in significantly less violent behavior than their male counterparts (Hatch & Faith, 1990), the number of females charged with violence has been increasing at twice the rate of males charged with violence over the last decade (Statistics Canada, 1998).

While the media addresses these rising crime rates through a portrayal of a new "tough" and "violent" female adolescent (Perrone & Chesney-Lind, 1998; Schissel, 1997), several theorists working in this area depict these young women as victims; victims of abusive families, victims of a male dominated justice system, and victims of a society more willing to "fear violent girls" than to recognize the poverty, despair, and other social ills plaguing their lives (Artz, 1998; Chesney-Lind & Sheldon, 1998; Reitsma-Street, 1999). In the end, we are left with the media's picture of the bad girl (Chisholm, 1997), academics' depiction of the poor girl (Reitsma-Street, 1991), and the practitioners' and policy-makers' "concern for the lack of information on girls" (Reitsma-Street, 1999, p. 335). As a result of these conflicting images of female youth entering the youth justice system, it is unclear how policy-makers and practitioners should deal with girls in their care. The calls for more research in this area are being heard throughout the justice system, from front-line workers, such as law enforcement officers and correctional staff, to administrative and judicial decision-makers (Department of Justice, 1998).

Obviously, there is a need for in-depth research focusing on serious female young offenders. In particular, the historical exclusion of females in research, and the contemporary conceptualization of female offenders as a homogenous group, has resulted in a limited understanding of the different types of female offenders (Sommers & Baskin, 1994). This theoretical and empirical void has become increasingly evident in Canada as criminal justice decision-makers struggle to deal with the "girl problem" in the midst of reforming the current *Young Offenders Act*.

One of the goals of the present research is to explore the differences between males and females, and between nonviolent and violent females in custodial settings. In order to develop effective strategies for dealing with the female youths who are filling our custody institutions, a holistic picture of the risks and needs embedded in their lives must be analyzed. In particular, the recent public and academic fascination with female young offenders has directed attention towards the identification of gender-specific risk factors. Hence, the current visibility of a population that has traditionally been "empirically invisible" (Simourd & Andrews, 1999) is necessitating the acceleration of systematic studies that either focus specifically on gender, or incorporate gender as a crucial variable.

Finally, the focus of the new criminal justice statute on serious and violent youth in Canada potentially increases the stakes, in terms of criminal justice sanctions, for a population that we do not yet fully understand (Reitsma-Street, 1999). While there is a small body of research linking female participation in violence to the same sets of variables as their male counterparts (Loucks & Zamble, 1999; Sommers & Baskin, 1994), numerous researchers have rejected this hypothesis. Instead, they argue that young females inhabit and experience different social worlds than do males (Artz, 1998; Reitsma-Street, 1991). Allegedly, these important social differences lead to distinct casual pathways to serious and violent offending for females. Only in the last few years have social science researchers begun to gather the systematic body of data on female offenders necessary to resolve this fundamental debate. Unfortunately, while researchers and practitioners are focusing their attention on an extremely complex gender debate, very little is being done to address the current needs of female youth in custody. In other words, there appears to be some general confusion surrounding what should be done with female young offenders; a confusion that may be explained, in part, by the lack of detailed information regarding the lives of young females in conflict with the law.

As such, the primary objectives of the current research are to: 1) compare male and female violent and nonviolent offenders on a range of commonly identified risk factors of youth violence and delinquency; 2) to gain further insight into a traditionally "empirically invisible" population of female youth who are coming into conflict with the law, and 3) to contribute to the body of research necessary for the effective treatment, management, and prevention of female young offending.

METHOD

Participants

A sample of 284 males and 55 females were selected from four youth custody institutions in Vancouver, Canada over a period of one year. In order to meet the criteria for inclusion in the study, the youth had to be serving a custodial sentence under the YOA; youths who were being held in remand at the four institutions were excluded. Moreover, youths who were sentenced only to a probation period were also excluded. All youth residing in the institutions were approached to participate in the study. The response rate was approximately 87%.

The interviews lasted approximately 90 minutes and addressed a range of family, school, peer, criminal justice, and psychological constructs, including attention deficit hyperactivity disorder and psychopathy. Each youth provided information regarding their social, educational, and criminal histories through a series of closed and open-ended questions. Collaborative file information from pre-disposition, psychological, and institutional reports was also reviewed and coded for each subject.

As shown in Table 1, the youth in the sample had an extensive history of involvement with the youth justice system. On average, females had spent 104 days in a custodial institution and they had been processed through the criminal justice system an average of four times. In comparison, males had spent an average of 190 days in custody and had been officially processed through the system an average of five times. Although there were no significant differences found between the average number of prior offences between males and females, the differences in relation to the average length of time spent in a custodial settings was significant, $t = 2.30$, df = 320, $p = .003$.

Measures of familial, educational, and abuse histories indicated an extremely high level of dysfunction across contexts for these youth. Less than half (48.2%) of the females were enrolled in school at the time of the offence, as compared to just over half of the males (55.3%). A large percentage of both females and males reported leaving home by their own volition, 87.8% of females and 77.9% of males. Similarly, a substantial percentage of the youth reported being kicked out of their home, with 60.0% of females and 47.0% of males indicating that they had been forced from their homes by a parent or guardian. A relatively small percentage of the youth were employed at the time of the offence. On average, a significantly greater percentage of males (33.9%) than females (19.6%) reported being employed at the time of the commission of their current offence. And, as shown in Table 1, there were significantly different levels of physical and sexual abuse between the males and females, with females having reported substantially more abuse than their male counterparts. Based on an overview of the measures in Table 1, it is evident that this group of adolescents had been exposed to a myriad of negative family, peer, and social influences.

In order to construct the violent and nonviolent offending profiles based on gender, the youth were divided into four categories: (1) Violent males, (2) Violent females, (3) Nonviolent males, and (4) Nonviolent females. A youth was placed in a violent category if she or he had ever been sentenced for a violent crime, i.e., murder, sexual assault, assault, robbery, and/or intimidation. Within the female offenders, there were 25 nonviolent and 30 violent offenders. Males divided into groups of 94 nonviolent offenders and 190 violent offenders. Comparisons were made using chi-square tests of independence for the categorical measures, and independent sample t-tests were used for interval level data. Due to the exploratory nature of the

Table 1: Sample Characteristics

Variable	Females (n = 55)	Males (n = 284)
Age (*M*)*	15.8	16.2
School factors		
Enrolled (%)	48.2	55.3
Times changed (*M*)	4.7	5.5
Trouble at school (%)***	83.3	96.5
Family factors		
Trouble at home (%)	92.6	88.9
Ever left home (%)	87.8	77.9
Age left home (*M*)*	11.8	12.8
Ever kicked out of home (%)	60.0	47.0
Age kicked out of home (*M*)	12.8	13.6
Number of places lived other than home (*M*)	6.3	5.8
Work factors		
Currently employed (%)*	19.6	33.9
Maternal employment (%)	61.5	58.0
Paternal employment (%)*	51.0	67.6
Abuse		
Physically abused (%)***	70.4	39.8
Sexually abused (%)***	54.8	11.4
Offence information		
Nonviolent offender (*n*)	25	94
Violent offender (*n*)	30	190
Number of prior convictions (*M*)	4	5
Total time spent in custody in days (*M*)	109	189

*$p < .05$. ***$p < .001$.

research, no control was used to correct for type-one errors. Future analysis will explore each set of variables through a more complex and in-depth multivariate analysis, however, the immediate goal was to construct and compare general profiles of this group of nonviolent and violent offenders, while paying specific attention to the role of gender.

RESULTS

Family variables

Measures of linear family history were compared across groups. In this case, a member of the youth's linear family included both immediate and extended family members. Levels of linear alcohol abuse, χ^2 (1, N = 118) = 3.61, $p < .05$, mental illness, χ^2 (1, N = 118) = 5.77, $p = .016$, and placement in foster care, χ^2 (1, N = 118) = 10.50, $p = .001$, were significantly higher among the nonviolent females than among nonviolent males. As shown in Table 2, nonviolent females had the highest levels of linear family dysfunction across all measures, excluding linear drug use (although the results were not statistically significant).

Measures of home separation indicated a high level of familial conflict across all of the groups. It is interesting to note that both males and females in the nonviolent categories were kicked out of their homes an average of seven times, while their violent counterparts were kicked out an average of four times, $t = 1.608$, df = 111, $p = .012$. Thus, it appears

Table 2: Family Variables

Variable	Females		Males	
	Nonviolent $n = 25$	Violent $n = 30$	Nonviolent $n = 94$	Violent $n = 190$
Family criminality				
Parental criminality	48.1	51.9	34.1	65.9
Sibling Criminality	8.0	16.7	26.6	24.2
Linear family history				
Drug abuse	70.8	56.7	71.3	55.7
Alcohol abuse	91.7	73.3	73.4	71.5
Foster care	68.0	46.7	32.3	35.3
Mental illness	44.0	30.0	20.4	16.9
Linear criminal record	80.0	66.7	71.3	70.1
Home separation				
Left home	94.7	81.9	83.9	75.9
Age left home	12.1	11.4	12.7	12.9
Times left	6.1	12.3	14.8	6.
Kicked out of home	50.0	68.2	57.4	42.3
Age kicked out	12.	13.3	13.4	13.6
Times kicked out	7.3	4.3	7.2	3.7
Number of places lived	6.5	6.1	2.1	2.4

that nonviolent offenders were forced from their homes more often than youths with a history of violent offending. Nonviolent females also reported being kicked out of their homes at a younger age than the other three groups of offenders. Although this difference was not statistically significant, it is consistent with other measures indicating early familial turmoil and high levels of dysfunction among this group.

Measures of parental employment also revealed some dramatic differences within the female categories, and across violent offenders. For instance, 81.5% of violent female offenders reported that their mothers were employed at the time of the interview, as compared to 47.6% of the nonviolent females, χ^2 (1, N = 48) = 6.10, p = .014). Violent females also reported a significantly higher percentage of maternal employment than did the males classified as violent offenders, χ^2 (1, N = 201) = 3.65, $p < .05$). Again, the nonviolent females reported the highest levels of both maternal and paternal unemployment across all categories. Using parental employment as a gross indicator of social class, it appears that the nonviolent females in this sample were coming from homes with the least amount of economic resources.

School variables

Similar to the findings with family variables, nonviolent females reported higher levels of overall dysfunction and conflict in school settings than the other groupings (See Table 3). Nonviolent females reported that they began skipping classes at an earlier age than violent females, t = 2.42, df = 35, p = .021. They also reported "getting into trouble at school" at an earlier age than violent females. The mean age at which nonviolent females stated that their problems at school began was age 9, as compared to the violent females whose behavior problems in school reportedly began at age 12, t = 2.30, df = 31, p = .028. In addition, nonviolent females reported changing schools much more frequently than their violent female counterparts, t = 1.96, df = 38, $p < .05$. There were no significant differences found between nonviolent females and males.

Interestingly, violent females reported beginning to skip school at an earlier age than did both the violent males, t = 2.49, df = 139, p = .014, and the nonviolent males, t = 2.15, df = 74, p = .035. Violent females also stated that they began getting into trouble at a later age than their violent males, t = 2.40, df = 135, p = .018, and nonviolent male counterparts, t = 1.96, df = 75, $p < .05$. They also reported changing schools less than both the violent males, t = 1.97, df = 157, $p < .05$. They also and the nonviolent males, t = 2.58, df = 79, p = .012.

Table 3: School Variables

	Females		Males	
	Nonviolent (n = 25)	Violent (n = 30)	Nonviolent (n = 94)	Violent (n = 190)
Enrolled (%)	40.0	56.7	54.3	55.8
Truancy				
Ever skipped class (%)	94.4	95.5	95.2	89.9
Skipping frequency (M)	1.7	2.1	2.2	2.4
Age of onset (M)	12.2	13.4	12.4	12.7
Behavior problems				
Trouble at school (%)	84.2	81.8	96.8	96.4
Age of onset (M)	9.4	11.9	10.4	10.1
Number of schools (M)	6.6	3.0	5.7	5.5

Abuse variables

As expected, females reported experiencing significantly higher rates of both physical and sexual abuse than their male counterparts across all categories. However, there were some surprising findings within the female violent and nonviolent categories. While the reporting of physical abuse across non-violent and violent females remained constant, with approximately 70% of both violent and nonviolent females reporting some type of physical victimization, nonviolent females reported having been sexually abused at a significantly higher rate than did their violent female counterparts. As shown in Table 4, 66.7% of nonviolent females reported being sexually abused at some point in their life, as compared to 44.8% of the females in the violent offender category, χ^2 (1, N = 53) = 2.53, p = .048. Similarly, a significantly higher percentage of nonviolent as compared to violent females reported that a member of their family had been a victim of sexual abuse, χ^2 (1, N = 52) = 2.57, $p < .05$.

There were no significant differences between nonviolent and violent males with respect to abuse, although, a higher percentage of nonviolent males reported being a victim of physical abuse, having a family member who was victimized physically, and having a family member who was sexually abused that their violent male counterparts. Conversely, a greater percentage of violent male offenders (12.8%) reported being sexually victimized than did nonviolent male offenders (8.7%).

In summary, it is clear that the females in this sample were far more likely to report being victimized both physically and sexually. However, the role that victimization plays in violent offending among both males and females is extremely unclear. Measures of physical abuse indicated relatively little difference *within* gender. While measures of sexual

Table 4: Abuse Variables

	Females		Males	
	Nonviolent (n = 25)	Violent (n = 30)	Nonviolent (n = 94)	Violent (n = 190)
Self				
Physical abuse (%)	70.8	70.0	42.4	38.4
Sexual abuse (%)	66.7	44.8	8.7	12.8
Linear family				
Physical abuse (%)	68.0	64.3	48.9	43.4
Sexual abuse (%)	54.2	32.1	17.6	14.7

victimization indicated significant differences within gender, they were in the opposite direction than would be predicted based on previous research (Chesney-Lind & Sheldon, 1998). That is, female nonviolent offenders were more likely to report being a victim of sexual abuse. This pattern was also apparent in the measures of linear family abuse. Clearly, a more in-depth analysis is needed to explore both the direct and indirect effects of abuse on youthful offending.

Substance abuse variables

Measures of substance abuse were the final set of variables compared across groups. As shown in Table 5, nonviolent females again appeared to be at the greatest risk across virtually every drug category. In particular, nonviolent females reported the highest levels of hard drug use. The use of cocaine appears to be extremely prevalent, with 82.6% of nonviolent females reporting frequent use of cocaine. Female nonviolent offenders reported higher levels of heroin use than did nonviolent male offenders, χ^2 (1, N = 89) = 5.03, p = .025, and violent male offenders, χ^2 (1, N = 172) = 12.02, p = .001. They also reported higher levels of cocaine use than did nonviolent males, χ^2 (1, N = 97) = 4.57, p = .033, and violent males, χ^2 (1, N = 187) = 12.10, p = .001. Although the differences in hard drug use were not significant among females, it is interesting to note that, based on percentages, they consistently reported higher usage. The extremely high percentages of nonviolent females using crack, heroin, and cocaine point to specific treatment issues for this group of young offenders.

DISCUSSION AND CONCLUSIONS

Overall, nonviolent female offenders reported the highest levels of dysfunction across familial, school, abuse, and drug use measures. The consistency of this finding indicates that the nonviolent females who were

Table 5: Substance Abuse Variables

	Females		Males	
	Nonviolent (n = 23)	Violent (n = 30)	Nonviolent (n = 94)	Violent (n = 190)
Marijuana	92.0	83.3	92.6	91.0
Crack	65.2	42.9	39.4	57.1
Heroin	56.5	53.6	30.3	22.1
Cocaine	82.6	60.0	58.1	43.9

interviewed in custody were the most disadvantaged in terms of economic, social, and educational resources. Nonviolent females appeared to be coming from families with the highest levels of dysfunction, as measured by alcohol use, mental illness, unemployment, and placement in foster care. Nonviolent females also reported the highest levels of parental unemployment across all four groups. In addition, they reported being kicked out of their homes both at the earliest age and with greater frequency.

Based on the results presented, it is apparent that this group of offenders requires an integrated model of intervention that addresses the myriad of problems impacting their lives. It is also important to note that, although our measures revealed the highest levels of dysfunction for females in the nonviolent offender category, the other three categories of offenders were not immune to these risk factors. Rather, a substantial proportion of all of the youth in the sample had backgrounds characterized by high levels of violence, substance abuse, and weak bonds to family and school.

Interestingly, there was a high degree of similarity among violent offenders, irregardless of gender. In general, relatively few significant differences were found between the profiles of violent females and those of their violent male counterparts. However, there were a number of significant differences found between the nonviolent and violent females, namely in relation to school and family measures. This type of aggregate comparison is useful in addressing the growing concern over violence committed by female youth and the lack of systematic research on risk factors associated with female violent offending. However, the exploratory nature of the present research findings points towards further analysis of the etiology of female violence, controlling for the myriad of intervening variables and interaction effects.

With respect to the nonviolent female offender category, some notable trends emerged. Despite the fact that the nonviolent females had extremely minor offending histories, they still spent an average of 92 days in a youth custody institution. In addition, a large percentage of their containment in custody, 65% on average, resulted from a simple breach, or an offence against the administration of youth justice.

Thus, when the high levels of dysfunction across familial, abuse, school, and drug measures are combined with these minor criminal histories and prolonged periods of incarceration, the exact role of the criminal justice system in these young women's lives is called into question. Arguably, it appears that custodial institutions are being used in many cases as a storage haven for "at- risk" and "neglected" youth, as opposed to an institution for criminal youth (Corrado, Odgers, & Cohen, 2000). If this is the case, and youth are being contained on grounds that are unrelated to both their offence history and current offence, the fundamental tenets and objectives of our "offence based" youth justice legislation must be revisited.

In Canada, the evolution over the last century from a welfare-based model of youth justice to a mixed justice model for dealing with young offenders has been viewed as progressive (Corrado & Markwart, 1994). The basis for this progressive outlook is rooted in a critical analysis of the abuse operant under the *Juvenile Delinquents Act* (1908) and the rights based orientation of current *Young Offenders Act* (1982) legislation. However, the preliminary findings of this present research provide some support for the argument that the containment of youth is still being justified on the basis of "best interest of the child" considerations, such as a dysfunctional family and minor delinquent transgressions.

As the proposals for the new youth *Criminal Justice Act* (Department of Justice, 1998) come forward, it is clear that the response of policy-makers to young offenders is crime control reforms. Although the need for early intervention initiatives has been recognized in the latest proposal (Department of Justice, 1998), the lack of attention paid to treatment and the special needs of youth currently in the system is a cause for significant concern. The results of this preliminary study clearly suggest a high level of familial, school, abuse, and substance abuse dysfunction. Arguably, the solution for these youth, namely the nonviolent offenders who pose little threat to society, cannot be realized solely through extended periods of incarceration, where treatment and reintegrative efforts are scarce. In particular, there is a need to critically examine the "rehabilitative" and "protective" role that custodial institutions may be playing, despite the rights-based underpinnings of the current youth justice legislation.

REFERENCES

Artz, S. (1998). *Sex, power, and the violent school girl.* Toronto: Trifolium.

Chesney-Lind, M., & Sheldon, R. (1998). *Girls, delinquency, and juvenile justice.* Pacific Grove: Brooks/Cole.

Chisholm, P. (1997). Bad girls. *Macleans*, December 8, 13–15.

Corrado, R., & Markwart, A. (1994). The Need to reform the YOA in response to violent young offenders: Confusion, reality, or myth? *Canadian Journal of Criminology*, *36*, 343–378.

Corrado, R., Odgers, C., & Cohen, I. (2000). The incarceration of female young offenders: protection for whom? *Canadian Journal of Criminology,* 42, 189–207.

Department of Justice. (1998). *Canada's youth justice renewal strategy: Prevention meaningful consequences rehabilitation.* Ottawa: Author.

Hatch, A., & Faith, K. (1990). The female offender in Canada: A statistical profile. *Canadian Journal of Women and the Law*, *3*, 432–456.

Juvenile Delinquents Act. S. C. 1908, c. 40.

Loucks, A., & Zamble, E. (1999). Some comparisons of female and male serious young offenders. *Women in Prison*, (6), January.

Perrone, P. & Chesney-Lind, M. (1998). Media presentations of crime in Hawaii: Wild in the streets? *http://www.cpja.ag.state.hi.us/rs/cts/mediajuv/.*

Reitsma-Street, M. (1991). A review of female delinquency. In A. Lescheid, P. Jaffe, & W. Willis (Eds.), *The Young Offenders Act : A revolution in Canadian juvenile justice.* Toronto: University of Toronto Press.

Reitsma-Street, M. (1999). Justice for Canadian girls: A 1990s update. *Canadian Journal of Criminology*, *41*, 335–364.

Schissel, B. (1997). *Blaming children: Youth crime, moral panics, and the politics of hate.* Halifax: Fernwood.

Simourd, L. & Andrews, D. (1999). Correlates of delinquency: A look at gender differences. *Women in Prison*, 6, January.

Sommers, I., & Baskin, D. (1994). Factors related to female adolescent initiation into street crime. *Youth and Society*, *25*, 468–489.

Statistics Canada. (1998). *Canadian dimensions—Youth and adult crime rates. http://www.statcan/english/Pgdb/State/Justice/legal*, 14.

Young Offenders Act. S. C. 180–81–82–83, c.110 [now R. S. C. 1985, c. Y-1].

Chapter 3

ARE JUVENILES GETTING A FAIR TRIAL?: THE JURY IS STILL OUT

Diane Warling, Michele Peterson-Badali and Jonathan Freedman

In North America, youth are being increasingly treated as adults in the legal system (Bala, 1994; Grisso, 1996). In Canada, youth aged 14 to 17 have the option of a jury trial when transferred to adult court. Furthermore, recent amendments to the Young Offenders Act in Canada have extended the right to a jury trial in *youth* court to youth charged with the commission of certain violent crimes. A central issue regarding jury trials for juveniles is the fact that these youth are not tried by a jury of their "peers," but by a jury of adults. A jury of one's peers is based on two premises: that the jury be made up of members from the defendant's community, and that the defendant is entitled to an impartial jury (Golash, 1992; Perez, Hosch, Ponder, & Trejo, 1993). The process of selecting an impartial jury has become a major endeavor, particularly in the American justice system. Jury selection procedures are often lengthy and cumbersome; yet throughout North America, certain procedures are followed in the hopes of securing an impartial jury.

A central concern regarding jury trials for young offenders is that a jury comprised only of adults may hold attitudes about young people that will result in a systematic bias in decision-making regarding juvenile defendants as compared to adult defendants. Indirect empirical support for this concern arises from studies reporting public attitudes of young offenders to be overly harsh, as well as from research highlighting extralegal biases in the jury decision making process.

Investigating the implications of jury trials for young offenders is particularly important given the widespread overestimation by the general public of the prevalence of youth crime (Corrado & Markwart, 1994), and the public's beliefs that youth should be held more accountable for their crimes and that the sentences for violent crime committed by juveniles should be more punitive (Baron & Hartnagel, 1996; Sprott, 1996; Stalans & Henry, 1994). This raises the possibility that adults' beliefs and attitudes toward youth crime may affect their perceptions of young defendants charged with the commission of a violent crime. This could have serious implications for whether youth tried by adult jurors would receive a fair trial by an impartial jury. Research needs to investigate whether youth tried by a jury (of adults) will be perceived differently than adults tried by jury. The main question of interest is whether the age of a defendant will affect verdict and/or sentencing decisions in a jury trial.

There is a large body of research which suggests that extralegal factors of a case (factors not legally relevant to the case at hand) can influence juridic decisions. For instance, researchers employing the jury simulation method have found that a variety of defendant characteristics can bias mock jurors, and in turn, influence decisions of guilt and/or sentencing (cf. Frederick, 1987). However, the effects of defendant characteristics on juridic decisions are often complex and dependent on a variety of factors (Bagby, Parker, Rector, & Kalemba, 1994; Kerr, Hymes, Anderson, & Weathers, 1995; MacCoun, 1990; Rector, Bagby, & Nicholson, 1993). It is difficult to extend much of this research to jury trials for youth as most of the jury bias research to date has examined characteristics of adult defendants. There is very little research that has examined the effects of defendant age on juror decision-making, particularly where youthful defendants are concerned.

Recent research examining the effects of defendant age in *capital* murder cases has found that adults acting as mock jurors have been more lenient with younger defendants as compared to older defendants (Crosby, Britner, Jodl, & Portwood, 1995; Finkel, Hughes, Smith, & Hurabiell, 1994). While the younger defendant appeared to have been granted some leniency with adult mock jurors, these studies reported a surprisingly high percentage of adults opting for executing child defendants as young as ten years of age (Crosby et al., 1995). This suggests that in severe cases, the crime itself may be viewed as more salient than the age of the defendant. Again, further research needs to investigate whether this is the case for *non-capital* trials to determine if adult perceptions of youth who commit violent crime affect their decision-making in a legal context.

In sum, the research on juror decision making regarding juvenile defendants in capital murder cases suggests that adults may be more lenient with youthful defendants as compared to adult defendants in rendering death sentences. However, public opinion surveys on adults' perceptions of youth crime would suggest that the general public may be more punitive with youthful defendants on trial as compared to adult defendants. It is unclear if adult jurors would tend to judge the evidence against a youthful defendant more harshly, or with more sympathy and lenience. Furthermore, it has yet to be established that adults' perceptions of youth who commit crime (whether it is punitive or sympathetic) will affect their ability to render an impartial verdict, or affect their sentencing recommendations, in a case involving a young defendant.

A series of studies is currently underway which has sought to answer several empirical questions regarding jury trials for juvenile offenders. The first question addressed is whether the age of a defendant will affect legal decision making. More specifically, will adults vote differently on a case involving a youthful defendant as compared to a case involving an adult defendant? Second, will adults' perceptions toward youth crime affect their decision in a simulated legal context? Is there a relationship between how people perceive youth who commit crime, and their decisions about a youth in a simulated trial, after general conviction proneness is taken into account? To address this question, the following information was collected: adults' general attitudes about the legal system which includes a measure of general conviction proneness; adults' perceptions of juvenile culpability; attitudes toward youth crime and young offenders; and demographic variables. These questions have been empirically addressed using the mock jury paradigm with jury eligible adults.

This research is comprised of two studies addressing whether and under what conditions defendant age affects juror verdict and sentencing decisions. Study 1 includes two samples of jury-eligible adults. The first sample includes undergraduate students that participated in a mock jury study independent of other students. However, it has been suggested that undergraduates are not an ecologically valid sample with respect to jury research, and thus may endorse different responses from that of a more representative sample of adults (Bornstein, 1999; Bray & Kerr, 1979; Diamond, 1997; Weiten & Diamond, 1979). Thus, data collection of a second sample comprised of adults from the general community is currently underway. As the size of this community sample remains too small for analyses, none have yet been completed. Future results from this non-deliberating, community adult sample will be compared to that of the non-deliberating student sample to examine whether there are statistically significant differences in juror decision making between undergraduates and adults from the general population, as suggested by a number of criticisms of mock jury research (cf. Bornstein, 1999; Diamond, 1997).

In Study 2, a different sample of undergraduates was included who were asked to deliberate in groups about a court case. The purpose of using a deliberating sample in Study 2 was to examine the effects of group deliberation on verdict and sentencing decisions, and assess possible effects of defendant age on the discussions during deliberation. This deliberating sample was also included to enhance the ecological validity of the research, as it has been suggested that mock jurors who deliberate arrive at different legal decisions when compared to mock jurors who render individual decisions about a case (cf. Bornstein, 1999; Diamond, 1997).

STUDY 1
METHOD

Sample

Participants were undergraduate students enrolled in a first or second year undergraduate psychology class at the University of Toronto, Canada, who were given course credit for their participation. There were 180 participants in the non-deliberating student sample, 60 in each of three defendant age conditions. Sixty-five percent were female, the average age of respondents was 20, most participants had no children, all had some university education, 64% were Caucasian, 30% were Asian, 2% were African-American, and the remaining participants identified themselves to be from other ethnic groups. As data collection is in progress for the sample of adults recruited from the community, results from this sample will not be presented.

Procedure

After giving consent, participants were informed that they would be given a description of a trial and would be asked to give their verdict in the case and answer several questions about it. They were also told that they would be asked to complete a brief demographics questionnaire, and a survey about their attitudes toward the legal system. Participants were told the study would take approximately 20 to 30 minutes of their time. Participants were run in small groups (one to five at a time), but were not permitted to discuss the case or questions with others in the room.

The defendant's age in the case vignette was varied, and the defendant was presented as either 13, 17, or 25 years of age. Participants received identical case vignettes (with only defendant age varied) and questionnaires. Case vignettes were distributed to participants such that the defendant's age progressed in sequence.

Materials

All participants were given a three-page written description of a case where a male defendant, Richard Smith, who was presented as 13-, 17-, or 25-years-old, was charged with second degree murder in the stabbing death of another male the defendant's stated age. The prosecution and defense each presented their opening statements and witnesses, with cross-examinations, as well as closing arguments. A final statement from the judge was given instructing the mock juror that to vote guilty, he/she must be convinced beyond a reasonable doubt that the defendant started the fight which led to the stabbing death of the victim, and deliberately intended to kill the victim.

The questions following the case vignette are found in Table I. These questions have been used in a number of jury simulation studies (cf. Freedman, Krismer, MacDonald, & Cunningham, 1994; Peterson-Badali, Chow, Abramovitch, & Freedman, 1997). Participants were asked to render an individual verdict of guilty or not guilty, rate the certainty of their decision on a 6-point Likert scale (from *absolutely certain* to *not at all certain*); and rate their *feeling* about whether the defendant was indeed guilty of the crime, regardless of their verdict, on a 7-point Likert scale (from *certain he was guilty* to *certain he was innocent*). Participants were then given a number of sentence lengths from which to choose should the defendant have been found guilty of the crime. Participants were then asked to indicate the defendant's age (as a manipulation check), and rate on a 4-point Likert scale how much they thought the defendant's age affected their decision regarding both their verdict and their sentencing recommendations (from *not at all* to *a great deal*). They were also asked to provide written comments regarding their response to these questions.

A brief demographics questionnaire followed, which included questions about the respondent's age, gender, country of citizenship, number of children, level of education, ethnicity, and level of religious commitment.

The next section consisted of a combination of three scales, and was called the Survey of Legal Attitudes. Participants were asked to rate their level of

Table 1: Questions Regarding the Case of Richard Smith

1. What would your verdict be in this case?
2. How certain are you of your decision?
3. Whether you voted guilty or not guilty, what is your *feeling* about whether Smith was guilty of murder?
4. Setting aside your own verdict, assume for a moment that Smith *was* found guilty of second degree murder, which of the following sentence lengths would you recommend, in terms of years of imprisonment? (Sentencing options were 2, 5, 10, 15 and 25 years of imprisonment.)
5. Without referring back to the case, how old was Smith?
6. How much do you think Smith's age affected your decision regarding the *verdict* you rendered? (Please comment on your response to question #6).
7. How much do you think Smith's age affected your decision regarding your *sentencing recommendations*? (Please comment on your response to question #7).

agreement, on a 5-point Likert scale (1 = *Strongly Agree*; 5 = *Strongly Disagree*), with 34 statements regarding the legal system, juvenile culpability, and youth crime.

The first scale in the survey was the Juror Bias Scale developed by Kassin and Wrightsman (1983). This questionnaire consists of 17 items (plus 5 "filler" items) that measure individual differences in pre-trial prejudice toward the guilt or innocence of an accused; 9 items reflect the probability of commission or subjective expectancy differences (e.g., "circumstantial evidence is too weak to use in court"), and 8 items reflect the reasonable doubt or "utility" component of the scale (e.g., "too often jurors hesitate to convict someone who is truly guilty out of pure sympathy"). A high score on this scale denotes greater pro-prosecution views, or greater conviction proneness. The Juror Bias Scale has been found in the past to be internally consistent (Cronbach's Alpha = .70 to .75) (Furnham & Alison, 1994). In the present study, internal consistency analyses revealed poor internal consistency among the 17-items of the scale. To increase the internal consistency of the scale, four items were dropped from the analysis (items 11, 13, 15, and 21). This final 13-item Juror Bias Scale was found to have moderate internal consistency (Cronbach's Alpha = .65).

The next scale in the Survey of Legal Attitudes included an adapted form of the Juvenile Culpability Scale, developed by Crosby, Britner, Jodl and Portwood (1995). The original scale consists of six items measuring adults' attitudes about the criminal accountability of juveniles, particularly regarding capital trials. Our adapted version contained eight items based on the original six which sought to measure perceptions of juvenile culpability not specific to capital murder cases (e.g., "compared to adults, teenagers (ages 12 to 17) do not have the maturity or life experience to appreciate fully all of the possible consequences of their actions, including criminal behavior" and "young offenders (ages 12 to 17) are more capable of reform than adult offenders"). The 8-item Juvenile Culpability Scale—Adapted Form used in the survey was found to be internally consistent (Cronbach's Alpha = .77).

The third scale included in the Survey was termed the Attitude Toward Youth Crime Scale and consisted of four statements about youth crime. These questions were thought to measure public perceptions of youth crime and appropriate juvenile justice responses to violent youth crime (e.g., "the sentences given to young people (ages 12 to 17) found guilty of criminal offences are generally too lenient" and "over the past ten years, youth crime has increased significantly"). The four items comprising the

Attitude Toward Youth Crime Scale demonstrated adequate internal consistency (Cronbach's Alpha = .71).

The final question of the Survey was adapted from the standard "Challenge for Cause" question from *Regina v. Parks* used in Canadian criminal courts in cases of suspected racial prejudice. In the survey, respondents were asked to answer "yes" or "no" to the following question: "do you hold any opinions, beliefs, or feelings that would make you unable to be a fair juror in a case involving a youth aged 12 to 17?"

RESULTS

Verdict

Overall, 65% or 117 of the 180 respondents voted not-guilty, and 35% rendered guilty verdicts. A series of chi-square tests was performed to examine the relationship between mock jurors' verdicts and the primary variable of interest—age of the defendant—as well as categorical demographic variables of interest such as gender and ethnicity. Respondents' verdict was not significantly related to the age of the defendant; 38% of the participants in the 13-year-old defendant condition voted guilty, 35% of participants in the 17-year-old defendant condition voted guilty, and 32% in the 25-year-old defendant condition voted guilty. Respondents' gender was the only (categorical) variable significantly related to verdict, χ^2 (1) = 6.96, $p < .01$, in that women were more likely to vote guilty than men, regardless of the age of the defendant.

A chi-square analysis of verdict and the response to the Challenge for Cause question revealed no relationship between participants' response to this question and their verdict in the case, regardless of defendant age. In general, very few people acknowledged bias against young people by answering yes to the Challenge for Cause question, with only 26 out of 180 (14.4%) answering yes to this question.

Overall, a majority of the respondents (63%) felt that the age of the defendant affected their verdict "not at all." However, a one-way ANOVA revealed that respondents who read the case involving the 13-year-old defendant were more likely to state that the defendant's age had affected their verdict (M = 1.9) than those who read cases involving either the 17-year-old (M = 1.3) or 25-year-old (M = 1.4) defendants, F (2, 177) = 5.66, $p < .01$.

Next, a logistic regression was performed with scores on the three scales of the Survey of Legal Attitudes, responses to the Challenge for Cause question, and respondents' gender as predictors and verdict as the outcome variable. Results indicated that scores on the Juror Bias Scale,

Wald = 11.37, $p < .001$; $R = -.20$, and respondents' gender, Wald = 4.86, $p < .05$; $R = .11$, significantly predicted verdict. Respondents likely to convict the defendant, regardless of his age, were those with a predisposition to convict and greater pro-prosecution biases, as indicated by higher scores on the Juror Bias Scale, as well as female mock jurors. It should be noted that neither variable accounted for much of the variance in verdict, however, as scores on the Juror Bias Scale accounted for 5% of the variance in verdict, and respondent's gender accounted for only 2% of the variance in verdict.

Sentencing

Overall, the average recommended sentence length was 10 years of imprisonment. However, sentence length was affected by defendant age, in that the older the defendant, the longer the sentence, F (2, 176) = 9.68, $p < .001$. Post hoc analyses revealed that the only significant pair-wise differences were between the 13-year-old defendant condition and the other two conditions where the defendant was presented as either 17- or 25-years of age. When this ANOVA was replicated with the sub-sample of participants who voted guilty ($n = 63$), the effect for defendant age on sentencing remained significant, F (2, 60) = 6.06, $p < .01$, but post hoc analyses revealed a significant difference only between the 13- and 25-year-old defendant conditions.

When asked if they believed the defendant's age affected their sentencing decision, most participants (65%) indicated that it did. Like verdict, there was an effect for defendant age, F (2, 175) = 19.78, $p < .001$, in that the younger the defendant, the more likely participants were to report that his age affected their sentencing recommendation.

To examine the relationship between sentence length and other variables of interest, a multiple regression analysis was performed. Variables entered simultaneously into the analysis were: defendant's age, and scores on the Juror Bias Scale, the Juvenile Culpability Scale—Adapted form, and the Attitude Toward Youth Crime Scale. Only two variables significantly predicted sentence length. Scores on the Juvenile Culpability Scale—Adapted form were found to be the best predictor of sentence length ($\beta = 0.370$, $p < .001$), and accounted for 14% of the variance in sentencing recommendations. The second significant predictor of sentence length was defendant age ($\beta = 0.291$, $p < .001$), which accounted for 8% of the variance in sentencing. Although scores on the Attitude Toward Youth Crime Scale were significantly correlated with sentence length ($r = -0.19$, $p < .01$), this scale shared significant variance with the Juvenile Culpability Scale—Adapted form, and thus did not significantly contribute unique variance to sentence length not accounted for by the Juvenile Culpability Scale—Adapted form. Those participants who believed juveniles are legally responsible for their criminal actions tended to endorse longer sentences, regardless of defendant age.

STUDY 2
METHOD

The purpose of this study was to examine the effects of group deliberation on verdict and sentencing decisions, and assess possible effects of defendant age on discussion during deliberation. Study 2 also sought to enhance the external validity of Study 1 by having participants deliberate, as is practice in actual jury trials.

The case vignette and following questionnaires used in Study 2 were identical to those used in Study 1. The defendant's age was varied *between* groups, and as in Study 1, he was presented as either 13, 17, or 25 years of age. Participants were asked to read the case summary privately, render an individual verdict, and then discuss the case with four or five other mock jurors. They were instructed to deliberate on the case and arrive at a group decision regarding verdict within 20 minutes (or less). Should the group members not be able to reach a unanimous verdict in the time allotted, they were informed that they would be considered a "hung jury." The group deliberations were audio taped. After the deliberations, the participants were asked to complete the demographics questionnaire and the Survey of Legal Attitudes independently.

Sample

The sample included 150 undergraduate students enrolled in an introductory psychology class at the University of Toronto. There were 27 deliberating mock juries in total, nine in each of the three defendant age conditions. Fifteen juries were comprised of 6 students, and 12 juries consisted of 5 students. This sample was found to be very similar demographically to the non-deliberating undergraduate sample in Study 1. Most participants were female (81%); the average age of participants in the sample was 20-years-old; no participants had children; 55% of the sample identified themselves to be Caucasian, 33% were Asian, 4% were African-American, and about 9% identified themselves to be of another ethnic group. In the deliberating sample, roughly 21%, or 31 of 150 participants answered "yes" to the Challenge for Cause question.

RESULTS

Overall, 21 mock juries rendered a unanimous Not Guilty verdict. The remaining 6 could not reach a unanimous verdict in the time given, and they were thus designated as Hung Juries. No group decision rendered a Guilty verdict.

Prior to deliberation, participants were asked to render individual verdicts. Twenty-five percent voted guilty before discussing the case with other members of the mock jury. A chi-square analysis on defendant age by pre-deliberation verdict revealed no significant relationship between the two variables. After deliberating in groups, there was an interesting effect of defendant age on group verdict. The mock juries in the 13-year-old defendant condition were almost as likely to reach a Hung Jury verdict ($n = 4$) as they were to return a unanimous Not Guilty vote ($n = 5$); whereas eight of the nine juries in each of the 17- and 25-year-old defendant conditions reached a unanimous Not Guilty verdict. However, this finding was not statistically significant, suggesting that defendant age did not significantly affect group verdicts. It will be interesting, however, to analyse the transcripts of the deliberations to identify any themes relating to the age of defendant, and to investigate possible reasons given for the discrepancy in Not Guilty jury verdicts between the case of the 13-year-old defendant and the two cases of the older defendant.

It is important to note that, for the student samples in both Study 1 and 2, there was not enough variability in some of the demographic variables to enter them into analyses (e.g., respondent age, level of education, and number of children).

DISCUSSION

It has been said that research needs to inform policy. In Canada, legal policy has been influenced by the public's perceptions of young offenders by increased transfers to adult court for youth charged with certain violent or repeat offences. Furthermore, public opinion has driven several amendments to the Young Offenders Act that have resulted in the significant lengthening of youth court sentences for serious crimes committed by young people, and most recently, to the introduction of new youth justice legislation. An unintended effect of these increased transfers and lengthened sentences for youth is that these youth are now entitled to a trial by jury.

This research grew out of a perceived need to explore whether youth are assured their right to a fair trial when tried by a jury of adults, as opposed to a judge or a jury of their "peers." The primary purpose of this research was to investigate whether a defendant's age in a simulated trial would affect adult verdicts and sentencing decisions when participants were presented with cases that involved both youthful and adult offenders. It was also of interest to examine the relationship between adults' perceptions of young offenders, and their decisions in court cases involving young defendants.

In response to the first research question, based on the data thus far, there is no evidence to suggest that adults are biased toward or against youth on trial in terms of their verdict decisions. Results from Study 1 using undergraduates as mock jurors suggest that the defendant's age does not significantly affect verdict when rendering individual decisions about a case. It is interesting that many jurors indicated that the age of the defendant did matter in rendering their verdict decisions, particularly with the younger defendants, but this was not reflected in their actual verdicts.

Adults did demonstrate age sensitivity with respect to sentencing. The younger defendants were consistently given lighter sentences by the mock jurors. This is consistent with public opinion research indicating that people value rehabilitation as a sentencing principle for young offenders (Hartnagel and Baron, 1994). This also corresponds to youth justice policy in Canada, which assumes that young people are more amenable to rehabilitation and change as compared to adult offenders. This finding is also similar to results regarding juvenile defendants in capital trials (Crosby et al., 1995; Finkel et al., 1994), which suggests adults may be more lenient with juveniles when rendering sentences.

The second research question pertained to attitudinal and demographic factors which may affect adults' legal decision-making. When acting as mock jurors, those participants who were more likely to convict an accused in general (as measured by the Juror Bias Scale) were also more likely to convict the defendant in the current study, regardless of his age. However, attitudes about youth crime and young offenders did not affect verdict. This suggests that specific attitudes about young offenders do not necessarily affect behavior (verdict) in a simulated legal context. Perceptions of juvenile culpability were positively related to sentence length, however. Those who held young offenders responsible for their actions were more likely to recommend longer sentences for the defendant in the study, indicating that there is a relationship between perceptions of culpability and punishment that was present regardless of the defendant's age.

Study 2 sought to examine the effects of group deliberation on verdict by having five or six participants discuss a court case, and arrive at a unanimous decision regarding the guilt of the accused. There was some suggestion that juries were less likely to return a unanimous Not-Guilty verdict for the youngest defendant than with the two older defendants (ages 17 and 25). Perhaps the standards for reasonable doubt were less stringent for the younger defendant. One participant commented during deliberation that the risks of wrongly convicting a youth are lower because (it was assumed that) youth typically serve shorter sentences for their crimes than adults. Analyzing the transcripts during deliberation may suggest other reasons for this finding.

Like most juror studies, the present simulation poses some ecological validity problems. Although some efforts are being made to enhance ecological validity, such as having participants deliberate, as well as an ongoing collection of a wider sample of more jury representative adults from the community, caution should and will be used in generalizing any findings to actual jury behavior.

It is important to note that this research is in its early phases. Further replication of the present design is needed, particularly with a more jury-representative sample. Other factors that may affect the outcome of jury trials with young offenders need to be explored. There is a need to investigate the specific cases involving youth that may be problematic when tried by a jury of adults. For instance, certain types of cases (e.g., gang-related crimes) may elicit perceptions that are age-specific and these may influence determinations of guilt or sentence. Also of interest would be to examine whether there are differences between judges and potential jurors in terms of susceptibility to age-based bias.

Although preliminary and in need of replication, the present findings do carry interesting implications for legal personnel and legislators. Lawyers representing youth need to be apprised of the empirical evidence regarding adults' perceptions of youth crime and youthful offenders. They also need to be informed of the ongoing research on the issues inherent in jury trials for juveniles, and under what conditions potential jurors may pose a threat to a youth's right to an impartial jury. This information might be helpful in advising their adolescent clients to opt for or against a trial by jury.

In Canada, there is new youth justice legislation on the horizon that will expand the sentencing options for youth. With such policy changes, adolescents as young as 14 years of age charged with certain violent offences, as well as those with a history of *repeat* violent offences, will be expected to receive adult sentences. This wider application of adult sentencing with juveniles may result in an increase in the number of youth granted the right to a trial by jury. The present study suggests that the use of jury trials will not necessarily disadvantage young defendants. However, it will be important for research in this area to continue so as to ensure that juveniles are ensured a fair trial if tried by jury.

REFERENCES

Bagby, R. M., Parker, J. D. A., Rector, N. A., & Kalemba, V. (1994). Racial prejudice in the Canadian legal system: Juror decisions in a simulated rape trial. *Law and Human Behavior, 18*, 339–350.

Bala, N. (1994). What's wrong with YOA bashing? What's wrong with the YOA?—Recognizing the limits of the law. *Canadian Journal of Criminology, 36*, 247–270.

Baron, S. W., & Hartnagel, T. F. (1996). "Lock 'em up":Attitudes toward punishing juvenile offenders. *Canadian Journal of Criminology, 38*, 191–212.

Bornstein, B. H. (1999). The ecological validity of jury simulations: Is the jury still out? *Law and Human Behavior, 23*, 75–91.

Bray, R. M., & Kerr, N. L. (1979). Use of the simulation method in the study of jury behavior. *Law and Human Behavior, 3*, 107–119.

Corrado, R. R., & Markwart, A. (1994). The need to reform the YOA in response to violent young offenders: Confusion, reality or myth? *Canadian Journal of Criminology, 36*, 343–378.

Crosby, C. A., Britner, P. A., Jodl, K. M. & Portwood, S. G. (1995). The juvenile death penalty and the Eighth Amendment: An empirical investigation of societal consensus and proportionality. *Law and Human Behavior, 19*, 245–261.

Diamond, S. S. (1997). Illuminations and shadows from jury simulations. *Law and Human Behavior, 21*, 561–571.

Finkel, N. J., Hughes, K. C., Smith, S. F., & Hurabiell, M. L. (1994). Killing kids: The juvenile death penalty and community sentiment. *Behavioral Sciences and the Law, 12*, 5–20.

Frederick, J. T. (1987). *The psychology of the American jury*. Charlottesville, Virginia: The Michie Company.

Freedman, J. L., Krismer, K., MacDonald, J. E., & Cunningham, J. A. (1994). Severity of penalty, seriousness of the charge, and mock jurors verdict. *Law and Human Behavior, 18*, 189–202.

Furnham, A., & Alison, L. (1994). Theories of crime, attitudes to punishment and juror bias amongst police, offenders and the general public. *Personality and Individual Differences, 17*, 35–48.

Golash, D. (1992). Race, fairness, and jury selection. *Behavioral sciences and the Law, 10*, 155–177.

Grisso, T. (1996). Society's retributive response to juvenile violence: A developmental perspective. *Law and Human Behavior, 20*, 229–247.

Hartnagel, T., & Baron, S. (1994). "It's time to get serious": Public attitudes toward juvenile justice in Canada. Research Discussion Paper No. 103. Population Research Laboratory, Department of Sociology, University of Alberta.

Kassin, S. M., & Wrightsman, L. S. (1983). The construction and validation of a juror bias scale. *Journal of Research in Personality, 17*, 423–442.

Kerr, N. L., Hymes, R. W., Anderson, A. B., & Weathers, J. E. (1995). Defendant-juror similarity and mock juror judgements. *Law and Human Behavior, 19(6)*, 545–567.

MacCoun, R. J. (1990). The emergence of extralegal bias during jury deliberation. *Criminal Justice and Behavior, 17*, 303–314.

Perez, D. A., Hosch, H. M., Ponder, B., & Trejo, G. C. (1993). Ethnicity of defendants and jurors as influences on jury decisions. *Journal of Applied Social Psychology, 23(15)*, 1249–1262.

Peterson-Badali, M., Chow, P., Freedman, J., & Abramovitch, R. (1997). *Juror decision making*. Unpublished manuscript, University of Toronto.

Rector, N. A., Bagby, R. M., & Nicholson, R. (1993). The effect of prejudice and judicial ambiguity on defendant guilt ratings. *The Journal of Social Psychology, 133*, 651–659.

Sprott, J. B. (1996). Understanding public views of youth crime and the youth justice system. *Canadian Journal of Criminology*, *38*, 271–290.

Stalans, L. F., & Henry, G. T. (1994). Societal views of justice for adolescents accused of murder. *Law and Human Behavior*, *18*, 675–696.

Weiten, W., & Diamond, S. S. (1979). A critical review of the jury simulation paradigm. *Law and Human Behavior*, *3*, 71–93.

PART 2

JURIES

Chapter 4

RACE AND THE CIVIL JURY: HOW DOES A JUROR'S RACE SHAPE THE JURY EXPERIENCE?

*Michael E. Antonio and Valerie P. Hans**

Lay participation in justice systems allows a broad range of the citizenry to be involved in legal decisions affecting a country's citizens. The legal systems of many democratic countries incorporate laypersons in some decision-making capacity, including lay judges or assessors (Diamond, 1990), mixed courts of law-trained and lay judges (Kutnjak Ivkovich, 1999), and the jury (Vidmar, 1999). Lay participation in the justice system has been justified on a variety of grounds. It is said to improve decision making, to reduce the impact of biased or corrupt judges, to keep the system responsive to changing community values, to better represent the diversity of citizen experiences and perspectives, and to enhance the legitimacy of the overall system in a democracy (Hans & Vidmar, 1986).

In countries such as Ireland and the United States, which have strong traditions of trial by jury, efforts to reduce or eliminate the use of lay decision makers are met with considerable controversy. Consider, for example, the debate over the introduction of the Diplock Courts, trial courts in Northern Ireland that handle terrorism cases by judge alone rather than by jury (Diplock Commission, 1972; Jackson & Doran, 1995; Quinn, 1999).

The representativeness of methods of lay participation

A key issue in the employment of lay participation in the justice system concerns the extent to which laypersons adequately represent the full range of the citizenry. Who sits as a lay judge or a juror, and the degree to which laypersons participate meaningfully in the decision-making process, are critical elements of its democratic nature. Research showing that lay judges are often marginalized when they decide cases together with professional judges suggests that mixed courts serve to limit the impact of lay perspectives on decision making (Kutnjak Ivkovich, 1999; Machura, 1999). Other evidence that lay participants in justice systems represent only a select portion of the public also raises concern about the ability of some methods of lay participation to reflect the views of the citizenry in legal decisions (Kutnjak Ivkovich, 1999).

From the perspective of representing the community, the institution of the jury appears to have some distinctive advantages over other methods of lay participation. Juries are chosen to represent the full range of the public. A unanimous verdict may be required so that every member of the jury must agree with the final decision. Finally, juries decide on verdicts independent of law-trained judges. All of these features should promote the democratic goals of lay participation in the legal system.

Self-report surveys of jurors indicate that serving on a jury promotes the legitimacy of the legal system. Jurors approach their task with seriousness (Diamond, 1993) and appear to be competent decision makers in the vast majority of trials (Guinther, 1988; Hans & Vidmar, 1986). After jury service, jurors express greater confidence in the jury system (Diamond, 1993).

Racial and ethnic minorities and the jury

Despite these apparent advantages of the jury system in serving democratic values, the actual participation of racial and ethnic minorities on juries is cause for concern. Racial and ethnic minorities have faced a variety of barriers to full involvement on the jury. Although the jury has long been lauded as a democratic institution, for most of its history the notion that the jury actually represented the full range of the citizenry was more myth than reality. In the Republic of Ireland, prior to 1976 there was a property qualification for jury service that excluded a substantial portion of the citizenry; furthermore, women were exempted from jury duty and juries were invariably all-male (Quinn, 1999). In 1976, the Republic of Ireland's Juries Act eliminated the property requirement and the gender exemption, providing instead that all citizens and registered voters between 18–70 years of age were eligible for jury service.

Similarly, the clear thrust of U.S. court cases and jury selection practice has been toward greater representativeness of the jury, at least in theory. A line of legal cases starting in 1880 held that the trial jury must be drawn from a representative cross-section of the population (Hans & Vidmar, 1986). No "cognizable" group may be systematically and purposefully eliminated from the pool or panel. The tide turned decisively toward greater representativeness with the Jury Selection and Service Act of 1968, a federal law that mandated voters' lists as the primary source for federal jury pools. Many states followed suit. Voters' lists do not fully capture all segments of the population, underrepresenting young people, the poor, transients, and racial minorities. However, they were an improvement over "key man" systems and other idiosyncratic methods of selecting the jury pool. Many jurisdictions began to take advantage of computerization, updating their jury pool lists more frequently, and combining the voters' list with drivers' license lists to obtain better representation of the community. Introduction of one day-one trial systems in many jurisdictions also improved representativeness by increasing the willingness of people to serve on jury duty when summoned. As a result of these changes, there has clearly been an improvement in jury representativeness compared to earlier times. Certainly, as a collective body, jurors are much more racially representative of the population than are law-trained judges. However, even given the strides that have been made, the representation of racial and ethnic minorities on juries continues to be a serious problem in some jurisdictions (Munsterman & Munsterman, 1983; Fukurai, Butler, & Krooth, 1993; King & Munsterman, 1996).

The fact that minorities are underrepresented on juries in comparison to their proportion of the population presents a serious challenge to the jury system (Fukurai et al., 1993). Psychological research on race and on the jury system points to ways in which a racially representative jury is likely to be a superior factfinder (Ellsworth, 1989; see Jones, 1997). Having a diverse jury should facilitate discussion and the generation of unique ideas that may not be considered by a judge or an all-White jury alone. Furthermore, mistaken or stereotyped judgments held by jurors of one race are able to be addressed by jurors of other races in the jury deliberation. Some scholars have argued that the presence of minorities in the deliberation will reduce the expression of prejudice (see, e.g., the discussion in Hans & Vidmar, 1986). There is also the legitimacy factor; verdicts reached by racially representative juries are more likely to be supported by all segments of the community. It is for such reasons that minority representation on the jury is of vital importance.

The quality of minority participation on juries

Changes over time indicate that although contemporary juries may not be completely representative of the community, they are likely to include some members of minority racial and ethnic groups. The purpose of this chapter is to examine the experience of minority jurors. Once a minority citizen is a member of the jury, is the experience comparable to that of White citizens?

In theory, each juror is formally equal, is entitled to voice his or her opinions in the jury room, and has an equal say in the final vote. However, some early research on jury decision making suggests that social inequalities in occupational, gender, and racial group status are reflected in jury deliberations (Hans & Vidmar, 1986). Jurors with higher social status outside the jury room participate more and are more likely to take leadership roles on the jury. A few studies have shown that jury members with lower educational achievements, income, and occupational status participate less often and are less influential than their colleagues who are higher on these dimensions (James, 1959; Hastie, Penrod, & Pennington, 1983). Given the disparities in education, occupation, and income between racial majority and minority groups, one might expect minority jurors to be at a disadvantage in the jury room. On the other hand, minority jurors likely have distinctive experiences and perspectives that may place them in an influential role during deliberations.

To explore whether a juror's racial and ethnic status was associated with different experiences as jurors, this study employed a data set of 1352 Arizona civil jurors, including 260 racial or ethnic minorities. Statistical analyses examined the effects of jurors' race and ethnicity on participation, perceived influence, and satisfaction with the jury experience.

In addition to the jurors' race and ethnicity, other factors that might affect jurors' perceptions of satisfaction with the deliberation were explored. First, case features such as trial complexity or having been able to discuss details of the trial before formal deliberation began could skew a juror's overall view of the discussion. Also, being required to reach unanimity or being able to submit a majority verdict was viewed as an important factor influencing satisfaction levels. In Arizona civil jury trials, a minimum of six out of the eight sitting jurors must agree on a verdict for it to be binding. Therefore, juries can differ on whether they reached a unanimous or nonunanimous verdict. To date how these issues influence jurors' levels of satisfaction by race have not been fully explored in prior research.

Juror satisfaction and case complexity, pre-deliberation discussions, and voting with or against the panel's verdict were all included as variables in statistical analyses. Additional factors including the dominance of other jurors, the degree to which the jurors saw themselves as influential in the deliberation, and jurors' income were examined as features impacting satisfaction levels as well.

Previous research reports that jurors look upon their experiences with the justice system positively. However, we could find no study that focused in much detail on how a juror's racial or ethnic identity affected his or her experiences and satisfaction with the deliberation process. Given that racial minorities experience and perceive discrimination at other stages of the justice system to a greater extent than do Whites, they may also experience or discern patterns of differential treatment during the deliberation process and, consequently, may be less satisfied with the discussion than Whites.

METHOD

The data to be used in this analysis were collected by the National Center for State Courts. The impetus for the study was to generate further knowledge regarding a novel Arizona jury trial reform that allowed civil jurors to discuss the evidence among themselves as the trial was going on, rather than wait until the final deliberations as is typical (see Hannaford, Hans, & Munsterman, 2000; Hans, Hannaford, & Munsterman, 1999). Half of the trials were randomly assigned to allow civil jurors to discuss the case as is permitted under present Arizona law, while the other half were randomly assigned to a control condition in which they were not permitted to discuss the evidence. Jurors who participated in the study completed extensive questionnaires about their perceptions of the trial and their experiences as jurors. Jurors from a total of 170 juries were examined in this study; the participation rate was close to 90%. Questionnaires were distributed to judges, attorneys, and litigants, but are not included in the present analysis, which focuses on juror perceptions.

Juror race and ethnic status

Race was the central factor in this analysis regarding juror's satisfaction with the jury experience. Fully 81% of the jurors identified themselves as White-Caucasian. Fourteen percent described themselves as Hispanic (either White or Nonwhite), and they were categorized as minorities. Other jurors identified themselves as members of different racial or ethnic groups, including African-American, Asian/Pacific Islander, and American Indian. Comparisons were made on two levels. First, non-Hispanic Whites and the responses of all racial minorities (including Blacks, White and non-White Hispanics, Native Americans, and Asian/Pacific Islanders) were compared regarding issues of juror satisfaction with trial deliberations. However, since this classification of racial minorities does not recognize the unique characteristics and distinctive traits of each ethnic group, a second comparison was made between non-Hispanic White and all Hispanic respondents.

Juror satisfaction scale

The present analysis focused on jurors' responses to questions regarding the trial and jury deliberation in which they participated. The central concern of this analysis was to determine whether there are racial differences among jurors' perceptions, experiences, and feelings of satisfaction with the deliberation process. A four-variable additive index was created to operationalize juror satisfaction using the following questions: 1) "How close and friendly would you say your jury was?" (1 = *very distant and unfriendly*, 7 = *very close and friendly*); 2) "How much personal conflict was there on your jury?" (*1 = a great deal*, 7 = *none*); 3) "How satisfied were you with the jury's deliberation?" (*1 = not at all satisfied*, 7 = *fully satisfied*), and 4) "How satisfied are you with the jury's decision?" (1 = *not at all satisfied*, 7 = *fully satisfied*). All of these variables were positively and significantly correlated with one another. Subjects' responses to these questions were combined to form one measure, a Juror Satisfaction Scale (α = .69). Scores on this measure ranged from 4 through 28 with a mean score of 24.23 and a median of 25.0.

Additional variables

In addition to race and satisfaction, several other factors warranted exploration. These included pre-deliberation discussions, case complexity, final verdicts, the juror's level of participation and influence, the juror's income, the extent to which the jury deliberations were dominated by a small number of other jurors, and whether the juror voted with the majority or was a holdout. Altogether 716 jurors who participated in the project were in trials that were randomly assigned to allow trial discussions, while 669 jurors were not. A case complexity measure was created from the judge's rating of complexity, the jurors' average rating of complexity, and the natural log of the total number of hours of the trial (Case Complexity Scale α = .78; Hannaford et al., 2000).

Sixty percent of the juries reached a verdict for the plaintiff, while the remainder decided on a defense verdict. To examine the issue of holdout jurors, respondents were asked "on the jury's final ballot, did you vote for the plaintiff, defendant, or unsure/did not vote." Jurors who identified themselves as voting for the losing party on the final ballot were identified as holdout jurors. In this study, 35 juries reached a majority verdict. Of these juries, there were 19 with either 1 or 2 White holdout jurors, 12 with 1 or 2 minority holdout jurors, and 4 with 1 White and 1 minority holdout juror each. It should be noted that missing data and "unsure" responses from jurors complicated the definition of the holdout juror. Approximately 10% of the jurors failed to answer the question regarding their final vote.

A two-variable additive index was created to operationalize juror influence using the following questions: 1) "How much did you talk in the final jury deliberation?" (1 = *very little*, 7 = *a great deal*), and 2) "How influential were you in the final jury deliberation?" (1 = *not at all influential*, 7 = *very influential*). Responses on these variables were combined to form one measure of perceived influence ($\alpha = .64$). Scores on this measure ranged from 2 through 14 with a mean score of 9.56 and median of 10.0.

In addition, the behavior of other jurors was likely to affect satisfaction levels. As a result, jurors' responses to the question, "How much would you say that one or two jurors dominated the final deliberations?" were examined. Possible responses ranged from 1 = *not at all* to 7 = *very much*. Lastly, juror's income, a proxy for social class, was assessed through a scale that provided ranges of annual income, including 1-under $10,000, 2-$10,000–$19,000, 3-$20,000–$29,000, 4-$30,000–$39,000, 5-$40,000–$49,000, 6-$50,000–$75,000, or 7-over $75,000.

RESULTS

Table 1 reports *t*-tests for levels of satisfaction with the jury experience by race/ethnicity. Mean scores close to one indicate that respondents were least content with a particular aspect of the jury experience, while scores ranging to seven suggest respondents were greatly satisfied with it. The first observation is that the overall satisfaction is quite high across racial groups. The overall Satisfaction Scale shows mean responses close to 24 on a 28-point scale. This table also shows how Whites' responses compared to all non-Whites' (or minority) responses. A *t*-test analysis indicates that Whites' and racial minorities' mean scores for satisfaction with the deliberation and perceived level of personal conflict on the panel were statistically different. In general, Whites were more satisfied with the deliberation and perceived less conflict on the panel than did racial minorities. Respondents' scores on the overall Satisfaction Scale indicate that overall Whites were slightly but significantly more satisfied with their jury experience than were racial minorities.

Also in Table 1, findings are reported regarding levels of juror satisfaction comparing White and Hispanic responses. From this table it can be determined that Whites perceived less personal conflict existing on the panel and were more satisfied with the trial deliberation than were Hispanic respondents. Also, as measured by the Satisfaction Scale, Whites were statistically significantly more satisfied with the jury discussions than were Hispanic respondents. In a parallel pattern to the White-minority comparisons, the comparisons for Non-Hispanic Whites and Hispanics shows overall high levels of satisfaction and small but significant differences between ethnic groups.

Table 1: Mean Satisfaction Levels with the Deliberation by Race/Ethnicity

	White $N = 1092$	Minority $N = 260$	t	White $N = 1092$	Hispanic $N = 190$	t
Closeness of Jury	5.80	5.70	1.323	5.80	5.70	1.037
Satisfaction with Deliberation	6.24	6.02	2.188*	6.24	6.03	2.023*
Satisfaction with Verdict	6.21	6.02	1.701	6.21	6.08	1.156
Low Conflict	6.14	5.88	2.590*	6.14	5.82	2.588**
Satisfaction Scale	24.38	23.61	2.658**	24.38	23.63	2.209**

*$p < .05$. **$p < .01$.

Linear regression comparisons (as illustrated in Table 2) were employed to determine whether predictors of juror satisfaction could be discernible through the data. When responses from the entire sample of jurors were examined it was found that case complexity, juror dominance, and a variable related to minority status were statistically significant predictors of juror satisfaction. That is, when jurors perceived their cases to be complex and when jurors reported one or more panel members dominating the deliberation their levels of satisfaction with the deliberation decreased. These data also illustrate that racial minorities were less satisfied with the deliberations than Whites, even taking into account other case variables influencing satisfaction.

The second regression analysis in Table 2 reports similar findings when comparing non-Hispanic White and Hispanic respondents. The data show that jurors became less satisfied with the deliberations when case complexity increased and when one or more fellow jurors dominated the discussions. In addition, being Hispanic was associated with decreased levels of satisfaction.

Table 2: Linear Regression Analyses of Juror Satisfaction

Predictors	*Beta*	t	*Beta*	t
Minorities	–.086	–3.109**	—	—
Hispanics	—	—	–.076	–2.700**
Trial Discussions	–.019	–.686	–.024	–.863
Complexity	–.069	–2.491*	–.087	–3.066**
Juror Dominance	–.272	–9.974***	–.284	–10.157***
Influence	.040	1.466	.045	1.623
Income	–.011	–.394	–.018	–.628
Constant	—	42.737***	—	42.547***
		$R^2 = .088$		$R^2 = .095$

*$p < .05$. **$p < .01$. ***$p < .001$.

Table 3: Linear Regression Analyses of Juror Satisfaction As a Function of Holdout Status and Racial Minority Respondents

	Jury Favored Plaintiff		Jury Favored Defendant	
Predictors	*Beta*	*t*	*Beta*	*t*
Minorities	–.095	–2.432*	–.120	–2.615**
Holdout	.015	.395	–.300	–6.710***
Trial Discussions	.012	.320	–.043	–.921
Case Complexity	–.088	–2.239*	.025	.544
Juror Dominance	–.275	–7.136***	–.196	–4.316***
Influence	.092	2.377*	.020	.452
Income	–.028	–.724	–.009	–.208
Constant	—	26.261***	—	28.793***
		$R^2 = .099$		$R^2 = .165$

*$p < .05$. **$p < .001$. ***$p < .001$.

Table 3 illustrates satisfaction levels as a function of holdout status and race. As shown, in panels reaching a verdict favoring the plaintiff, jurors were less satisfied with the deliberation when they perceived other jurors to be dominant and the case to be complex. However, the more influential jurors perceived themselves to be, the more satisfied they were with the trial discussions. Also illustrated in this table, racial minorities were less satisfied with the trial discussions than were White respondents.

The second regression analysis reported in Table 3 shows juror satisfaction levels when the panel rendered a verdict for the defendant. These data show that juror dominance is a significant predictor of decreased satisfaction with the jury experience. Other findings showed that jurors voting against the majority and racial minority jurors were less satisfied with trial discussions than Whites.

Table 4 illustrates findings regarding satisfaction levels as a function of holdout status and Hispanic ethnicity. This table reports findings similar to the above table controlling for holdout status and racial minorities. When the panel favored the plaintiff, jurors were less satisfied with trial deliberations in complex cases and when other jurors dominated the discussions. In addition, findings showed jurors were more satisfied when they believed they were influential during the discussions, and Hispanics were less satisfied with the deliberations than were Whites. When the panel favored the defendant, holdout jurors voting for the plaintiff and those who perceived others dominating the discussions were less satisfied

Table 4: Linear Regression Analyses of Juror Satisfaction as a Function of Holdout Status and Hispanic Respondents

	Jury Favored Plaintiff		Jury Favored Defendant	
Predictors	*Beta*	*t*	*Beta*	*t*
Hispanics	–.096	–2.390*	–.109	–2.261*
Holdout	.028	.698	–.234	–4.974***
Trial Discussions	.009	.240	–.048	–.989
Case Complexity	–.102	–2.534*	.009	.190
Juror Dominance	–.287	–7.290***	–.214	–4.463***
Influence	.082	2.069*	.056	1.172
Income	–.038	–.937	–.017	–.351
Constant	—	26.052***	—	28.547***
		R^2 = .107		R^2 = .126

*$p < .05$ ***$p < .001$.

with the trial deliberations. Lastly, Hispanic ethnic status was shown to be significant as well, in that Hispanics were less satisfied with the discussions in comparison to Whites.

DISCUSSION

The present analysis identified differences between White and racial and ethnic minority jurors in their perceptions of their jury experience. What made this work unique was that it did not solely poll jurors regarding their perceptions of the deliberation. Rather, this analysis examined what factors affected levels of satisfaction and compared those responses along racial lines. Overall, there were significant differences in the levels of satisfaction with trial deliberations as reported by White and racial minority respondents, including Hispanics. These findings suggest that Whites, in general, were more satisfied with their jury experience than were racial minority groups.

Despite the significant pattern of comparatively lower satisfaction among minority jurors, it's important to point out that both Whites and minorities for the most part were satisfied overall with their jury experience. The mean score for the Satisfaction Scale was 24.23 out of a possible 28, indicating a high level of satisfaction, and the mean scores for White and minority jurors differed by less than one scale point. The averages for both Whites and minorities were above the midpoint on most individual items. In general, jurors reported feeling satisfied with the deliberation and verdict, and believed fellow juror members were friendly and attentive to their points of view.

These findings are noteworthy especially when compared to other public opinion studies regarding differences between racial and ethnic groups. Such research has shown individuals from different racial and ethnic groups vary widely in their beliefs of fair treatment existing within the courts (National Center for State Courts, 1999). Race is a significant predictor of confidence in the courts. Furthermore, perceptions of judicial bias vary systematically with the race of the respondent, with Whites more likely than African–Americans and Hispanics to believe that "Judges are generally fair and honest in deciding cases" (National Center for State Courts, 1999).

Our findings identified other factors that affected satisfaction with the jury experience. When jurors perceived their cases to be complex, when one or more panel members were viewed as domineering, and when jurors were holdouts voting against the majority decision, overall levels of satisfaction with jury deliberations decreased.

One of the most interesting findings in this analysis concerns juror holdout status. When jury panels rendered final verdicts for the defendant, holdout jurors and racial minorities (including Hispanics) reported decreased levels of satisfaction with the deliberation. In comparison, when jury panels decided in favor of the plaintiff, racial minority group jurors were still less satisfied with the trial discussions; however, holdout jurors were not less satisfied with the deliberation than were jurors voting in the majority.

It would have been interesting to determine whether the race or ethnicity of the parties was related to minority jurors' satisfaction. Although litigant surveys were distributed as part of the overall study, the response rate was low and there were too few litigants who identified themselves as racial or ethnic minorities ($N = 16$) to undertake separate analysis of their cases or to use litigant race as an explanatory variable.

Overall, this analysis has generated important findings for the study of juries. It was shown here that racial minority and White jurors did perceive the dynamics of trial deliberations differently. For whatever reasons, the jury experience for racial minorities is not as positive as it is for Whites.

Future endeavors

The present analysis has been unique in its focus on jurors and how jurors' perceptions and satisfaction differ by racial and ethnic identity. While there are typically just a handful of racial minorities who sit on jury panels, it is of utmost importance to determine what impact their presence has on the trial deliberation and new studies should be designed to examine this issue further.

We did not ask explicitly about whether any jurors observed or experienced differential treatment linked to their racial or ethnic characteristics. Was the decreased satisfaction due to behavior of Whites toward minorities? White jurors may have been more dominant or less tolerant when other jurors (especially racial minorities) expressed contradictory positions. Or, were there other aspects of the jury experience that led to the decreased satisfaction of minority jurors? In future research it will be especially important to examine dimensions of the trial, particularly the race and ethnicity of trial participants.

The identification of features of the trial or deliberation that are associated with decreased satisfaction for minority jurors is an important task for psycholegal scholars. Psychological research indicates that the full and robust deliberation of a diverse jury is a significant element of jury competence. Mere presence on the jury is not enough. Even if we reach the point of fully representative juries, the ability of racial and ethnic minorities to present distinctive points of view will depend on ensuring equality within the jury room as well.

REFERENCES

Diamond, S. S. (1990). Revising images of public punitiveness: Sentencing by lay and professional English magistrates. *Law & Social Inquiry*, *15*, 191–221.

Diamond, S. S. (1993). What jurors think: Expectations and reactions of citizens who serve as jurors. In R. Litan (Ed.), *Verdict: Assessing the civil jury system* (pp. 282–305). Washington D. C.: The Brookings Institution.

Diplock Commission. (1972). *Report of the Commission to consider legal procedures to deal with terrorist activities in Northern Ireland.* London: HMSO.

Ellsworth, P. (1989). Are twelve heads better than one? *Law & Contemporary Problems*, *52*, 205–224.

Fukurai, H., Butler, E., & Krooth, R. (1993). *Race and the jury: Racial disenfranchisement and the search for justice.* New York: Plenum Press.

Guinther, J. (1988). *The jury in America.* New York: Facts on File Publications.

Hannaford, P. L., Hans, V. P., & Munsterman, G. T. (2000). Permitting jury discussions during trial: Impact of the Arizona reform. *Law and Human Behavior*, *24*, 359–382.

Hans, V. P., Hannaford, P. L., & Munsterman, G. T. (1999). The Arizona jury reform permitting civil jury trial discussions: The views of trial participants, judges, and jurors. *University of Michigan Journal of Law Reform*, *32*, 349–377.

Hans, V. P., & Vidmar, N. (1986). *Judging the jury.* NY: Plenum.

Hastie, R., Penrod, S., & Pennington, N. (1983). *Inside the jury.* Cambridge, Mass: Harvard University Press.

Jackson, J. D., & Doran, S. (1995). *Judge without jury: Diplock trials in the adversary system.* Oxford: Clarendon.

James, R. (1959). Status and competence of jurors. *American Journal of Sociology*, *64*, 563–570.

Jones, J. M. (1997). *Prejudice and racism* (2nd ed.). NY: McGraw-Hill.

King, N., & Munsterman, G. T. (1996). Stratified juror selection: Cross-section by design. *Judicature*, *79*, 273–278.

Kutnjak Ivkovich, S. (1999). *Lay participation in criminal trials: The case of Croatia.* San Francisco: Austin & Winfield.

Machura, S. (1999, May). Interaction between lay assessors and professional judge in German mixed courts. Paper presented at the conference, Lay participation in the criminal trial in the 21st century, at the International Institute for Higher Studies in the Criminal Sciences, Siracusa, Italy.

Munsterman, G. T., & Munsterman, J. (1986). The search for representativeness. *Justice System Journal*, *11*, 59–78.

National Center for State Courts. (1999). *How the public views the state courts: A 1999 national survey*. Williamsburg: National Center for State Courts.

Quinn, K. (1999, May). Lay participation in the criminal trial in the 21st century: Country study: Republic of Ireland. Paper presented at the conference, Lay participation in the criminal trial in the 21st century, at the International Institute for Higher Studies in the Criminal Sciences, Siracusa, Italy.

Schwarzer, W. W. (1990). Reforming jury trials. *University of Chicago Legal Forum*, *1990*, 119–146.

Snortum, J., Klein, J., & Sherman, W. (1976). The impact of an aggressive juror in six and twelve member juries. *Criminal Justice and Behavior*, *3*, 255–262.

Strodtbeck, F., James, R., & Hawkins, C. (1957). Social status in jury deliberations. *American Sociological Review*, *22*, 713–718.

Vidmar, N. (1999). Foreword. *Law & Contemporary Problems*, *62*, 1–5.

AUTHOR NOTE

* The data analyzed in this chapter were collected under State Justice Institute grant SJI-96–12A-B-181 to the National Center for State Courts. Correspondence may be addressed to either author at: Department of Sociology and Criminal Justice, University of Delaware, Newark, DE 19716 (email addresses are *miantoni@udel.edu; vhans@udel.edu*).

Chapter 5

JUROR COMPETENCE AND PROCESSING STYLE IN MAKING SENSE OF COMPLEX TRIAL INFORMATION

Elizabeth A. Charman, Terry M. Honess and Micheal Levi

All trials place particular demands on jurors, but complex trials have been seen to increase these demands to the point where the competency of the lay juror has been challenged (Horowitz, ForsterLee, & Brolly, 1996; Penrod & Heuer, 1997). The research described in this chapter is concerned with the role of processing styles in juror competence in complex cases, and involves a simulation of the recent Maxwell fraud trial in the U.K. where the acquittal of all defendants gave fresh impetus to the view that "something must be done" about fraud juries (Doran & Jackson, 1997).

The Maxwell trial was complex by any standard and met all of the criteria proposed by Heuer and Penrod (1994). Based on judges' commentaries on a number of trial variables, Heuer and Penrod identified three main components of complexity: evidence complexity, legal complexity and, quantity of information. Further, they suggested that each component of complexity might impact differentially on juror processing with consequent effects on juror competence.

A cognitive-contextual framework for delineating jurors' understanding of complex material is presented in Figure 1. This serves to summarize relevant research and place our own into context. Two processing modes are identified in this framework as mediating juror understanding. These are taken from the Heuristic Systematic Processing Model or HSM (Chaiken, 1987; Chaiken, Liberman, & Eagly, 1989; Eagly & Chaiken, 1993). Systematic processing involves close scrutiny of information; it is relatively comprehensive and analytic. Heuristic processing involves less detailed scrutiny and, at times, the individual may follow simple persuasion heuristics like "experts can be trusted" or implicit assumptions such as "there is no smoke without fire". Although systematic processing is more thorough, heuristics can be helpful when the subject matter is complex (Bodenhausen & Lichtenstein, 1987).

Necessarily related to juror understanding is the nature of the trial evidence and the way in which it is presented (see Figure 1). For example,

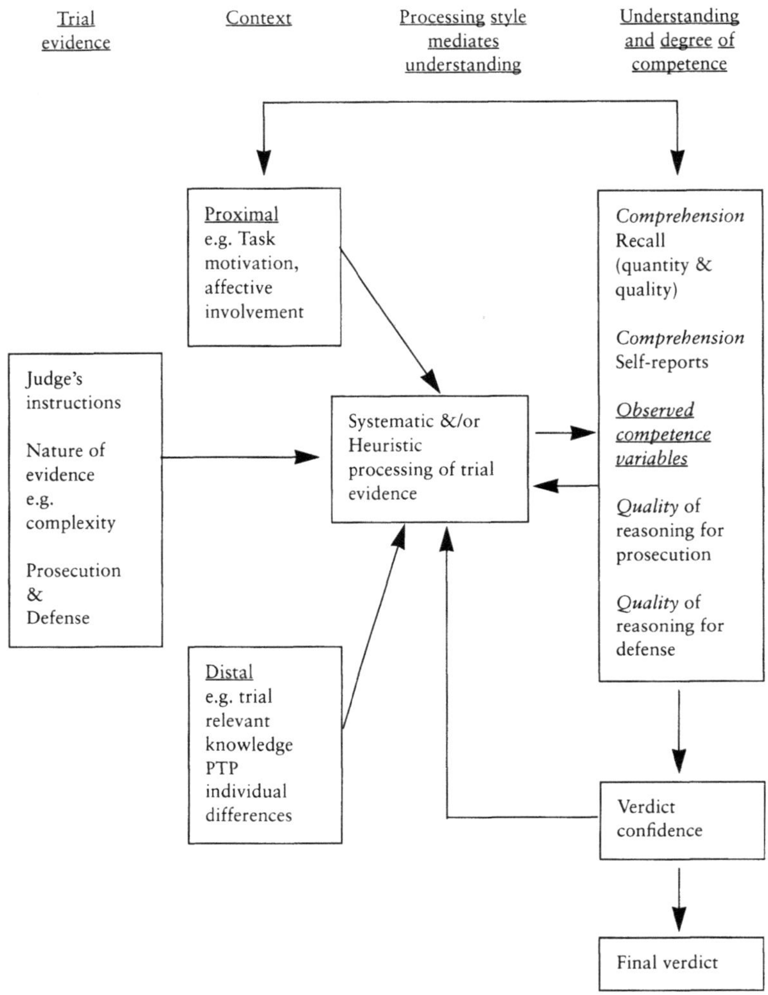

FIGURE 1: A COGNITIVE-CONTEXTUAL FRAMEWORK FOR DELINEATING INDIVIDUAL JURORS' UNDERSTANDING OF COMPLEX MATERIAL

the elaboration of judicial instructions (Diamond & Casper, 1992); testimony complexity (Cooper, Bennet, & Sukel, 1996); and changes in case management, such as access to trial transcripts (Bourgeois, Horowitz, & ForsterLee, 1993), can all have powerful effects. The possible mediating role of processing style is supported by studies such as these. Bourgeois et al. (1993) show that systematic processing can be enhanced when evidence is presented in less technical language; and Cooper et al. (1996) show that participants were more persuaded by an expert witness with relatively strong credentials when testimony was highly complex (i.e., reliance on heuristics).

Two sets of contextual factors that impact on processing style are identified in the Figure 1 framework: proximal and distal. Proximal factors are defined as those that are introduced within the immediate context of the trial (or trial simulation). These include both pretrial variables (e.g., degree of motivation or affective involvement) and requirements during evidence presentation (e.g., note taking, see Forsterlee & Horowitz, 1997). Maheswaran and Chaiken (1991) demonstrate that higher motivation leads to the activation of the more thorough systematic processing, and Johnson and Eagly (1989) show that affective involvement decreases the likelihood of the consideration of alternative interpretations.

Distal factors include pretrial knowledge, e.g., knowledge about the financial world, information from exposure to pretrial publicity, and individual differences. The last have been shown to impact on juror processing, especially in respect of consideration of complex information (Graziano, Panter, & Tanaka, 1990; Moore & Gump, 1995; Smith, Penrod, Otto, & Park, 1996).

The key outcome of such processing is juror understanding. Both empirical research (e.g., Kuhn, Weinstock, & Flaton, 1994) and professional opinion (e.g., the U.K. Home Office consultation document, 1998, sec. 2.12.) suggest two categories of competence: The first is comprehension, for which there are well-established indicators such as quantity and quality of recall. Difficulties in comprehension may spark different processing strategies, hence the feedback arrow in Figure 1. The second category is quality of reasoning. This is important within the HSM—the juror's "evaluative elaboration" of information plays the primary role in mediating the acceptance or rejection of argument (Chaiken, 1987; Petty & Cacioppo, 1986). Measurement of quality of juror reasoning is less well established and typically relies on verdict outcome (e.g., Bourgeois et al., 1993), hence one necessary aim of the research reported here was to identify what constitutes quality in reasoning.

The juror's exposure to, and understanding of, trial evidence will feed back into proximal factors (see Figure 1), especially task motivation and possible affective involvement. Understanding will lead to a verdict decision, held with a particular level of confidence. In general, a more competent juror would be expected to demonstrate increasing confidence and coherence in argument (see Pennington & Hastie, 1993a for criteria concerning "the best fitting" interpretation). More particularly, it is expected that mediation though "evaluative elaboration" of evidence, leading to well informed judgment, results in more firmly held positions (Petty & Cacioppo, 1986). Confidence will itself impact on the differential activation of systematic and heuristic processing (see Figure 1) because once a "sufficiency threshold" (Chaiken et al., 1989) for a final verdict has been reached, effortful processing will become minimal.

In investigating particular aspects of the framework presented in Figure 1, we sought to establish the reliability and validity of a new self-report measure of heuristic and systematic processing style.[1] The questionnaire items followed HSM theory, but were made relevant to the jury process, e.g., "I judged each piece of evidence in relation to what I had already learned about the case" would indicate systematic processing, and "I thought that some things—such as the sort of person Kevin Maxwell is—were much more revealing than the details about who had done what and when" would indicate heuristic processing.

The hypotheses tested here are

1. Greater comprehension difficulties will be associated with both poorer evidence recall and poorer quality reasoning.
2. The use of heuristics will be associated with (a) less competent reasoning and (b) more comprehension difficulties
3. Competence, revealed through (a) fewer comprehension difficulties and (b) higher quality of reasoning, will be associated with greater confidence in judgement.
4. HSM questionnaire scores of systematic processing will be associated with fewer comprehension difficulties and more competent reasoning. The converse is expected for heuristic processing scores

METHOD

Preparation of trial evidence: The video simulation

Verbatim transcripts of the opening statements of the Maxwell trial were used to prepare a video simulation, complemented by our observations of the real trial proceedings. The video followed precisely the format used in the trial. It consisted of the charges (two counts of "conspiracy to defraud" for Kevin Maxwell and one count for the other three defendants) which were read by the Clerk to the Court, followed by the judge's briefing, and the opening statements of the prosecution and the defense counsel in which they presented their main arguments and evidence. The judge's briefing followed standard practice in the UK, it dealt with procedural arrangements Directions as to the application of the law in relation to verdicts are given at the end of the trial.

The opening statements lasted four days of the trial proper. Editing the verbatim transcripts for breaks and time when the jury was not present, the complete video simulation lasted for more than six hours of continuous play. The documentary evidence—a significant part of the prosecution opening statement—was reconstructed using the verbatim descriptions by counsel of these documents.

No more than four participants were tested at any one time, since each required a trained interviewer.

Participants and procedure

Participants were recruited through public notices and were paid £25 for their participation. All 50 participants met the eligibility criteria for jury service in the U.K. They were told they were to be jurors in a fraud trial and that it was their task to listen to the evidence presented and to reach a verdict in respect of one of the defendants, Kevin Maxwell (who was the key prosecution target). Data were collected at four points during the video presentation. The first three covered the opening statement for the prosecution, the fourth the defense case. At each point, participants were asked to provide a summary of their knowledge and views in the light of all of the evidence presented to date. They were also required to provide a dichotomous verdict (guilty or not guilty only) and to rate their confidence in this verdict on a scale from 1 (*not at all confident*) to 10 (*extremely confident*). Each participant was assigned an interviewer who was able to probe for more information on reasons for verdicts and confidence levels and any changes or lack of changes in these between interview sessions. The interviewers were not present during the video simulation.

Following the video simulation, participants were given a questionnaire, to be returned by post, about their experience as a mock juror. This included whether, on the whole, they felt they had followed or lost the thread of the prosecution case and the defense case. Participants also completed the HSM questionnaire at this time.

Content analysis of participants' transcripts

All typed transcriptions of the full interview text were subject to detailed content analysis. Standard quantitative content analysis was employed, and satisfactory inter-rater reliability was established. The repetition of any argument within a time period was not counted. The first two authors and two graduate assistants carried out the ratings. The final four category sets follow; each was coded independently of the other three sets.

A. Reasoning during presentation of prosecution evidence (six categories):

1. Strong pro-prosecution assertions—e.g., "you can see the lies building up ... the letters he wrote were damning";
2. Tentative pro-prosecution assertions—e.g., "sounds like he knew what was going on, but I'm not really sure";
3. Doubt about the defendant's guilt, supported by alternative interpretations of the evidence—e.g., "although he was trying to shuffle funds, maybe it was bad management rather than fraud";
4. Doubt about the defendant's guilt, related to standard of proof—e.g., "there's been a lot of evidence on defrauding banks, but not specifically on defrauding the Pension Fund";
5. Doubt based on relatively weak, indirect considerations—e.g., "I think it's unfair, he's being made a scapegoat";
6. Suspension of judgement until the defense case has been presented (i.e., recognition of possible alternative accounts)—e.g., "I need to hear the other side of the story first".

Reasoning of the type described in categories 1, 3, and 4 is informed by probative matters (equivalent to the "strong" argument described by Petty & Cacioppo, 1986) and therefore meets a necessary condition for higher competence. Correspondingly, lower competence is described in category 5, which relies on indirect non-probative matters. Lower competence is also evident in the use of category 2—which involves only "weak evaluative elaboration". Category 6 is indicative of competence because alternative possibilities are acknowledged, there is no pre-emptive "satisficing model" of reasoning (Kuhn et al., 1994).

B. Reasoning during presentation of defense evidence (four categories): These categories were generated from the response of participants to the specific set of counter-arguments presented by the defense counsel: participants either approved or rebutted these arguments. However, the counter-arguments presented by the defense were of two types. The first type was argument directly relevant to the charges or the evidence, such as the legality of the transfer and ownership of the pension funds or the defendant's knowledge of the details of financial transactions. The second type was argument that was indirect or tangential to the charges or evidence, such as Robert Maxwell's "good name" (at the time) or Kevin Maxwell's youth and inexperience. This led to the development of four reasoning response categories:

1. Approval of direct counter-argument—e.g., "Yes, maybe the defense are right—he had not been told of the company's obligation to repay that debt."
2. Rebuttal of direct counter-argument—e.g., "he had to sign those deals, so he must have known what was going on."
3. Approval of indirect counter-argument—e.g., "the defense is right, the banks should take some of the blame."
4. Rebuttal of indirect counter-argument—e.g., "I don't think his youthfulness is a defense."

Higher competence is manifest by reasoned consideration of defense arguments that are related directly to the evidence (categories 1 and 2—strong evaluative elaboration). It is also indicated by rejection of arguments *not* related directly to the evidence (category 4)—for example, questioning the relevance of the proposition that "if only Robert Maxwell hadn't died, the financial empire wouldn't have collapsed". Such propositions have parallels with the lower competence counterfactual "lures" used in malpractice simulations (e.g., Bourgeois et al., 1993). In contrast, lower competence is manifest in Category 3: the approval of arguments not based on probative matters.

C. Use of heuristics in consideration of either defense or prosecution (one category)

This is reasoning that moved beyond direct consideration of trial evidence. Their use makes the details hang together in a meaningful, though not necessarily accurate, way (Chaiken et al., 1989). For example, "like father, like son..."

D. Comprehension in consideration of either defense or prosecution (one category).

Major difficulties were related to perceived complexity of the information—e.g., "just too difficult to digest", the level of detail—e.g., "all that financial detail goes over my head", and level of technicality—e.g., "I simply don't understand financial ins and outs".

RESULTS

Prior to statistical inference, the requisite assumptions of normality for all variables was established with appropriate logarithmic transformations. The rare "not guilty" verdicts were coded at confidence level zero; hence, in the data presented here, higher confidence scores always reflect greater confidence in guilt. This is consistent with the proposition (Dane, 1985) that probability of zero guilt reflects a true presumption of innocence.

Table 1 presents information on the number of participants who used each type of reasoning, the mean use of each type, and verdict confidence, for each of the three stages of the prosecution case. Table 2 provides a matrix of correlations for all aspects of the prosecution case, including reasoned argument. Table 3 presents data on the mean use of each type of reasoning for the defense case, and the correlations between them.

Comprehension difficulties: Two measures of comprehension are referred to in these results: Unsolicited references to major comprehension difficulties and post-trial reports of whether or not participants felt they had "lost the thread" of (a) the prosecution case and (b) the defense case. Post-trial reports indicated more difficulty with the prosecution: 22 participants reported they had "lost the thread" of the prosecution case compared to only 3 in respect of the defense case. For the prosecution case, these reports were consistent with on-line reports: Participants who had "lost the thread" of the prosecution case had referenced more difficulties during the prosecution case, $t = 3.50$, $p < .01$.

Just over half of the participants (see Table 1) made unsolicited references to at least one major difficulty during consideration of prosecution evidence and, as predicted (Hypothesis 1), the incidence of comprehension difficulties was associated with poorer recall. This was evident at each time stage, and for the prosecution case as a whole, $r = -.28$, $p < .05$. Also as predicted, major comprehension difficulties were associated significantly with the poorer quality tentative anti-defendant reasoning (see Table 2).

Use of Heuristics: There was support for Hypothesis 2, that comprehension difficulties were associated with greater use of heuristics (see Table 2). Also as predicted, the use of heuristics was associated with less competent reasoning—that based on non-evidential considerations ("Kevin shouldn't have to take responsibility on his own, others are to blame too")—see Table 2. There was also evidence of continuity of processing style between the prosecution and the defense case in that participants making use of heuristics during the prosecution case were

Table 1: Number of Respondents Using Each Reasoning Type, and Their Verdicts for the Three Stages of the Prosecution Case

	Stage One	Stage Two	Stage Three	All Prosecution	
no of guilty	46/50	48/50	48/50	As Verdict at Stage 3	
Confidence *M* (*SD*)	5.70 (2.59)	6.64 (2.50)	6.84 (2.48)		
Reasoning	Stage one	Stage two	Stage three	All prosecution	
	n	n	n	n[a]	*M* (*SD*)
Strong pro-prosecution	42	44	45	49	4.56 (2.23)
Tentative pro-prosecution	15	8	6	25	0.62 (0.73)
Doubt re. alternatives	19	9	12	26	0.92 (1.08)
Doubt re. standards proof	8	12	5	18	0.52 (0.79)
Doubt re. Weaker considerations	3	7	5	13	0.34 (0.63)
Doubt re. need to await defence	23	15	14	36	1.06 (0.87)
Use of heuristics	12	10	9	18	0.80 (1.55)
Comprehension difficulties[b]	15	15	14	27	1.33 (1.81)

[a] Number of respondents using each reasoning type at some time during the prosecution case.
[b] Unprompted reported difficulties which were part of reasoning accounts.

much more likely to make use of heuristics in considering the defense case ($r = 0.62, p < .01$).

Confidence: Consistent with hypothesis 3, confidence in guilt was related to the use of the higher competence strong pro-prosecution reasoning at each stage, $r = .45$, .46 and .42, $p < .01$ in all instances. This picture is amplified by the correlation matrix for all forms of reasoning used in considering the prosecution case (see Table 2, column 9). There was a clear positive relationship between confidence and strong pro-prosecution assertions, but no such relation with the weaker tentative assertions. Similarly, there were significant negative relations between confidence in guilt and the more competent doubt referencing alternatives and standard of proof, but that between confidence and the lower competence doubt based on weak considerations was not significant.

Although *t*-tests show significant differences between relevant correlations (e.g. .53 vs. –.05 for strong and weak pro-prosecution assertions), a more convincing overview of this set of relations is found using regression techniques. With confidence as the dependent variable, and entering the 5 reasoning variables into the equation and then employing backward regression selection procedures, the best fitting model eliminated the two weaker reasoning variables but included the more competent variables: Strong pro-prosecution, $\beta = 0.387, p < .01$, doubt referencing alternatives, $\beta = -0.292, p < .01$, and doubt referencing standards of proof, $\beta = -0.146, p < .10$.

Table 2: Correlation matrix for all aspects of the complete prosecution case

	1	2	3	4	5	6	7	8	9	10	11
1 Strong pro-prosecution		–.312*	–.403**	–.261	–.100	.053	.169	–.041	.533**	–.163	.060
2 Tentative pro-prosecution			.067	–.044	–.318*	–.008	–.186	.337*	–.054	.162	–.161
3 Doubt–alternatives				.144	.225	–.098	.171	–.011	–.435**	–.001	–.056
4 Doubt–standards proof					–.009	–.249	.011	.100	–.292*	–.116	–.131
5 Doubt–weak considerations						.112	.323*	–.203	–.088	–.016	.333*
6 Doubt–await defence							.097	–.195	.104	.357*	.025
7 Use of heuristics								.303*	.238	–.045	.511**
8 Comprehension difficulties									–.053	.024	.174
9 Verdict confidence										–.003	.139
10 Self-report Systematic											–.106
11 Self-report Heuristic											

* $p < 0.05$ (2-tailed).
** $p < 0.01$ (2-tailed).

There was also support for Hypothesis 3 from reasoning related to the defense case Just one of the four reasoning categories—approval of indirect counter argument—reflects lower competence. Of particular interest, therefore, is the comparison between confidence and this lower competence indicator on the one hand, and confidence and the more competent approval of *direct* counter-argument on the other hand (see Table 3). The confidence link with the more competent reasoning category proved to be stronger, –.57 vs. –.35, t (47) = 1.47, $p < .10$.

Post trial HSM questionnaire scores: Direct support for hypothesis 4 comes from a comparison of those who reported they had followed the thread of the prosecution case with those who had not. Those who followed the case scored higher on systematic (M = 28.45, SD = 5.60 vs. M = 25.95, SD = 3.84), t (49) = 1.70, $p < .05$, one tail.

Turning now to the relation between questionnaire scores and competence in reasoning, there was some, but not extensive support. For example, systematic scores were associated with the higher competence reference of needing to wait for the defense, and heuristics scores with the lower competence doubt referencing weak considerations (see Table 2).

DISCUSSION

Where comprehension difficulties were experienced, it was shown that these were associated with poorer evidence recall, lower quality reasoning (e.g., "sounds like he knew what was going on, but I'm not really sure"), the greater use of heuristics (e.g., "like father, like son..."), and higher heuristic questionnaire scores. The relationship between comprehension difficulties and the use of heuristics is important as it demonstrates that a key HSM proposition (Chaiken et al., 1989) does generalize to juror decision making.

A direct relationship between competence and confidence could clearly be seen with regard to the quality of reasoning employed. Use of strong argument based on evidential matters (higher competence reasoning) was associated with higher confidence in judgment in both the prosecution and the defense. Conversely, use of weaker reasoning or that based on non evidential matters (lower competence reasoning) had relatively little impact on confidence. This is consistent with the ELM dual process model of Petty and Cacioppo (1986) in which stronger argument leads to more confident positions which, although open to change, have greater temporal persistence, and greater resistance to weak counter argument.

There was one further link between comprehension difficulties and verdict outcome that had not been predicted, though it is potentially

Table 3: Descriptive statistics and correlation matrix for reasoning about the defence

	M (*SD*)	1	2	3	4	5	6	7	8
1 Rebuttal of direct counter	0.52 (0.74)		.437**	–.310*	–.211	.082	.327*	.316*	–.220
2 Rebuttal of indirect counter	0.46 (0.71)			–.353*	–.242	.244	.447**	.162	–.084
3 Approval of direct counter	0.44 (0.61)				.014	–.021	–.572**	–.069	.030
4 Approval of indirect counter	0.28 (0.57)					.211	–.348*	–.199	.271
5 Use of heuristics	0.42 (0.73)						.030	–.062	.320*
6 Verdict confidence[a]	4.86 (3.76)							.271	–.039
7 Self-report systematic	(4.81) 27.2								–.106
8 Self-report heuristic	23.9 (4.88)								

[a] 36/50 guilty verdicts. Confidence always refers to confidence in guilt.
* $p < 0.05$. ** $p < 0.01$ (2-tailed).

important for our understanding of juror decision making. It was expected that comprehension difficulties would lead to lower confidence in guilt and consequently, an increased likelihood of a not guilty verdict. Comprehension difficulties with the prosecution statement lent some support to this. However, in respect of the defense case, none of those who reported they had "lost the thread" returned a non guilty verdict, nor did it lead to a lowering of confidence in guilt. In contrast, each of the 14 participants who returned a not guilty verdict reported they had followed the thread of the defense case. This finding merits replication, and perhaps attests to the importance of distinguishing the impact of complexity for different facets of trial evidence as suggested by Heuer and Penrod (1994).

In spite of the assumption within HSM theory that heuristic and systematic processing should be seen as orthogonal, or at least asymmetrical, higher competence was generally associated with systematic processing, and lower competence with heuristic processing. In particular, associations between comprehension difficulties, the spontaneous use of heuristics, weaker forms of reasoning, and the heuristic scores on the HSM scale, suggest a cluster of factors implicating low competence. It was not possible to explore causal pathways with the current data set, but it is plausible that if comprehension difficulties activate heuristic processing, a circular process involving the cluster of factors implicating low competence, once initiated, may be difficult to remedy.

REFERENCES

Bourgeois, M. J., Horowitz, I. A., & ForsterLee, L. (1993). Effects of technicality and access to trial transcripts on verdicts and information processing in a civil trial. *Personality and Social Psychology Bulletin*, *19*, 220–227.

Chaiken, S. (1987). The heuristic model of persuasion. In M. P. Zanna, J. M. Olson, & C. P. Herman (Eds.), *Social influence: The Ontario Symposium* (Vol. 5., pp. 3–39). Hillsdale, NJ: Erlbaum.

Chaiken, S., Liberman, A., & Eagly, A. H. (1989). Heuristic and systematic processing within and beyond the persuasion context. In J. S. Uleman & J. A. Bargh (Eds.), *Unintended thought* (pp. 212–252). New York: Guilford Press.

Cooper, J., Bennett, E. A., & Sukel, H. L. (1996). Complex scientific testimony: How do jurors make decisions? *Law and Human Behavior*, *20*, 379–394.

Diamond, S. S., & Casper, J. D. (1992). Blindfolding the jury to verdict consequences: Damages, experts, and the civil jury. *Law and Society Review*, *26*, 513–563.

Doran, S., & Jackson, J. (1997). The case for jury waiver. *Criminal Law Review*, 167.

Eagly, A. H., & Chaiken, S. (1993). *The psychology of attitudes*. London: Harcourt Brace Javanovich.

Forsterlee, L., & Horowitz, I. A. (1997). Enhancing juror competence in a complex trial. *Applied Cognitive Psychology*, *11*, 305–319.

Graziano, S. J., Panter, A. T., & Tanaka, J. S. (1990). Individual differences in information processing strategies and their role in juror decision making and selection. *Forensic Reports*, *3*, 279–301.

Heuer, L., & Penrod, S. (1994). Trial complexity: A field investigation of its meaning and its effects. *Law and Human Behavior*, *18*, 29–51.

Home Office (1998). *Juries in serious fraud trials*. London: Home Office

Horowitz, I. A., Forsterlee, L., & Brolly, I. (1996). Effects of trial complexity on decision making. *Journal of Applied Psychology*, *81*, 757–768.

Johnson, B. T., & Eagly, A. H. (1989). Effects of involvement on persuasion: A meta analysis. *Psychological Bulletin*, *106*, 290–314.

Kuhn, D., Weinstock, M., & Flaton, R. (1994). How well do jurors reason? *Psychological Science*, *5*, 289–296.

Maheswaran, D., & Chaiken, S. (1991). Promoting systematic processing in low motivation settings: Effect of incongruent information on processing and judgment. *Journal of Personality and Social Psychology*, *61*, 13–25.

Moore, P. J., & Gump, B. B. (1995). Information integration in juror decision making. *Journal of Applied Social Psychology*, *25*, 2158–2179.

Pennington, N., & Hastie, R. (1993). Reasoning in explanation based decision making. *Cognition*, *49*, 123–163.

Petty, R. E., & Cacioppo, J. A. (1986). The elaboration likelihood model of persuasion. In L. K. Berkowitz (Ed.), *Advances in experimental social psychology* (Vol. 19, pp. 123–205). San Diego, CA: Academic Press.

Penrod, S. D., & Heuer, L. (1997). Tweaking common-sense: Assessing aids to jury decision making. *Psychology, Public Policy, and Law*, *3*, 259–284.

Smith, B. C., Penrod, S. D., Otto, A. L., & Park, R. C. (1996). Jurors' use of probabilistic evidence. *Law and Human Behavior*, *20*, 49–82.

Endnote

1. For full details of the questionnaire contact T. M. Honess@city.ac.uk

Chapter 6

EFFECTS OF CRIMINAL MOTIVATION, ABILITY, AND OPPORTUNITY ON MOCK JURORS' VERDICTS

*Paul Skolnick and Jerry I. Shaw**

Prosecutors have long tried to demonstrate that criminal defendants had the motive, ability, and opportunity to commit the crime of which they are accused. For example, in the infamous O. J. Simpson trial, prosecutors Marcia Clark and Christopher Darden went to great lengths to document the accused's history of spousal abuse and jealousy (motive), to demonstrate his general physical fitness on a videotape (ability), and to establish a time line that made it possible for Simpson to have committed the crime (opportunity). Although this strategy failed to win a conviction in the Simpson case for a variety of other reasons (see Cowan & Fairchild, 1997), it would appear to be a sound legal strategy.

Each of these factors has been investigated in the social psychological literature, with motivation, by far, receiving the most attention (Geen, 1995; Reeve, 1997). Ability has been studied in several contexts, including the effects of self-efficacy expectations on task performance (Schunk, 1981), causal ascriptions for achievement outcomes (Weiner, 1986), and therapeutic interventions for perceived failure (Försterling, 1988). Opportunity has been examined mostly in antisocial contexts, such as the opportunity to steal (Diener, Fraser, Beaman, & Kelem, 1976), to aggress (Donnerstein & Hallam, 1978), and to cheat (Diener & Wallbom, 1976).

The same three factors have also been examined in the legal literature. Motivation has been studied in terms of profiles of certain types of criminals (e.g., rapists, drug couriers, hijackers) and psychological syndromes, such as battered spouse and rape trauma syndromes (see Monahan & Walker, 1998). With respect to ability, a distinction has been made between physical and mental ability. There is an extensive legal literature that considers mental ability, either in terms of insanity (mental ability at the time a crime is committed) or competence (mental ability at the time the accused is brought to trial). For a summary of this literature, the interested reader is referred to Grisso (1986) or Sales and Shuman (1996). Physical ability and criminal opportunity have been considered by criminologists (e.g., Sheley, 1991; Yablonsky, 1990).

The social psychological studies of motivation, ability, and opportunity are typically unrelated to the law and the legal studies of these factors are seldom empirical. Thus, there is a dearth of empirical studies relating ability, motivation, and opportunity to the legal context. An examination of the indices of three current textbooks in psychology and law (Bartol & Bartol, 1994; Horowitz, Willging, & Bordens, 1997; Wrightsman, Nietzel, & Fortune, 1998) failed to produce a single entry related to these three factors. Owing to the lack of empirical studies documenting the importance of these factors, the authors conducted a mail survey of law school deans throughout the country requesting them to rate the importance of establishing these three factors for criminal prosecution. The deans concurred that all three factors were extremely important, but that motivation was less vital than the others. This may be true because ability and opportunity are viewed as necessary conditions for the crime to occur, whereas motivation is merely a sufficient condition. Capricious criminal acts can be committed with no apparent motive, but would seem impossible in the absence of either ability or opportunity.

The present study investigates the relative importance for criminal prosecution of establishing criminal motivation, physical ability, and opportunity by manipulating each of these three factors (high vs low). Since all three factors are important, main effects are expected for each with more guilty verdicts obtained when each factor is high than when it is low. Furthermore, since the standard of proof that applies in criminal cases is "reasonable doubt," it is expected that the absence of any of these elements may create such a doubt, making more probable not guilty verdicts. Thus, it is hypothesized that guilty verdicts will be most prominent only when all three factors have been established. However, since motivation is merely a sufficient condition to establish guilt, whereas ability and opportunity are necessary conditions, it is predicted that motive will have an effect only when both ability and opportunity have been established. Ability and opportunity should have an effect whenever the other element is present, regardless of motivation.

METHOD

Participants

Mock jurors were 112 jury-eligible introductory psychology students at California State University, Northridge, who participated in partial fulfillment of their course requirements. Approximately one-third of the participants were men and two-thirds women.

Design and procedure

The experiment was conducted as a 2 × 2 × 2 (Motive × Ability × Opportunity) factorial design. Individuals were randomly assigned to read one of eight versions of a hypothetical murder scenario which varied according to experimental condition. Each of the eight groups resulting from this procedure contained 14 participants with the proportion of men and women approximately as described above.

Participants received an authentic-looking case transcript that described the fictitious trial of a male defendant accused of murdering his former wife. The case transcript was adapted from practice advocacy materials contained in Seckinger (1992). The cover page of each transcript presented the grand jury indictment against the defendant, Roger Saunders, who was accused of stabbing his ex-wife, Helen Wilson Saunders, to death on the front porch of her home. In all cases, Saunders had entered a plea of not guilty to the charge of first-degree murder.

A summary of case evidence followed which was identical in all conditions and served as a template to introduce the basic facts of the case. This consisted of testimony by three witnesses, as well as four exhibits that included photos of the murder scene and the victim. The victim's stepmother testified that Helen lived with her and on the night of the murder had returned home alone from the movies at about 10:00 pm. Her stepmother heard noise on the front porch, looked out a bedroom window and saw a shadowy figure attack Helen. The porch light was on, enabling the stepmother to get a clear view of the attacker's face who she identified as her ex-stepson, Roger Saunders. She also testified that she saw him speed away in a white automobile that she recognized as belonging to Saunders. A neighbor corroborated the stepmother's testimony, also identifying Roger Saunders as the assailant and the white car as belonging to him. The first police officer at the scene testified that the victim was lying in a pool of blood on the front porch when he arrived. He stated that no weapon was found at the crime scene, but that the coroner's report concluded that Helen had been killed by a serrated, six-inch hunting knife. Based on an interrogation of Helen's stepmother and her neighbor, Saunders was subsequently arrested. A knife similar to the one indicated in the coroner's report was found in his house and advanced forensic techniques permitted the coroner to estimate that the probability the knife was the actual murder weapon was at least 80%.

The remainder of the case evidence came from witness testimony that established each of three factors regarding the defendant's motivation, ability, and opportunity to commit the crime. In the High Motivation scenario, the victim's stepmother testified that Saunders had a quick temper and was easily angered. She reported that Roger and Helen had frequent arguments and that on several of these occasions, Roger had physically assaulted Helen. After they divorced and Helen had returned to live with her stepmother, Roger would frequently visit, often flying into a rage in an attempt to get her to reconcile with him. Roger's last visit was the night before Helen's murder when Helen rejected his offer to get back together despite Roger's threats that she would regret it if she refused. A bartender testified that Saunders had entered the Silver Dollar Bar at about 8:00 pm on the evening of the murder. Saunders was extremely agitated and told the bartender that he was going to make certain that if he could not have his former wife back, no one else could have her either. Testimony in the Low Motivation condition was given by the same two individuals, except that Roger and Helen's relationship had been described as nonconfrontational and friendly even after their divorce. Neither witness mentioned any threats by Saunders to harm his ex-wife. Additionally, Roger Saunder's testified that he was extremely upset by his wife's murder and that he would never do anything to harm her.

The High Ability scenario was based on testimony from Saunders and his doctor. Saunders explained he was an avid hunter and that the knife found at his house was used on hunting trips. He admitted that he had won several hunting competitions that required expert use of hunting knives, but he contended that the knife had been stored in a display case since the Spring prior to Helen's murder. The doctor testified that he had given Saunders a complete physical examination just prior to the murder and had found him in excellent health, with exceptional endurance and muscle tone. The doctor rendered the expert opinion that Saunders had the physical strength and ability to commit the murder. Testimony in the Low Ability scenario was from the same two individuals. Saunders asserted that he had broken his preferred arm and that it had been immobilized in a cast since two weeks prior to his ex-wife's murder. He also claimed that he had developed painful arthritis in his hands making it very difficult to grip a knife with sufficient strength to harm anybody. He contended that the knife found at his house had been a gift and, since he was unfamiliar with the use of such knives, it had been stored in a display case ever since he received it. The doctor confirmed that he had been treating Saunders for severe arthritis of his fingers and hands for several years and that Saunders' broken arm was in a cast the night of the murder. The doctor also stated that Saunders was in poor health and that he had poor muscle tone and physical endurance due to the debilitating arthritis and inactivity from the broken arm. The doctor rendered the expert opinion that Saunders lacked the physical strength and ability to commit the murder.

The High Opportunity scenario included testimony from two witnesses. The bartender testified that Saunders had left the Silver Dollar Bar at 9:15 pm on the night of the murder, thereby affording the opportunity for Saunders to have committed the murder at 10:00 pm. Roger Saunders' neighbor testified that he saw Saunders return home at 9:30 pm that night. The neighbor established that Saunders' house was only a 15 minute drive from the murder scene and that he could have easily left home and driven there prior to when the murder was committed at 10:00 pm. The same two individuals testified in the Low Opportunity scenario, in which the bartender stated that Saunders had left the Silver Dollar Bar at 9:45 pm on the night of the murder. The neighbor testified that he saw Saunders return home at 10:00 pm that night and that since Saunders house was a 15 minute drive from the murder scene, he could not have arrived there prior to when the murder was committed. In addition, Saunders testified in this scenario that he had left the bar at 9:45 pm and had exchanged greetings with his neighbor when he arrived home 15 minutes later prior to going immediately to bed for the night.

All case summaries next included closing arguments for the prosecution and the defense. Depending on condition, the prosecution and defense each reiterated the appropriate evidence supporting their side's contention of high or low motivation, ability, and opportunity. This was followed by juror instructions that defined the charge of murder in the first degree, described the "reasonable doubt" standard of proof, and admonished the mock jurors to consider all of the available evidence.

Dependent measures

Mock jurors then received a verdict form on which they returned either a "Not guilty" or a "Guilty" verdict. This was followed by a juror opinion form that requested their sentencing preferences and two evaluative judgments. Mock jurors who found the defendant guilty were asked to indicate which of three sentencing options they recommended: life in prison with possible parole; life in prison without parole; or the death penalty.

Mock jurors next rated how responsible the defendant was for his ex-wife's murder on a 9-point scale ranging from (1) *Not at all responsible* to (9) *Totally responsible*. A second item asked the mock jurors to render a personal evaluation of the defendant on 10 personality traits, including trustworthiness, likability, competence, ethics, considerateness, attractiveness, intelligence, warmth, sensitivity, and industriousness. Each trait was rated on a 9-point scale with higher ratings signifying more positive evaluations. Ratings for the 10 traits were averaged for each mock juror to yield a personal evaluation score.

Three additional items were included as a check on the effectiveness of the motivation, ability, and opportunity manipulations. Each of these was rated on 9-point scales, ranging from No motive, ability, or opportunity (1) to High motive, ability, or opportunity (9). Another item asked mock jurors to assess the strength of the overall evidence presented against the defendant from Weak (1) to Strong (9).

Finally, demographic attributes of the mock jurors were recorded on a juror background form requesting their sex, age, year in college, university major, and ethnic background. After completing the postquestionnaire, mock jurors were debriefed as to the nature of the experiment, given credit for their participation, and dismissed.

RESULTS

Manipulation checks on the three independent variables indicated that our manipulations were very successful. Mock jurors in the high motive conditions rated the defendant's motive as significantly higher than did those in the low motive conditions, $F\ (1{,}104) = 41.86$, $p < .001$. The mean for the high motive condition was 7.41, and for the low motive condition, 4.46. Similarly, the manipulation of opportunity was successful in that mock jurors in the high opportunity conditions rated the defendant's opportunity higher than did those in the low opportunity conditions, $F\ (1{,}104) = 50.02$, $p < .000$. The means for high and low opportunity were 7.73 and 4.91 respectively. Finally, there was a significant difference in perceived ability between mock jurors in the high and low ability conditions, $F\ (1{,}104) = 85.25$, $p < .000$. The mean scores for ability in the high and low conditions were 8.08 and 4.79 respectively.

A $2 \times 2 \times 2$ hierarchical log linear analysis (motive $\times$ ability $\times$ opportunity) was conducted on juror verdicts. Table 1 presents the data. Overall mock jurors judged the case to be a very close one: they found the defendant guilty in 54 cases and not guilty in the remaining 58 cases. As expected, polarized verdicts were obtained in the cases where motive, ability, and opportunity were all high, where 83% voted guilty, and where all three factors were low, where 92% voted not guilty. In the remaining cases where only one or two of the three factors were high, the guilty/not guilty split was approximately 50%, $\chi^2\ (N = 112, 3) = 17.4$, $p < .001$.

Table 1: Mock Juror Verdicts as a Function of Defendant Motive, Ability and Opportunity

		High Opportunity		Low Opportunity	
Motive	Ability	Guilty	Not Guilty	Guilty	Not Guilty
High	High	12	2	9	5
	Low	5	9	7	7
Low	High	7	7	5	9
	Low	8	6	1	13
Total		32	24	22	34

There was a significant main effect for motive indicating that the defendant was found guilty more often when he was perceived to have a strong motive (33 cases) than when his motive was weak (21 cases), $\chi^2 = (1, N = 112) = 5.65$, $p < .018$. The main effect for ability was likewise significant, with the defendant being found guilty more often when his ability was high (33 cases) than when it was perceived to be low (21 cases), $\chi^2 = (1, N = 112) = 5.65$, $p < .018$. Finally, there was a significant main effect for opportunity such that there were more guilty verdicts when the defendant was perceived to have high opportunity (32 cases) than when opportunity was low (22 cases), $\chi^2 = (1, N = 112) = 3.97$, $p < .046$. None of the interactions was significant in this analysis.

If mock jurors found that the defendant was guilty, they were then asked to recommend a sentence. Their choices were life with the possibility of parole, life without parole, or death. A second $2 \times 2 \times 2$ hierarchical log linear analysis (motive × ability × opportunity) was conducted on sentencing for those mock jurors that voted guilty. Table 2 presents the data.

Table 2: Juror Sentencing Recommendations as a Function of Defendant Motive, Ability and Opportunity

		High Opportunity			Low Opportunity		
Motive	Ability	Life With Parole	Life With No Parole	Death Penalty	Life With Parole	Life With No Parole	Death Penalty
High	High	0	12	0	2	4	3
	Low	1	4	0	2	3	2
Low	High	2	3	2	2	3	0
	Low	4	2	2	1	0	0
Total		7	21	4	7	10	5

This analysis yielded a significant main effect for motive in that the defendant was given more severe punishment when his motive was high than when it was low, $\chi^2 = (2, N = 54) = 8.32, p < .016$. The main effect for opportunity approached significance in that mock jurors recommended more severe punishment to defendants when they had high opportunity than when their opportunity was low, $\chi^2 = (2, N = 54) = 4.97, p < .084$. These two variables of motive and opportunity also significantly interacted with each other, $\chi^2 = (2, N = 54) = 9.49, p < .009$. Sentences were more lenient when both factors were either high or low and less lenient when one factor was high and the other was low. Although the death penalty was seldom recommended by mock jurors (only 9 cases overall), it was recommended only when opportunity was high and motivation low (4 cases), or the reverse, when opportunity was low and motivation high (5 cases). The remaining main effect for ability, as well as the other interaction effects, were not significant.

Mock jurors were asked to rate the defendant on a 9-point scale measuring attribution of responsibility. A 2 × 2 × 2 (motive × ability × opportunity) analysis of variance was conducted on this dependent variable. Results revealed significant main effects for all three independent variables. Defendants with strong motivation were perceived as more responsible than defendants with weak motivation (6.6 vs 5.0; $F\ (1,104) = 9.15, p < .003$). Defendants with high ability were seen as more responsible than defendants with lower ability (6.5 vs. 5.1; $F\ (1,104) = 7.19, p < .009$). Finally, defendants with ample opportunity were rated as more responsible than were defendants with little opportunity (6.5 vs. 5.1; $F\ (1,104) = 7.19, p < .009$). None of the interactions was significant on attribution of responsibility.

A final 2 × 2 × 2 analysis of variance was conducted on mock jurors' personal evaluation of the defendant. The only significant main effect in this analysis was the main effect for motivation. When the defendant was highly motivated, mock jurors evaluated him less positively than when he had little motivation (3.7 vs 4.9; $F\ (1,104) = 29.37, p < .000$. Thus, personal evaluations were dependent on perception of the defendant's motive, but were unrelated to any other factor.

DISCUSSION

Consistent with our hypothesis, the data show that motive, ability, and opportunity are extremely important factors in mock jury decision-making. It is clear that to maximize the likelihood of obtaining a guilty verdict, prosecutors must establish all three factors. If one or more of these factors is missing, the likelihood of a guilty verdict is reduced 33%–37%. From this it follows that defense attorneys need only concentrate on their strongest point. If it can be shown that evidence for any of the three factors is weak, the chances for a favorable verdict of not guilty, or at least a hung jury, are markedly increased.

It was anticipated that establishing a defendant's motive would be viewed as less important in verdict decisions than documenting either ability or opportunity. No evidence was found to support this. Mock jurors' verdicts were as strongly affected by motivation evidence as by ability and opportunity. Since this contradicts the perceptions of legal professionals obtained in our survey, as well as the logical conclusion that motive is sufficient, but not necessary to convict, this merits additional commentary. If motivation is viewed as explaining an action, whereas ability and opportunity make an action possible, then mock jurors appear reluctant to convict when they lack a clear explanation. Apparently, jurors need a reason why a crime was committed to warrant a conviction even if all other evidence strongly points toward guilt. It appears that legal professionals respond logically to the evidence, whereas jurors may respond more psychologically.

Although motivation had an independent effect on verdicts, its effect on sentencing options was dependent on opportunity. When opportunity was high, mock jurors recommended more severe punishment for a guilty defendant whose actions were capricious, rather than motivated. Alternatively, when opportunity was low, highly motivated criminal acts were punished more severely. Note the death penalty was recommended only in these two cases. Though speculative, this interaction may be explained in terms of perceived dangerousness by mock jurors. That is, opportunistic, but unmotivated criminals are viewed as unpredictable and therefore as more dangerous. Likewise, criminals whose motivation is so strong as to commit a crime with little opportunity, are also perceived as unpredictable and dangerous. The theoretical notions proposed here that opportunistic and/or highly motivated criminals are perceived as dangerous and that dangerous criminals should be severely punished merit attention in subsequent research.

Finally, attribution of responsibility was dependent upon all three factors, but personal evaluation was dependent only upon perceived motive. Since responsibility judgments mirrored verdict decisions, this implies either that mock jurors first make a judgment about criminal responsibility and then base their verdict on this judgment; or, alternatively, they may render their verdict decision based on other factors and then justify it by inferring responsibility. In contrast, since personal evaluation was affected only by motive information, mock jurors apparently did not base their verdicts on the likability of the defendant.

REFERENCES

Bartol, C. R., & Bartol, A. M. (1994). *Psychology and law* (2nd ed.). Pacific Grove, CA: Brooks-Cole.

Cowan, G., & Fairchild, H. H. (Eds.). (1997). The O. J. Simpson trial: Research and theory on the dynamics of ethnicity. *Journal of Social Issues*, *53*, 409–595.

Diener, E., Fraser, S. C., Beaman, A. L., & Kelem, R. T. (1976). Effects of deindividuation variables on stealing on Halloween trick-or-treaters. *Journal of Personality and Social Psychology*, *33*, 178–183.

Diener, E., & Wallbom, M. (1976). Effects of self-awareness on antinormative behavior. *Journal of Research in Personality*, *10*, 107–111.

Donnerstein, E., & Hallam, J. (1978). Facilitating effects of erotica on aggression against women. *Journal of Personality and Social Psychology*, *36*, 1270–1277.

Försterling, F. (1988). *Attribution theory in clinical psychology*. Chichester, N. Y. Wiley.

Geen, R. G. (1995). *Human motivation: A social psychological approach*. Belmont, CA: Brooks-Cole.

Grisso, T. (1988). *Evaluating competencies: Forensic assessments and instruments*. New York, NY: Plenum Press.

Horowitz, I. A., Willging, T. E., & Bordens, K. S. (1998). *The psychology of law*. New York, NY: Addison-Wesley.

Monahan, J., & Walker, L. (1998). *Social science in law: Case materials*. (4th ed.). Westbury, N. Y.: The Foundation Press.

Reeve, J. M. (1997). *Understanding motivation and emotion* (2nd ed.). Orlando, FL: Harcourt Brace.

Sales, B. D., & Shuman, D. W. (Eds.). (1996). *Law, mental health, and mental disorder*. Pacific Grove, CA: Brooks-Cole.

Schunk, D. H. (1981). Modeling and attributional effects on children's achievement: A self-efficacy analysis. *Journal of Educational Psychology*, *73*, 93–105.

Seckinger, J. H. (1992). State v. O'Neill, problems and case file (5th Ed.). *National Institute for Trial Advocacy*.

Sheley, J. F. (1991). *Criminology: A contemporary handbook*. Belmont, CA: Wadsworth.

Weiner, B. (1986). *An attributional theory of motivation and emotion*. N. Y.: Springer.

Wrightsman, L. S., Nietzel, M. T., & Fortune, W. H. (1998). *Psychology and the legal system* (4th ed.). Pacific Grove, CA: Brooks-Cole.

Yablonsky, L. (1990). *Criminology: Crime and criminality*. New York: Harper & Row.

Author note

* The authors wish to thank Edward Binder for his skillful role in helping to develop stimulus materials and in collecting and coding the data for statistical analysis. Correspondence regarding this chapter should be addressed to Paul Skolnick, Department of Psychology, California State University, Northridge, Northridge, CA 91330. Electronic mail may be sent by Internet to paul.skolnick@csun.edu.

PART 3

CIVIL AND CRIMINAL COURT

Chapter 7

COMPLEX MEDICAL LITIGATION AND HINDSIGHT BIAS: STRATEGIES TO REDUCE FACTFINDERS' RETROSPECTIVE ATTRIBUTIONS OF FAULT

Merrie Jo Stallard, Joseph M. Price and Francis C. Dane

The belief in a factfinder's ability to render a fair and impartial verdict is a cornerstone of most judicial systems. As part of their task, factfinders are expected to be able to set aside biases and, consequently, base their verdicts only on the evidence presented (Menon, 1995; Sand, Siffert, Loughlin, Reiss, & Batterman, 1977). However, researchers and legal experts have long questioned the typical factfinder's ability to comprehend and reach a fair decision when faced with a complex court case (Strawn & Munsterman, 1982). Many argue that one's ability to render a fair and impartial verdict is affected by a number of potentially extra-legal biasing factors, including opening and closing arguments (Pitera, 1991; Pyszczynski & Wrightsman, 1981). Thus, inexperienced factfinders, such as jurors, are instructed not to consider the content of arguments as evidence. However, there still exist extra-legal biases that are difficult to eliminate simply with the use of standard procedures.

In virtually every legal system, factfinders render a verdict after the event in question has already occurred and the final outcome, typically negative, is known. The problem inherent in this structure of the legal system, especially in certain types of litigation (*inter alia*, medical malpractice, medical mass tort cases), is that the negative outcome is the cause of the lawsuit. This "after-the-fact" structure encourages factfinders (judges and jurors) to be more susceptible to the human judgment phenomenon known as hindsight bias (Fischhoff, 1975; Hawkins & Hastie, 1990). When factfinders engage in hindsight bias, they are going beyond the "facts of the case" and are using extra-legal factors when determining their verdict.

Hindsight bias

Hindsight bias is the tendency for individuals with outcome knowledge to judge a priori decisions or actions in light of their post hoc knowledge (Fischhoff, 1975). For example, people who are told that a particular outcome had actually occurred believe the prospective odds of occurrence are higher than do people who know only that the particular outcome is one of several possible outcomes. Baron and Hershey (1988) described the pervasiveness of hindsight bias when evaluating a variety of decisions, including malpractice suits, liability cases, and regulatory decisions. Hindsight bias has been demonstrated in a variety of experimental settings and populations, including the legal arena (Casper, Benedict, & Kelly, 1988; Casper, Benedict, & Perry, 1989; Christensen-Szalanski & Willham, 1991; Hawkins & Hastie, 1990).

Explanations of hindsight bias

Several motivational and cognitive explanations have emerged to account for hindsight bias (Hawkins & Hastie, 1990). Motivational theorists invoke needs or desires, while cognitive theorists invoke cognitive-decision strategies (Rachlinski, 1998). Motivational theories have little demonstrated validity (see Hawkins & Hastie, 1990, for a review of motivational-based studies), but the cognitive strategy of what Fischhoff (1975) originally described as "creeping determinism" has received considerable empirical support.

Creeping determinism is the process by which outcome information is automatically integrated into an individual's knowledge about the factual events preceding the outcome. Because individuals tend to revise events so that the "beginning and middle are causally connected to its end" (Wasserman, Lempert, & Hastie, 1991, p. 31), it is difficult to imagine how alternate outcomes could occur (Fischhoff, 1975; Schkade & Kilbourne, 1991). Consequently, facts that are consistent with an event's outcome are rated as more important and more pertinent to the outcome (Baron & Hershey, 1988; Fischhoff, 1975). Lowe (1992) summarizes this "causal linkage" of hindsight bias by noting that it is tantamount to processing information "backwards," i.e., from outcome to antecedent.

Everyone engages in hindsight bias, but people are more prone to engage in hindsight under certain circumstances, specifically absent topic-specific knowledge. Uninformed individuals are most likely to use cognitive heuristics, including hindsight bias, to process information (Klayman & Ha, 1987). In their meta-analysis of hindsight studies, for example, Christensen-Szalanski and Willham (1991) demonstrated that effect sizes for hindsight bias in studies involving familiar tasks were significantly smaller than in studies involving unfamiliar tasks.

Relevant or specific knowledge enables one to imagine alternate outcomes, which apparently is one of the few reliable ways to reduce hindsight bias (Agans & Shaffer, 1994; Arkes, 1989; Tversky & Kahneman, 1982). Arkes,

Guilmette, Faust, and Hart (1988), for example, asked subjects to consider the opposite outcome, a strategy first suggested by Lord, Lepper and Preston (1984), and found the increased probability estimates for the alternative outcomes reduced hindsight bias.

Limitations in complex medical litigation

The complexity of most medical litigation almost guarantees that factfinders do not have the technical, scientific, and medical testimony background necessary to prevent hindsight bias. Even with the help of adversarial expert witnesses, factfinders often do not have sufficient understanding of the scientific principles underlying the competing theories to evaluate the validity of those theories (Menon, 1995). Factfinders who lack such understanding are ill-equipped to arrive at a just verdict, and no amount of judicial instructions can substitute for the years of education required to become proficient in scientific reasoning. Thus, most factfinders who must decide between two equally incomprehensible scientific theories are likely to disregard both and decide the case on some other basis (Price & Kelly, 1996). Given factfinders' shortcomings with respect to understanding medical and scientific testimony, it is easy to understand how hindsight bias influences decisions as they reason from the (negative) outcome and incorporate that outcome in their decisions. Medical mass tort cases serve as classic examples of hindsight bias among factfinders.

Medical products inevitably involve the use of a drug or medical device that is ingested, implanted, infused, or inserted into human beings. Most of the recipients suffer from pre-existing adverse medical conditions that necessitate use of these products. It is axiomatic that such products have side effects and other dangers associated with their use; safety is traditionally judged by balancing the risks associated with the product against the benefits to be gained by its use. Inevitably, some recipients of the drug or device will suffer side effects either related to or separate and independent from the use of the product. When many recipients experience such effects, mass-tort liability suits are often filed.

Factfinders, when faced with ill or injured plaintiffs and deep-pocket defendants, are often unable to discard the outcome of injury or death and examine facts in a prospective, as opposed to retrospective, manner ("Developments in the law," 1995; Rachlinski, 1998). Similar effects have been identified in medical malpractice suits (Arkes & Schipani, 1994). Thus, factfinders who lack the requisite scientific and medical expertise to avoid hindsight are likely to unfairly benefit injured plaintiffs.

Debiasing techniques

Fischhoff (1982) reviewed a variety of debiasing strategies that have produced limited success (e.g., Arkes et al., 1988; Davies, 1987; Wood, 1978). Arkes (1989), however, noted that many of them "seem to be either impractical or impossible to use in the context of court testimony" (p. 449–450). More recent attempts to reduce hindsight bias in the courtroom have produced mixed results (Kamin & Rachlinski, 1995; Stallard & Worthington, 1998). Jury instructions failed to reduce jurors' hindsight bias (Kamin & Rachlinski, 1995), while Stallard and Worthington (1998) successfully reduced hindsight bias by incorporating debiasing arguments into the defense attorney's presentation through which a specific alternative outcome was presented. Arkes (1989) noted that criminal defense attorneys use similar techniques to provide jurors with scenarios that do not implicate their clients. A number of additional proposals have been suggested for reducing hindsight bias, including bifurcation, special masters, blue-ribbon juries, and court-appointed experts (Wexler & Schopp, 1989; "Developments in the law," 1995). As will become apparent, however, these proposals have been met with considerable criticism.

Bifurcation. Bifurcation has been proposed to separate causation, liability, and damages in order to overcome the scientific and medical knowledge shortcomings of factfinders (Poythress, Schumacher, Wiener, & Murrin, 1993; Wexler & Schopp, 1989). Bifurcation also limits the number of issues the jury must decide in a single trial ("Developments in the law," 1995). At least one commentator has suggested that trial bifurcation "produce[s] superior outcomes" (Sanders, 1993, p. 75), and many judges feel that bifurcation increases fairness of the verdicts ("Judges' Opinions on Procedural Issues," 1989). Bifurcation has also been suggested as one procedure to reduce the tendency to engage in hindsight (Dawson, et al., 1988; Hawkins & Hastie, 1990). In the United States, bifurcation is done pursuant to Federal Rules of Civil Procedure 42(b) (1999) or its state court counterparts.

Perhaps one of the most effective uses of bifurcation involved litigation over the anti-nausea drug, Bendectin, prescribed for pregnant women, which was claimed to cause fetal malformations ("Bendectin Litigation," 1988). In that case, U.S. District Judge Carl Rubin tried the question of causation first in a consolidated action that included 1,100 cases. After hearing only the causation issue, the factfinders decided that Bendectin did not cause the alleged defects. One of the more controversial aspects of the case was Judge Rubin's decision to prohibit the child plaintiffs from appearing in the courtroom during the causation phase. It seems reasonable to conclude that this decision reduced hindsight bias that would have occurred had the jury been able to see the malformed children who were alleged to be the "outcome" from the drug.

Bifurcation, however, does not solve the problem of factfinders who do not possess the necessary technical expertise to understand complex evidence. Some also argue that separating issues removes the factfinders' ability to weigh strengths and weaknesses of liability and damage arguments against one another ("Developments in the law," 1995). Wexler and Schopp (1989) also acknowledge that it would be naïve to assume that the factfinders would be completely unaware that a negative outcome precipitated the trial.

Special Masters. Special masters are individuals, appointed at any stage of a trial, to serve as factfinders and provide neutral advice to an otherwise ill-equipped judge (Wilkinson, Zielinski, & Curtis, 1998; Farrell, 1994). In the United States, however, the use of special masters should be exceptional rather than normal trial procedure (Federal Rules of Civil Procedure Rule 53(b), 1999).

One of the objections to appointing special masters is the claim that reducing hindsight bias comes at the expense of invading the judge's or juror's traditional fact-finding responsibility by eliminating the need for factfinders to evaluate technical evidence ("Developments in the law," 1995). Additionally, some have argued that giving special masters adjudicatory authority violates the U. S. constitutional requirement that civil cases in federal court be tried and decided by Article III judges (Farrell, 1994). Others argue that taking the fact-finding role from jurors eliminates incorporation of the values of the community, which is traditionally viewed as part of the role of the jury in protecting against arbitrary decisions by tenured judges (Fournier, 1980; "Developments in the law," 1995).

Blue-Ribbon Juries. The use of blue-ribbon juries containing scientifically and technologically competent individuals has been proposed as a remedy for factfinders' technical incompetence (Drazan, 1989; Fournier, 1980; "Developments in the law," 1995; Luneburg & Nordenberg, 1981; Menon, 1995). Because there is no federal authority permitting blue-ribbon juries, both parties must consent. In the Bendectin case, for example, Judge Rubin suggested the use of a blue-ribbon panel but the plaintiff rejected the idea.

While all of the above strategies can reduce hindsight bias in scientific and technical complex medical products liability litigation, none of these procedures has been regularly employed (Champagne, Shuman, &

Whitaker, 1996). Courts seem reluctant to usurp the power of the factfinder despite the recognition of a lack of scientific and medical capability as well a tendency to reach a decision that incorporates the outcome. One additional debiasing technique, court-appointed scientific panels, has gained recent attention in the largest, most complex mass tort medical products liability case to date, the silicone gel breast implant litigation.

Court-Appointed Scientific Panels. In the United States, Rule 706 of the Federal Rules of Evidence permits the appointment of expert witnesses of the court's own selection to present evidence to the trier(s) of fact. There is also broad inherent authority of the court to appoint experts who enable the court to carry out its duties, including the authority to appoint a technical advisor to consult with the court during the decision making process pursuant to Rule 104 of the Federal Rules of Evidence (Cecil & Willging, 1994). Both the use of court-appointed experts under Rule 706 and technical advisors under Rule 104 have received renewed attention since the U.S. Supreme Court's ruling in *Daubert v. Merrell Dow Pharmaceutical, Inc.* (1993), which required judges to be "gatekeepers" to "insure that any and all scientific testimony or evidence admitted is not only relevant but reliable" (p. 2795). Various requirements for the admissibility of scientific evidence were enunciated in which judges were required to do a preliminary assessment of the reasoning or methodology underlying proposed testimony to determine its validity and application to the facts in issue.

Reactions to Daubert were mixed. Some felt the test was too vague to apply. Federal judges protested that they were ill-equipped to fulfill the Daubert-mandated role of scientific gatekeepers since many of them were no more scientifically adept than lay jurors. Some judges continued to just apply general acceptance criteria, while others used the standards of testability, peer review, error rate and general acceptance mentioned in Daubert, and others applied their own standards to the issue of scientific admissibility (Price & Rosenberg, 1998).

At the time that Daubert was decided, the most challenging piece of complex medical products liability litigation in the history of jurisprudence was starting to wend its way through the courts—i.e., silicone gel breast implants. Silicone, a synthetic polymer, had long been employed as an implantable biomaterial. Silicone gel breast implants were first marketed in the early 1960s, and by the early 1990s there was a long history of safe use without scientific evidence to the contrary (Angell, 1997).

In 1982 a series of anecdotal reports first appeared in which a possible link between silicone gel breast implants and various traditional autoimmune diseases was hypothesized. Later, atypical autoimmune diseases were included. These anecdotal reports did not include scientific methodology, involved small populations, and could not rule out other potential causes of these autoimmune diseases and symptoms. Because the claims made in this litigation involved diseases and symptoms that also occurred among women without breast implants, epidemiological studies were required to determine whether silicone gel breast implants were associated with such diseases. No such research was available when the initial suits were filed, but authors of 25 epidemiological studies have since concluded that no association between silicone gel breast implants and autoimmune diseases exists (e.g., Gabriel et al., 1994; Sanchez-Guerrero et al., 1995).

Despite this scientific analysis, lawsuits alleging a relationship between breast implants and autoimmune disease continued to clog the courts. These cases were presented to jurors who lacked sufficient knowledge to understand highly technical scientific studies presented simultaneously with sympathetic, ill, or injured plaintiffs. Early silicone breast implant trials manifested considerable hindsight bias, resulting in large verdicts for plaintiffs who had otherwise scientifically groundless claims (e.g., *Hopkins v. Dow Corning Corp.*, 1994). Thus, even though there has never been an epidemiological study to support the plaintiffs' theories, factfinders continue to find for plaintiffs who claim to have suffered autoimmune diseases as a result of their silicone gel breast implants (*Meister v. Bristol-Myers Squibb*, 1999).

Another confounding factor has been media coverage of silicone gel breast implants. Many factfinders have been exposed to popular versions of the horrors of silicone gel breast implants that are incorporated into their decisions. When engaging in hindsight, for example, the outcome information also activates the representative heuristic—i.e., the degree to which salient features of the one category are similar to the features presumed to be characteristic of that category (Tversky & Kahneman, 1982). When faced with a negative outcome factfinders search their memories for similar circumstances, including various media reports. Because such reports are recalled from memory, factfinders believe such media reports are representative of information about the relevant topic. Thus, while disregarding the objective science to the contrary because it is impossible to understand, factfinders are unable to disassociate media information from the plaintiff's illness when reaching their decisions.

Recently, in conformance with the dictates of the Daubert opinion, several judges have appointed independent scientific expert panels to review the voluminous scientific literature relevant to this litigation and report their scientific conclusions. Members of these panels, serving as expert witnesses, can educate the knowledge-starved factfinders toward a better understanding of the relevant science, potentially offsetting the tendency of factfinders to reason from outcome to antecedent.

In 1996, for example, Judge Robert Jones of the U.S. District Court in Portland, Oregon, appointed a panel of technical advisors to assist him in analyzing the association of breast implants and connective tissue disease. Following extensive analysis, hearings and expert testimony, the panel reported its conclusions to Judge Jones and he then issued his opinion, concluding that the plaintiffs' claim of an association between breast implants and autoimmune disease was "at best an untested hypothesis." These claims were then stricken from the case (*Hall v. Baxter Health Care Corp.*, 1996). Similarly, Judge Jack Weinstein, U.S. District Court for the Eastern District of New York, conducted his own hearings, analyzed the reports from Judge Jones' technical advisors, and reached the same conclusion ("Breast Implants," 1997). At the same time, Judge Sam Pointer (1996), Chief Judge of the United States District Court for the District of Alabama and the judge to whom all federal silicone gel breast implant cases were assigned for multi-district litigation, appointed a similar panel chosen by an independent selection committee of scientists and lawyers. They exhaustively examined thousands of pages of scientific literature on the subject, listened to testimony from expert witnesses chosen by the parties, and invited their own panel of experts to discuss the causation question. After two years of work, the panel released a report explaining their conclusion that silicone gel breast implants "do not alter incidence or severity of autoimmune disease..." or "precipitate novel immune responses or induce systemic inflammation" (Diamond, Hulka, Kerkvliet, & Tugwell, 1998). The findings of these expert witnesses has been supported by at least two other major analyses of this controversy. The Independent Review Group (1998) appointed by the U.K. Department of Health and the Institute of Medicine-National Academy of Sciences (1999) also concluded that there was no scientific basis to plaintiffs' autoimmune claims.

The four scientists appointed to Judge Pointer's panel have now been deposed in extensive videotape depositions and the testimony contained therein is available for use in federal and state courts in future silicone gel breast implant cases. Those courts will hear motions pursuant to Daubert to dismiss plaintiffs' claims on the ground that there is no reputable science to support the claims. In the event that those motions are denied, this neutral court-appointed expert testimony will be presented to the factfinders that hear the cases. One question to be answered is whether the testimony by these neutral experts will either eliminate or reduce the hindsight bias which has plagued these cases to date.

Previous experience with court-appointed experts leads us to predict that factfinders (jurors and judges) will decide cases consistent with the advice and testimony of court-appointed experts. Cecil and Willging (1994), for example, report that, in a survey of 58 cases that included seven jury trials, only two judges indicated that the result was not consistent with the guidance given by the court-appointed expert. In many of the cases, the testimony of court-appointed experts dominated the proceedings. Brekke, Enko, Clavet, and Seelau (1991), however, found that the court-appointed expert did not overwhelm and unduly influence jurors, at least after jurors deliberated. They also found that court-appointed (non-adversarial) expert testimony content was not as well received by the jurors, and recognition recall of expert testimony was higher in adversarial than non-adversarial conditions. It remains to be seen whether this distinction has meaning for Judge Pointer's national science panel. The panel had its own court-appointed counsel who questioned them at the videotaped depositions. Then the parties were each allowed to cross-examine the panel members. This approach may make the adversarial/non-adversarial distinction moot. However, Poythress, Schumacher, Wiener, and Murrin (1993) found that the use of court-appointed and court-paid experts was competitive with, and frequently rated superior to, the adversary system model.

Brekke et al., questioned the advisability of informing jurors that an expert is court appointed. Alternately, Cecil and Willging (1994) demonstrated the significant impact in favor of a verdict consistent with the court-appointed expert testimony. A priori, it seems irrelevant whether factfinders are aware of an expert's appointed status as long as the expert is sufficiently informative to enable the factfinders to entertain plausible alternate outcomes. Additional research is required to determine whether this is the case for all types of court-appointed expert testimony. Further, courts are usually reluctant to appoint experts because many judges believe that the adversarial system requires them to defer to party presentation of evidence, that it would be difficult to find truly neutral experts, and that the cost may be prohibitive (Cecil & Willging, 1994).

Despite these concerns, it appears that the opportunity exists in many complex scientific cases to use either court-appointed expert(s) or technical advisors. The benefit of such court-appointed experts is that they are neutral, they can help the court and jury understand specialized issues beyond their expertise, and they can help to eliminate or significantly reduce hindsight bias. Neutral experts, by virtue of their expertise, are not likely to incorporate the outcome in their decisions. They will be able to focus on the scientific and technical issues without being distracted by the after-the-fact damages or injuries claimed by the plaintiff. Use of such experts and advisors could, in combination with other debiasing techniques such as voir dire, opening statement, closing argument, and jury instructions, go a long way toward eliminating or reducing this systemic defect involving complicated torts.

REFERENCES

Agans, R. P., & Shaffer, L. S. (1994). The hindsight bias: The role of the availability heuristic and perceived risk. *Basic and Applied Social Psychology*, *15*, 439–449.

Angell, M. (1994). Do breast implants cause systemic disease? Science in the courtroom. *The New England Journal of Medicine*, *330*, 1748–1749.

Arkes, H. R. (1989). Principles in judgment/decision making research pertinent to legal proceedings. *Behavioral Sciences & the Law*, *7*, 429–456.

Arkes, H. R., Guilmette, T. J., Faust, D., & Hart, K. (1988). Eliminating the hindsight bias. *Journal of Applied Psychology*, *73*, 305–307.

Arkes, H. R., & Schipani, C. A. (1994). Medical malpractice v. The business judgment rule: Differences in hindsight bias. *Oregon Law Review*, *73*, 587–638.

Baron, J., & Hershey, J. C. (1988). Outcome bias in decision evaluation. *Journal of Personality and Social Psychology*, *54*(4), 569–579.

Bendectin Litigation, 857 F2d 290 (6th Cir. 1988).

Breast Implants, 942 F. Supp. 958 (1997).

Brekke, N. J., Enko, P. J., Clavert, G., & Seelau, E. (1991). Of juries court appointed expert: The impact of non-adversarial vs. adversarial expert testimony. *Law & Human Behavior*, *15*, 451–475.

Casper, J. D., Benedict, K., & Kelly, J. R. (1988). Cognition, attitudes and decision-making in search and seizure cases. *Journal of Applied Social Psychology*, *18*, 93–113.

Casper, J. D., Benedict, K., & Perry, J. L. (1989). Juror decision making, attitudes, and the hindsight bias. *Law and Human Behavior*, *13*, 291–310.

Cecil, J. S., & Willging, T. E. (1994). Court appointed experts. *Moore's Federal practice: Reference manual on scientific evidence* (pp. 547–555). San Francisco: Matthew Bender & Co. Inc.

Champagne, A., Shuman, D. W., & Whitaker, E. (1996). The problem with empirical examination of the use of court-appointed experts: A report of non-findings. *Behavioral Sciences and the Law*, *14*, 361–365.

Christensen-Szalanski, J. J., & Willham, C. F. (1991). The hindsight bias: A meta-analysis. *Organizational Behavior and Human Decision Processes*, *48*, 147–168.

Daubert v. Merrill Dow Pharmaceutical, Inc., 113 S Ct. 2786 (1993).

Dawson, N. V., Arkes, H. R., Siciliano, C., Blinkhorn, R., Lakshmanan, M., & Petrelli, M. (1988). Hindsight bias: An impediment to accurate probability estimation in clinicopathologic conferences. *Medical Decision Making*, *8*, 259–264.

Davies, M. F. (1987). Reduction of hindsight bias by restoration of foresight perspective: Effectiveness of foresight-encoding and hindsight-retrieval strategies. *Organizational Behavior & Human Decision Processes*, *40*, 50–68.

Developments in the law: Confronting the new challenges of scientific evidence. (1995). *Harvard Law Review, 108*, 1482–1605.

Diamond, B. A., Hulka, B. S., Kerkvliet, N. I., & Tugwell, P. (1998). Silicone breast implants in relation to connective tissue diseases and immunologic dysfunction: A report by a national science panel to the honorable Sam C. Pointer Jr., Coordinating Judge for the Federal Breast Implant Multi-District Litigation. *http://earth.fjc.gov/BREIMLIT/mdl926.htm*

Drazan, D. (1989). The case for special juries in toxic tort litigation, *Judicature*, Feb–March. 292–297.

Farrell, M. G. (1994). Special masters. *Moore's Federal Practice: Reference Manual on Scientific Evidence* (pp. 580–581). San Francisco: Matthew Bender.

Federal Rules of Civil Procedure Rule 42(b), 1999.

Federal Rules of Civil Procedure Rule 53(b), 1999.

Fischhoff, B. (1975). Hindsight ≠ foresight: The effect of outcome knowledge on judgment under uncertainty. *Journal of Experimental Psychology: Human Perception & Performance, 1*, 288–299.

Fischhoff, B. (1982). Debiasing. In D. Kahneman, P. Slovic & A. Tversky (Eds.), *Judgment under uncertainty: Heuristics and biases* (pp. 422–444). Cambridge: Cambridge University Press.

Fournier, C. W. (1980). The case for special juries in complex civil litigation. *Yale Law Journal, 89*, 1155–1160.

Gabriel, S. E., O'Fallow, W. M., Kurland, L. T, Beard, G. M., Woods, J. E., & Melton, L. J. (1994). Risk of connective-tissue disease and other disorders after breast implantation. *New England Journal of Medicine, 330*, 1697.

Hall v. Baxter Healthcare Corp., 947 F. Supp. 1387 (D. Ore. 1996).

Hawkins, S. A., & Hastie, R. (1990). Hindsight: Biased judgments of past events after the outcomes are known. *Psychological Bulletin, 107*(3), 311–327.

Hopkins v. Dow Corning Corporation, 33 F3d 1116 (9th Cir 1994).

Independent Review Group. (1998). Report: Silicone gel breast implants. *http://www.silicone-review.gov.uk/silicone/index.htm*

Institute of Medicine—National Academy of Sciences (1999). Safety of silicone breast implants. *www.nap.edu*

Judges' Opinions on Procedural Issues: A survey of state and federal trial judges who spend at least half their time on general civil cases. (1989). *Boston University Law Review, 69*, 731.

Kamin, K. A., & Rachlinski, J. J. (1995). Ex post ≠ ex ante: Determining liability in hindsight. *Law & Human Behavior, 19*(1), 89–104.

Klayman, J., & Ha, Y. (1987). Confirmation, disconfirmation and information in hypotheses testing. *Psychological Review, 94*(2), 211–228.

Lord, C. G., Lepper, M. R., & Preston, E. (1984). Considering the opposite: A corrective strategy for social judgment. *Journal of Personality and Social Psychology, 47*, 1231–1243.

Lowe, D. J. (1992/1993). An empirical examination of the hindsight bias phenomenon in evaluation of auditor decisions (Doctoral dissertation, Arizona State University, 1992). *Dissertation Abstracts International, 53*, A2444.

Luneburg, W. V., & Nordenberg, M. A. (1981). Specially qualified juries and expert non-jury tribunals: Alternatives for coping with complexities of modern civil litigation. *Virginia Law Review*, 67, 887.

Meister v. Bristol-Myers Squibb, CA 92-2660 (D.C. 1999).

Menon, J. W. (1995). Adversarial medical and scientific testimony and lay jurors: A proposal for medical malpractice reform. *American Journal of Law and Medicine, 21*, 281–300.

Pitera, M. J. (1991). *The effects of closing arguments on mock jurors' decisions.* Unpublished master's thesis, University of Kansas.

Pointer, S. C., U.S. District Court Alabama. In re: Silicone Gel Breast Implant Products Litigation (MDL 926). Order No. 31E : Directions to National Science Panel Under FRE 706 (1996).

Poythress, N. G., Schumacher, J., Wiener, R., & Murrin, M. (1993). Procedural justice judgments of alternative procedures for resolving medical malpractice claims. *Journal of Applied Social Psychology, 23*, 1639–1658.

Price, J. M., & Kelly, G. G. (1996). Junk science in the courtroom: Causes, effects, and controls. *Hamline Law Review, 19*, 395–408.

Price, J. M., & Rosenberg, E. S. (1998). The war against junk science: the use of expert panels in complex medical-legal scientific litigation. *Biomaterials, 19*, 1425–1432.

Pyszczynski, T. A., & Wrightsman, L. S. (1981). The effects of opening statements on mock juror's verdicts. *Journal of Applied Social Psychology, 11*, 301–313.

Rachlinski, J. J. (1998). A positive psychological theory of judging in hindsight. *University of Chicago Law Review, 65*, 571–625.

Sanchez-Guerrero, J., Colditz, G. A., Karlson, E. W., Hunter, D. J., Speizer, F. E., & Liang, M. H. (1995). Silicone breast implants and the risk of connective-tissue diseases and symptoms. *New England Journal of Medicine, 332*, 1666.

Sand, L. B., Siffert, J. S., Loughlin, W. P., Reiss, S. A., & Batterman, N. (1997). *Modern federal jury instructions* (Vol. 4). San Francisco: Matthew Bender.

Sanders, F. (1993). From science to evidence: the testimony on causation in the Bendectin Cases. *Stanford Law Review, 1*, 75.

Schkade, D. A., & Kilbourne, L. M. (1991). Expectation-outcome consistency and hindsight bias. *Organizational Behavior and Human Decision Processes, 49*, 105–123.

Stallard, M. J., & Worthington, D. L. (1998). Reducing the hindsight bias utilizing attorney closing arguments. *Law and Human Behavior, 22*, 671–683.

Strawn, D. U., & Munsterman, G. T. (1982). Helping juries handle complex cases. *Judicator, 65*, 444–447.

Tversky, A., & Kahneman, D. (1973). Availability: A heuristic for judging frequency and probability. *Cognitive Psychology, 5*, 207–232.

Tversky, A., & Kahneman, D. (1982). Judgment under uncertainty: Heuristics and biases. In D. Kahneman, P. Slovic, & A. Tversky (Eds.) *Judgment under uncertainty: Heuristics and biases* (p 3–20). Cambridge: Cambridge University Press.

Wasserman, D., Lempert, R. O., & Hastie, R. (1991). Hindsight and causality. *Personality and Social Psychology Bulletin, 92*, 683–700.

Wexler, D. B., & Schopp, R. F. (1989). How and when to correct for juror hindsight bias in mental health malpractice litigation: Some preliminary observations. *Behavioral Sciences & the Law, 7*, 485–504.

Wilkinson, J. C., Zielinski, F. D., & Curtis, G. M. (1994). A bicentennial transition: Modern alternatives to seventh amendment jury trials in complex cases. *Kansas Law Review, 37*, 61.

Wood, G. (1978). The knew-it-all-along effect. *Journal of Experimental Psychology, 4*, 345–353.

Chapter 8

A COMPARISON OF AMERICAN AND CANADIAN CONCEPTUALIZATIONS OF COMPETENCE TO STAND TRIAL

Patricia A. Zapf and Ronald Roesch

It has been a generally accepted legal principle in Western jurisprudence that incompetent individuals should not be allowed to proceed with a trial (*Blackstone*, 1783; *Frith's Case*, 1790). The notion that an individual must be competent to proceed in the criminal justice system originated in English common law and has been traced to the 17th century (Winick, 1983). Its roots are found in the common law prohibition on trials in absentia and in the difficulties encountered by the courts when the defendant remained mute[1] (either "mute by visitation from God" or "mute of malice") and failed to plead to the charges (Winick, 1983).

Although it is a legal principle that evolved at a time when defendants were expected to represent themselves in most criminal matters (and, in fact, representation by counsel was prohibited in certain types of cases) it is still important today despite the fact that representation by counsel is now guaranteed by the Sixth Amendment to the U. S. Constitution. The Group for the Advancement of Psychiatry (1974) listed four justifications for the incompetency doctrine in the United States: to safeguard the accuracy of any criminal adjudication, to guarantee a fair trial, to preserve the integrity and dignity of the legal process, and to be certain that the defendant, if found guilty, knows why he or she is being punished (pp. 888–889). In addition, two legal scholars, professors Bonnie (1993) and Winick (1983, 1985, 1996), offer modern justification for the incompetency doctrine which includes three principles: dignity, reliability, and autonomy.

Bonnie (1992, 1993) argued that trying defendants who lack a meaningful understanding of the criminal process would offend the moral dignity of this process. Winick (1983, 1985, 1996) relates this justification of the incompetency doctrine to the legitimacy of the criminal justice system; that is, the need to ensure the respect and confidence in the criminal process by the public. What both of these scholars are arguing is that the criminal process must be seen as reasonable and legitimate by the public in order for the public to have respect for and confidence in the process. Allowing a defendant, who is unable to meaningfully understand the nature of the process and who cannot understand the proceedings, to proceed to trial would not be seen as reasonable and legitimate by the public and would, therefore, offend the dignity of the process and would undermine the public's confidence in and respect for the criminal process. If the public loses respect for and confidence in the criminal process, then the process becomes meaningless and the criminal justice system is no longer viewed as a legitimate means of ensuring the safety and protection of society.

Bonnie (1993) and Winick (1985) each argue that society has an independent interest in the reliability of the criminal process. That is, society has an interest in ensuring that erroneous or unjust convictions do not occur and that the criminal process occurs in a similar manner for different defendants or for the same defendant across time. Allowing a defendant, who is unable to recognize or communicate relevant information to counsel and is therefore unable to assist in his or her own defense, to proceed with trial would undermine the reliability of the criminal process as well as society's interest in the reliability of this process (Bonnie, 1993).

Finally, Bonnie (1993) and Winick (1992) present the notion of the preservation of individual autonomy as a final justification for the incompetency doctrine. Bonnie (1993) indicates that although counsel may be responsible for making certain types of decisions regarding the defense to be presented, the nature of the criminal justice system[2] requires that the defendant must make certain key decisions. Since these decisions cannot be made by anyone but the defendant, it is necessary that the defendant be capable of understanding the issue and the possible consequences, and of making an informed decision. Thus, the incompetency doctrine is necessary in order to ensure the preservation of individual autonomy.

Given that dignity, reliability, and autonomy have each been proposed as elements that are necessary to the criminal justice system, it therefore appears that there is sufficient modern justification for the incompetency doctrine. In North America, however, this differs from the initial justification in English common law. Although both the United States and Canada have their roots in English common law and the argument can be made that the modern justification for the incompetency doctrine holds true for both countries, case law in the two jurisdictions has led to somewhat different conceptualizations of the legal standards for competence to stand trial. The purpose of this chapter is to examine the evolution of the standards for competency to stand trial that have evolved in both Canada and the United States and to compare and discuss the possible impact of the resulting two conceptualizations.

Canadian conceptualization of fitness[3] to stand trial

In Canada, the issue of competence to stand trial has been interpreted through early English common law as meaning that individuals charged with a criminal offence must be able to understand the nature of the proceedings and assist counsel in order to participate in their own defence and have a fair trial (see *Regina v. Pritchard*, 1836; *The Queen v. Berry*, 1876). The presence of a mental disorder may pose a serious impediment to an accused's understanding of the proceedings and ability to assist counsel; therefore, it is important that an individual who has a mental disorder at the time of trial be able to participate in his or her own defence. If this is not possible the individual is said to be unfit to stand trial. The judicial proceedings are then suspended until the accused becomes fit to stand trial. Until recently, individuals who were found unfit to stand trial were committed to inpatient facilities for an indeterminate period until they became fit, at which time they then returned to court.

Prior to 1992 there was no codified definition of the term unfit to stand trial. The criteria that were used were taken from case law. Specifically, the case of *Regina v. Pritchard* (1836) has often been cited as the "'classic test' for the determination of fitness to stand trial" (Lindsay, 1977, p. 306). The judge in *Pritchard* ruled that there were three issues that must be determined to assess whether a defendant was fit to stand trial:

> First, whether the prisoner is mute of malice or not; secondly, whether he can plead to the indictment or not; thirdly, whether he is of sufficient intellect to comprehend the course of the proceedings on the trial, so as to make a proper defence—to know that he might challenge any of you to whom he may object—and to comprehend the details of the evidence, which in a case of this nature must constitute a minute investigation. (p. 304)

Lindsay (1977) reviewed Canadian case law and concluded that there are three questions that follow from the criteria set out in *Pritchard* (1836) that are usually asked in order to determine an individual's fitness. First, "does the accused understand the nature and object of the proceedings? (i.e., does he understand that this is a criminal trial; does he understand what an oath is; does he know what the offence is, etc.?)" (p. 306). Second, "does the accused understand what his relationship is to the proceedings? (i.e., does he understand that he and not somebody else is on trial; that he has the right to rebut the charges; that he may be incarcerated if he is found guilty etc.?)" (p. 307). Third, "is the accused able to assist in his defence? (i.e., can he communicate with his counsel; is he capable of giving evidence himself, if necessary; can he make strategic decisions with respect to the conduct of his defence etc.?)" (p. 307). Lindsay concluded that these three questions identify important areas to assess when determining an individual's fitness to stand trial even though "the concept of unfitness does not embrace any single standard" and its meaning varies according to "the type of mental defect, the nature of the proceedings and the way in which defence counsel relates to his client and conducts his defence" (p. 307). It appears, therefore, that the three criteria set out in *Pritchard* and delineated through case law parallel three abilities: the ability to understand, to appreciate, and to communicate with counsel.

Lindsay (1977) also discussed the scope of the unfitness rule and stated that the courts have had considerable difficulty in applying the rule of unfitness to particular situations with any degree of consistency. He indicated that the courts have adopted two contradictory approaches in applying the rule of fitness to particular cases. The first he called the *rationality test* and the second the *narrow test*. The former approach uses a broad scope and has the court make a qualitative assessment of an accused's mental capacity to assist in his or her defence in a rational way or to have a rational understanding of the proceedings. The latter approach uses the notion that only the accused's cognitive ability be examined. Accused individuals are said to be able to assist counsel in their own defence if they are capable of relating the events surrounding an alleged offence to their lawyers. This test is limited only to the actual cognitive abilities of the individual and ignores the reasons behind any decision. Lindsay, in 1977, noted that although Canada had yet to "articulate explicitly a single test for defining the scope of the fitness rule, it is submitted that the weight of authority follows the wider view of the rationality test enunciated by the Supreme Court of the United States in *Dusky*" (pp. 314–315).

In 1992, the *Criminal Code of Canada* was amended. Many changes were made to the legal procedures related to the determination of fitness to stand trial. Explicit guidelines were set out in Section 2, which include a definition as well as standards for the determination of fitness to stand trial. *Unfit to stand trial* is a legal term that is now defined as follows. A defendant is unfit to stand trial if he or she is:

> Unable on account of mental disorder to conduct a defence at any stage of the proceedings before a verdict is rendered or to instruct counsel to do so, and, in particular, unable on account of mental disorder to (a) understand the nature or

> object of the proceedings, (b) understand the possible consequences of the proceedings, or (c) communicate with counsel.(C. C. C., §. 2, 1992)

It appears that these criteria are close in nature to those delineated by Lindsay (1977) with one possible exception. That is, the second standard as codified in section two of the *Criminal Code* reads "understand the possible consequences of the proceedings" whereas the second standard delineated by Lindsay in his review of case law is more along the lines of whether or not the accused understands his or her *relationship* to the proceedings. Upon further review, it appears that these two criteria are somewhat different from each other. Understanding the possible consequences of a proceeding and understanding one's relationship to a proceeding are slightly different variations on possibly the same theme. It is theoretically possible for someone to understand the possible consequences of something while not understanding his or her relationship to it. A defendant may understand in a detached and unaffected way the possible consequences of being found guilty of a crime but still not understand his or her relationship to the proceedings that will determine his or her guilt. It appears that Lindsay may have been alluding to the necessity that a defendant have the ability to *appreciate* but that the recently codified standard simply requires that a defendant have the ability to *understand* the consequences of a proceeding without any appreciation of the personal importance of that proceeding. Though arguably a subtle distinction, given that recent court decisions surrounding the competency issue have served to narrow the standards for competence (e.g., *Regina v. Taylor*, 1992; *Regina v. Whittle*, 1994), it is one that may become important in the future.

Since 1992 there have been finer distinctions made in case law with respect to the recently codified standards. In *Regina v. Taylor* (1992), the Ontario Court of Appeal decided "the test to be applied in determining the accused's ability to communicate with counsel is one of limited cognitive capacity" (p. 553). This means that it is not necessary that accused individuals be able to act in their own best interests, but rather, must only be able to recount the necessary facts pertaining to the offence to counsel so that counsel can present a proper defence. The appellate judges in *Taylor* decided that the "'limited cognitive capacity' test strikes an effective balance between the objective of the fitness rules and the constitutional right of the accused to choose his own defence and to have a fair trial within a reasonable time" (p. 567). This case serves to narrow the criteria used to assess fitness to stand trial. The Canadian criteria for unfitness, therefore, currently appear to follow the narrow test described earlier by Lindsay (1977).

American conceptualization of competence to stand trial

Just as the early Canadian courts relied upon English common law, so too did the early American courts. The issue of competency within the United States extends as far back as the early 1800s. In 1835, the defendant in *United States v. Lawrence* was found unfit to stand trial after his failed attempt to assassinate President Jackson. Some 60 years later, the appellate court in *Youtsey v. United States* (1899) held that "it is not 'due process of law' to subject an insane person to trial upon an indictment involving liberty or life" (p. 941). Since that time, various courts in the United States have essentially ruled that the issue of competency is "fundamental to an adversary system of justice" (*Drope v. Missouri*, 1975, p. 172; see also *Dusky v. United States*, 1960; *Godinez v. Moran*, 1993).

The Group for the Advancement of Psychiatry (1974) wrote a report on competency to stand trial that documented some of the competency-related questioning conducted by the trial judge in Milton Richard Dusky's first trial on the issue of competency. From the trial judge's questions, it appears that some of the necessary elements to be considered competent to stand trial included that the defendant: be oriented to time, place, and person; know who his or her attorney is; know what he or she has been charged with; and know (to some extent) or express a knowledge of some of the incidents leading up to the commission of the offense that he or she was alleged to have committed. In addition, from this report it appears that prior to the U. S. Supreme Court's prevailing decision regarding competency to stand trial (i.e., *Dusky v. United States*, 1960) the court was operating under the assumption that to be considered competent to stand trial an individual "must possess sufficient capacity to comprehend the nature and object of the proceedings and his [or her] own position in relation to those proceedings; and to be able to advise counsel rationally in the preparation and implementation of his [or her] own defense" (GAP Report, 1974, p. 916). The standard for competency that was subsequently decided upon by the U. S. Supreme Court in the Dusky case appears to be slightly more vague than the standard that was operated on by the trial judge in his case.

Unlike the situation in Canada where the standard for fitness to stand trial was only recently codified in 1992, the U. S. Supreme Court established the modern standard for competency to stand trial in the United States in 1960 in *Dusky v. United States*. Although the exact wording is different from state to state, each state uses some variation of the *Dusky* standard to define competence to stand trial (Favole, 1983). The Court, in *Dusky*, held that for a defendant to be considered competent to stand trial, he or she must have "sufficient present ability to consult with his attorney with a reasonable degree of rational understanding" and "a rational as well as factual understanding of the proceedings against him" (p. 402). This decision reflects the need for a defendant to have both understanding as well as rationality, although the term "reasonable degree of rational understanding" was left undefined by the Court. In addition, some jurisdictions have interpreted the requirement of having "a rational as well as factual understanding of the proceedings" as meaning that an individual must possess the ability to appreciate the personal importance of the proceedings (Roesch & Golding, 1980). Given that the abilities required of defendants to be considered competent include understanding, appreciation, and rationality, it therefore appears that the United States follows the wider rationality test described above by Lindsay (1977).

Comparison of the Canadian and American conceptualizations of competency

Although the Canadian and American criminal justice systems are both grounded in English common law, the two countries have somewhat different legal systems. In the U. S., each state has its own criminal code and, therefore, its own provisions for determining competence to stand trial. Although there are many similarities in terms of the provisions for competency to stand trial and the procedures used by each of the states and Canada with respect to determining competency, there are also some differences. Specifically, there appear to be three fundamental differences between the United States and Canada in terms of their respective current applications and conceptualizations of competence.

First, the *scope* of the standards for competency to stand trial is different between the USA and Canada. As previously discussed, Lindsay (1977) delineated two contradictory approaches that the courts have used in applying the competency standards to particular cases: the rationality test and the narrow test. The former approach uses a broad scope and has the court make a qualitative assessment of the accused's mental capacity to assist in his or her defense in a rational way or to have a rational understanding of the proceedings whereas the latter approach uses a narrow scope and considers only an accused's cognitive ability and ignores the reasoning behind any decision. The application of the competency standard to particular cases by the U. S. courts appear to follow the broader rationality test. This is in direct opposition to the Canadian application of the competency standard, which follows the narrow test and does not take an accused's rationality into consideration. Although Lindsay, in 1977, submitted that the weight of authority in Canada appeared to be following the wider rationality test enunciated by the U. S. Supreme Court in *Dusky*, since the codification of the Canadian competency standards in 1992 it appears that this has changed and that the Canadian courts are currently following the narrow test. Given this change in the *application* of competency standards in Canada but not in the United States, it can be concluded that the scope of the competency standards are now different between the two countries.

The second difference, which follows directly from the first, is that the Canadian standard, in terms of its conceptualization of competency, does not take into consideration the rationality of the defendant. In fact, the Canadian courts, in recent years, have specifically ruled that a defendant's inability to be rational or to act in his or her own best interests should not be taken into consideration when making a determination of competency to stand trial. Therefore, not only is the scope of the two standards (that is, their application) different within each of the two countries, but in addition, the American conceptualization of competency specifically includes and takes into consideration a cognitive ability that the Canadian standard does not. That is, the ability of the defendant to be rational. The word "rational" is not used in the codified Canadian standard and, furthermore, in both *Taylor* (1992) and *Whittle* (1994), the Canadian courts have ruled that the test to be used in determining fitness was one of "limited cognitive capacity" and specifically stated that a defendant's ability (or inability) to act in a rational manner or in his or her own best interests should not be considered by the court in determining competency to stand trial. This is in contrast to the decision of the U. S. Supreme Court in *Dusky* (1960), which reflected the need to take into consideration the rationality of the defendant when making a determination of competency. Given that the United States includes in its standard for competency a cognitive ability that Canada specifically excludes from its standard, and given that this cognitive ability (rationality) is a higher-order ability than the ability to understand[4] (which is considered necessary by both the USA and Canada), it can be argued that the American standard of competency is a stricter standard to satisfy than is the current Canadian standard.

Finally, the argument can be made that the Canadian conceptualization of competence does not take the ability of an individual to appreciate the personal importance of the proceedings into consideration. Specifically, there is no use of the word "appreciate" in the codified Canadian standard for fitness to stand trial and, furthermore, the court, in its recent decisions, does not appear to be concerned with an individual's ability to appreciate the personal importance of the proceedings. For example, in *Whittle* (1994) the court opined that to be considered fit to stand trial an accused must be "capable of communicating with counsel to instruct counsel, and understand the function of counsel and that he can dispense with counsel even if this is not in the accused's best interests ... it is not necessary that the accused possess analytical ability" (p. 923). In addition, as previously discussed, in *Taylor* (1992) the appellate court overturned the decision of the trial court, which found Taylor unfit due to the fact that he was "unable to perceive his own best interests" (p. 552). The appellate court indicated that to be considered fit to stand trial an accused must be cognizantly aware of the charges, the officers of the court, the possible pleas, and the possible outcome of the proceedings and that the inability to perceive one's own best interests or how these interests should be addressed in the trial are not of concern. It appears that the courts are using a very narrow definition of competency and that they are attempting to adhere strictly to the codified definition of fitness. Accused individuals in Canada must only be able to understand the nature and object of the proceedings as well as the possible consequences of those proceedings. In many states, the standards for competency to stand trial are such that an accused individual must be able to appreciate the personal relevance of the proceedings (see Roesch & Golding, 1980). Given that the Canadian conceptualization of competency does not appear to take into consideration the ability of an individual to appreciate the personal importance of the proceedings and the American conceptualization does, and given that the ability to appreciate appears to be a higher-order ability than the ability to understand (which both countries take into consideration), it seems logical to conclude that the U. S. has a stricter standard of criminal competency than does Canada. As a result, one would expect that it would be possible for the same individual to be found incompetent with respect to the American standard of competence but competent with respect to Canadian standard of competence.

To summarize, not only is there a difference between the United States and Canada in terms of the *application* of their respective competency standards to specific cases, but there are also differences between the two countries in terms of how each *conceptualizes* competency and the abilities that are necessary to be considered competent to stand trial.

Specifically, the United States appears to conceptualize competency in such a way that, to be considered competent to stand trial, an accused must be able to communicate and must have the ability to understand, appreciate, and reason. Conversely, in Canada, competency is conceptualized in such a way that, to be considered competent to stand trial, an accused must only be able to communicate and possess the ability to understand. Arguably, the Canadian standard appears to be a much less stringent standard of competency.

CONCLUSION

A review of the application and conceptualization of the standards for competence to stand trial reveal that there appear to be certain fundamental differences between the United States and Canada. Given these differences, it appears that the United States has a higher standard of competency than does Canada. Preliminary research has indicated that these apparently theoretical differences between the two countries may actually be more than simply theoretical. That is, these differences may actually translate into a measurable difference in terms of the same individual being found competent with respect to the Canadian standards and incompetent with respect to the American standards (Zapf, 1999).

One possible implication of this difference in standards of competence to stand trial is that the American criminal justice system may be experiencing a greater burden than that experienced by the Canadian criminal justice system. A higher standard of competence in the United States would be directly related to an increased number of individuals being found incompetent by the courts, thereby, placing a higher demand on both the legal and mental health systems. An increased number of individuals deemed incompetent by the courts might mean that more court time is being used for these individuals (e.g., a series of hearings to determine competence/restoration of competence), and that more mental health resources are being used to assess and restore competence (i.e., inpatient/outpatient treatment programs). Obviously, these increased burdens are speculative in nature and further research is needed to determine the exact nature of the differences between the two countries in terms of the individuals involved and the impact on the criminal justice systems.

Conversely, it may be the case that some proportion of defendants in Canada may be proceeding to trial with perhaps less than optimal capabilities. The extent to which defendants require the ability to appreciate and the ability to be rational to cope with the demands of a criminal trial with legal representation and assistance is unclear.

Certainly, future research would need to investigate the lowest-order abilities required of a legally-represented defendant to be able to participate in his or her own defence in such a manner as to satisfy current justification for the incompetency doctrine before such questions could be addressed.

REFERENCES

Blackstone, W. (1783). *Commentaries on the laws of England* (9th ed.). London: W. Strahan.

Bonnie, R. J. (1992). The competence of criminal defendants: A theoretical reformulation. *Behavioral Sciences and the Law, 10*, 291–316.

Bonnie, R. J. (1993). The competence of criminal defendants: Beyond *Dusky* and *Drope. University of Miami Law Review, 47*, 539–601.

Criminal Code of Canada, R. S. C., C–46 (1985).

Drope v. Missouri, 420 U. S. 162 (1975).

Dusky v. United States, 362 U. S. 402 (1960).

Favole, R. J. (1983). Mental disability in the American criminal process: A four issue survey. In J. Monahan & H. J. Steadman (Eds.), *Mentally disordered offenders: Perspectives from law and social science*. New York: Plenum.

Frith's Case, 22 How. St. Tr. 307 (1790).

Godinez v. Moran, 509 U. S. 389 (1993).

Group for the Advancement of Psychiatry. (1974). *Misuse of psychiatry in the criminal courts: Competency to stand trial.* New York: Author.

Lindsay, P. S. (1977). Fitness to stand trial: An overview in light of the recommendations of the Law Reform Commission of Canada. *Criminal Law Quarterly, 19*, 303–348.

Regina v. Pritchard, 7 Car. & P. 304, 173 E. R. 135 (1836).

Regina v. Taylor, 77 C. C. C. (3d) 551 (Ont. C. A. 1992).

Regina v. Whittle, 2 S. C. R. 914 (1994).

Roesch, R., & Golding, S. L. (1980). *Competency to stand trial.* Urbana, IL: University of Illinois Press.

The Queen v. Berry, 1 Q. B. D. 447 (1876).

United States v. Lawrence, 26 F. Cas. 887 (D. C. Cir. 1835).

Winick, B. J. (1983). Incompetency to stand trial: Developments in the law. In J. Monahan & H. J. Steadman (Eds.), *Mentally disordered offenders: Perspectives form law and social science* (pp. 3–38). New York: Plenum.

Winick, B. J. (1985). Restructuring competency to stand trial. *UCLA Law Review, 32*, 921–985.

Winick, B. J. (1992). On autonomy: Legal and psychological perspectives. *Villanova Law Review, 37*, 1705–1777.

Winick, B. J. (1996). Incompetency to proceed in the criminal process: Past, present, and future. In D. B. Wexler & B. J. Winick (Eds.), *Law in a therapeutic key: Developments in therapeutic jurisprudence*. Durham, NC: Carolina Academic Press.

Youtsey v. United States, 97 F. 937 (6th Cir. 1899).

Zapf, P. A. (1999). *An investigation of the construct of competence in a criminal and civil context: A comparison of the FIT, the MacCAT-CA, and the MacCAT-T*. Unpublished Dissertation, Simon Fraser University, Burnaby, BC.

Notes

1. Two categories were identified: "mute by visitation of God" and "mute of malice." Winick (1983, 1996) details the consequences of each of these two categories wherein individuals determined to be in the former category were spared a torturous ritual and individuals determined to be in the latter were not. The former category initially included the "deaf and dumb" but was gradually expanded to include "lunatics."

2. Although Bonnie only specifically discusses the American criminal justice, the argument can be made that the same holds true of the Canadian criminal justice system.
3. Fitness is an equivalent term for competence that is used in Canada, England, and other countries.
4. Some preliminary research by Zapf (1999) indicates that the ability to appreciate and the ability to reason are higher-order abilities when compared to the ability to understand.

Chapter 9

THE MACARTHUR COMPETENCE ASSESSMENT TOOL—FITNESS TO PLEAD: EVALUATION OF A RESEARCH INSTRUMENT FOR ASSESSING FITNESS TO PLEAD

Akintunde Akinkunmi, Louise Cumbley, Galya Goodman and Robert Blizard

In England and Wales, a finding that a patient is unfit to plead can result in compulsory admission to hospital for treatment under the Mental Health Act (1983) or the Criminal Procedure (Insanity and Unfitness to Plead) Act (1991). It is a statutory requirement that two psychiatrists' opinions are presented to the court as to whether or not the defendant is fit to stand trial once this issue has been raised. However, the clinical assessment of fitness to stand trial can delay the legal process, and it can also consume considerable resources of both the healthcare and criminal justice systems. It is therefore essential that the clinician's evaluation be both a valid and reliable one.

At present, fitness procedures are based on criteria that were set down in case law in the mid-19th century (*R. v. Pritchard*, 1836). These, essentially, are whether the defendant could plead to the indictment, knew that he or she was able to challenge a juror and was of sufficient intellect to comprehend the course of proceedings of the trial and the details of the evidence. Later cases have raised the question as to whether or not the defendant was capable of properly instructing his counsel because of his or her mental illness. Although the process of dealing with unfit defendants was reviewed in the Butler Committee's report to the Home Office (1975), there has been relatively little clinical research in this area (Grubin, 1991).

It may be argued that the typical assessment procedure is too subjective and unreliable as a method of fitness assessment for clinical as well as research purposes. Indeed, there has been little research examining the validity and reliability of current assessment procedures used in England and Wales (Grubin, 1991). Grisso (1986) described four important characteristics that must be considered in developing the competency to stand trial evaluation. The evaluation procedure should (1) ensure that each of the relevant legal constructs must be captured; (2) have quantitative measures that reflect performance in discrete legal domains (3) include flexible, in-depth enquiries on legal issues which are guided by coherent legal theory and (4) be administered in a standardized fashion which promotes inter and intra-rater reliability.

The MacArthur Structured Assessment of the Competencies of Criminal Defendants (MacSAC-CD) has been validated by Hoge et al. (1997). The results demonstrated that the MacSAC-CD had satisfactory psychometric properties, and construct validity, as well as potential for clinical application. They also found that the instrument was able to distinguish between identified groups of fit and unfit defendants. Modest correlations were found with clinician's judgments of competency to assist counsel ($r = .38$) and decisional competence ($r = .39$) which to some extent supports the construct validity of the questionnaire in assessing these abilities. It was found that scores on the MacSAC-CD correlated negatively with measures of degree of psychopathology and cognitive functioning.

A clinical instrument resulting from this research, the MacArthur Competence Assessment Tool-Criminal Adjudication (MacCAT-CA) was evaluated by Otto et al. (1998). This instrument was found to have strong internal consistency and construct validity. Norms from 729 subjects' performance on the questionnaire were derived to inform judgements regarding the competency of defendants. With the consent of the authors of the MacCAT-CA, the tool has been modified to test abilities according to each of the criteria for fitness to stand trial in England and Wales. It has been subjected to review, both by experienced forensic psychiatrists and legal practitioners with a view to ensuring that its content captures all the relevant legal criteria for England and Wales. This process led to the development the MacArthur Competence Assessment Tool—Fitness to Plead (MacCAT-FP). The present study examines the usefulness of this as a research instrument in assessing fitness to stand trial.

METHOD

Design

The independent variables were (1) whether the subject was admitted to a psychiatric hospital awaiting trial under the provisions of section 48/49 of the Mental Health Act (1983), or awaiting trial in prison, and (2) whether the hospital subject was seen at Time 1, two weeks after admission, or Time 2, six weeks after admission, (hospital group only). The dependent variables were the scores achieved on the questionnaire measures administered. For the hospital group, these measures include two psychiatrists' opinions of the subject's fitness to stand trial; one of the patient's responsible psychiatrist (RMO) and the other of an independent psychiatrist.

Participants

Data were collected from two groups of participants: a) patients awaiting trial who were admitted to one of three Secure Units under Section 48/49 of the Mental Health Act (1983); and b) prisoners awaiting trial who were randomly selected from a London prison as a control population. A total of 75 subjects have so far taken part in the study; 55 in the prison group (all males) with a mean age of 33.9 years and 20 in the hospital group (16 males, 4 females) with a mean age of 30 years.

The hospital group subjects were the first 20 patients admitted to one of the three hospitals who fulfilled the criteria described above. Participants were excluded from the hospital group if they were deemed to be too disturbed to be seen, if the interviewer felt that the subject was unable to give valid consent to participating in the study due to the severity of the mental illness, or if the subject was categorized as suffering from severe mental impairment or psychopathic disorder. Subjects were excluded from the prison group if they had been receiving psychiatric treatment whilst awaiting trial or were currently on drug and alcohol detoxification programs. Those assessed who received a Brief Psychiatric Rating Scale (Overall & Gorham, 1962) score two standard deviations above the mean for this group were excluded from the prison group as the possibility of mental illness, diagnosed or otherwise, could not be discounted. There have been four subjects excluded on this basis to date. Finally, non-English speakers who did not have a conversational grasp of English or deemed to need an interpreter were excluded from the present study.

Measures

The MacCAT-FP consists of a 22-item clinical instrument based on a hypothetical scenario of two men who get into a fight, and one is then charged with assaulting the other. The questionnaire was initially divided into three fitness to stand trial related areas: *Understanding*, *Reasoning*, and *Appreciation*. These three categories were devised by Hoge et al. (1997) and are based on a theoretical model of abilities underlying the legal requirements for adjudicative competence in the United States. For the purposes of this initial validation study, the same three categories were retained.

The Brief Psychiatric Rating Scale (Overall & Gorham, 1962) was also administered. This is a standardized interview-based assessment that provides a reliable and valid estimate of the subject's current metal state. The symptoms and behavior were rated on their occurrence during the previous week and during the interview situation.

To estimate participants' cognitive-intellectual abilities, two reading-based tests were administered; the National Adult Reading Test (NART) (Nelson, 1982) and the Schonell Graded Word Reading Test (Schonell GWRT) (Schonell, 1942). The scores on these tests are combined to provide an estimate of pre-morbid intellectual functioning (or IQ). Both the NART and the Schonell GWRT have good reported validity and reliability (O'Carroll, 1987; Crawford, Parker, Stewart, Besson & De Lacey, 1989; Schlosser & Ivison, 1989b; Schonell, 1942).

The Responsible Medical Officer (RMO) and an independent Forensic Psychiatrist gave their opinions of the patient's fitness to plead according to the traditional Pritchard criteria. Each criterion was rated as either fulfilled, unfulfilled or doubtful, and an overall opinion of the subjects fitness to plead was rated as definitely yes, definitely no, probably yes or probably no. Both the RMO and the independent doctor were blind to the MacCAT-FP scores when assessing the subjects.

Procedure

For those in the hospital group for the first assessment, a risk assessment was competed with a member of the nursing staff to ensure that the patient was suitable for the interview process. The subjects were first informed about the aims of the study and issues regarding confidentiality. Once informed consent was established, the measures were administered. The prison group subjects were given all the assessment measures during one assessment. The hospital group was given the MacCAT-FP and the BPRS only during the first assessment (two weeks after admission), and all the measures during the second assessment, six weeks after admission.

RESULTS

Psychometric properties

We present analyses of three psychometric properties of the MacCAT-FP measures: internal consistency, inter-rater reliability and correlations among the measures.

Internal Consistency. Co-efficient alpha and item-scale correlations were calculated for each of the three categories. The α's are reported in Table 1. All of these equal or exceed the accepted values for research measures ($r > .70$; Nunally, 1978, p. 245) but slightly below the recommended values for decision-making instruments ($r > .90$; Nunally, 1978; p. 246).

Table 1: Internal Consistency of the Categories of the Maccat-Fp

Categories	
Understanding	.73
Reasoning	.77
Appreciation	.77

Correlations Among Measures

Correlations were computed between the three categories used in the MacCAT-FP. Table 2 demonstrates a strong correlation between Understanding and Reasoning but neither correlate well with Appreciation.

Table 2: Correlations Between Questionnaire Categories

	Understanding	Reasoning
Understanding		
Reasoning	.75	
Appreciation	.54	.66

Inter-rater reliability. The two researchers carrying out the data collection examined a random sample of 12 subjects and their assessments were compared to those of the consultant psychiatrist running the project. The coefficients for the agreement between the raters ranged from .73 to .95 for the MacCAT-FP measures and the agreement for the BPRS ranged from .89 to .94.

Validation against the psychiatrists' opinions

Using a ROC analysis, the two physicians' opinions were compared to the scores on the MacCAT-FP. The ROC analysis demonstrated that the performance of the MacCAT-FP's, measured by the area under the curve, was 0.844, significantly better than chance (Figure 1). Here the area under the curve is taken to measure the likelihood that the MacCAT-FP can be used to correctly distinguish between fit and unfit subjects.

Construct validity

The two groups were compared on their performance on the MacCAT-FP categories. The results are displayed in Table 3. The Prison group perform significantly better on all the categories at Time 1. When the Prison group are compared to the Hospital Group at Time 2, the differences in scores are no longer significant ($r = .975$).

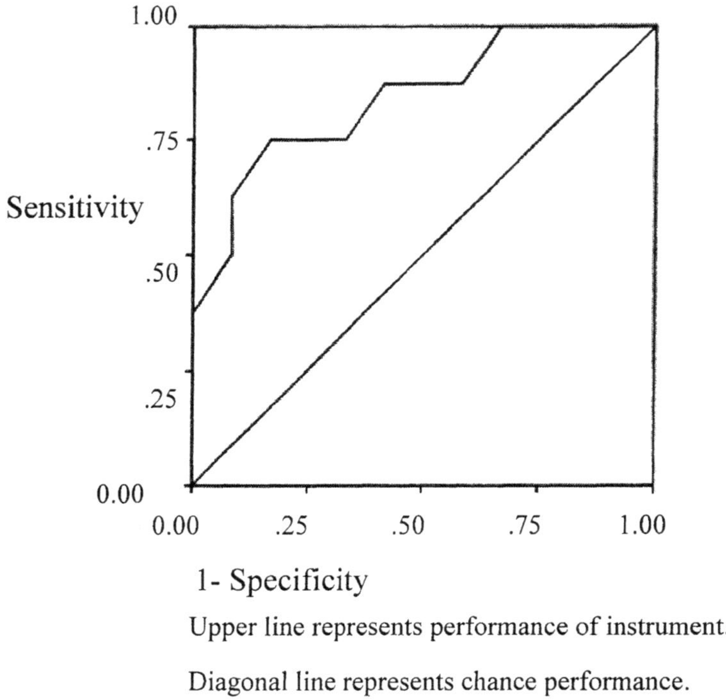

FIGURE 1: ROC CURVE COMPARING MACCAT-FP AGAINST PSYCHIATRIST OPINIONS

In terms of the effects of mental state and intellectual functioning, Table 5 shows the differences in BPRS scores and estimates of IQ. There is a significant difference between the BPRS scores for the hospital group and the prison group but as expected there is no significant difference in the two groups' intellectual functioning. There is also a significant difference between the hospital group's BPRS scores at Time 1 and Time 2 showing that there is a significant improvement in their mental state after 6 weeks of treatment.

Table 3: Means and SDs for Each Group of Subjects

	Hospital Group		Prison Group	
Category	*M*	*SD*	*M*	*SD*
Understanding***	9.10	3.75	2.98	.74
Reasoning***	8.38	5.05	3.53	.72
Appreciation***	6.24	4.39	0.90	985
Total***	23.71	11.54	7.02	.58

***$p < .001$.

Table 4: Comparison Between the Groups for Mental State and IQ

	Hospital Group ($n = 21$)	Prison Group ($n = 51$)
BPRS (time 1)**	45.90	26.16
IQ*	102.00	93.23

*$p < .05$. **$p < .001$.

Table 5: Changes in Scores Between Time 1 and Time 2

N = 16	BPRS	Understanding	Reasoning	Appreciation	Total
Time 1	44.25	9.94	9.25	6.38	25.56
Time 2	39.69	1.81	1.38	8.25	31.31
p value	.02*	.013	.74	.11	.003**

*$p < .05$. **$p < .01$.

When looking solely at the hospital group, there appears to be changes over time to which the MacCAT-FP is sensitive (Table 5). The group did not improve significantly on the three individual categories although the trend is an improving one. The group improved significantly on the MacCAT-FP total score within the six weeks.

DISCUSSION

The psychometric properties of the MacCAT-FP so far look encouraging. The inter-rater reliability, internal consistency and correlations are all within acceptable limits. When looking at the validation using the physician's opinions, the results demonstrate that the MacCAT-FP is able to discriminate between the fit and unfit subjects within the hospital group significantly better than chance.

In terms of the construct validity, the results are equally encouraging. The prison group perform significantly better than the hospital group on all the categories. The MacCAT-FP is able to distinguish between the groups of known fit (prison group) and unfit (hospital group) defendants and this distinction is significant.

In terms of the sensitivity to change in the hospital, group scores improve significantly in terms of their mental state and the total score on the MacCAT-FP. By the sixth week of admission, the hospital group does not differ significantly from the prison group on their BPRS scores, demonstrating that the period of treatment has significantly improved their mental state. However, the numbers for the hospital group are still small and therefore any results from the study so far needed to be treated with caution.

The MacCAT-FP, once validated, may be adapted for clinical application where it may be used by various professionals as a screening tool in police stations or Court Psychiatric Assessment Schemes. Further research is needed to examine the clinical effectiveness of this instrument and how it may be adapted for use with other populations such as juveniles.

REFERENCES

Crawford, J. R., Parker, D. M., Stewart, L. E., Besson, J. A. O., & De Lacey, G. (1989). Prediction of WAIS IQ with the National Adult Reading Test: Cross validation and extension. *British Journal of Clinical Psychology*, *28*, 267–273.

Grisso, T. (1986). *Evaluating competencies: Forensic assessments and instruments*. New York: Plenum.

Grubin, D. H. (1991). Unfit to plead in England and Wales, 1976–88: A survey. *British Journal of Psychiatry*, *158*, 540–548.

Hoge, S. K., Bonnie, R. J., Poythress, N., Monahan, J., Eisenberg, M., & Feucht-Haviar, T. (1997). The MacArthur adjudicative competence study: Development and validation of a research instrument. *Law and Human Behavior*, *21*, 141–179.

Home Office & Department of Health & Social Security (1975). Report of the Committee on Mentally Abnormally Offenders (The Poulter Report) Cmnd 6244. London HMSO.

Nelson, H. E. (1991) *National Adult Reading Test (NART): Test Manual*. Windsor: Nfer-Nelson.

Nunally, J. C. (1978). *Psychometric theory*. New York: McGraw-Hill.

O'Carroll, R. E. (1987). The inter-rater reliability of the National Adult Reading Test (NART): A pilot study. *British Journal of Clinical Psychology*, *26*, 229–230.

Otto, R. K., Poythress, N. G., Nicholson, R. A., Edens, J. F., Monahan, J., Bonnie, J., Hoge, S., & Eisenberg, M. (1998). Psychometric properties of the MacArthur Competence Assessment Tool—Criminal Adjudication. *Psychological Assessment*, *10*, 427–455.

Overall, J. E., & Gorham, D. R. (1962) The Brief Psychiatric Rating Scale. *Psychological Reports*, *10*, 799–812.

R. v. Pritchard, 7 C & P 303 (1836).

Schlosser, D., & Ivison, D. (1989). Assessing memory deterioration with the Wechsler Memory Scale, the National Adult Reading Test, and the Schonell Graded Word Reading Test. *Journal of Clinical and Experimental Neuropsychology*, *11*, 785–792.

Schonell, F. (1942). *Backwardness in the basic subjects*. London: Oliver and Boyd.

Author Note

Many thanks to all the consultants who helped with the research. We would like to thank Dr. H.G. Kennedy, Dr. L. Hamilton, Dr. D. James, Dr. G. Duffield, Dr. N. De Taranto, Dr. N. Boast, Dr. T. McClintock, Dr. M. Whittle, Dr. K. Cleary and Dr. M. Lock, Dr. M. Maier, Dr. J Dent and Dr. D Moscovitch. Thanks are also due to Mr. C. Leigh, Ms. B. Taylor, Mr. M. Conte and Mr. K. McGann for helping us with our work within the hospitals. We would also like to thank Ms. P. Carr for her help in recruiting prison subjects. We are particularly grateful to Mr. R Blizzard for statistical advice.

Chapter 10

PUBLIC OPINION, SENTENCING, AND PAROLE: INTERNATIONAL TRENDS

Julian V. Roberts and Michael Hough

Public attitudes play a pivotal and controversial role in the administration of justice, but nowhere is the influence of these attitudes more apparent than in the area of penal policy and judicial practice. The views of the public have helped to determine the shape of sentencing and parole reform in most western nations over the past 30 years. Many examples of this influence exist, including the "Three Strikes" sentencing laws in the US, similar legislation for burglary, drug dealing, and serious crimes of violence in the United Kingdom, and mandatory firearms sentences in Canada. As well, adverse public reaction has been a factor in the movement to abolish parole in the US and, more recently, Canada (Greenspan, Matheson, & Davis, 1998).

It is also likely that judicial attitudes and behaviour have been shaped by the views of the public, although this is much harder to document, as judges are far less inclined to acknowledge the influence of community views upon their decisions than are politicians, for example. Nevertheless, there is evidence that judges consider the views of the public when imposing sentence. A recent national survey of judges in Canada found that almost half the sample acknowledged that before imposing a community-based sanction they consider the effect that the sentence will have on the views of the public (Roberts, Doob, & Marinos, 1999).

In light of this relationship between public opinion, penal policy, and practice, it is no surprise that public opinion surveys in several jurisdictions have repeatedly addressed the issues of sentencing and parole. Indeed, the first empirical investigation into public attitudes towards punishment was published almost a century ago (Sharp & Otto, 1909). The steady accretion of opinion data relating to these critical areas of criminal justice since then suggests that we are now in a position to draw some general conclusions about the nature of public attitudes to punishment, and that is the purpose of this chapter. We review public opinion surveys from the United States, Canada, the United Kingdom, and Australia with particular emphasis on the most recent findings. After summarizing some of the most important trends, we explore the policy implications for the field of criminal justice. First, however, we briefly summarize public knowledge of these critical criminal justice issues.

Public knowledge

Proportion of Recorded Crime Involving Violence. It is important to understand that public reaction to punishment is a response to erroneous perceptions of the crime rate. Polls reveal that most members of the public, in all the countries surveyed, perceive the crime problem to be worse than it is. One illustration of this can be found in public estimates of the amount of violent crime. The percentage of crime involving violence varies slightly across jurisdictions with the latest statistics revealing that 12% of recorded crime in England and Wales involve violence, and 11% of criminal incidents in Canada involve violence (Povey & Prime, 1999; Statistics Canada, 1999). The public, however, believe this statistic to be much higher. Table 1 summarizes the responses from representative polls that have posed this question to members of the public in Australia, Canada, and the United Kingdom (Doob & Roberts, 1988; Hough & Roberts, 1999; Indermaur, 1987). As can be seen, there is a remarkable degree of concordance between the responses from people in different countries. This consistency is all the more compelling since the surveys were conducted several years apart.

Crime Trends. The public is no more accurate when asked questions about crime trends. In 1996, a representative sample of Americans was asked whether there was "more or less crime in the US than a year ago." 80% of respondents stated that the crime rate had increased, when in reality there had been a 9% decline (U.S. Department of Justice, 1997). When Canadians were asked the same question in 1998, 77% were of the opinion that crime rates were increasing, when in fact statistics showed the greatest decrease in crime in well over a decade (Statistics Canada, 1998). The data from England and Wales show a similar pattern. In 1996, a representative sample of the British public was asked about crime trends

Table 1: Public Estimates of Percentage of Crime Involving Violence in Three Jurisdictions

	Australia	Canada	England and Wales
Accurate	9%	4%	3%
Small over-estimate	17%	15%	18%
Large over-estimate	73%	74%	77%
Don't know	1%	8%	3%
Total	100%	100%	100%

Sources: see text.

over the previous two years. In reality, crime rates had dropped by 10%. The public, however, had a rather different view: 76% thought that there was more crime, while only 4% were correct (Hough & Roberts, 1998). These trends carry clear implications for our understanding of public reactions to sentencing and parole. Since crime control figures strongly in public expectations of criminal justice, as discussed below, it is important to realize that people hold exaggerated views concerning the magnitude of the problem that the sentencing process is supposed to address.

Sentencing and parole. It is surprising that so little work has been done on the issue of public knowledge of sentencing and parole. Most researchers have simply explored the nature of public attitudes and have ignored the knowledge on which these opinions are based. This is regrettable because only by having a firm understanding of public knowledge can we truly understand public opinion. That said, enough research has been conducted to give us some insight into the extent of public knowledge of the courts and the parole system. The results of this research paint a portrait of a public that holds systematically distorted views of the sentencing and parole systems.

The general finding is that most people have little accurate knowledge of the statutory framework of sentencing, including the number and nature of minimum and maximum penalties, sentencing patterns at the trial court level, sentencing alternatives available to the court, parole-related statistics, including the parole grant rate, and the recidivism rate of prisoners released on parole (Roberts & Stalans, 1997; Roberts & Stalans, 1998). While disappointing, this result is not that unexpected. After all, the public probably have little concrete knowledge of many areas of public policy. How accurate are people about the costs of health care, the magnitude of the national debt, or the volume of immigration? These and many other issues crowd the newspapers on a daily basis, and there is often a confusing blizzard of statistics, particularly when the issue is polarized by politicians. For example, the same statistics relating to the benefit and costs of immigration to the host country are often hotly disputed by political parties with different positions on whether the number of immigrants should be increased or decreased.

Criminal justice has an additional element: it is fraught with ideology. This sets it apart from many other social issues. For example, while there are "left" and "right" approaches to health care, with one stressing universal access and a single state-run system while the other favours creation of private and public systems, the issue is not as highly politicized, and the public is not as divided on the critical issues. Nor does health care contain a host of competing interests as the primacy of the patient's interests is accepted by all.

In criminal justice, however, there is a clear ideological split, as identified over 30 years ago by Packer (1968) in his distinction between due process and crime control. Moreover, there are many competing interests in any criminal proceeding, such as the interests of the victim, the accused or offender, the immediate community in which the offence occurred, and the State. All too frequently, the interests of these parties come into conflict. The most obvious conflict involves the rights of the victim and the rights of the accused or offender (Roach, 1999). When victims claim standing in a criminal trial, or in a parole hearing, the offender's rights may be compromised. Most members of the public support the crime control model and concept of justice, and regard the system as providing far too many due process rights to the accused at the expense of the victim. This perspective influences the information that people acquire. The result is that public misperception of the courts and parole is not random; the errors people make are consistently in one direction, and that is towards a perception of leniency, as the following examples make clear.

Public Estimates of Incarceration Rates and Average Sentence Lengths. Surveys conducted in Canada in the mid-1980s asked respondents to estimate the incarceration rates for a number of offences. Results indicated that most people under-estimated the severity of sentencing patterns (Doob & Roberts, 1983). Comparable results emerge from the 1996 British Crime Survey. Respondents were asked about three offences: rape, mugging, and burglary. People tended to under-estimated the incarceration rate, most by a considerable margin. Thus, while the actual imprisonment rate for mugging in England and Wales was approximately 70% at the time that the survey was conducted, two-thirds of the public estimated that the rate was under 45% (Hough & Roberts, 1999). Other research has shown that the public also under-estimate the length of custodial sentences (Canadian Sentencing Commission, 1987). Results from surveys conducted in other countries show similar trends.

Public Knowledge of Parole Trends. Public knowledge of parole is no more accurate. Earlier research conducted by the Canadian Sentencing Commission (1987) found that only a third of the Canadian public could identify parole using a simple multiple choice test. A recent Canadian study asked members of the public to estimate the percentage of inmates granted release on parole. Although the true statistic was 42%, only 14% of the public were even approximately correct when asked to provide an estimate. A third of the sample generated what could be termed a large over-estimation (Roberts, Nuffield, & Hann, 1999). Further analyses have demonstrated that the two misperceptions go hand in hand. People who under-estimate incarceration rates, as well as the average sentence imposed, also over-estimate the parole rate. In both instances, people perceive the criminal justice system to be more lenient than is in fact the case.

Perhaps the two most important conclusions from these results are the following: (a) polls which explore public attitudes towards sentencing and parole need to consider the systematic misperceptions that the public hold; and (b) an important goal for the criminal justice system is to improve the state of public knowledge. (Roberts & Stalans, 1997).

Effects of Knowledge upon Public Opinion. The research that demonstrates poor public knowledge of sentencing and parole is only important if knowledge of criminal justice affects attitudes towards these areas of criminal justice. There are some social issues on which peoples' attitudes appear unaffected by knowledge, or the passage of legal reform. Abortion in the US would appear to be one such issue. However, research that has provided subjects with information about sentencing has demonstrated significant differences in opinion when respondents are provided with more or better information about the issues.

United States. Some studies use a pre-post, within-subjects design in which the same subjects are asked their views before and after receiving information. For example, Doble and Klein (1989) asked respondents to sentence an offender convicted of robbery. First, however, respondents were given only two sentencing options to consider. They could either sentence the offender to prison or to probation. Seventy-eight percent of the sample favored incarceration for the offender. Then, in the post-test, the same subjects were given seven sentencing alternatives. These alternatives were those which were available to the court in the State in which the research was conducted. These additional sentences included intensive probation and house arrest, among others. When subjects were asked to impose a sentence on the second occasion, support for prison as a sanction declined to 46%.

United Kingdom. A more ambitious pre-post experiment involving public knowledge and attitudes was conducted in the United Kingdom. A representative sample of the public was invited to attend a "Deliberative Weekend". Participants listened to two days of informative seminars about the criminal justice system. Prior to receiving this material, subjects had been asked a number of questions about their attitudes to crime and justice. At the end of the weekend, these questions were posed a second time. Results indicated significant shifts in terms of public attitudes towards some important criminal justice topics. For example, prior to the weekend, 78% of the sample agreed that "longer sentences help to fight crime". After the weekend, only 55% agreed with this opinion, a statistically significant shift (Fishkin, 1993). However, this kind of research design is open to criticism on the grounds of "demand characteristics". In other words, subjects clearly knew that they were in some kind of experiment. This kind of research design is also open to criticism on the grounds that the direction of change is likely to be heavily dependent on the advocacy skills of speakers, rather than the substantive quality of their arguments. A better experimental approach would employ a between-subjects design.

In the latest exploration of the knowledge-opinion relationship, Hough and Roberts (1998) tested the effects of information using a sub-sample of the 1996 British Crime Survey comprising some 8,000 respondents. Half the sample were simply asked to sentence an offender convicted of robbery, while the other half were provided with a complete "menu" of sentencing options available to the judge. Subjects were randomly assigned to experimental conditions. Without the menu of sentencing options, over two-thirds of the sample favored imprisonment. However, when they were given the list of potential dispositions, the percentage of respondents endorsing the incarceration of the offender declined significantly to 54%. This experiment makes it clear that part of the public support for incarceration as a sanction can be attributed to lack of familiarity with the alternative dispositions available to a sentencing judge.

Canada. The public's lack of information is not restricted to the sentencing options. Other research has manipulated the amount of information about the case to examine whether this affects public sentencing preferences. Doob and Roberts (1983) conducted a content analysis of news media sentencing stories and found that most were very brief and provided little information about the offender, and almost none about the judicial reasoning underlying the sentence that was imposed. This finding led to a series of experiments in which subjects were randomly assigned to read either a very brief account of a case or a more complete description. When people were given the more comprehensive account of a case, they were significantly less likely to favor incarcerating the offender.

Finally, another experiment by the same authors (Doob & Robert, 1983) compared the reactions of two groups of subjects, one of whom had been asked to read a summary of court documents pertaining to an assault trial, the other group were asked to read a newspaper account of the same case. Subjects randomly assigned to the media version were significantly less satisfied with the sentence imposed by the judge and gave significantly more negative ratings to the judge and the offender. Since the amount of information was comparable in the two conditions, in that both accounts included details such as the offender's criminal record and the circumstances surrounding the commission of the offence, the difference may be attributable to the interpretation placed upon events by the newspaper. So, it is not simply the volume of information about a sentencing decision that affects public reactions, but also the way in which this information is reported.

Public attitudes to sentencing

A consistent finding across many jurisdictions is that the public hold negative opinions of the courts. There has been little change over the past two decades in responses to the simple and simplistic question of "Are sentences too lenient, too harsh or about right?." Within the period 1996–1998, over three-quarters of the polled public in Australia, Canada, the United States, and the United Kingdom expressed the view that sentences are too lenient (Roberts & Hough, 1999). The widely held belief that sentences are too lenient comes about through biased recall of very serious crimes, and excessive news media coverage of lenient sentences (Stalans, 1993). Findings from several surveys identify important qualifications to the public's apparent dissatisfaction with the severity of sentencing trends.

Reactions to specific cases compared to general questions. One important limitation of most public opinion polls is that they pose a general question, such as are sentences too harsh or too lenient?, or are you in favor of or opposed to parole? These kind of questions suffers from at least two weaknesses. First, they fail to capture the complexities of the issue, such as sentences for which kinds of crimes and for which kinds of offenders? More importantly, such questions generate a response from the public that is at odds with their reactions to specific cases. This has been demonstrated in a number of surveys that have included both kinds of questions. Two recent examples will illustrate the point, one from the area of sentencing and the other relating to parole.

Using the British Crime Survey (BCS) respondents, Hough and Roberts (1999) first posed the general question "Are sentences too harsh, too lenient or about right?". Four respondents out of five responded that sentences were too lenient. Then respondents were given a description of a an actual case and were asked to impose a sentence. The crime involved a burglary of a private residence by a man with several previous convictions for the same crime. The offender had actually been sentenced to two years in prison. However, the sentencing preferences of the BCS respondents were far less harsh. Only half the sample chose imprisonment at all, and of these, the average term of custody imposed was only 12 months (Hough & Roberts, 1999). Clearly, when the public says sentences are too lenient, this does not necessarily mean that the public are much harsher than the courts.

The same phenomenon can be demonstrated for parole. When asked their opinion about parole, most members of the public will express their dissatisfaction. Thus, in a survey in Canada (Roberts et al., 1999) results indicate (a) that very few respondents had much confidence in the parole system, and (b) most Canadians think that too many prisoners are released on parole. However, results are quite different when members of the public are asked to consider a specific parole application. The case provided to the subjects was based upon a typical parole application made by a prisoner serving a relatively long sentence for burglary. The individual was making his application after having served the minimum period of one-third of their custodial disposition in prison. These details are important because questions of this nature can be crafted to generate a sympathetic reaction from the public. In this case, however, care was taken to ensure that the individual was representative of the inmate population.

Upon hearing of the specific case, three-quarters of the respondents supported the release of the inmate at the earliest eligibility date in his sentence of imprisonment (Roberts et al., 1999). Earlier research demonstrated the same phenomenon in Canada (Cumberland & Zamble, 1992). This last point is worth making because other survey data show that in addition to their opposition to the parole system, people believe that offenders get parole too early in the sentence. Most people would prefer that inmates serve a greater proportion of their custodial sentence in prison. These findings, with respect to case histories, are important to the sentencing process because at the end of the day, sentencing is about individual cases, and not categories of offences or offenders.

Public attitudes to parole

The tenor of public reaction to parole can be summarized as follows. First, people tend to express far less confidence in the parole system than other branches of criminal justice. Much of their dissatisfaction, however, springs from erroneous perceptions of the parole grant rate, and exaggerated fears of the likelihood of recidivism by prisoners serving time in the community on parole. For example, a survey using a representative sample of the public in Canada found that three-quarters of respondents over-estimated the recidivism rate. This finding was true in 1985, and when the poll was replicated over a decade later (Roberts et al., 1999). As well, when people consider re-offending, they are thinking about violent offences, even though statistically, non-violent recidivism is ten times as likely as violent recidivism.

Once confronted with a specific parole application, the public tends to be supportive of parole, particularly if the applicant is perceived to be a non-violent offender. In fact, there is strong evidence that the public adopt a bifurcated approach to parole, favouring parole by a strong margin if the offender is non-violent, and opposing by an equally strong margin if he is serving time for a crime of violence. There is even evidence from a jurisdiction in which the public have direct input into parole eligibility dates that the public are supportive of parole even for offenders serving life for the most serious category of murder (Roberts, Nuffield, & Hann, 1999).

In Canada, all offenders convicted of first degree murder are sentenced to life imprisonment with no possibility for parole before having served 25 years in custody. However, according to section 745.6 of the criminal code, most of these life prisoners may apply for a jury review of their parole eligibility dates after having served 15 years. The jury has the power to reduce the number of years that must be served before parole eligibility from 25 to 15. To date, 80% of these parole eligibility reviews have resulted in a favorable decision from juries (Roberts & Cole, 1999). As a result of these reviews, inmates serving life for first degree murder have become eligible for parole much earlier than the 25 year point in their sentences. These trends suggest that the public are not implacably opposed to parole, even for offenders convicted of the most heinous crimes.

Discussion

It is clear that no single theoretical explanation or perspective can adequately account for the nature of public attitudes towards sentencing and parole. The existence of such strikingly similar international trends suggests that the criminal justice response to crime is not determinant of public opinion since the level of severity and the nature of sentencing varies widely across the countries surveyed in this chapter, yet the tenor of public opinion is invariant. Researchers must look elsewhere to explain public punishment preferences.

One valuable source of insight is the literature examining the way that members of the public acquire and assimilate information relevant to their attitudes. A number of studies have demonstrated that information processing reflects cognitive "shortcuts" that affect the nature of the attitude held. One example of this is that people tend to change their views when the decision-making context changes. Thus, altering the nature of prior questions on a survey affects responses to subsequent questions (Tourangeau & Rasinski, 1988). With respect to attitudes to sentencing, the context in which questions are asked will determine the nature of the subject's response.

As well, the existence of strongly held opinions can serve as a template by which subsequently acquired information relevant to those opinions is evaluated. A classic research example is the study by Lord, Ross, and Lepper (1979), in which evaluations of capital punishment studies were affected by the subjects' pre-experimental attitudes towards the death penalty. In a similar way, evaluations of the appropriateness of specific sentencing decisions are going to reflect global attitudes towards the leniency of the courts. A harsh or appropriate sentence that does not fit the cognitive template of judicial leniency is likely to be dismissed as an aberration, while an overly-lenient sentence is likely to conform to the template and be retained longer.

Finally, understanding the origin and nature of public attitudes towards the courts and the correctional system also requires knowledge of the news media's treatment of sentencing and parole. That treatment emphasizes lenient dispositions and an indulgent parole system. This image is transmitted to a public made receptive to such a message by years of skewed criminal justice stories.

Research and policy lessons

There are a number of lessons to be drawn from the emerging international findings in this area. First, despite differences in the extent of the crime problem, and the nature of the criminal justice response across different jurisdictions, there are important commonalities in terms of public reaction. For example, people tend to be critical of the sentencing and parole systems, believing them to be more lenient than is in fact the case. These beliefs reflect a broader perception that the criminal justice system is tilted more in the direction of protecting the rights of the offender than in responding to crime.

Second, while different research designs have been used, no single research tool is sufficient to obtain a veridical portrait of public opinion. Policy-makers wishing to design penal policies that reflect community values cannot rely on the results of opinion polls the way that political parties track public support by means of polls measuring voting intention. Divining the true nature of public opinion, with respect to sentencing and parole, requires a more complex analysis that incorporates the findings from different research methods. These methods include representative polls, qualitative analyses such as Focus Groups, as well as hybrid techniques such as the Deliberative Poll.

Unfortunately, interpreting public opinion by means of simplistic survey questions remains popular with politicians and policy-makers. Two recent examples can be found in criminal justice legislation emanating from the US and Canada. As noted earlier, the "Three-Strikes" sentencing laws were introduced in America on a wave of public support. A poll conducted in 1994 found overwhelming support for such punitive recidivist sentencing statutes as four-fifths of the polled public supported a law mandating life imprisonment as the punishment for offenders convicted of a serious felony for the third time (Lacayo, 1994). More recent and more sophisticated research on public attitudes to the three-strikes legislation has shown that there is far less support for the concept than would be indicated by the simple poll. Applegate, Cullen, Turner, and Sundt (1996) demonstrate that citizens only endorse three-strikes policies that focus on the most serious offenders and that allow considerable flexibility in application.

In Canada, a single poll has been instrumental in aiding passage of legislation in June 1999 which, if it becomes law, could result in the imposition of consecutive terms of imprisonment for offenders convicted of multiple counts of murder or sexual assault. This legislation is likely to have a significant impact on sentencing practices in Canada. For example, an offender convicted of two counts of murder may now be sentenced to 50 years without parole. Since the average age of a life prisoner on admission is 39, the proposed Bill will probably mean imprisonment for the rest of the offender's natural life. Life without parole was rejected by the Canadian Parliament when it reformed the sentencing arrangements for offenders convicted of murder in 1976. Now, this option has re-emerged as a result of this Bill. It is not at all clear that the public support this Bill to the extent indicated by a single poll as public reaction to consecutive and concurrent sentencing simply cannot be determined by a single, simple question on an opinion survey.

Perhaps the most important policy lesson is that there is a clear need to provide the public with more and better information about issues related to sentencing and parole. Part of the misperception about sentencing involves a link between sentencing patterns and crime rates. In the light of this connection, it is important to educate the public about trends in crime, and the proportion of crime that involves violence. Otherwise, people will continue to believe that crime rates are increasing inexorably, particularly rates of violent crime, and they will be inclined to attribute this increase to leniency in sentencing. The result will be increasing calls for harsher sentencing, appeals for which politicians appear only too eager to respond.

REFERENCES

Applegate, B., Cullen, F., Turner, M., & Sundt, J. (1996). Assessing public support for three-strikes-and-you're-out laws: Global versus specific attitudes. *Crime and Delinquency*, *42*, 517–534.

Canadian Sentencing Commission (1987). Sentencing reform: A Canadian approach. Ottawa: Supply and Services Canada.

Cumberland, J., & Zamble, E. (1992). General and specific measures of attitudes toward early release of criminal offenders. *Canadian Journal of Behavioural Science*, *24*, 442–455.

Doob, A. N., & Roberts, J. V. (1983). *An analysis of the public's view of sentencing*. Ottawa: Department of Justice Canada.

Doble, J., & Klein, J. (1989). *Punishing criminals: The public's view. An Alabama survey*. New York: Edna McConnell Clark Foundation.

Greenspan, E., Matheson, A., & Davis, R. (1998). Discipline and parole. *Queen's Quarterly*, *105*, 9–28.

Fishkin, J. (1995). *The voice of the people*. New Haven, CN: Yale University Press.

Hough, M., & Roberts, J. V. (1998). *Attitudes to punishment: Findings from the British Crime Survey*. Home Office Research Study 179. London: Home Office.

Hough, M., & Roberts, J. V. (1999). Sentencing trends in Britain: Public knowledge and public opinion. *Punishment and Society*, *1*, 7–22.

Indermaur, D. (1987). Public perception of sentencing in Perth, Western Australia. *Australia and New Zealand Journal of Criminology*, *20*, 163–183.

Lacayo, R. (1994). Public support for three-strike. *Time Magazine*, 41–53.

Lord, C., Ross, L., & Lepper, M. (1979). Biased assimilation and attitude polarization: effects of prior theories on subsequently considered evidence. *Journal of Personality and Social Psychology*, *37*, 2098–2109.

Packer, H. (1968). *The limits of the penal sanction*. New York: Oxford University Press.

Povey, D., & Prime, J. (1999). *Recorded crime statistics in England and Wales, April 1998 to March 1999*. Home Office Statistical Bulletin No. 18/99. London: Home Office.

Roach, K. (1999). *Due process and victims' rights: The new law and politics of criminal justice*. Toronto: University of Toronto Press.

Roberts, J. V., & Cole, D. P. (1999). *Making sense of sentencing*. Toronto: University of Toronto Press.

Roberts, J. V., & Doob, A. N. (1990). News media influences on public views of sentencing. *Law and Human Behavior*, 14, 451–468.

Roberts, J. V., Doob, A. N., & Marinos, V. (1999). *Judicial attitudes to conditional terms of imprisonment: Results of a national survey*. Ottawa: Department of Justice Canada.

Roberts, J. V., Nuffield, J., & Hann, R. (1999). *Parole and the attitudes and behaviour of the public*. Ottawa: Department of Criminology, University of Ottawa.

Roberts, J. V., & Stalans, L. S. (1997). *Public opinion, crime and criminal justice*. Boulder: Co: Westview Press.

Roberts, J. V., & Stalans, L. S. (1998). Crime, criminal justice and public opinion. In M. Tonry (Ed.), *The handbook of crime and punishment*. New York: Oxford University Press.

Sharp, F., & Otto, M.. (1909). A study of the popular attitude towards retributive punishment. *International Journal of Ethics*, *20*, 341–357.

Stalans, L. S. (1993). Citizens' crime stereotypes: Biased recall, and punishment preferences in abstract cases: the educative role of interpersonal sources. *Law and Human Behavior*, *17*, 451–470.

Statistics Canada. (1998). *Canadian crime statistics, 1997*. Ottawa: Supply and Services Canada.

Tourangeau, R., & Rasinski, K. (1988). Cognitive processes underlying context effects in attitude measurement. *Psychological Bulletin*, *103*, 299–314.

U. S. Department of Justice (1998). *Sourcebook of criminal justice statistics*. Washington, D. C.: Bureau of Justice Statistics.

Chapter 11

THE SYNDROME EVIDENCE PHENOMENON: TIME TO MOVE ON?

Ian Freckelton

A variety of forms of psychological evidence has been adduced in the courts over the past 25 years in attempts to disabuse triers of fact of misconceptions that allegedly they may have harbored. The mainstream forms of such evidence have included "rape trauma syndrome" ("RTS") evidence, "battered woman syndrome" ("BWS") evidence, "child sexual abuse accommodation syndrome" ("CSAAS") evidence, "repressed memory syndrome" ("RMS") evidence, "false memory syndrome" ("FMS") evidence, "premenstrual syndrome"[1] ("PMS") evidence, "cult indoctrinee syndrome" ("CIS") evidence and latterly even "Vietnam Veteran syndrome" ("VVS") evidence and "false victimization syndrome" ("FVS") evidence. It is timely after a quarter of a century of syndrome evidence to ask whether the experiment is or should be coming toward its conclusion. Are there better means than syndrome evidence to introduce counterintuitive information into the courts?

In this chapter, by reference primarily to rape trauma syndrome, child sexual abuse accommodation syndrome and battered woman syndrome, the "Big Three" of the syndrome phenomenon, I argue that the attempt by the use of syndromes to introduce counterintuitive mental health expert evidence was misconceived, intellectually lacking in rigor and inappropriately driven by evidence entrepreneurs pursuing political objectives through the courts. Firstly, much of the information sought to be conveyed was neither medical nor scientific. By assuming the nomenclature of pathology, wrong messages were given in an attempt to secure evidentiary admissibility. By asserting empirical validation, again misimpressions were created to bolster the insights sought to be communicated. In the translation of working hypotheses that had a practical utility in the therapeutic context into the forensic milieu, each of the syndromes in due course was betrayed as lacking proper scientific credentials. The expectation had been created that the syndromes were diagnostic and could assist the criminal courts in their dichotomous task of determining guilt and innocence. They were shown not to be and the disillusionment created in the courts in many jurisdictions has set back the reception of psychological evidence substantially.

The subsequent backlash by scholars and the courts was deserved. However, the most unfortunate result of the adverse reaction to the syndrome phenomenon, captured by Dershowitz's throw-away epithet "the abuse excuse"[2] has been that clinical insights which formed the core of most of the syndromes now risk not being conveyed to triers of the fact with the result that sources of error which might otherwise have been factored out of the decision-making process remain. New modes of effectively communicating myth-dispelling information need to be explored.

A short history of syndrome evidence

The syndrome phenomenon started in 1974 with the writings, directed toward a clinical audience, of Burgess and Holmstrom[3], asserting that a characteristic range of behaviors followed upon sexual assaults upon women. It was not long before a forensic relevance was alighted upon for such contentions; they could assist the prosecution in criminal actions to account for delays in reporting and for behavior on the part of complainants seemingly inconsistent with their having been engaged in involuntary sexual interaction.

Hot on the heels of Burgess and Holmstrom came assertions by the legal academic, Delgado,[4] that a range of predictable factors were responsible for and followed upon people joining totalitarian religious organizations labeled "cults". This time, the initial focus of the syndrome's proponent was legal, not therapeutic. It was upon legal legitimization for interfering with people's ongoing membership of such groups and facilitating civil action against those responsible for pressured recruitment and retention of devotees.

Then in the early 1980s the best known of the syndromes was born, battered woman syndrome. Drawing upon the work of Seligman, Walker contended that a paralyzing sense of helplessness frequently resulted from the serial infliction of domestic violence upon women, a helplessness on occasion paradoxically characterized by retaliatory violence on the part of the woman.[5] The syndrome was soon used to support legal defences of self-defence, provocation and duress for women who committed serious assaults and homicides, and then later to assist them when charged with matters such as social security frauds, and when endeavoring to sue their battering partner in the civil courts. Walker herself was regularly employed as an expert witness from the mid-1980s.

At the same time, legal writers argued that premenstrual symptoms could also result in an altered perception of reality, similar to that resulting from the serial beating giving rise to battered woman syndrome, such as to qualify for defences to criminal acts, or at least such as to mitigate the moral culpability of women responsible for their commission.

During the same period, Summit argued that a range of consequences for children could therapeutically be identified from repeated sexual abuse.[6] Prosecution lawyers soon sought to utilize his "syndrome", seeking to explain away frequent delays in reporting, poor quality disclosure and erratic giving of evidence by child victims. In the 1990s he was to attempt to withdraw his syndrome from such uses.[7]

The 1990s saw the phenomenon of "repressed memory syndrome", again a "prosecution" syndrome seeking to account for the failure of victims of sexual and other abuse to report or disclose promptly what had happened to them—in essence, the explanation went, for long periods after they have been exposed to certain kinds of stressors women and children often do not remember what has happened to them. They only "recover their memories after cues such as are to be encountered in intensive psychotherapy. Detractors of recovered memories themselves coined a syndrome, at first tongue-in-cheek, to describe the phenomenon in which patients/clients come to believe in confabulated memories of abuse—"false memory syndrome."

The 1990s generated moves to reclassify battered woman syndrome as battered person syndrome, so as to include victims within gay and lesbian relationships, battered children, battered husbands, battered older persons, and so on. The 1990s also continued to generate new coinages of syndromes with a forensic application,[8] one of the most recent and one of the more dubious being an amalgam construct entitled by its creators "False Victimization Syndrome."[9]

The forensic need for expert syndrome evidence

In sexual assault cases, the perfect forensic scenario rarely presents itself from the point of view of the prosecution. Ideally, the complainant was unaffected by any intoxicating substances at the time of the rape, and was not intellectually or psychiatrically disabled. She/he disclosed promptly and complained to the police straightaway. Not only that, she/he was physically injured so there is evidence corroborative of non-consensual activity. If the victim is a child, merely scientific proof of seminal fluids in a body cavity is good enough. Preferably from the point of view of the prosecution, the complainant is detailed and precise in respect of all the interactions between them and the assailant. They do not retract. They were visibly distressed to all who saw them after the rape and they consistently thereafter shunned the company of the perpetrator. In short they complain promptly; they are sober, "normal", physically injured, visibly upset, clear, precise and consistent. They fulfil all the stereotypes of the rape victim.

The fact that few complainants are of such a kind leaves a range of problems for the justice system in determining whether assertions of sexual assault are proved beyond reasonable doubt. There are rape myths that need to be grappled with, and there are complexities and subtleties of human affection and interaction that consistently yield ambiguous and unanticipated answers. Not surprising then that prosecutors should embrace with alacrity any tool that might make more understandable the greatest impediments to complainants' credibility: their delay in complaining and reporting, their lack of total and consistent recollection of the indignities perpetrated on them and in some cases their continued association with the assailant.

In respect of women who assert in court that they have engaged in retaliatory violence, from the point of view of tapping into common community attributions about "real victims", ideally they defend themselves by proving that they have done so when immediately threatened with serious physical risk or in response to provocation such as that to which any normal person would respond belligerently. Again, though, this is not how it often happens. Life, gender and relationships are more complex than that. As a community we are accustomed, perhaps enured to men's violence, but we are confronted and alarmed by women who take up arms. Our tendency in such cases is to assume mental instability of significant proportions or to suspect sinister premeditation. The law dealing with violence has been generated by men about men's explosive reactions to threats from other men and provocative words uttered by men, and sometimes by women. It has been predicated on assumptions of equalities of strength and legitimations of violence, but within stereotypes of acceptability. It has not adapted easily to scenarios of chronic violence or oppression perpetrated by males against females (or males) of inferior physical capacity. It has not catered readily to the psychological consequences of long term abuse and threat of abuse. Again, not surprising that those defending women accused of violence, especially premeditated murderous violence, should seize any tool for giving to triers of fact an appreciation of scenarios of domestic battery, dilemmas and perceptions probably well outside their experience. It was such considerations that laid a fallow forensic field for the generation of most of the syndromes that have bedeviled the courts for a quarter of a century.

The historical context of syndrome evidence

Syndrome evidence needs to be historically contextualized. The 1970s saw the rise of feminism and of the victims' rights movement. Their collocation saw many socio-legal changes: the start of sexual assault centres, the commencement of the refuge movement, legislative change to protect women from violent and threatening partners by court orders, and lobbying to change the definition of rape, including acknowledging that rape can and does occur within marriage. For the first time the criminal justice system treated women's sexual integrity and privacy as more than an asset for their parents and their spouses. Attention by lobbyists then turned to adverse aspects of criminal procedure so far as female victims of sexual assault were concerned—the availability of counseling records to the defence, the ability of the defence to cross-examine the complainant about other sexual activities and the unfairness within the trial process. The plight of the woman being misunderstood because of her reactions subsequent to being raped was adopted as part of the platform of feminist trial process reformists. Supplying a means of insight into the mythologies of rape and the misconceptions prevalent within the community about the impact of sexual assault became part of the lobbying agenda for feminist evidence entrepreneurs who were pursuing the political objective of improving the lot of complainants in sexual assault cases and optimizing the potential for such prosecutions to be successful.[10] Securing convictions and proper punishment for sex crimes became part of the wish list of those advocating broader recognition of rights for women within the general community and, particularly, within the forensic domain. Ironically, latterly it has linked in with the law and order lobby.

Another aspect of the social movements that focussed upon the need for perpetrators of sexual assault to be made accountable through the trial process and punished more severely was that which centered upon children. Societies for the Prevention of Cruelty to Children and then children's advocacy movements piggy-backed on the work done on behalf of women in relation to the trial process. Once again evidence entrepreneurialism became apparent in the lobby to improve the appreciation by forensic decision-makers of the dynamics and impact of child sexual abuse. This gave rise to lobbying to secure the admissibility of the syndrome known as child sexual abuse accommodation syndrome on the part especially of protection workers, dealing with abuse of children.

Another aspect to the social changes brought about by feminist and victimology focus on the criminal justice system was a consciousness starting in the 1980s of the potential for miscarriages of justice when women killed their abusive partners. Infamous cases in which battery had been horrendous, longterm and even fatal for women were highlighted. This in turn gave a fillip to the movement for the creation of domestic violence and intervention orders by the courts to make it a criminal offence for a man to make contact with a woman who had obtained such orders. However, on some occasions women who had long been the subject of domestic violence killed their partners in circumstances that did not readily fit the traditional, male-oriented criteria for the defences of self-defence or provocation. This in turn focussed the attention of feminist law reformers on the criteria for the defences and upon means of giving to forensic decision-makers a porthole of understanding into the dynamics and effects of longterm domestic violence upon its victims. Enter the evidence entrepreneurs again and the forensic adaptation of battered woman syndrome.

The development of the forensic syndromes

Rape Trauma Syndrome. In 1974 Ann Burgess and Lynda Holmstrom coined the term "rape trauma syndrome" to describe the emotional, behavioral and psychological reactions typically exhibited by female victims of sexual assault. They contended that rape victims generally experience two phases of response to their violation. The first, they said, was characterized by the experience by the victim of disorganization in lifestyle with emotional reactions ranging from fear, humiliation and embarrassment to anger and a desire for revenge. Although fear of physical violence and death dominates the victim's feelings, they contended, self-blame is also very prominent. During this phase, when the victim feels the impact of the rape most severely, they identified that the victim may exhibit one of two widely divergent emotional styles. In the "expressed style", feelings of fear, anger, and anxiety are manifested through crying, sobbing, smiling, restlessness, and tenseness. In "the controlled style", feelings are masked by a calm, composed, or subdued demeanor.

According to Burgess and Holmstrom, the second phase involves a long-term process of physical and emotional reorganization. This phase begins two to three weeks after the attack. Symptoms may include change in residence, travel to sources of support in other cities, nightmares, and various phobic reactions. Although all victims do not experience the same symptoms in the same sequence, the researchers identified that victims consistently experience the disorganization phase, and that many victims thereafter experience mild to moderate symptoms in the reorganization process. Few victims, they said, report no symptoms.[11]

Their analysis has legitimately attracted significant criticism of its profoundly flawed methodology. The critique has focussed upon the self-selecting and probably unrepresentative group whom the researchers studied, namely those who sought treatment for the effects of rape at a city hospital; the absence of controls or comparison groups; the failure to employ standardized psychometric testing instruments; and the inadequate documentation of the reliability of measuring devices that were used. Extraordinarily, by today's standards, at least, the researchers factored out of their analyses victims who they said had been unable by reason of youth or disability to provide consent and women who had initially consented to sex but withdrew their consent or were forced into different kinds of sexual acts by violence or threat.

A forensic relevance of rape trauma syndrome is its potential to explain firstly a disinclination on the part of a victim of rape to report by reason of the distress caused by the sexual assault, whether overtly manifested or not. A second forensic utility of the syndrome is to shed light on why the woman may not exhibit the kind of expressed emotion which might otherwise be expected of her. In other words the syndrome seeks to draw attention to the diversity of responses in victims of sexual assault. A key to Burgess and Holmstrom's interpretation of the modest data which they generated lies within their perception that women exhibit two contrasting modes of dealing with their feelings in the short-term aftermath of sexual assault. This has the potential to be counterintuitive, disabusing of the expectation that "real victims" will manifest their distress in a demonstrative fashion, will disassociate themselves from the offender, and will decline, or at least not seek out, (in the short term) subsequent sexual encounters. However, the forensic utility of the syndrome, as formulated by Burgess and Holmstrom, could not properly go much further than this. It was not regarded by them as diagnostic, simply descriptive of the reactions of many victims of sexual assault.

What occurred, though, in its translocation into the legal environment was a desire on the part of prosecution lawyers to invite jurors to exercise more than counterintuitive logic; what they wanted to do was to invite jurors to conclude on the basis of the syndrome's characteristics being satisfied that therefore the woman had been raped. At least, six major difficulties beset such an approach:

- It is based upon a biased sample of women who may or may not have responded in a way characteristic of the greater percentage of women who did not present at hospitals seeking assistance for the psychological sequelae of rape. So it may not be accurate;
- It is an averaging—a significant percentage of even Burgess and Holmstrom's sample did not respond in accordance with the syndrome. A number of them were excluded from analysis by the criteria that the researchers employed. That did not mean they had not been raped, simply that they had not met the researchers' eligibility criteria or had dealt with the assault in their own way, perhaps not by exhibiting the most common responses;
- There is total diversity lying between the expressed and controlled styles, meaning that the fact that a woman did or did not register distress after an interaction with a sexually assaultive male may or may not be of consequence in evaluating whether it was non-consensual;
- The registering of distress simply establishes that something traumatic, probably of a sexual nature, occurred, not necessarily that the complainant was raped. Interestingly, some research suggests that the responses of women the subject of attempted rape are much the same as those who are the subject of rape perpetrated to finality;[12]
- The syndrome makes no attempt to cater to complainants' various cultural and racial backgrounds;
- The syndrome deals exclusively with females, not acknowledging those males who are the subject also of sexual assault.[13]

The inevitable happened in 1989 with the absence of the syndrome's characteristics being used by the defence against sexual assault complainants to suggest that the sexual intercourse that had taken place had been consensual.[14] This remains a relatively rare attempted forensic use of the syndrome but highlights the potential for the stereotypes created by the syndrome to be used against those whom the syndrome was created to assist therapeutically.

Cult Indoctrinee Syndrome. In 1977 Delgado coined the term "cult indoctrinee syndrome" to describe the process and the psychological impact of abusive cult membership:

(1) sudden, drastic alteration of the individual's value hierarchy, including abandonment of previous academic and career goals;

(2) reduction of cognitive flexibility and adaptability, the victim answering questions mechanically, substituting stereotyped cult responses for his own;
(3) narrowing and blunting of affect. Love feelings are repressed, the victim appearing emotionally flat and lifeless;
(4) regression of behavior to childlike levels, the victim becoming dependent on cult leaders and desiring that they make all decisions for him;
(5) physical changes including weight loss and deterioration in the victim's physical appearance and expression;
(6) possible pathological symptoms, including dissociation, delusional thinking, and various other types of thought disorder.[15]

It has not to this date been applied in the courts.[16]

Child Sexual Abuse Accommodation Syndrome. In 1983 Roland Summit identified a "sexual abuse accommodation syndrome" experienced by children who had been sexually molested by members of their family, identifying as its characteristics: secrecy; helplessness; entrapment and accommodation; delayed, conflicted and unconvincing disclosure; and retraction of disclosures.[17]

The syndrome was used regularly in courts both to dispel myths about the responses displayed by children being regularly sexually assaulted in the home and to suggest that in fact departure from expected responses on the part of victims might be indicative of sexual abuse of children actually taking place—in other words, contrary to the usual experience of life and the standard expectations acted upon in the courts, imprecise, delayed, conflicted disclosure was suggestive of a complainant's assertions of assault being correct.

However, by 1992 Summit recanted,[18] asking for his "syndrome" no longer to be referred to as such and blaming trial lawyers for importing it as a diagnostic instrument into the courts.[19] He emphasized that the syndrome originated not as a "laboratory hypothesis or as a designated study of a defined population. It emerged as a summary of diverse clinical consulting experience, defined at the interface with paradoxical forensic reaction. It should be understood without apology that the CSAAS is a clinical opinion, not a scientific instrument."[20] He acknowledged that his syndrome was non-diagnostic, lambasted the notion that the presence or absence of its indicia could indicate whether a child had been sexually assaulted, and bewailed lawyers' preparedness to seize on the syndrome as a forensic weapon.[21]

Battered Woman Syndrome. In 1984 Lenore Walker published her influential book, *Battered Woman Syndrome*,[22] identifying three phases in the typical cycle of domestic violence against women and maintaining that Seligman's experimental work on dogs to which electrical shocks had been applied and which thereafter became "helpless" was transferable as a concept to battered women. Her work has been subjected to continuing conceptual critique in relation to the syndrome. From the early 1990s in face of attack that it was not a medically recognized phenomenon, she has increasingly sought resort in its being a form of post-traumatic stress disorder in an attempt to secure its admissibility.[23]

Many criticisms of Walker's cycle of violence have been made by researchers and commentators. The most prominent grievance directed toward the syndrome is that it pathologizes or medicalizes women's reactions to domestic violence.[24] Critics such as Scutt[25] have contended that the phenomenon that Walker described is no more than a social reality, frequently utilized by males to control and oppress women. Women's reactions in face of the manipulation and brutalization are not "diseased" or abnormal. It is the situation that is deviant; the woman simply survives and adapts in face of violence.[26]

Fundamental to Walker's theory is the idea that women in domestically abusive relationships are like the dogs to which electric shocks were applied in Seligman's experiments. Significantly, Seligman warned against extrapolation between species.[27] Moreover, Walker's interpretation of the Seligman experiments is selective and questionable.[28] Seligman and co-researchers formulated a complex construct of "learned helplessness", one that went a distance beyond mere "acquired passivity", as the term tends to be used by Walker. As they have developed the theory over 25 years, it has three elements: (1) critical environmental conditions; (2) translation of these conditions into expectations; and (3) alteration of psychological processes by the expectations. Seligman and colleagues in later publications have pointedly distanced themselves from the use by Walker and others of their earlier data. In 1993, for instance, Petersen, Maier, and Seligman, referring to Walker, maintained that "we think matters are again misunderstood by this theorist". They accept that domestic violence can induce passivity but they repudiate this alone as constituting "learned helplessness" according to their model. In addition, they argue that socialization of women can induce passivity and a receptivity to abuse but again they distinguish this from "learned helplessness". They argue that the passivity of many women in violent homes may be instrumental, the potential being present for a range of explicit reinforcements to their passivity.[29]

A significant question exists about whether women who remain in domestically violent relationships can routinely be characterized as suffering from learned helplessness or as helpless. Walker's data in fact demonstrate that around 20% of the women in her selection said that they left their home immediately after a battering incident, about 25% left the batterer frequently, about 49% immediately sought "outside help" after being assaulted,[30] and 39% reported taking out a restraining order against their husband at some point.[31]

Moreover, it has already been argued in North American and Australian courts that particular victims of domestic violence could not properly avail themselves of expert evidence on battered woman syndrome because they had not been sufficiently beaten or beaten for long enough to have developed the syndrome. The inference sought then to be drawn (usually on behalf of the prosecution) is that the woman's actions are in fact premeditated, malicious and calculated—not the result of the injurious effects of long-term violence. This was the tack of what was ultimately the successful prosecution argument in *Osland v R*.[32] The point at which a woman "qualifies" for the forensic indulgences potentially to be extended by the categorization as a "battered woman" is not an easy one to pinpoint and is frequently the subject of considerable forensic argument.

The correctness of dividing the cycle of violence into three phases has been questioned by some commentators, together with the description of the phases, particularly attributes of the second phase in which the battering incident occurs.[33] A telling array of criticisms may be made of the conduct of the interviews by Walker's researchers, including the fact that interviewers were aware of the hypotheses being tested, this having the potential to impact upon both recording and interpretation of answers.[34] In addition, a variety of findings are conflated without apparent justification and without statistical tests of significance being applied.[35]

As a construct, BWS may misrepresent many women's experiences of violence. It is based largely on the experiences of Caucasian women of a particular social background. Their "passive" responses may be different from those of women with different economic or ethnic backgrounds."[36] In addition, it fails to cater to women who did not live with their partners or have not undergone the full cycle of violence on at least two occasions. Its definitional parameters remain unclear and whether it comprehends the lot of male victims of domestic violence is unclear.[37]

The strength of battered woman syndrome is that it provides a means of disabusing jurors of myths related to domestic violence. Wilson J. in *Lavallee v R*.[38] usefully summed up the issues:

> How can the mental state of the appellant be appreciated without it? The average member of the public (or of the jury) can be forgiven for asking: Why would a woman put up with this kind of treatment? Why should she continue to live with such a man? How could she love a partner who beat her to the point of requiring hospitalization? We would expect the woman to pack her bags and go. Where's her self-respect? Why does she not cut loose and make a new life for herself? Such is the reaction of the average person confronted with the so-called "battered-woman syndrome". We need help to understand it and help is available from trained professionals.

Wilson noted[39] the commendation of the value of such testimony by the New Jersey Supreme Court in *State v Kelly*[40] where it had been said that such evidence: "is aimed at an area where the purported common knowledge of the jury may be very much mistaken, an area where jurors' logic, drawn from their own experience, may lead to a wholly incorrect conclusion, an area where expert knowledge would enable the jurors to disregard their prior conclusions as being common myths rather than common knowledge."

The road of battered woman syndrome has been rocky, however, with a retreat in latter years by Walker into proclaiming the syndrome to be simply a subset of PTSD. Its scientific credentials have never been clearly established and the paradox lying between the asserted learned helplessness of the women who suffer it and the small number of those women who then erupt out of their helplessness into violence against their batterer has never been satisfactorily explained. The absence of a clear definition of the syndrome that incorporates this aspect into a few women's reactions has cast a pall over its forensic legitimacy to a point where in 1997 Faigman and Wright persuasively denounced the syndrome as "bad science", incapable of being properly tested, inappropriately medicalising women's experiences and perverting the concept of learned helplessness.[41] A key point which they and other commentators make is that a new stereotype has been created by the syndrome—of the "real battered woman" who exhibits symptomatology consistent with the syndrome. Once again, deviation from the descriptors used by the researchers, perhaps for cultural, ethnic or personality reasons, has potentially adverse repercussions for women. The difficulty with the syndrome is that it has been so woolly in its parameters, so little grounded in reality that it has few empirical boundaries to support it. Its scientific illegitimacy has been revealed and the fact that it has been employed in a diagnostic context when unequipped for the task has left it wanting in terms of capacity to assist courts to any meaningful degree. Its use-by date is fast being reached by evidence entrepreneurs and courts alike.

Premenstrual Syndrome. By the mid-1980s scholars such as Luckhaus were arguing that what was then known as "premenstrual syndrome" and is now classified under DSM-IV as "premenstrual dysphoric disorder" should be able to be applied as a defence in the criminal courts.[42] However, the feasibility of so using it came under increasing scrutiny during the 1990s and few serious attempts have been made to assert its relevance save occasionally in the sentencing context.[43]

Repressed and False Memory Syndromes. In the early 1990s the Freudian notion that memories of trauma can be repressed and later retrieved by a trigger, often occurring in the therapeutic milieu, prompted the forensic entity of "repressed memory syndrome".[44] Hot on its heals doubters coined the term "false memory syndrome" to describe the phenomenon whereby people come to believe, largely through clinically inappropriate interaction, that they have been abused when in fact all that they have done is to confabulate innocently in response to cues while in a highly suggestible state. Psychological and psychiatric associations in a number of countries have now offered warnings to practitioners about therapeutic processes with the potential to induce erroneous memories. Repressed memory cases flourished briefly in the courts in the mid-1990s, especially in the United States, but have now largely receded in face of a series of civil actions brought against mental health practitioners for inducing psychiatric injuries by the negligent implantation of false memories.

False Victimization Syndrome. The flow of proffered syndromes continued in the late 1990s. In Meloy's 1998 book, *The Psychology of Stalking*,[45] Mohandie, Hatcher and Raymond, for instance, endeavor to build upon the notions of "hysterical paralysis", Munchausen's Sydnrome and Munchausen's Syndrome by Proxy to construct "False Victimization Syndrome". It purports to describe various kinds of stalking perpetrators and merges into a kind of offender profiling. The categories of forensic syndromes, it seems, are not closed but ever more flexible.

COURTS' APPROACHES TO SYNDROMES

A number of different jurisdictions have had occasion to deal with the admissibility of the "Big Three Syndromes", and it is by reference to the tenor of those decisions that it is possible to garner a flavor of where syndrome law is headed.

New Zealand Courts' approaches to syndrome evidence

New Zealand appellate and superior courts have had occasion to rule on the admissibility of child sexual abuse accommodation evidence, repressed memory syndrome evidence and battered woman syndrome evidence. They have taken a relatively benign attitude toward battered woman syndrome evidence[46] but focussed particularly upon the symptomatology exhibited by the woman and noted its capacity to provide an explanation of why women might remain in abusive relationships.

It is in New Zealand law in relation to child sexual abuse accommodation syndrome evidence that most international interest lies. In 1989 the Court of Appeal in *R v Accused* expressed concern that it was not yet possible to establish properly that children subject to sexual abuse "demonstrate certain characteristics or act in peculiar ways which are so unmistakable that they can be said to be concomitants of sexual abuse; or that expert evidence in this field was able to indicate with a sufficient degree of compulsion, features which establish that the evidence of the complainant was indeed truthful."[47] The grievance highlighted was therefore the non-diagnostic quality of child sexual abuse accommodation syndrome, as well as its inability to provide a definitive tool for determining whether a complainant's evidence was accurate.

Shortly after the *R v Accused* decision, a legislative amendment applying to trials of sexual offences allowed expert evidence, amongst other things, on "the question whether any evidence given during the proceedings by any person (other than the expert witness) relating to the complainant's behavior is from the expert witness's professional experience or from his or her knowledge of the professional literature, consistent or inconsistent with the behavior of sexually abused children of the same age group as the complainant."[48]

Australian Courts' approaches to syndrome evidence

Australian appellate courts have had occasion to make rulings on the admissibility of battered woman syndrome, on child sexual abuse accommodation syndrome and on false memory syndrome. In 1991 the South Australian Court of Criminal Appeal followed the Canadian decision of *Lavallee* and permitted evidence of battered woman syndrome in relation to the defence of duress. A number of later decisions also admitted battered woman syndrome in relation to self-defence claims and provocation defences by women charged with murder. However, by 1995 a less sympathetic approach on the part of the courts (perhaps not coincidentally at the height of the controversies relating to repressed memory syndrome) can be discerned. In *DPP v Secretary*[49] the accused stood trial for murder and pleaded self-defence, alleging a long history of domestic abuse. The accused conceded that after an argument the deceased went to sleep. She walked outside to the utility grabbed a gun and a bullet, re-entered the house, walked past her children, aimed the gun and shot the deceased. She maintained that she feared for her life and was concerned about what he was going to do if she did not kill him while he slept. The Crown did not object to the accused leading expert evidence from a psychiatrist in relation to battered woman syndrome. Kearney J. commented, "Despite the various cases in which expert evidence of 'battered woman syndrome ' has been admitted, it is not clear to me that this novel scientific evidence can properly be said to be a recognized area of expertise for forensic purposes, as opposed to its use for therapeutic purposes. Those purposes are not the same. The need for caution in the admission of such evidence, referred to by King C.J. in *R v. Runjanjic* at p. 44 is very real."

Then in the first case on the subject which has reached the Australian High Court,[50] Kirby J. voiced a range of serious concerns about the syndrome being referred to in such terms, in relation to its scientific credentials and in relation to its definitional ambit. In particular, he queried whether it could also be applied to battered men, an issue that has many important ramifications to take the gendered approach to the syndrome that has been prominent. It is clear that the syndrome henceforth will be scrutinized with great care before evidence in respect of it is admitted to support claims of self-defence, provocation or duress.

A series of Australian cases has taken up where the New Zealand authorities on child sexual abuse accommodation syndrome left off and have ruled on its admissibility in terms of its relating to matters of credibility, being oath-helping and being non-diagnostic.[51] No cases have admitted the evidence, a number finding that to do so would be premature in light of the concerns articulated by the New Zealand Court of Appeal. In the most significant decision on the subject, though, that of the New South Wales Court of Criminal Appeal in *F v. The Queen*, the Court's concern was particularly focussed upon the failure of the syndrome to be diagnostic and on its potential to induce nothing more than confusion in the jurors' minds:

> Presumably the corollary of the proposition that some children delay in complaining of sexual abuse is that other children do not delay. Presumably the corollary of the proposition that some children, for good and sufficient reason, make complaints which are inconsistent, is that other children make complaints which are consistent. From one point of view, the evidence, if taken at face value, might be regarded by a jury as destroying the utility of seeking to test the evidence of a complainant by examining the circumstances and the content of complaints.[52]

The Court expressed its dissatisfaction about the parameters of what the expert's counterintuitive information was conveying to the jury. It queried whether the evidence was intended to suggest that inconsistency in stories told by a complainant can never reflect adversely on the reliability of a complainant, and, if not, in what circumstances such inconsistency would be a useful guide to a complainant's reliability. It also expressed reservations about the employment of the term "syndrome", noting that it "is one that is not always associated with scientifically rigorous analysis".[53] The Court commented that, "It is not easy to understand why one would need any such term to describe the phenomenon whereby victims of crime, whether of a sexual or any other nature, who feel helpless or powerless, delay in making complaints, or deciding to let the truth out piece by piece."[54] The Court expressed the view that if the term were to be used, then the label should be accompanied by some explanation of how cases where delay or inconsistency are to be attributed to the syndrome should be distinguished from those where delay or inconsistency indicate unreliability on the part of the complainant—"So far as appears from the evidence of Dr P., the 'syndrome' is non-diagnostic. It is not possible to tell when delay or inconsistency in complaint is a manifestation of the syndrome, as distinct from an indication of unreliability.".[55] Gleeson C.J. frustratedly exclaimed that the conclusion of the expert's evidence appeared to be that "some children conceal abuse when they feel threatened; some children conceal abuse when they feel safe; some children disclose abuse when they feel threatened; some children disclose abuse when they feel safe."[56] The Court raised the bar high against the admissibility of counter-intuitive evidence for the future, declining to say that such evidence would never be admissible, but holding that while evidence from an expert may be admitted to restore the credibility of a complainant, this is subject to the conditions that the subject matter be a fit subject for expert opinion, that the evidence be given in proper form and that it be given by a suitably qualified expert. The Court made the strong point that as yet the syndrome had not been shown to be "fit subject for expert opinion".[57]

However, the Australian approach has not been uniform. The Victorian Court of Appeal in *R v Bartlett*[58] held that a trial judge should have permitted expert opinion evidence about the risks and fallibilities of repressed memory syndrome evidence after a complainant had testified that she had made no early complaint of sexual assaults because she had only recently "remembered" them thanks to psychotherapeutic intervention. Winneke P., giving the Court's judgment held that, "the questions of whether there is such a phenomenon as 'suppressed memory' and, if so, whether it is likely to provide accurate recall; or whether recall of events suppressed for many years are likely to be affected or displaced by other similar events, are questions which must surely be outside the ken of the lay person."[59] The Court held that the evidence should have been admitted so that the jury could have been placed in a better position to evaluate the complainant's evidence. It may be that the fact that it was a defendant who was seeking to adduce the clarificatory and arguably counter-intuitive evidence played a role in the court's approach. On the other hand, it might be said that the opinions sought to be introduced were not so much counter-intuitive, which is what expert evidence about repressed memory syndrome would have been, as necessary to make understandable how it was that the complainant made the assertions that she did in her examination-in-chief. As of 1999, it can be said that there is no consistent approach in Australia toward the admissibility of counter-intuitive syndromal evidence.

English Courts' approaches to syndrome evidence

Relatively little case law has been generated at an appellate level in England in relation to syndrome evidence. The best known case is the decision of the Court of Appeal in *R v Thornton (No 2)*[60] where, on referral, the Court held that the fact that the appellant had been suffering from battered woman syndrome was a relevant characteristic which could have been taken into account by the jury had it been placed before them. The Chief Justice, Lord Taylor, found that the syndrome has relevance to the provocation defence in criminal proceedings in terms of providing an enhanced understanding as to why a woman might lose control as a result of what might otherwise be considered a minor incident and so as to understand better what impact sustained domestic violence may have had upon a woman's personality.

Canadian Courts' approaches to syndrome evidence

The Canadian courts have proved to be the most receptive courts in the western world to counterintuitive evidence, in particular to syndrome evidence. As already indicated, the decision of the Supreme Court in *R. v. Lavallee*[61] provided a highly influential authority for subsequent Australian decisions in relation to battered woman syndrome. However, the decision and subsequent cases which have applied it have not been without controversy. Feminists at first heralded the decision as an example of judicial sensitivity to gender difference[62] but concerns were raised by some that those living with beating husbands were being classified as suffering a pathology.[63] Shaffer in 1996,[64] having considered authorities subsequent to *Lavallee*, commented that "battered woman syndrome may be developing in ways that should concern feminists. The cases indicate that at least some of the players in the criminal justice system understand battered woman syndrome as deviance and expect battered women to exhibit a purely passive demeanor. In part this may explain why, in cases in which women killed their violent partners, *Lavallee* does not yet appear to have widened the doctrine of self-defence to the degree that feminists had hoped."

In respect of child sexual abuse accommodation syndrome, the Canadian approach has similarly been welcoming to expert evidence, the Supreme Court endorsing Summit's 1983 opinions in the decision of La Forest J. in *KM v HM*[65] and holding that expert testimony about child development and the characteristics of sexually abused children is admissible in *DR, HR and DW v The Queen*.[66]

United States Courts' approaches to syndrome evidence

From 1982, some 20 United States state Supreme Courts have admitted evidence of rape trauma syndrome from a variety of professionals.[67] The decision of the California Supreme Court in *People v. Bledsoe*[68] has been established as the dominant justification for evidentiary admission—to disabuse jurors of widely held misconceptions about rape and rape victims. However, the extent and nature of these myths has not been clearly enunciated. Moreover, the admission of the evidence has opened some unwelcome doors, including to weakening of the rape shield, to enable explanations other than the rape to account for current symptomatology—including prior adverse sexual encounters.[69] It can also open up possibilities for court orders that the victim be psychiatrically examined by an expert for the defence and for access to counseling records unless this is sufficiently clearly precluded by statute.[70] In addition, expert evidence as to the fact that a complainant does not satisfy the criteria for the syndrome has been permitted to be adduced by the defence.[71]

In respect of battered woman syndrome, the approach of United States courts has similarly been diverse. In general, latitude in terms of admissibility has been extended in respect of counterintuitive information about myths relating to domestic violence and about the principles of learned helplessness, as adopted by witnesses testifying on the Walker model. In general, the trend has been toward admissibility.[72] However, Ewing has pointed out that battered woman syndrome evidence is frequently refused admission—for a number of reasons, varying from the expertise of the proffered witness, to its being too close to answering the ultimate issue, relating in substance to the credibility of the complainant, or being more prejudicial than probative. In his analysis published in 1990 of 85 cases where a battered woman claimed self-defence, expert evidence was only admitted in 26 of the 45 cases in which it was offered.[73]

The repercussions of the syndrome phenomenon

The admission of syndrome evidence has been promoted by representatives of the women's movement and others as a goal.[74] Its exclusion has been bemoaned as a defeat for feminists and an insightless maintenance of the status quo for a masculocentric legal system.[75]

At its best, rape trauma syndrome evidence educates judges and juries about the diversity of perhaps surprising responses of women to having been sexually assaulted and enables them to view the complainant's post-assault conduct in a broader and more sensitive socio-cultural context. At its worst, though, the syndrome substitutes one set of rape myths for another, creating an expectation of post-rape pathology on the part of the woman, and attempting ex post facto reasoning—because the women subsequently behaved in a certain way after the alleged rape, it is more likely than not that she was raped, unless it can be shown that there were other explanations for her behavior, such as a prior rape, mental instability or a history of antagonism toward the defendant. The syndrome proceeds from an assumption of complainants' lack of credibility and ironically in an attempt to redress it creates new, and inaccurate stereotypes of the credible complainant—the woman who behaves consistently with the new Burgess and Holmstrom categories of rape victim, and ideally who seeks professional help for the pathology that has been engendered by the sexual assault. As Stefan accurately points out, "Women who are not inclined to seek professional help or have no access to it because of economic or other pressures still have no credibility."[76] Not only this, but if they cannot procure or have procured for them an expert of whatever ilk to testify that there is a syndrome into whose parameters they fit, they risk again being discarded as a complainant without credibility.

Construction of counter-intuitive frameworks

Where the syndromes have fallen down most problematically is in their construction of false expectations, rendered into disease-sounding language in order to secure their admissibility. They have created new assumptions and expectations in the process of trying to puncture myths and misconceptions. Worst of all, their counterintuitive element, which is their best quality, has been misused in a number of countries, with connivance from evidence entrepreneurs, to construct diagnoses of victims from whose symptomatology victims depart at their peril.

The tragic truth is that each of the syndromes has at its core an important insight about the diversity of response to experience and trauma. Women continue to associate with their assailants for a plethora of social, economic, relational and other reasons. They continue to be sexually active after being raped again for many reasons. They do not complain or report for good and multiple causes—including social pressures, ongoing fears, guilt, confusion, denial, threats from the assailant, and dread of the medical, prosecutorial and legal processes, to name just a few.

Women remain in abusive relationships for a host of reasons other than suffering some unclear condition of "learned helplessness". It can be because they love their assailant, and believe him when he says it will never happen again; because they have learned from experience to fear the consequences for themselves and their children of unsuccessful attempts to leave; because they feel unequal to the process of leaving and starting again; because of economic, familial and cultural processes, again to name just a few. The fact that they have remained does not connote acceptance of what has happened. Nor does it mean that they are not and have not for some time been living in mortal danger. It just reflects the limited options that they have perceived themselves as having. They sometimes initiate the proximate trigger to the male's violence because they cannot bear the tension any longer, because they need to feel some control over the otherwise uncontrollable, because in doing so they may defuse what might be a worse explosion. Women in abusive relationships for a long time learn the intimate patterns in the escalation of risk. They learn better than those not privy to their relationship what is likely to instigate an explosion, when things are worse than ever before, when a threat made some time previously is likely to be carried out. They know this because of the subtle dynamics that exist within their dyad whose characteristics others are unlikely to appreciate unless the woman is able to educate them to the dysfunctional relationship's subtleties.

There is a substantial number of reasons why children fail to make early complaints or reports of sexual and physical assaults, few of them have anything to do with pathology. So deviant may their pattern of interacting with their abuser be that they may have no understanding that sexual contact with adults is other than normal. More likely is that they have long been subject to the "guilty secret" between the perpetrator and themselves and by manipulation lack the objectivity and the confidence to tell anyone. They may well believe what they have been told—that no-one will believe them and that they and/or the perpetrator will get into trouble for disclosing. They may have tried previously to tell a close family member, such as their mother, and not been believed—this is hardly such as to engender confidence that strangers will accept as true what they are saying and put a stop to it happening any more. Although, the sexual abuse may have been of longstanding, nonetheless it is only part of their life and they will have had to continue to interact with peers, teachers, family members and so on. They will have adapted to their reality. The result is that there may have been a lengthy delay in their complaining or reporting and that their doing so may only have been instigated by an incident that gave them the resolve to tell or because they have found a person in whom they have confidence and feel will believe them. Again, this has nothing to do with the truthfulness of their disclosure. In addition, the dynamics of the abuse, the time over which it has occurred, the identity of the perpetrator and other factors will all impact upon the likely quality of the disclosure and the capacity of the child to be precise about individual incidents. Finally, there will generally be many pressures upon the child to abandon disclosing and to retract—from perceptions, or the reality, of disbelief by those to whom disclosure is made, from pressures from the perpetrator or family members, from the sheer difficulty of the process for a young person. Again, halting, erratic, self-contradictory or imprecise disclosures do not necessarily betoken lack of truthfulness on the part of the child complainant.

Courts need such counter-intuitive information, lest they reason wrongly from the behavior of the victim of sexual or physical abuse. They need to appreciate informedly the diversity of victim behavioral profiles post-assault. Unfortunately, for the most part syndrome evidence has failed in accomplishing this pedagogical end and has in some ways exacerbated the position of victims by creating more and different attributions of "the real victim" than existed previously. It has stereotyped and medicalized women and children subject to abuse in the home, creating amongst lawyers expectations of diagnostic pathologies in victims that frequently are not met or are not satisfied with adequate precision.

Three options appear to exist to redress the informational deficit of triers of fact, be they judges or jurors. The first is to confine expert evidence previously described as syndrome evidence to truly counterintuitive provision of information about the diversity of experience in situations of physical and sexual abuse. This would promote the right of affected parties to remove sources of potential error from the fact-finding processes of judges and jurors. The second is that by law judges be mandated to direct jurors (and, where the trials are judge-alone, themselves) of inferences that they should not necessarily make—by reason of delays in reporting and complaining, staying at the site of domestic violence and so on. While this sounds somewhat negative, it has the potential to accomplish the original apparent objective of counterintuitive evidence, namely to factor out potential sources of error, generated by misunderstanding and erroneous assumptions. The judicial direction solution mooted 12 years ago by Walker and Monahan in an article entitled "Social Frameworks: A New Use of Social Science in Law",[77] was that judicial charges encapsulate the counterintuitive information sought to be communicated to juries. With the increasing problems being confronted by the phenomenon of syndrome evidence, their suggestion deserves further analysis. Its negative aspects are that it may be too little, too late, being merely a judge's direction coming at the end of the evidence. It would therefore be subject to the limitations on the extent to which such directions are taken into account by juries. We know from social science research that first impressions and settled modes of analysis are not easily displaced and that it is difficult to evaluate whether judicial instructions of such a subtle and complex variety would effectively disabuse jurors of stereotypes, assumptions and modes of analysis which might have become the norm in the course of a multi-day or multi-week trial.

The third option is that routinely expert witnesses be called, not to give evidence about the circumstances of the case, but simply to provide myth-dispelling evidence pertinent to the issues of the case. Ideally, they would be court-appointed experts, this freeing them from the temptation to orient their testimony toward one side or the other in the conflict. Again, there is a timing difficulty about such evidence. If given at the start of the trial, it may not deal with the actual issues as they emerge in the course of evidence being adduced. It might also receive inappropriate prominence. If given at the end of the trial, it may once again be infelicitously late, but at least it would be prior to the judge's summing up and instructions on matters of law to jurors. This means that it could receive further support from the judge in his or her address to the jury.

Useful research might well be undertaken on the efficacy of each of these modes of reducing the difficulties that exist by reason of the potential for wrong assumptions to be made by triers of fact without the provision of appropriate counterintuitive information. In respect of each, the information needed by courts is as to what are the misperceptions that may be harbored by lay people, how widespread such sources of misunderstanding are, what the real state of knowledge is in respect of the area and whether the provision of such counterintuitive information is likely to dispel the myth effectively. These are not easy questions. But posing them, wrestling with answering them and confronting the difficulties that they pose may well prove to be a more constructive exercise than pursuing any further the demonstrably flawed syndrome approach.

Notes

1. Also known as "Late Luteal Phase Dysphoric Disorder".
2. See in particular A. Dershowitz, "The PMS Defense Feminist Setback" in A Dershowitz, *The Abuse Excuse*, Little, Brown & Co, New York, 1994.
3. A.W. Burgess and L. L. Holmstrom, "Rape Trauma Syndrome" (1974) 131 *American Journal of Psychiatry* 981.
4. R. Delgado, "Religious Totalism: Gentle and Ungentle Persuasion under the First Amendment" (1977) 51 *Southern California Law Review* 1.
5. L. E. Walker, *The Battered Woman*, Harper & Row, New York, 1979; LE Walker, *Battered Woman Syndrome*, Springer, New York, 1984.
6. R. C. Summit, "The Child Sexual Abuse Accommodations Syndrome" (1983) 7 *Child Abuse and Neglect* 177.
7. R. C. Summit, "Abuse of the Child Sexual Abuse Accommodation Syndrome" (1992) 1(4) *Journal of Child Sexual Abuse* 153.
8. See E. Turk, "Abuses and Syndromes: Excuses or Justifications?" (1997) 18 Whittier Law Review 401; T. Y. Foster, "From Fear to Black Rage" (1997) 38 William and Mary Law Review 1851; R. P. Mosteller, "Syndromes and Politics and in Criminal Trials and Evidence Law (1996) 46 *Duke Law Review* 461.
9. For a listing, see I. Freckelton, "Syndrome Evidence" in I Freckelton and H Selby (ed), *The Law of Expert Evidence*, LBC Information Services, Sydney, 1999; K. Mohandie, C. Hatcher and D. Raymond, "False Victimization Syndromes in Stalking" in J. R. Meloy (ed), *The Psychology of Stalking*, Academic Press, San Diego, 1998.
10. See S. A. Dobbin and S. I. Gatowski, "The Social Production of Rape Trauma Syndrome as Science and as Evidence" in M. Freeman and H. Reece, *Science in Court*, Ashgate, Dartmouth, 1998.
11. By contrast the earlier findings of Sutherland and Scherl had been a distillation of three phases of response to rape: "acute", "outward adjustment" and "integration and resolution": S Sutherland and D. Scherl, "Patterns of Response Among Victims of Rape" (1970) 40 American Journal of Orthopsychiatry 503.
12. See e.g. J. V. Becker et al, "The Effects of Sexual Assault on Rape and Attempted Rape Victims" (1982) 7 *Victimology* 106 at 112.
13. Casey and Craven comment that, although studies on the effect of sexual assault on males are sparse, "anecdotal reports suggest that coerced sexual intercourse is as harmful to men as it is to women": P. Casey and C. Craven, *Psychiatry and the Law*, Oak Tree Press, Dublin, 1999 at p. 123.
14. *Henson v State*, 535 NE 2d 1189 (Ind 1989).

15. R. Delgado, "Religious Totalism: Gentle and Ungentle Persuasion under the First Amendment" (1977) 51 *California Law Review* 1 at 70–71. See also R. Delgado, "Religious Totalism as Slavery" (1979) 9 *New York University Review of Law and Social Change* 51; R. Delgado, "Cults and Conversion: The Case for Informed Consent" (1982) 16 *Georgia Law Review* 533; R. Delgado, "When Religious Exercise is not Free: Deprogramming and the Constitutional Status of Coercively Induced Belief" (1984) 37 *Vanderbilt Law Review* 1072.
16. For an analysis of its forensic shortcomings, see I Freckelton, "Cults, Coercion and Psychological Consequences" (1998) 5(1) *Psychiatry, Psychology and the Law* 1.
17. R. C. Summit, "The Child Sexual Abuse Accommodation Syndrome" (1983) 7 *Child Abuse and Neglect* 177.
18. See I. Freckelton, "Child Sexual Abuse Accommodation Evidence: the Travails of Counter-intuitive Evidence in Australia and New Zealand (1997) 15 *Behavioral Sciences and the Law* 245.
19. R. C. Summit, "The Rehabilitation of the Child Sexual Abuse Accommodation Syndrome" (1992) 1(4) *Journal of Child Sexual Abuse* 147; R. C. Summit, "Abuse of the Child Sexual Abuse Accommodation Syndrome" (1992 1(4) *Journal of Child Sexual Abuse* 153.
20. Summit, op cit. at 155.
21. Summit, op cit. at 157.
22. L. E. Walker, *The Battered Woman Syndrome*, Springer, New York, 1984; see also L.E. Walker, *The Battered Woman*, Harper and Row, New York, 1979.
23. See, for example, L. E. Walker, "Post-Traumatic Stress Disorder in Women: Diagnosis and Treatment of Battered Woman Syndrome" (1991) 28(1) *Psychotherapy* 21; L. E. Walker, "Understanding Battered Woman Syndrome" (1995) 31(2) *Trial* 30.
24. J. Stubbs and J. Tolmie, "Race, Gender and the Battered Woman Syndrome: An Australian Case Study" (1995) 8 *Canadian Journal of Women and the Law* 122; E. A. Sheehy, J. Stubbs and Tolmie, "Defending Battered Women on Trial: The Battered Woman Syndrome and its Limitations" (1992) 16 *Criminal Law Journal* 369; J Stubbs "Battered Woman Syndrome: An Advance for Women or Further Evidence of the Legal System's Inability to Comprehend Women's Experience" (1991) 3(2) *Contemporary Issues in Criminal Justice* 267; J. Stubbs, "The (Un)reasonable Battered Woman" (1992) 3(3) *Contemporary Issues in Criminal Justice* 359; J. Walus-Wigle and J. R. Meloy (1988), "Battered Woman Syndrome as a Criminal Defense" *Journal of Psychiatry and Law* 389; I Freckelton, "When Plight Makes Right: the Forensic Abuse Syndrome" (1994) 18 *Criminal Law Journal* 29; F. Goodyear-Smith, "Re Battered Woman's Syndrome" [1998] *New Zealand Law Journal* 39; McDonald, "Battered Woman Syndrome" (1997) *New Zealand Law Journal* 436.
25. J. A. Scutt, *Women and the Law*, Law Book Co, Sydney, 1990; J. A. Scutt, "No Syndrome': the Reality for Battered Women" (1992) *Impact* 18.
26. See also Stefan, op cit.
27. M. E. P. Seligman, *Helplessness: On Depression, Development and Death*, Freeman, San Francisco, 1975.
28. See A. Coughlin, "Excusing Women" (1994) 82 *California Law Review* 1.
29. C. Petersen, S. F. Maier and M. E. P. Seligman, *Learned Helplessness: A Theory for the Age of Personal Control*, Oxford University Press, New York, 1993.
30. Walker 1984, p. 170, Table 11.
31. Walker 1984, Table 17, p. 179.
32. (1998) 159 ALR 170; [1998] HCA 75.
33. See e.g. D. Dutton and S. Painter, "The Battered Woman Syndrome: Effects of Severity and Intermittency on Abuse" (1994) 12 *Behavioral Sciences and the Law* 215.
34. D. Faigman, "The Battered Woman Syndrome and Self-Defence: A Legal and Empirical Dissent" (1986) 72 *Virginia Law Review* 67; D. Faigman and A. Wright, "The Battered Woman Syndrome in the Age of Science" (1997) 39 *Arizona Law Review* 67.
35. M. McMahon, "Battered Woman Syndrome" (1999) 6(1) *Psychiatry, Psychology and Law* 23; Faigman 1986, op cit.

36. *Osland v R* (1998) 159 ALR 170 at 213–4; [1998] HCA 75 at para 161; see also S. Beri, "Justice for Women Who Kill: A New Way?" (1997) 8 *Australian Feminist Law Journal* 113.
37. See I. Freckelton and H. Selby, *The Law of Expert Evidence*, LBC Information Services, Sydney, 1999.
38. (1990) 55 CCC (3d) 97 at 112.
39. Ibid at 113.
40. 478 A 2d 364 at 378 (1984) .
41. D. Faigman and A. Wright, "The Battered Woman Syndrome in the Age of Science" (1997) 39 *Arizona Law Review* 67 at 105–107.
42. L. Luckhaus, "A Plea for PMT in the Criminal Law" in S. Edwards (ed), *Gender, Sex and the Law*, Croom-Helm, Oxford, 1985; see also P. Easteal, *Women and Crime: Premenstrual Issues*, No. 31, Trends and Issues, Australian Institute of Criminology, Canberra, 1991.
43. See the useful analyses by McSherry: B. McSherry, "The Return of the Raging Hormones Theory: Premenstrual Syndrome, Postpartum Disorders and Criminal Responsibility" (1993) 15(3) *Sydney Law Review* 292; B. McSherry, "Premenstrual Syndrome and Criminal Responsibility" (1994) 1(2) *Psychiatry, Psychology and the Law* 139.
44. For an analysis of the forensic construct, see I. Freckelton, "Repressed Memory Syndrome: Counterintuitive or Counterproductive?" (1996) 20(1) *Criminal Law Journal* 7.
45. K. Mohandie, C. Hatcher and D. Raymond, "False Victimization Syndromes in Stalking" in J. R. Meloy (ed), *The Psychology of Stalking*, Academic Press, San Diego, 1998.
46. See, e.g., *R v Jai Fong Zhou*, unreported, High Court Auckland, 8 October 1993; *R v Wang* [1990] 2 NZLR 529 and *Ruka v Department of Social Welfare* (1996) 14 CRNZ 196.
47. *R v Accused* [1989] 1 NZLR 714, applying *R v B* [1987] 1 NZLR 362 at 368: "As child psychology grows as a science it may be possible for experts int hat field to demonstrate as matters of expert observation that persons subjected to sexual abuse demonstrate certain characteristics or act in peculiar ways which are so clear and unmistakable that they can be said to be the concomitants of sexual abuse. When that is so the courts may admit evidence as evidence of direct observation."
48. Evidence Act 1908 (NZ), s23G.
49. Unreported, Supreme Court of the Northern Territory, 1 December 1995, at p. 50.
50. *R v Osland* (1998) 73 ALJR 173; 159 ALR 170.
51. See *Ingles v The Queen*, unreported Tasmanian Court of Criminal Appeal, 4 May 1993; *R v C* (1993) 60 SASR 467; 70 A Crim R 378; *J v The Queen* (1994) 75 A Crim R 522 and *F v The Queen* (1995) 83 A Crim R 502.
52. A Crim R at 507.
53. Ibid at 508.
54. Ibid at 508.
55. Ibid at 508.
56. Ibid at 508.
57. Ibid at 509.
58. [1996] 2 VR 687.
59. Ibid, at 695.
60. [1996] 2 All ER 1023.
61. (1990) 55 CCC (3d) 97.
62. D. Martinson et al, "A Forum on Lavallee v R: Women and Self-Defence" (1991) 25 *UNCL Rev* 23; C. Boyle, "The Battered Wife Syndrome and Self-Defence" (1990) 9 *Can J Fam L* 171.
63. M. Shaffer, R v Lavallee. A Review Essay" (1990) 22 *Ottawa L Rev* 607; I Grant, "The 'Syndromization' of Women's Experience" (1991) 25 *UBC L Rev* 51.
64. M. Shaffer, "The Battered Woman Syndrome Revisited: Some Complicating Thoughts Five Years After R v Lavallee" (19997) 47 *University of Toronto Law Journal* 1 at 33.
65. (1992) 96 DLR (4th) 291.
66. (1996) 107 CCC (3d) 289.
67. Varying from psychologists (*see e.g. People v Reid*, 475 NYS 2d 741 at 742 (Sup Ct 1984); *State v Teeter*, 355 SE 2d 804 at 807 (NC Ct App 1987); *People v Taylor*, 536 NYS 2d 825 at 828 (App Div 1988); *People v Housley*, 8 Cal Rptr 2d 431 at 434 (Ct App 1992); *Rivera v State*, 840

P 2d 933 at 938 (Wyo 1992); to psychiatrists (see e.g. *State v Huey*, 699 P 2d 1290 at 1293–4 (Ariz 1995); *People v Randt, 530 NYS 2d 266 at 268 (App Div 1988)*; to psychiatric nurses (*State v Liddell*, 685 P 2d 918 at 922 (Mont 1984); to social workers (*Simmons v State*, 504 NE 2d 575 at 578 (Ind 1987); *State v Roles*, 832 P 2d 311 at 313–4 (Idaho Ct App 1992; cp *State v Goodwin*, 357 SE 2d 639 at 641 (NC 1987), counsellors (see e.g. *State v Radjenovich*, 674 P 2d 333 at 335 (Ariz Ct of App 1983); *State v Bubar*, 505 A 2d 1197 at 1200 (Vt 1985); *State v MCCoy*, 366 SE 2d 731 at 733 (W Va 1988); workers at sexual assault centres (see e.g. *People v Whitehead*, 531 NYS 2d 48 at 49; *State v Robinson*, 431 NW 2d 165 at 171 (Wis 1988); *People v Douglas*, 538 NE 2d 1335 at 1343 (Ill App Ct, 1989); *People v DeSantis, 456 NW 2d 600 at 609 (Wis 1990); People v Davis*, 585 NE 2d 214 at 217–8 (Ill App Ct 1992), and even police officers (see e.g. *Scadden v State*, 732 P 2d 1036 at 1044 (Wyo 1987); *State v Roles*, 832 P 2d 311 at 314 (Idaho Ct App 1992).
68. 681 P 2d 291 (Val 1984).
69. P. Frazier and E. Borgida, "Rape Trauma Syndrome Evidence in Court" (1985) 40 *American Psychologist* 984; T. M. Massaro, "Experts, Psychology, Credibility and Rape" (1985) 69 *Minnesota Law Review* 395 at 441.
70. See *In re Pittsburgh Action Against Rape*, 428 A 2d 126 (Pa 1981).
71. See e.g. *Henson v State*, 535 NE 2d 1189 (Ind 1989).
72. R. Brown, "Limitations on Expert Testimony on the Battered Woman Syndrome in Homicide Cases: the Reality of the Ultimate Issue Rule" (1990) 32 *Arizona Law Review* 665; K. L. Duncan, "Lies, Damned Lies and Statistics? Psychological Syndrome Evidence in the Courtroom After Daubert" (1996) 71 *Indiana Law Review* 753; Faigman and Wright, 1997, op cit.
73. C. P. Ewing, "Psychological Self-Defense: A Proposed Justification for Women Who Kill" (1990) 14 *Law and Human Behavior* 579.
74. See, for example, P Easteal, "Battered Woman Syndrome:Misunderstood?" (1992) 3(3) *Current Issues in Criminal Justice 356*; M. Torrey, "When Will We Be Believed? Rape Myths and the Idea of a Fair Trial in Rape Prosecutions" (1991) 24 *University of California Davis Law Review* 1013 at 1014, 1062; P. Wilk, "Expert Testimony on Rape Trauma Syndrome: Admissibility and Effective Use in Criminal Rape Prosecution" (1984) 33 *American University Law Review 417, at 449.*
75. See K. Kinports, "Evidence Engendered" (1991) *University of Illinois Law Review* 414 at 444.
76. Op cit. at 1333.
77. (1987) 73 *Virginia Law Review 559.*

Chapter 12

CONDITIONAL RELEASE ATTITUDES: LAYPERSONS' PERCEPTIONS OF THE PURPOSES, EFFECTIVENESS, AND ACCEPTABILITY OF EARLY RELEASE BY OFFENSE TYPE[1]

Joti Samra and Ronald Roesch

Public opinion toward the legal system is important to study for several reasons. It has been demonstrated that policy-makers have enacted particular laws with public opinion being the driving force (Gottfredson & Taylor, 1984). Furthermore, public opinion on legal issues is taken into account by judges when rendering decisions (Gibson, 1980). Discontent with the criminal justice system (e.g., courts) and awarded sentences may result in undesirable effects such as public withdrawal from participation in the criminal justice system, and reluctance on the part of the public to report crimes and appear as witnesses (Roberts & Edwards, 1989). A consistent finding in the literature has been the public's perception of the criminal justice system, and sentencing in particular, as being too lenient (Blumstein & Cohen, 1980; Brillon, 1988; Broadhurst & Indermaur, 1982; Doob & Roberts, 1988; Roberts, 1992; Skovron, Scott, & Cullen, 1988; Sprott, 1996). Although overall research on legal attitudes has been growing, the literature on laypersons' attitudes toward Conditional Release (CR[2]) specifically is limited. This neglect in the literature is problematic as, unlike more restrictive forms of corrections (such as incarceration), public support is inherently critical to the implementation, operation, and success of community correctional procedures such as CR (Senese, 1992; Sigler & Lamb, 1995). Public opinion may also be instrumental in CR-related social policy reforms (e.g., regarding which offenders should receive parole, and when; Roberts, 1988).

The research that does exist suggests that, overall, public opinion toward CR is not favorable. For example, Brillon, Louis-Guérin, and Lamarche (1984) found that only 8% of their sample favored parole release for "every case." Furthermore, a nationwide poll reported that 62% of those surveyed felt that the present parole system is too lenient (*Ottawa Citizen*, as cited in Roberts, 1988). However, there is indication that the majority of the public (i.e., 63%) favor the theoretical principles of early release, but are opposed to the operation of the current system

(Zamble & Kalm, 1990). For example, many favor the conditional abolition of parole (e.g., not to be granted to certain types of offenders), or the extension of the time lapse prior to parole eligibility (i.e., Roberts, 1988 reported that, on average, the public felt offenders should serve 74% of their sentence prior to parole eligibility).

Limitations in existing research

In addition to there being relatively little literature on the assessment of CR attitudes, several limitations plague the research that does exist. The primary limitations that will be highlighted relate to: (a) ambiguity regarding the types of offenders and types of release that CR attitudes are directed toward; (b) laypersons' inaccurate estimations of release and recidivism rates of offenders on CR; and, (c) laypersons' inaccurate knowledge of CR definitions.

With respect to the first limitation, the existing indices of attitudes have, for the most part, consisted of an insufficient number of questions (i.e., often only one or several questions are posed). Consequently, there exists considerable ambiguity in terms of the types of offenders (e.g., by offense type) and types of release (e.g., Day or Full Parole) that respondents' attitudes are directed toward. For example, although 65% of Roberts' (1988) sample indicated that only certain types of offenders should be eligible for Full Parole, the reasons for this are unclear. Specifically, there is ambiguity regarding whether these figures represent a desire to deter certain types of offenders from future crime, or whether they reflect perceptions that serving only one-third of the sentence prior to parole eligibility is an inadequate punishment for the type of crime committed. Also, by virtue of there being only a limited number of questions that are asked, the questions that are utilized tend to be quite broad and non-specific. However, global questions are not the best indicators of attitudes, and more specific questions have been found to reveal more complex, liberal, flexible, and less punitive legal attitudes on the part of the public (Applegate, Cullen, Link, Richards, & Lanza-Kaduce, 1996; Diamond & Stalans, 1989; McCorkle, 1993; Skovron et al., 1988; Thomson & Ragona, 1987; Zamble & Kalm, 1990), leading researchers to suggest that more detailed questions be asked (Keil & Vito, 1991).

The second limitation relates to inaccurate perceptions of the CR system. Despite only minor fluctuations in actual statistics, the public overestimates the proportion of offenders who are released on CR, and incorrectly perceives parole boards as having become more lenient over time (Roberts, 1988). The public also overestimates the rates, nature, and severity of crimes committed (e.g., perceiving there to be more violent crimes; Brillon et al., 1984; Diamond & Stalans, 1989; Graber, 1980), and believes that a higher proportion of offenders recidivate on CR than is actually the case (Roberts, 1988). This may be partially attributable to findings that the public's knowledge of crime and sentencing is often derived from selective and non-representative sources such as the media, family, and friends (Broadhurst & Indermaur, 1982; Diamond & Stalans, 1989).

Regarding the third limitation, Roberts (1988) found that two-thirds of his sample incorrectly identified the definition of Full Parole on a multiple-choice question with four responses (with a 25% probability of being correct by chance alone). The validity of the results are questionable in cases wherein respondents are unclear as to the definition of the very thing on which their attitudes are being assessed.

Sentencing purposes

It has been suggested that the public may view sentences as too lenient because they espouse a different purpose of sentencing as compared to key players in the legal system, such as judges (Roberts & Edwards, 1989). It may be that the public's perceptions of the purpose(s) of CR may account for negative attitudes toward this aspect of the sentencing process. The primary sentencing purposes that have been highlighted in the literature are: specific deterrence (i.e., deterring that offender from committing future crimes); general deterrence (i.e., deterring others from committing future crimes); incapacitation (i.e., physically preventing the offender from engaging in crime through supervision); rehabilitation (i.e., through training, educating, or counseling, so that the offender becomes a law-abiding citizen); and, retribution (i.e., punishing the offender; see generally Roberts & Edwards, 1989). To date, public perceptions of the purposes of Conditional Release have not been empirically examined.

Present study

The purpose of this study was to examine the following: (a) perceptions of the purposes/goals (i.e., general deterrence, specific deterrence, incapacitation, rehabilitation, or punishment) of various types of CR; (b) perceptions of the effectiveness of various types of CR (i.e., Day Parole, Full Parole and Statutory Release); (c) reasons for being opposed to and in favor of CR; (d) extent of support for various types of CR across offense categories (i.e., murder, sexual assault/abuse, physical assault, robbery, break and enter/theft, drug offenses, and traffic offenses); and, (e) opinions on the acceptable proportion of their sentence that offenders should serve prior to release eligibility, by offense type. To address limitations in the existing research, respondents were provided with definitions of the various forms of Conditional Release. Differences between participants who were provided with Correctional Service of Canada (CSC, 1995) statistics on the number, percentage, and types of CR violations and participants who were not provided with this information were examined, as were differences according to participants' personal experiences with crime.

METHOD

Respondents

Respondents were 206 undergraduate students enrolled in a mid-sized Canadian university. The control and experimental groups did not differ in terms of important demographic characteristics ($ps > .05$); hence, the entire sample is described collectively.

Respondents' mean age was 20.3 years ($SD = 4.5$). The sex distribution was skewed, with 141 of the participants being female (68.4%), and 65 male (31.6%). Fifty percent[3] of the participants identified themselves as Caucasian, 27% as Asian, and 14% as East Indian. Most participants (90%) were single. Approximately one-third (36%) reported not belonging to any religious group; 18% identified themselves as Catholic, 18% as Christian, 10% as Sikh, and 5% as Buddhist. Seventy-nine percent of respondents reported attending religious activities *never, occasionally*, or only *on special holidays*. Almost half (45%) of the respondents did not affiliate themselves with any political party, 30% affiliated themselves with the Liberal party, 13% with NDP, 7% with Reform, and 3% with the Conservative party. Most respondents (96%) reported being moderately, or less than moderately active in politics.

Questions on personal experiences with crime revealed that almost half (46%) had themselves been a direct victim of a crime in the past. Three-quarters of the respondents (71%) reported knowing someone who had been a victim of a crime, and one-third (37%) reported having been a direct witness of a crime. Forty-six respondents (22%) reported personally knowing someone who had been Conditionally Released in the past; of these respondents, 63% reported that, to the best of their knowledge, that individual had been successful in meeting his or her conditions of release. Only 9% of respondents reported that they, or someone close to them, was or had been a criminal justice employee. Finally, 82% indicated being only moderately, or less than moderately, familiar with the workings of the Canadian criminal justice system.

Questionnaire and procedure

Participants were presented with a questionnaire assessing (a) perceptions of the purposes (i.e., specific deterrence, general deterrence, incapacitation, rehabilitation, and retribution) and effectiveness of various types of CR, (b) reasons for being opposed to and/or in favor of CR (assessed via an open-ended question), (c) degree of support for various types of CR, across offense categories, and (d) opinions on the length of time that should be served prior to release eligibility, by offense type.

To improve upon limitations with existing research, all participants were provided with an information sheet that presented an overview of the CR system, as well as definitions of relevant CR terms (i.e., Escorted and Unescorted Temporary Absences, Day Parole, Full Parole, and Statutory Release). Participants in the experimental group were also provided with CSC (1995) statistics (i.e., both percentages and absolute numbers) on the following: (a) number of offenders incarcerated on any given day; (b) of these offenders, the percentage who have not previously served federal terms; (c) annual costs associated with incarcerating/supervising offenders; (d) number of offenders on CR on any given day; (e) proportion of offenders who are granted various forms of CR; (f) proportion of offenders who violate conditions of CR; and, (g) the types of offenses committed by offenders on CR.

Questionnaires were randomly distributed to students. Two-thirds of the students participated for course credit; the remaining volunteered for inclusion in the study after being approached for participation in one of their classes.

RESULTS

Purposes and effectiveness of CR

Respondents were asked (via an open-ended question) about their perceptions of the most important purpose of having a CR system. An overwhelming majority of respondents (88%) stated that rehabilitation/reintegration was the most important purpose of CR. The remaining respondents cited specific deterrence (5%), cost-effectiveness (3%), incapacitation (3%), and reduction of overcrowding (1%) as being the most important purposes of CR.

Perceptions of the effectiveness of the various types of CR were assessed via a 5-point Likert scale, with respondents being asked how effective they

Table 1: Perceptions of the Effectiveness of Types of CR and Incarceration

	Day Parole	Full Parole	Statutory Release	Incarceration (Jail)
Specific Deterrence	25%	17%	18%	54%
General Deterrence	14%	9%	11%	63%
Incapacitation	48%	23%	22%	75%
Rehabilitation	69%	47%	38%	29%
Punishment	16%	11%	11%	75%

Note. Respondents were asked *To what extent do you think Day Parole/Full Parole/Statutory Release/Jail is effective in achieving the following goals?*. Perceptions of effectiveness were rated on a 5-point Likert response scale (i.e., *extremely ineffective, ineffective, neither effective nor ineffective, effective*, and *extremely effective*). Reported percentages reflect responses of either *effective* or *extremely effective*.

thought Day Parole, Full Parole, and Statutory Release were with respect to the following: specific deterrence; general deterrence; incapacitation; rehabilitation; and, punishment. In order to have a baseline to compare responses against, respondents were also asked to report their perceptions of the effectiveness of incarceration (so that perceptions of the effectiveness/ ineffectiveness of CR would not be confounded with perceptions of the effectiveness/ineffectiveness of the criminal justice system as a whole). Almost two-thirds (69%) felt that Day Parole is effective in achieving the goal of rehabilitation, whereas only one-third (29%) felt that incarceration is effective in meeting this goal (see Table 1). The perceptions of the effectiveness of CR with respect to rehabilitation were lower for both Full Parole (47%) and Statutory Release (38%).

A series of t-tests[4] revealed that perceptions of the effectiveness of the various purposes of CR did not differ according to the condition to which the respondent was assigned. There were also no differences according to whether the respondent reported ever being a direct victim of crime, knowing a victim of a crime, or having witnessed a crime. The one significant difference found was that individuals who reported having witnessed a crime in the past were more likely to view Day Parole as being ineffective in achieving the goal of incapacitation, $t(201) = -3.12$, $p < .0025$.

Reasons for being opposed to/in favor of CR

Respondents were asked to indicate their reasons for being opposed to or in favor of CR via open-ended questions. The primary reasons cited for being opposed to CR related to risk/harm to society (e.g., that offenders would reoffend or be enticed to reoffend; 41%). Other reasons included perceptions that CR is an ineffective/lenient punishment (29%), CR is granted too easily or incorrect CR decisions may be made (10%), and CR occurs too early in offenders' sentences (5%). Fourteen percent of respondents reported that they were opposed to CR only for certain types of offenders (i.e., violent and sexual offenders; 14%).

Reasons for being in favor of CR included perceptions that CR is rehabilitative (49%), it gives offenders a second chance (22%), it provides specific deterrence (i.e., to that particular offender; 5%), and it allows for the monitoring/supervision of offenders (4%). Respondents also reported being in favor of CR as it is cost effective (4%), it allows innocent or unfairly sentenced offenders to be released (4%), and because most offenders do not recidivate upon release (1%). Eleven percent reported feeling that CR is acceptable for minor offenses.

Support for CR by offense type

Respondents were asked to indicate their degree of support for various types of CR, by offense type. Cronbach's alphas were obtained separately for the Day Parole, Full Parole, and Statutory Release items. As reliability was high within each of the types of CR (i.e., αs = .85, .85, and .86, respectively), an average percentage of degree of support was obtained across the seven offense types within each of the types of CR. Using these average percentages, analyses were conducted to determine whether the control and experimental respondents differed on their degree of support for CR. T-tests revealed no differences between the two groups on their degree of support for Day Parole, Full Parole, or Statutory Release (ps > .05). Thus, percentages are reported for all respondents as a whole.

Table 2: Support for CR by Offense Type

	Day Parole		Full Parole		Statutory Release	
	Against	In Favor	Against	In Favor	Against	In Favor
Murder	84%	7%	86%	6%	85%	7%
Sexual assault/abuse	91%	4%	90%	2%	89%	3%
Physical assault	62%	24%	64%	36%	61%	19%
Robbery	45%	36%	44%	34%	40%	37%
Break and Enter/Theft	34%	45%	37%	34%	35%	47%
Drug offenses	32%	50%	31%	47%	29%	48%
Traffic offenses	13%	78%	14%	77%	12%	77%

Note. Respondents were asked *How do you feel about offenders who have committed the following crimes being considered for Day Parole/Full Parole/Statutory Release?*. Degree of support was assessed via a 5-point Likert scale (i.e., *strongly against, against, neither in favor nor against, in favor,* and *strongly in favor*). Responses were classified as being *Against* if the respondent reported being *strongly against* or *against*; responses were classified as being *In Favor* if respondents answered *in favor* or *strongly in favor.*

It is evident from Table 2 that there is high consistency across the types of CR within each of the offense types. Thus, degree of support does not vary by the type of release being considered as much as it does by the type of offender for whom release is being considered.

T-tests revealed that being a victim of crime, knowing a victim of crime, and witnessing the commission of a crime did not impact the degree of support for Day Parole, Full Parole, or Statutory Release ($ps > .05$).

Acceptability of time to release eligibility by offense type

Respondents were asked to indicate the percentage of offenders' sentences that should be served prior to eligibility for the various forms of CR, by offense type. Reliability of the Day Parole, Full Parole, and Statutory Release items was high (i.e., $\alpha s = .93, .91$, and $.79$, respectively), so an average score was obtained across the seven offense types within each type of CR. There were no differences between the control and experimental groups on the average score for the Day Parole, Full Parole, or Statutory Release items (as assessed by t-tests; $ps > .05$), so results are presented for all subjects. On average, respondents reported that 66% of offenders' sentences should be served prior to eligibility for Day Parole, 73% should be served prior to Full Parole eligibility, and 78% should be served prior to Statutory Release eligibility (see Table 3). Similar to the results obtained on degree of support for CR, perceptions of the acceptable time that should be served prior to release eligibility varied as a function of the nature of the crime, with the time lapse being shorter for less serious crimes.

T-tests prior to release eligibility revealed that perceptions of the acceptable time length that should be served did not differ as a function of whether the respondent reported being a victim of a crime, knowing a victim of a crime, or having witnessed a crime ($ps > .05$).

Table 3: Perceptions of Time that Should be Served Prior to Release Eligibility by Offense Type

	Day Parole	Full Parole	Statutory Release
Murder	86%	91%	96%
Sexual assault/abuse	84%	90%	92%
Physical assault	71%	78%	83%
Robbery	63%	71%	76%
Break and Enter/Theft	59%	66%	71%
Drug offenses	56%	63%	69%
Traffic offenses	43%	50%	56%
All Offenses	66%	73%	78%

Note. Respondents were asked *For the following offences, please indicate the percentage of the offender's sentence that you think should be served before the offender becomes eligible for Day Parole/Full Parole/Statutory Release.*

DISCUSSION

The purpose of this study was to improve upon limitations in the existing research and assess support for various types of Conditional Release (i.e., Day Parole, Full Parole, and Statutory Release) across offense type. A second aim was to examine laypersons' perceptions of the effectiveness and purposes of various types of early release, neither of which have been the subject of previous empirical investigation. Findings revealed that support for Day Parole, Full Parole, and Statutory Release varied significantly depending upon the type of offense committed. Personal experiences of criminal victimization and provision of information on CR statistics did not impact degree of support or perceptions of the effectiveness of CR.

Purposes and effectiveness of CR

Rehabilitation was overwhelming cited as being the most important purpose of offering offenders Conditional Release. This is important, as it demonstrates that the public's perception of the purpose of CR mirrors the Correctional Service of Canada's mandate: "To contribute to the maintenance of a just, peaceful, and safe society by means of decisions on the timing and conditions of release that will best facilitate the rehabilitation of offenders and their reintegration into the community as law-abiding citizens" (Corrections and Conditional Release Act, 1992, s. 100, pp. 42–43).

Perceptions of the effectiveness of various types of CR and incarceration in achieving the goals of specific deterrence, general deterrence, incapacitation, rehabilitation, and retribution were also examined. Interestingly, most respondents (69%) felt that Day Parole was most effective in achieving the goal of rehabilitation, and incarceration was least effective (29%). Perceptions of the rehabilitative effectiveness of different forms of CR decreased as the amount of supervision decreased, with only half (47%) of the respondents feeling Full Parole was effective in achieving rehabilitation, and only one-third (38%) feeling that Statutory Release was effective.

Reasons for being opposed to/in favor of CR

Examination of the reasons respondents provided for being opposed to and in favor of CR may serve to explain why support and perceptions of rehabilitative effectiveness varied across the different forms of CR. Primary reasons that were cited for being opposed to CR were that offenders would reoffend or be enticed to reoffend (41%) and that CR is an ineffective or too lenient punishment (29%). Thus, there appear to be two distinct aspects that contribute to negative attitudes toward certain types of Conditional Release—risk of reoffense concerns, and a desire for a certain level of retribution. Day Parole seems to be viewed as a more effective and more acceptable alternative to incarceration than the other forms of CR are, primarily due to the higher level of supervision provided to offenders. This higher level of supervision may provide the public with the security that offenders would be less likely to recidivate when they are more closely monitored.

The primary reason cited by respondents for being in favor of CR was that it is rehabilitative. Although rehabilitation was viewed as being the most important purpose of a Conditional Release system, it appears that respondents had a need to balance the importance of this goal with a desire to provide appropriate punishment to offenders for their crimes. Thus, it seems that decreased support for Full Parole and Statutory Release is also attributable to these forms of CR providing inappropriate retribution to offenders.

Attitudes by offense type

The type of crime an offender has committed significantly impacted attitudes toward CR. Fourteen percent of respondents stated being against CR only for certain types of offenders (most typically violent and sexual offenders), and 11% reported feeling CR is completely acceptable for offenders who have committed only minor offenses. Type of offense committed had a strong influence upon the degree of support for Day Parole, Full Parole, and Statutory Release—for example, the percentage of respondents indicating support for Day Parole ranged from 7% to 78%, depending upon the offense committed; similar ranges were observed for Full Parole (6% to 77%) and Statutory Release (7% to 77%).

When asked about the acceptable proportion of sentences that should be served prior to eligibility for early release, offense type again demonstrated a significant influence upon responses, with the time lapse being significantly shorter for less serious crimes. On average, respondents' perceptions of the acceptable proportion of the sentence that should be served prior to CR eligibility was 66% for Day Parole, 73% for Full Parole, and 78% for Statutory Release. These figures are significantly higher than the present CSC criteria for release eligibility.[5]

Implications

Most importantly, these findings reveal that when support for CR is assessed very globally, resultant attitude indices are likely to be inaccurate and hence invalid. When conducting research on attitudes toward CR, it is important to delineate the types of release that the questions are directed toward, as there exist differential support levels and perceptions of effectiveness across Day Parole, Full Parole, and Statutory Release. There is also a great degree of variability in CR attitudes based upon the type of offender the attitudes are directed toward, pointing to the importance of also taking this variable into account.

Somewhat surprisingly, provision of CR statistics on application, grant, release, and recidivism rates for offenders was found to not moderate the nature of respondents' attitudes.[6] It may be that attitudes toward CR are quite robust, and invariable to the assuaging influence of information such as CR statistics. It is likely that most respondents held pre-existing beliefs and perceptions of the CR system (i.e., schema) prior to completing the study materials in the present study. Schema refer to meaningful categories that organize knowledge of social objects (e.g., "Conditional Release"), and consist of interconnected sets of beliefs, information, and examples of those social objects (Alcock, Carment, & Sadava, 1994; Nisbett & Ross, 1980). Schema impact the coding of ambiguous information (with new information being over-assimilated into existing schema, thereby strengthening the schema), and also lead to errors and distortions in memory (Nisbett & Ross, 1980). It is possible that if respondents' held pre-existing negative Conditional Release schema, subsequent CR-related information that they were presented with would be incorporated in a correspondingly negative manner. It is unlikely that the evaluative nature (i.e., positive or negative) of pre-existing schema would be easily or speedily amenable to modification by the provision of a few statistics. Examination of the possibility of robust, pre-existing attitudes toward the legal system or CR schemata may prove to be a fruitful avenue for future study in order to examine this possibility. The affect-laden nature of CR attitudes may further make CR-related schema resistant to modification (see also Ellsworth & Gross, 1994).

Alternatively, it is possible that there was a cognitive dissonance effect, wherein individuals presented with CSC statistics found this information to be incompatible with their pre-existing attitudes, and thus were motivated to discount it. Participants' pre-existing knowledge of CR was not assessed; however, differences in this knowledge may have interacted with the provision of statistics in some manner. Assessment of pre-existing

CR knowledge may prove this variable to be an important predictor of attitudes, and as such warrants attention in future studies.

Personal experiences with crime were found to not impact the degree of support for CR, or perceptions of the acceptable proportion of offenders' sentences that should be served prior to CR eligibility. The reasons for these findings are unclear; however, it is tenable that a ceiling or floor effect on some of the dependent variables may have restricted the range of possible responses that could be provided by respondents. Further investigation of this possibility is warranted. Finally, future research using a non-university sample that is more representative of the general public is also recommended.

Concluding remarks

Overall, findings revealed that most participants support the concept of CR. In fact, one form of CR (i.e., Day Parole) was viewed as a more attractive alternative to incarceration in terms of attaining the goal of rehabilitation. However, there was diminished support for the less restrictive forms of CR (i.e., Full Parole and Statutory Release). Perceptions of acceptability of length of sentence that should be served prior to CR eligibility revealed robust dissatisfaction with the timing of both Day Parole and Full Parole eligibility times (i.e., on average, participants felt that two-thirds of offenders' sentences should be served while incarcerated). These areas of reported dissatisfaction are important considerations for relevant policy- and decision-makers in this area. To conclude, there are many different purposes to consider in sentencing and Conditional Release decisions—although the North American criminal justice system, and perhaps even society as a whole, espouses the view that rehabilitation should be the paramount goal, there is also a need to appropriately punish offenders for the nature of their crime. Respondents' views that there should be variable eligibility for early release dependent upon the nature of the crime committed is certainly an issue worthy of consideration by the criminal justice system.

REFERENCES

Alcock, J. E., Carment, D. W., & Sadava, S. W. (1994). *A textbook of social psychology* (3rd ed.). Scarborough, Ontario: Prentice-Hall.

Applegate, B. K., Cullen, F. T., Link, B. G., Richards, P. J., & Lanza-Kaduce, L. (1996). Determinants of public punitiveness toward drunk driving: A factorial survey approach. *Justice Quarterly*, *13*, 57–79.

Blumstein, A., & Cohen, J. (1980). Sentencing of convicted offenders: An analysis of the public's view. *Law and Society Review*, *14*, 223–261.

Brillon, Y. (1988). Punitiveness, status and ideology in three Canadian provinces. In M. Hough & N. Walker (Eds.), *Public attitudes to sentencing: Surveys from five countries* (pp. 84–110). Aldershot, England: Gower.

Brillon, Y., Louis-Guérin, C., & Lamarche, M. C. (1984). *Attitudes of the Canadian public towards crime policies*. Montreal: Centre International de Criminologie Compareé.

Broadhurst, R., & Indermaur, D. (1982). Crime seriousness ratings: The relationship of information accuracy and general attitudes in Western Australia. *Australia and New Zealand Journal of Criminology, 15*, 219–234.

Correctional Service of Canada. (1995). *Basic facts about corrections in Canada: 1994 edition*. Ottawa: Minister of Supply and Services.

Corrections and Conditional Release Act, S. C. 1992, c. 20, ss. 100–102.

Diamond, S. S., & Stalans, L. J. (1989). The myth of judicial leniency in sentencing. *Behavioral Sciences and the Law, 7*, 73–89.

Doob, A., & Roberts, J. V. (1988). Public punitiveness and public knowledge about facts: Some Canadian surveys. In M. Hough & N. Walker (Eds.), *Public attitudes to sentencing: Surveys from five countries* (pp. 111–133). Aldershot, England: Gower.

Ellsworth, P. C., & Gross, S. R. (1994). Hardening of the attitudes: Americans' views of the death penalty. *Journal of Social Issues, 50*, 19–52.

Gibson, J. L. (1980). Environmental constraints on the behavior of judges: A representational model of judicial decision-making. *Law and Society Review, 14*, 343–370.

Gottfredson, S. D., & Taylor, R. B. (1984). Public policy and prison populations: Greater awareness of the views and goals of the public—which is less punitive than generally assumed. *Judicature, 68*, 190–201.

Graber, D. (1980). *Crime news and the public*. New York: Praeger.

Keil, T. J., & Vito, G. F. (1991). Fear of crime and attitudes toward capital punishment: A structural equations model. *Justice Quarterly, 8*, 447–464.

McCorkle, R. C. (1993). Research note: Punish and rehabilitate? Public attitudes toward six common crimes. *Crime and Delinquency, 39*, 240–252.

Nisbett, R. E., & Ross, L. (1980). *Human interference: Strategies and shortcomings in social judgment*. Englewood Cliffs, NJ: Prentice-Hall.

Roberts, J. V. (1988). Early release from prison: What do the Canadian public really think? *Canadian Journal of Criminology, 30*, 231–249.

Roberts, J. V. (1992). Public opinion, crime, and criminal justice. In M. Tonry (Ed.), *Crime and justice: A review of research* (Vol. 16, pp. 99–180). Chicago: University of Chicago Press.

Roberts, J. V., & Edwards, D. (1989). Contextual effects in judgments of crimes, criminals, and the purposes of sentencing. *Journal of Applied Social Psychology, 19*, 902–917.

Senese, J. D. (1992). Intensive supervision probation and public opinion: Perceptions of community correctional policy and practice. *American Journal of Criminal Justice, 16*, 33–56.

Sigler, R. T., & Lamb, D. (1995). Community-based alternatives to prison: How the public and court personnel view them. *Federal Probation, 59*, 3–9.

Skovron, S. E., Scott, J. E., & Cullen, F. T. (1988). Prison crowding: Public attitudes toward strategies of population control. *Journal of Research in Crime and Delinquency, 77*, 931–948.

Sprott, J. B. (1996). Understanding public views of youth crime and the youth justice system. *Canadian Journal of Criminology, 38*, 271–290.

Thomson, D. R., & Ragona, A. J. (1987). Popular moderation versus governmental authoritarianism: An interactionist view of public sentiments toward criminal sanctions. *Crime and Delinquency, 33*, 337–357.

Zamble, E., & Kalm, K. L. (1990). General and specific measures of public attitudes toward sentencing. *Canadian Journal of Behavioural Science, 22*, 327–337.

Notes

1. The authors wish to express their gratitude to Kristin Carey for her aid in data collection, and Sharie Kouril for her aid in manuscript preparation.

2. In Canada, Conditional Release includes Escorted Temporary Absences, Unescorted Temporary Absences, Day Parole, Full Parole, and Statutory Release (see Correctional Service of Canada, 1995).
3. Percentage sums across categories may be incomplete, as figures are not reported in cases where the number of participants within each respective category was small (i.e., $N < 10$).
4. The critical significance level was set at .0025, as a Bonferroni correction using a family-wise error rate of .05 was conducted.
5. At present, on average, one-third of the sentence minus six months must be served prior to eligibility for Day Parole, one-third of the sentence must be served prior to Full Parole eligibility, and two-thirds of the sentence must be served prior to Statutory Release eligibility.
6. Similar findings have been obtained in the literature on death penalty attitudes; the reader is referred to Ellsworth and Gross (1994) for a review of that literature and possible explanations for those findings.

Chapter 13

JUDGES' DECISION-MAKING FROM WITHIN

Ramon Arce, Francisca Fariña, Mercedes Novo and Dolores Seijo

Sentencing has been defined as the corner stone of the judicial system (Sallmann & Willis, 1984). Though traditionally research on judicial decision-making has primarily focused on the jury, in recent years attention has increasingly shifted toward the construction of a specific model that explains judges' decision-making. A key issue has been to explain the disparity in sentencing among judges. McFatter (1986) defines disparity as any variation in the severity of the judge's sentencing for similar offences or the disparity among different judges for the similar cases. Fitzmaurice and Pease (1986) state that disparity occurs when people who share similar characteristics and commit similar crimes receive different sentences. Brantingham (1985) distinguishes two types of judicial disparity. First order disparity occurs when a judge is consistent in similar cases, but is consistently different from other judges. Second order disparity occurs if a judge is inconsistent in similar cases.

It should be noted that the assessment of disparity is closely linked to the methodological approach of the study. Thus, some studies have focused on the analysis of disparity in sentencing in similar cases (e.g., Austin & Williams, 1977; Green, 1961); other researchers have centered on the inconsistency among judges in sentence severity in similar cases (Diamond & Zeisel, 1975; Partdridge & Eldridge, 1974). Alternatively, others have sought to assess the variance of extralegal factors, having controlled the legal factors, in a scale of sentence severity (Hagan, 1974; Hogarth, 1971).

With reference to the decision to incarcerate, there is considerable disparity among judges. Thus, Gaudet, Harris, and St. John's (1933) review of 7000 sentences of six judges in the state of New Jersey, showed that variation in the decision to incarcerate ranged from 34% to 58%. Likewise, Partdridge and Eldridge (1974) observed discrepancies in the judges' decision to sentence to imprisonment in 16 of the 20 case studies. In 1975, Diamond and Zeisel's study of data from the "Sentencing Council" of Chicago revealed a 30% disparity in the decision to incarcerate.

Disparity not only affects the decision to incarcerate. Sutton (1978) has found variations both in the decision to incarcerate, and the length of the prison term by federal district courts. In determining the length of the prison term, previous convictions and whether the conviction was by jury trial were the strongest correlates in multivariate analysis. On the other hand, the strongest correlates of the decision to incarcerate were the offender's prior criminal record, with method of conviction and type of offence less strongly related. Similarly, Green's (1961) study of sentencing by 18 judges in 1437 cases registered from 1956 to 1957, concluded that legal factors, such as the type of offence, the number of convictions, previous criminal record, and recommendations to the court accounted for most of the disparity. Moreover, Green observed that disparity was inversely correlated with the severity of the offence i.e., the disparity being greater in milder offences.

As for legal factors, several authors (e.g., Ostrom, Werner, & Saks, 1978) have pointed out that the weight of the evidence rests on two dimensions: reliability and validity. Reliability in a trial is determined by factors such as witness credibility, the consistency of the evidence and the likelihood that certain events occurred. As for validity, it is determined by the relevance of a particular fragment of evidence. The dimension "validity" was measured by assessing the importance of different testimonies, and lawyers' skill on judgement making (in the direct- and cross-examination of prosecution and defense witnesses), while the defense and prosecution's opening and closing statements constitute the instrument for the evaluation of the dimension "reliability". Opening statements enable lawyers to establish a cognitive schemata which influences the juror's processing and interpretation of the evidence (Lingle & Ostrom, 1980) as well as judgement-making (Pyszczynski, Geenberg, Mack, & Wrightsman, 1981), whereas the closing statements provide a consistent and logical account of events, without which the likelihood of a contrary verdict increases (Carson, 1984).

An alternative approach seeks to attribute disparity to extralegal variables. For example, Finegan (1978) and Stewart (1980) have reported a positive relationship between the physical appearance of the accused and leniency in sentencing. In contrast, Douglas, Weber and Braybrook (1980), and Konecni and Ebbesen (1979) claimed there was no correlation between an attractive appearance and a favorable decision. Another variable that has often been attributed to be responsible for disparity is the gender of the accused. Studies undertaken in Britain have tended, with the odd exception, to confirm greater leniency in sentencing for women than for men (Hedderman, 1994). The data obtained in the USA seems rather contradictory (Kapardis, 1997). Further discrepancies in the literature can be found in relation to the race of the accused. Most empirical studies carried out in Britain have not detected a relationship between race and sentence severity (e.g., Brown & Hullin, 1992; Jefferson & Walker, 1992). On the other hand, studies undertaken in the United States, have reported racial discrimination in sentence severity (Elion & Megargee, 1979; Hood, 1992). Kleck (1985) insisted that there is no racial discrimination in sentencing, but rather that researchers tend to over-dimensionalize the weight of race in sentencing. The judge's personal characteristics and the influence they may have on the sentence have also come under scrutiny. Once again, there seems to be no unanimity regarding the correspondence between sentence severity and the judge's personal variables; Palys and Divorski (1986) have detected a relationship, whereas Konecni and Ebbesen (1979) have not. Consequently, further studies are required to determine the extralegal variables not only in terms of the sex, race, etc of the accused, but also of the role of gender, political allegiance, religion, social class, and other characteristics of the judge. Where there seems to be some consensus in the literature is in relation to sentencing disparity mediated by the penal philosophy of the judge, which may be driven to rehabilitation or retribution of the offender (Gottfredson & Stecher, 1979; Hogarth, 1971).

The mixed approach combines the evaluation of legal and extralegal factors. For example, Diamond (1981) states that the most influential factors in the decision to incarcerate were the gender of the accused, and the severity of the crime, personal characteristics of the judge such as age and education, and the conflict between mitigating and aggravating circumstances of the offence. A further line of investigation has been to determine the variables influencing sentencing, how they account for disparity in sentencing, and how judges evaluate the weight of each of these variables. Diamond observed that judges tended to consider the same variables, and even assigned the variables the same positive or negative valence, but weighed them up differently. Likewise, Ebbesen and Konecni (1981) found that variability in sentencing ranged from 9% to 33%, and that four factors appeared to be responsible for systematic variations in sentencing: the type of offence; previous convictions; the legal circumstances of the accused from the time of arrest to the sentence, and the probation officer's recommendations. Given that the judge's decision comply with the probation officer's recommendations in 84% of cases, the authors argue that disparity rests more on the strategies employed by the probation officer than those used by the judge.

In a recent seminal study of two courts which had been previously classified as severe or lenient according to their previous record on sentencing in the same case types and on the basis of personal interviews, Hommel and Lawrence (1992) found that sentence severity was greater in the former than in the latter. This finding highlights that legal or extralegal factors cannot entirely account for disparity in sentencing, and that the interaction between both factors can only explain 20% of the variance.

We should point out that the discrepancies reported in the findings are, to a certain degree, the result of the comparison of different case types, and evidence (Kapardis, 1997). Bearing in mind the systematic disparity in sentencing, and the inconsistency of the findings reported in the literature, our study aims to homogenize legal factors by presenting the same case to a group of judges which allows us to isolate and evaluate first order disparity i.e., inter-judge inconsistency. To determine the weight of the factors involved in reaching a verdict and sentencing, the reliability and validity assigned to the evidence by the judge was assessed

METHOD

Participants

A total of 52 Spanish judges with a minimum of one year's experience in Appeal and High Court were randomly selected from the Spanish directory of judges. The sample included 73.0% males and 26.9% females. The average age was 34.6 years.

Materials

Participants were given a written transcript of a real trial where the defendant was accused of raping a woman. The key evidence was the victim's identification of the defendant in the street, and once again, in the police lineup that did not offer judicial guarantees. The defendant provided an alibi supported by a witness; nevertheless there was some doubt as to his guilt. The case included testimonies of several witnesses (three from defense council: the two alibi witnesses, and the accused; and two from the prosecution council: the police officer and the victim) who were submitted to direct- and cross-examination, as well as the lawyers' summing-up.

According to Fraga (1998), the evidence of this case was counterbalanced, so from a total of 345 jurors, 43.7% reached a not-guilty verdict, and 56.3% a guilty verdict.

Procedure

The participants were administered a questionnaire with sociodemographic data (age, gender, place of residence, and years of experience). Thereafter, the participants were asked to read the transcript of the trial and then complete a questionnaire designed to evaluate judgment making in terms of verdict and sentence. The analysis of the mechanisms underlying judgement-making was undertaken using a 5-point Likert-type scale, including questions on: witness credibility, the importance of testimonies for judgement making, the defense's skill (direct- and cross-examination), the prosecution's skill (direct- and cross-examination), defense's opening and closing statements (plausibility), and prosecution's opening and closing statements (plausibility). Judges also were asked to reconstruct the events as they thought they had occurred.

Analysis of the protocols

Since the aim was to evaluate possible differences in cognitive processing in the reconstruction of events, a system of categories was used that has proven to be useful and reliable in other studies (e.g., Fraga, 1998). This system enables us to examine the underlying processes that influence judgement making. There are two category lists, one referring to general, and the other to specific cognitive activity. The former deals with the number of words, general and specific thoughts, (the unit of analysis is the grammatical sentence, and it is specific when it is related to the case and general when it does not). Given that specific cognitive activity interacts with the content of the case in question, the two coders were previously asked to codify a list of categories obtained from other studies (Arce, Fariña, Novo, & Real, 1996; Fraga, 1998). Moreover, a procedure based on successive approximations was used to identify new categories related to the case in question. The list and description of the productive categories in our study are as follows:

Contextual incrustation: Total number of incrustations (that is, information taken from other cases and included as evidence in the reconstruction of events) related to other physical or social situations referring to similar cases as well as references to the law of precedence and jurisprudence.

Description of interactions: Total number of descriptions of interrelated actions and reactions.

Contextual information: Total number of references made to places, dates, time periods, etc.

Physical causal relationships: Total number of physical-causal events, when there is a presumed nexus between two physical events.

Temporal causal relationship: Total number of temporal-casual relationships, when there is the existence of temporal continuity between two events.

Number of pro-accused statements

Number of statements against the accused

Number of words
Number of general statements referring to the law of precedence and legal issues
Number of specific statements referring to the law of precedence and legal issues

Training of coders

The two coders who participated in the experiment were trained, and the correlations between coders served to contrast and correct any bias. One of the coders had previous experience in other studies that had used the same coding system with similar categories (Arce et al., 1996).

Reliability

Together, both coders analyzed all of the protocols of the categories that measure the cognitive processes. One week later, 10% of the protocols were coded again in order to determine the inter- and within-encoder consistency. The consistency was calculated using the correlation (see Table 1).[1]

RESULTS

Verdict

Strikingly, of the 52 judges under study, half reached a Not Guilty verdict, and the other half, a Guilty verdict. Gender of judge was not a significant predictor in verdict, χ^2 (1) = .43, ns. This is the main extralegal variable associated with bias in cases of rape.

Evidence evaluation

The results reveal significant differences in both multivariate, F (7,44) = 21.83, $p < .001$; ES = .777, and univariate (see Table 2) evaluation of evidence reliability mediated by the verdict factor.

The results for evidence reliability reveal that this variable accounts for 77.7% of the variance in the verdicts. Moreover, the univariate effects

Table 1: Average Inter- and Within-Encoder Consistency of Cognitive Processes

Cognitive Processes	Correlation	*p*
Pro-accused statements	.95	.001
Statements against accused	.77	.001
Temporal causal relations	.98	.001
Physical causal relations	.99	.001
Description of interactions	.99	.001
Contextual incrustation	1.00	.001
General statements	.96	.001
Specific statements	.80	.001
Words	1.00	.001

Table 2: Univariate Effects for the "Reliability" Dimension

Variable	MS	F(1, 50)	p	η^2	Mng	Mg
Accused	21.27154	35.30148	.000	.42378	3.1	1.7
1st defense witness	5.40593	5.87603	.019	.10907	2.1	1.5
2nd defense witness	12.41400	12.07161	.001	.20095	3.3	2.3
Victim	5.70704	60.44356	.000	.55737	3.4	4.2
1st prosecution witness	9.52920	8.00117	.007	.14288	2.8	3.7
Defense statements	8.16302	5.68200	.021	.10585	3.2	2.4
Prosecution statements	9.92208	6.39172	.015	.11751	2.7	3.6

Note. M_{ng} = Mean not-guilty group; M_g = Mean guilty group.

illustrate that the verdict was in line with credibility assigned to the different items of evidence. Thus, a Not Guilty verdict rested on more reliability attributed to the defendant's testimony, and to the defense's first and second witnesses, and to the defense's statements. Conversely, Guilty verdicts rested on the reliability of the victim's testimony, and the prosecution's statements and the testimony of the prosecution's first witness. In short, the demands of the task entailed the choice between two groups of items that were mutually exclusive.

The verdict reached modulated the validity assigned to the evidence, F (7,44) = 4.64; $p < .001$; ES = .425, and explained 42.5% of the variance. Moreover, the univariate effects showed that some items of evidence were influenced by the verdict reached (see Table 3). Thus, the results indicate that when reaching a Not Guilty verdict, judges assigned more weight to the defendant's testimony, and the first witness of the defense, and less importance to the victim's testimony, whereas the inverse relationship was observed for those judges who favored a Guilty verdict. In other words, the task demands require the choice of one of two separate sets of evidence that is in line with a corresponding verdict.

As for the evaluation of the defense and prosecution council, the results highlighted that neither were crucial for reaching a verdict.

Table 3: Univariate Effects for the "Validity" Dimension

Variable	MS	F(1, 50)	p	η^2	Mng	Mg
Accused	6.61068	5.41372	.024	.09770	3.3	2.6
1st defense witness	5.22746	7.55262	.008	.13123	1.9	1.3
2nd defense witness	2.52494	1.63463	.207	.03166	2.7	2.2
Victim	10.86343	10.73587	.002	.17676	3.3	4.3
1st prosecution witness	.11615	.07072	.791	.00141	3.0	2.8
Defense's skill	1.61379	1.04170	.313	.02039	2.1	1.7
Prosecution's skill	.00599	.00413	.949	.00008	1.7	1.6

Table 4

Sentence (Months)	N	Percentage	Verdict
00	26	50	Not guilty
60	1	1.9	Guilty
72	2	3.8	Guilty
120	6	11.5	Guilty
144	4	7.7	Guilty
156	3	5.8	Guilty
180	1	1.9	Guilty
216	1	1.9	Guilty
240	1	1.9	Guilty
288	1	1.9	Guilty
300	1	1.9	Guilty
No answer	5	9.6	Guilty

Note. Mean = 67.9; mode = .00; Standard deviation = 86.19.

Sentencing disparity

Table 4 shows the results for the decision to incarcerate, and the length of sentence. The decision to incarcerate exhibited considerable disparity, that is, 50% were against and 40.4% in favor of incarceration (9.6% did not respond). Similarly, no homogeneity was observed in the length of the sentence that ranged from 5 years (60 months) to 25 years (300 months).

Reconstruction of events

Multivariate analysis revealed significant differences in general cognitive activity mediated by the verdict, $F\ (3,48) = 4.27533$; $p < .01$; ES = .211, which explains 21.1% of the variance. The univariate effects (see Table 5) exhibit differences modulated by the verdict in the variable general statements, which were only observed in the reconstruction of events that are in line with a Guilty verdict.

Likewise, specific cognitive activity was mediated at the multivariate level by the verdict, $F\ (6,465) = 6.60595$; $p < .001$; ES = .468, which explains 46.8% of the variance. The univariate effects (see Table 6) illustrate that guilty verdicts require more arguments against the defendant, to establish more physical causal relations, and contextual incrustations. In other words,

Table 5: Univariate Effects of the General Cognitive Activity Modulated by the Verdict

Item of Evidence	MS	$F(1, 50)$	p	η^2	Mng	Mg
General statements	15.16667	9.26680	.004	.15636	1.08	0.00
Specific statements	326.62507	2.06491	.157	.03966	8.25	23.28
Words	7.15430	.00114	.973	.00002	97.04	97.78

Table 6: Univariate Effects of the Specific Cognitive Activity Modulated by the Verdict

Item of Evidence	MS	$F(1,50)$	p	η^2	Mng	Mg
Description of interactions	532.08974	3.25374	.077	.06110	6.33	12.75
Pro-accused statements	49.26007	2.52151	.119	.04801	3.42	1.46
Statements against accused	101.14469	10.27272	.002	.17044	.16	2.96
Physical causal relations	17.23260	12.77616	.001	.20352	.16	1.32
Temporal causal relations	518.35897	2.17975	.146	.04177	6.16	12.50
Contextual incrustation	30.00733	11.15415	.002	.18239	1.08	2.61

a guilty verdict needs more specific cognitive activity in such a way that it relates the evidence with the guilty verdict. Moreover, a guilty verdict is based more on the integration of information rather than on the exclusion, if we bear in mind that, in the reconstruction of events of guilty verdicts, there are as many pro-innocence arguments as in the reconstruction of not-guilty verdicts.

DISCUSSION

The findings of this study support once again disparity in the judges' decision to incarcerate as well as in the length of sentencing. The mechanisms underlying disparity in the decision to incarcerate rest, to a large extent, on the credibility and validity assigned to the evidence. In addition, the reconstruction of events is mediated by the verdict reached. It appears that judges are required by the task demands to search for cognitive balance in the mental reconstruction of events, given that any imbalance would not be cognitively acceptable. This tendency towards congruency takes the form of an episodic schemata (Hastie, Penrod, & Pennington, 1983), which is different and incompatible for each verdict reached. Furthermore, the verdict influences both general and specific cognitive activity. Likewise, reliability and validity are also means to ensure congruency. From a legal approach (Hastie et al., 1983; Wigmore, 1935), reliability is related to the opportunity, bias, confidence, temporal and inter-witnesses consistency, and/or the plausibility. Alternatively, from an extralegal approach, the literature also includes variables that influence the assignment of reliability and, consequently, validity, including personal characteristics of the decision maker such as: ideology, gender, racial attitudes; and information processing by the decision maker such as: errors in the encoding, storage, and retrieval of information. The relationship between the personal characteristics of judgment makers and sentencing has been reviewed. As for the decision maker's information processing, after analyzing the content of all the sentences of the same court, heuristics that served as the basis for the interpretation and congruence of the events were observed in 80.83% of cases (Arce et al., 1996). In conclusion, judges had a greater tendency to apply heuristic processing rather than the expected systematic information processing (Chaiken, 1980).

Finally, this study has also implications for lawyer's practice. Through the previous simulation of the case, legal practitioners can identify and assess the reliability and validity of the evidence for judgment making, and the reconstruction of the events. This procedure will enable legal practitioners to prepare strategies for direct- and cross-examination, to reinforce or undermine the reliability of items of evidence, and to design a reliable episodic schemata of the events (for a description of the procedure, see Hastie, 1997).

REFERENCES

Arce, R., Fariña, F., Novo, M., & Real, S. (1996). *Cognition and judicial decision making.* VI European Conference on Psychology and Law, Siena, Italy.

Austin, W., & Williams, T. A. (1977). A survey of judges' responses to simulated legal cases: Research note on sentencing disparity. *Journal of Criminal Law and Criminology, 368*, 306–310.

Brantingham, P. L. (1985). Sentencing disparity: An analysis of judicial consistency. *Journal of Quantitative Criminology, 1*, 281–305.

Brown, Y., & Hullin, R. (1992). A study of sentencing in the Leeds Magistrates' Courts: The treatment of ethnic minority and white offenders. *British Journal of Criminology, 32*, 41–53.

Carson, D. (1984). Putting the expert in expert witness. In D. J. Müller, D. E. Blackman, & A. J. Chapman (Eds.), *Psychology and law.* New York: Wiley.

Chaiken, S. (1980). Heuristic versus systematic information processing and the use of source versus message cues in persuasion. *Journal of Personality and Social Psychology, 39*, 752–766.

Diamond, S. S. (1981). Exploring the sources of sentence disparity. In B.D. Sales (Ed), *The trial process.* New York: Plenum Press.

Diamond, S. S., & Zeisel, H. (1975). Sentencing Council: A study of sentence disparity and its reduction. *University of Chicago Law Review, 43*, 109–149.

Douglas, R., Weber, T., & Braybrook, E. K. (1980). *Guilty, your worship: A study of Victoria's magistrates'courts. Occasional Monograph, 1. Legal Studies Department.* Melbourne, Australia: La Troube University.

Ebbesen, E., & Konecni, V. J. (1981). The process of adult felons: A causal analysis of judicial decision. In B. D. Sales (Ed.), *The trial process.* New York: Plenum Press.

Elion, V. H., & Megargee, E I. (1979). Facial identity, length of incarceration, and parole decision-making. *Journal of Research in Crime and Delinquency, 16*, 232–245.

Finegan, J. (1978). *The effects of non-legal factors on the severity of sentence in traffic court.* Unpublished doctoral thesis. University of Toronto.

Fitzmaurice, C., & Pease, K. (1986). *The psychology of judicial sentencing.* Manchester: Manchester University Press.

Fraga, A. (1998). *Memoria, conciencia y formación de juicios.* Unpublished doctoral thesis, University of Santiago de Compostela.

Gaudet, F. J.; Harris, G. S., & St. John, C. W. (1933). Individual differences in the sentencing tendencies of judges. *Journal of Criminal Law, Criminology and Penal Studies, 23*, 811–817.

Gottfredson, D. M., & Stecher, B. (1979). *Sentencing policy models.* New Jersey: Rutgers University Press.

Green, E. (1961). *Judicial attitudes in sentencing.* London: Macmillan.

Hagan, J. (1974). Extra-legal attributes and criminal sentencing: An assessment of a sociological viewpoint. *Law and Society Review, 8*, 357–383.

Hastie, R. (1997). Implicaciones del "Strory Model" en la conducta de los abogados y jueces en los juicios. In R. Arce, & F. Fariña (Eds.), *Psicología e investigación judicial*. Madrid: Fundación Universidad Empresa.

Hastie, R., Penrod, S., & Pennington, N. (1983). *Inside the jury*. Cambridge, Mass.: Harvard University Press.

Hedderman, C. (1994). Decision-making in court: Observing the sentencing of men and women. *Psychology, Crime and Law, 1*, 165–173.

Hogarth, J. (1971). *Sentencing as a human process*. Toronto, Canada: University Toronto Press.

Homel, R. J., & Lawrence, J. A. (1992). Sentencer orientation and case details. *Law and Human Behavior, 16*, 509–537

Hood, R. (1992). *Race and sentencing: A study in the crown court. A report for the commission for racial equality*. Oxford: Oxford University Press.

Jefferson, T., & Walker, M. A. (1992). Ethnic minorities in the criminal justice system. *Criminal Law Review*, 83–95.

Kapardis, A. (1997). *Psychology and law: A critical introduction*. Cambridge: Cambridge University Press.

Kleck, G. (1985). Life support for ailing hypotheses: Modes for summarizing the evidence for racial discrimination in sentencing. *Law and Human Behavior, 9*, 271–284.

Konecni, V. J., & Ebbesen, E. (1979). External validity for research in legal psychology. *Law and Human Behavior, 3*, 39–70.

Lingle, J. H., & Ostrom, T. M. (1980). Thematic effect of attitude on the processing of attitude relevant information. In R. E. Petty, T. M. Ostrom, & T. C. Brock (Eds.), *Cognitive responses in persuasion*. Hillsdale, N. J.: LEA.

McFatter, R. M. (1986). Sentencing disparity: Perforce or perchance? *Journal of Applied Psychology, 16*, 150–164.

Ostrom, T. M., Werner, C., & Saks, M. J. (1978). An integration theory analysis of jurors' presumptions of guilt or innocence. *Journal of Personality and Social Psychology, 36*, 436–450.

Palys, T. S., & Divorski, S. (1986). Explaining sentencing disparity. *Canadian Journal of Criminology, 28*, 347–362.

Partdridge, A., & Eldridge, W. (1974). *The second circuit sentencing study*. New York: Federal Judicial Center.

Pyszczynski, T., Geenberg, J., Mack, D., & Wrightsman, L. S. (1981). Opening statements in a jury trial: The effect of promising more than the evidence can show. *Journal of Applied Social Psychology, 11*, 434–444.

Sallmann, P., & Willis, J. (1984). Criminal justice in Australia. Melbourne: Oxford University Press.

Stewart, J. E. (1980). Defendant's attractiveness as a factor in the outcome of criminal trials: An observational study. *Journal of Applied Social Psychology, 10*, 348–361

Sutton, L. (1978). *Variations in federal criminal sentences: A statistical assessment at the national level*. Washington, D. C.: National Criminal Justice Information and Statistics Service.

Wigmore, J. H. (1935). *A student's textbook of the law of evidence*. Mineola, N. J.: Foundation Press.

Author Note

Preparation of this chapter was supported in part by Programa Sectorial de Promoción General del Conocimiento (DGICYT); code: PB96–0944.

1. We should bear in mind that this index is not accurate since it is not sensitive to the correspondence of the counts, thus the exact correspondence of the counts was verified. With this safeguard, Carrera and Fernández–Dols (1992) report that a correlation greater than .70 is reliable.

PART 4

EYEWITNESS EVIDENCE AND TESTIMONY

Chapter 14

CHILDREN'S RECALL OF THE UNFORTUNATE FAKIR: A FURTHER TEST OF THE ENHANCED COGNITIVE INTERVIEW

Pär Anders Granhag and Emma Spjut

Most professionals working within the field of law enforcement (and related areas) would agree that interviewing a witness or a victim is a very delicate task, especially so if the witness or victim is a child (Ceci & Bruck, 1993; 1995; Poole & Lamb, 1998). Furthermore, although police officers seem to agree that witnesses usually provide central leads in criminal investigations, they also report that they often find witnesses' statements to be incomplete (Kebbel & Milne, 1998). Hence, to develop interview techniques that facilitate the elicitation of both correct and complete statements is of paramount importance. In the last decade, much research has focused on one such technique: the Cognitive Interview (for a recent review see Köhnken, Milne, Memon, & Bull, 1998). The present study focuses on the use of the Cognitive Interview to enhance children's recall.

The Cognitive Interview (CI) and the Enhanced Cognitive Interview (ECI)

In the mid-eighties, Geiselman and Fisher introduced the Cognitive Interview (Geiselman, Fisher, MacKinnon, & Holland, 1986). The CI is based upon two well-known principles from cognitive psychology. The first principle is the multicomponent view of the memory trace (e.g. Bower, 1967). In short, this principle suggests that memory traces are multi-featured, and that if some features aren't accessible using one type of retrieval probe, another type of probe might unlock the memory. The second principle is known under the name of "encoding specificity" (e.g. Tulving & Thomson, 1973). The idea behind this principle is that the most effective retrieval probes are those that successfully reinstate the original encoding environment. Obviously, the multicomponent view of the memory trace and the encoding specificity principle are inter-related. Using these two principles as the point of departure, Geiselman and Fisher derived four mnemonics: (1) the "report everything" instruction, which encourages the interviewee to report as many details as she or he can; (2) the "mental reinstatement of context" instruction, which asks the interviewee to mentally recreate both the internal (e.g. feelings) and external (e.g. physical surroundings) context of the to-be-remembered event; (3) the "recalling-of-the-event-in-an-alternative-temporal-order" instruction (e.g. reverse order recall); (4) the "change-perspective" instruction, which encourages the interviewee to try to recall the event from the perspective of another witness.

In an attempt to make the original Cognitive Interview more useful in applied forensic contexts, the technique has been further developed. In short, over the last years different principles from the interpersonal communication paradigm have been incorporated into the original CI, e.g. a "verbal warm-up" before the actual interview and an appropriate use of pauses (e.g., Fisher & Geiselman, 1992; McCauley & Fisher, 1996). In all, a multitude of different principles have been suggested and used in different combinations. They all meet under the generic term, the *Enhanced Cognitive Interview.*

The cognitive interview and children's recall

To what extent can the Cognitive Interview technique be used to enhance children's recall? To date, nine studies have been published which focus on the Cognitive Interview and children's recall. In eight of these studies it was found that children in the CI (or ECI) condition recalled significantly more correct information than did children in a control interview (Structured Interview or Standard Interview) (Chapman & Perry, 1995; Geiselman & Padilla, 1988; Hayes & Delamothe, 1997; Köhnken, Finger, Nietschke, Höfer & Aschermann, 1992, cited in Memon, 1998; McCauley & Fisher, 1996; McCauley & Fisher, 1995; Memon, Wark, Bull, & Koehnken, 1997; Saywitz, Geiselman & Bornstein, 1992). In only one study did the difference between recalled correct information in the CI-condition and recalled correct information in the control-condition fail to reach a significant level (Memon, Cronin, Eaves & Bull, 1993). Critically, in three of the nine studies it was revealed that the children in the ECI condition recalled a significantly higher degree of incorrect information than did the children in the control interview (Hayes & Delamothe, 1997; Köhnken et al., 1992, cited in Memon, 1998; McCauley & Fisher, 1995).

There is an obvious challenge in modifying the CI/ECI technique so that the increase in incorrect information is reduced without any reduction of correct recall. With this as the research objective, Geiselman and Padilla (1988), as well as Saywitz et al. (1992), noticed that children had a difficult time using components three and four in the original CI (i.e., the recalling of events in a variety of "different-temporal-orders" and the "change-perspective" component). They therefore suggested that these two components should be excluded for those situations where CI is used with children. To avoid abrupt answers, it has been suggested that children should be "warmed up" before the actual interview. This can be done by letting the child, in detail, talk about an event that s/he is very familiar and comfortable with (see, for example, Fisher & Geiselman, 1992; McCauley & Fisher, 1996). For a large selection of other potential "child-friendly modifications" of the original CI see Geiselman and Padilla (1988).

The present study

In the present study, we contrasted three different interview techniques: (a) the Enhanced Cognitive Interview (ECI), (b) the Structured Interview (StrI) and (c) the Standard Interview (SI). We know of no previous research, focusing on children's recall, where all three interview techniques have been contrasted for the same material. Furthermore, we tried to counteract the problem that has been exposed in previous research on the use of the ECI to enhance childrens' recall, (i.e., a concomitant increase in incorrect recall) by incorporating a large number of potentially memory enhancing principles from the interpersonal communication paradigm. All in all, we had three main predictions:

Prediction 1:
Children in the ECI-condition will recall more correct information compared to children in the StrI- and the SI-condition (see, for example, Hayes & Delamothe, 1997; McCauley & Fisher, 1996; Memon et al., 1997).

Prediction 2:
Children in the StrI-condition will recall more information compared to children in the SI-condition.

Prediction 3:
There will be no differences between the three techniques in terms of incorrect information and confabulations (see, for example, Geiselman & Padilla, 1988; Hayes & Delamothe, 1997; McCauley & Fisher, 1996; Memon et al., 1993).

METHOD

Participants

Interviewees. A total of 32 children, 16 girls and 16 boys (age 9–10 years), participated in the study. All children were recruited from a local public school. The parents or guardians of each child were contacted through the school by a letter asking for their consent. Children from two different classes participated and each class was paid 1 500 SEK (approximately $200 USD). Each child was randomly assigned to one of the three interview conditions.

Interviewers. A total of nine psychology students volunteered to conduct the interviews (six women and three men). Six of these nine interviewers (those allocated to the StrI- and ECI-condition) went through a one-day training program. The training program included both a theoretical and a practical phase. The three persons in the SI-condition received a "basic interview instruction package" to study at home. Each interviewer conducted between three and five interviews.

Materials

The to-be-remembered-event used was a 15-minute performance by a professional fakir. The fakir, among other things, played with fire and placed himself on a bed of nails. Judging from the spontaneous reactions, the children experienced the fakir's performance as both fascinating and scary. The "tremendus et fascinas-index" was in a substantial way elevated by the fact that the fakir managed to hurt himself during his performance. From an experimental point of view, we were lucky that his injury also caused a fair amount of bloodshed. The performance was video-recorded by two separate cameras.

Procedure

The Enhanced Cognitive Interview. The three interviewers in the ECI-condition were asked to follow the instructions given in Table 1. First, and before the actual interview, each child practiced "detailed-story-telling" by giving a detailed description of his/hers morning routines. Next, the interviewer gave the child a number of important instructions (see Table 1). For example, the child was informed that if a particular question was repeated during the interview, it should not be taken as a sign that the previous answer to that question was incorrect. In addition, the interviewers were instructed to use the two first components of the original Cognitive Interview (i.e., the "mental-reinstatement-of-context" instruction and the "report-everything" instruction).

The structured interview. The three interviewers in the StrI-condition were, with one important exception, instructed to follow the same guidelines as did the interviewers in the ECI-condition. Critically, the interviewers in the StrI-condition did not use the first two components of the original Cognitive Interview (see Table 1).

Table 1: Specifications of the Three Interview Techniques

	SI	StrI	ECI
Instructions to the interviewer			
– Establish rapport		x	x
– Do not interrupt the witness		x	x
– Avoid leading questions		x	x
– Ask open-ended questions		x	x
– Ask one question at the time		x	x
– Pause after the interviewee's response		x	x
– Use age-appropriate language		x	x
– Listen actively		x	x
– Ask witness-compatible questions		x	x
– Ask specific questions based on the interviewee's free-recall		x	x
Instructions to the interviewee (given by the interviewer)			
Inform the child that:			
– you want him/her to do a "verbal-warm-up" before the actual interview		x	x
– it's okay to answer "I don't know"		x	x
– s/he should not make up any answers		x	x
– s/he should ask the interviewer to be more specific if s/he doesn't understand a question		x	x
– the previously given answer isn't wrong if a question is repeated		x	x
– encourage the child to generate information on his/her own initiative		x	x
–s/he should try to be concentrated all through the interview		x	x
– you want him/her to follow the "mental-reinstatement-of-context" instruction			x
– you want him/her to follow the "report-everything" instruction			x
Order of the interview			
– a Free-recall-phase	x	x	x
– a Specific-question-phase	x	x	x

The Standard Interview. The three interviewers in the SI-condition were instructed to first ask the child to describe what s/he remembered of the performance (the Free-recall-phase). Then followed a phase in which the interviewer was free to ask as many specific questions about the performance as s/he found necessary (the Specific-question-phase).

RESULTS

Interjudge reliability

All 32 interviews were transcribed and then coded by one coder. The coding was based on a scoring-schedule comprising 189 information units categorized into 46 Object-related, 113 Action-related and 30 Person-related information units. The coding was done to trace both correct and incorrect information, as well as confabulations. Five interviews were randomly selected to be coded by a second coder. The interjudge-reliability calculated proved to be 97.2%, that is, 211 of the total 217 information units found in the selected five interviews, were coded identically between the two coders (Cohen's Kappa = 0.70).

Correct information, incorrect information and confabulations

To compare the three techniques (ECI, StrI and SI), we conducted one between-subjects one-way ANOVA for each of the three dependent measures (correct information, incorrect information and confabulations).

An overall test showed that the three techniques differed in terms of correct information, $F(2,29) = 26.66$, $p < .001$. Tukey post hoc tests showed that the number of correct answers for ECI ($M = 65.42$) was significantly higher than the corresponding mean for StrI ($M = 41.8$) and SI ($M = 28.3$) ($p < .05$ holds for all significant differences showed by post hoc tests). Furthermore, post hoc tests showed that the children in the StrI-condition recalled significantly more correct information than did the children in the SI-condition. Differently put, the ECI generated 56% more correct information than did StrI, and no less than 131% more correct information than did SI. In turn, the StrI generated 48% more correct information than did the SI. We found no significant differences for incorrect information and confabulations (see Table 2).

As can be noted in Table 2, the number of incorrect details and the number of confabulations were very low, this independently of the type of interview technique used. The children in the StrI-condition gave somewhat more incorrect information ($M = 2.50$) than did the children in the ECI- and SI-conditions ($M = 1.92$ and $M = 1.90$, respectively), however, the overall test conducted showed no significant effect ($F(2,29) = .42$ $p = .659$). In only four cases (out of the 32 interviews), we found confabulations (1 for the ECIcondition, 1 for the StrI-condition and 2 for the SI-condition).

Table 2: Means for Correct, Incorrect, and Confabulations for All Three Conditions

Technique	Correct Info M (%)	Incorrect Info M (%)	Confabulations M (%)
Enhanced Cognitive interview	65.40 (34.6%)	1.92 (1.0%)	0.08 (0.04%)
Structured interview	41.80* (22.1%)	2.50 (1.3%)	0.10 (0.05%)
Standard interview	28.30* (15.0%)	1.90 (1.0%)	0.20 (0.10%)

Note. The percentages given within brackets are based on the 189 information-units found in the fakir's performance.
*$p < .05$ compared with the ECI condition.

The coding, based on the scoring-schedule comprising the 189 different information units, showed that there was quite a large number of details that the children didn't tell. In the ECI-condition the children left out, on the average, 123.6 information units (or 65.4%). The corresponding figures for the StrI-condition was 147.2 units (or 77.9%), and for the SI-condition 160.7 units (or 85%).

The contribution of the free-recall- and the specific-question-phases

To get a more detailed picture, we separated the information told in the *Free-recall-phase* from the information told in the *Specific-question-phase* (see Table 3). We did this with the following restriction: if a specific information unit was told in the Free-recall-phase and then again told in the Specific-question-phase, it was not counted twice.

For correct information, the overall test showed significant effects both for the Free-recall-phase, $F(2,29) = 16.39$, $p < .001$, and the Specific-question-phase, $F(2,29) = 6.25$, $p < .05$. Post hoc test revealed that children in both the ECI-($M = 32.80$) and the StrI-condition ($M = 25.40$) remembered more information in the Free-recall-phase than did children in the SI-condition ($M = 6.40$). However, the difference between the ECI- and the StrI-condition was not significant. Analyzing the Specific-question-phase, we found that the children in the ECI-condition ($M = 32.70$) were significantly better than the children in the StrI-condition ($M = 16.40$), while the SI-condition ($M = 21.90$) did not differ from the other two conditions. We found no significant differences for incorrect information.

Object-, action- and person-related information

The 189 original information units comprising the fakir's performance were divided into three separate categories: (a) *Object-related* (46); (b) *Action-related* (113) and (c) *Person-related* information (30). An

Table 3: Means for Correct and Incorrect Information for the Free-Recall-Phase and the Specific-Question-Phase

Interview Technique	Correct Info. Free-recall	Correct Info Specific-Question	Incorrect Info Free-recall	Incorrect Info Specific-Question
ECI	32.80 (17.3%)	32.70 (17.3%)	0.17 (0.1%)	1.75 (0.9%)
Structured Int.	25.40* (13.4%)	16.40* (8.7%)	0.70 (0.4%)	1.80 (1.0%)
Standard Int.	6.40* (3.4%)	21.90 (11.6%)	0.00 (0.0%)	1.90 (1.0%)

*$p < .05$ compared with the ECI condition.

Table 4: Means for the Correct Information for the Categories Object-, Action- and Person-Related Information

Interview	Object-related Info	Action-related Info	Person-related Info
ECI	18.83	38.00	7.75
Structured Int.	10.20*	26.30*	5.00
Standard Int.	7.30*	14.90*	6.20

*$p < .05$ compared with the ECI condition.

overall test showed significant differences for Object-related information, $F(2,29) = 13.33$, $p < .001$, as well as for Action-related information, $F(2,29) = 31.30$, $p < .001$. Post hoc tests revealed that children in the ECI-condition ($M = 18.83$) were significantly better at remembering Object-related information compared to both children in the StrI-condition ($M = 10.20$) and the children in the SI-condition ($M = 7.30$). Also for Action-related information, the children in the ECI-condition ($M = 38.00$) performed significantly better than did the children in the StrI-($M = 26.30$) and the SI-condition ($M = 14.90$). Furthermore, StrI generated significantly more correct Action-related information than did SI. We found no significant differences for Person-related information (see Table 4).

Number of questions and duration

A one-way between-subjects ANOVA indicated that there were no significant differences between the three techniques in terms of the number of questions put in the Specific-question-phase (see Table 5). However, we found a significant difference in terms of the duration of the interviews, $F(2,29) = 31.17$, $p < .001$. Tukey post hoc tests revealed that the interviews in the ECI-condition ($M = 27.11$ min) lasted significantly longer than the interviews both in the StrI-condition ($M = 14.07$ min) and the SI-condition ($M = 8.03$ min). The difference in duration between the StrI- and the SI-condition only approached significance ($p = .068$).

Furthermore, we found significant differences in duration between the techniques for both the Free-recall-phase ($F(2,29) = 10.31$, $p < .001$), and the Specific-question-phase ($F(2,29) = 18.42$, $p < .001$). Post hoc tests showed that the Free-recall-phase for both the ECI-condition ($M = 3.44$ min) and the StrI-condition ($M = 3.06$ min) took significantly longer to conduct than did the same phase in the SI-condition ($M = 0.59$ min). The difference between the ECI- and the StrI-condition was not significant. In addition, post hoc tests revealed the Specific-question-phase for ECI-

Table 5: Means in Terms of Number of Questions in the Specific-Question-Phase and Duration of the Interviews

Interview	Number of Questions	Duration Overall	Duration Free-recall	Duration Specific-question
ECI	30.92	27.11 min	3.44 min	15.53 min
Structured Int.	19.30	14.07 min*	3.06 min	6.00 min*
Standard Int.	33.70	8.03 min*	0.59 min*	6.20 min*

Note. Duration overall includes instructing the witness, the Free-recall-phase and the Specific-question-phase.
$^*p < .05$ compared with the ECI condition.

condition (M = 15.53 min) took significantly longer to conduct compared with the StrI-(M = 6.00 min) and the SI-condition (M = 6.20 min). The duration for the Specific-question-phase did not differ between the StrI- and the SI-condition.

Correlations

(i) For the ECI-condition alone, we found a significant correlation between the number of questions asked in the Specific-question-phase and the number of correct details given in the same phase (r = .84, p < .001); that is, the more questions asked, the better the recall.

(ii) Only for the StrI-condition, we found a significant correlation between the overall duration of the interviews and the amount of correct information recalled (r = .73, p < .05); that is, the longer the duration, the better the performance.

(iii) In terms of the correlations between the duration for the Free-recall-phase and the number of correct details reported in the same phase, only the correlation for the StrI-condition was significant (r = .84, p < .01). In other words: the longer the duration, the better the recall.

(iv) For both the StrI- and the SI-condition, we found significant correlations between the number of questions put (in the Specific-question-phase) and the duration of the same phase (r = .70, p < .05 and r = .90, p < .001, respectively). In other words, the more questions put, the longer the interview. Noteworthy, for the ECI-condition this correlation was close to zero (r = .004).

Sub-analysis of critical information

As mentioned above, the fakir's performance was broken down into 189 information units. This set of units comprised both information that was more, and information that was less, critical for the performance. This made possible a sub-analysis that answered the question whether the children's memory performance differed, as a consequence of interview technique, for the most critical information in the scenario. To answer this question, we employed eight coders to watch the fakir's performance (on video). Their instructions were to identify what they considered to be critical information in the performance (both in terms of Object-, Action- and Person-related information). The coders were free to select as many information units as they found necessary. All information units that were mentioned by at least five coders were then categorised as *critical information units*. In the end, this left us with 56 critical information units.

A one-way ANOVA showed that there was a significant difference between the three interview techniques in terms of critical information, $F(2,29) = 25.38$, $p < .001$. Post hoc tests revealed that the children in the ECI-condition ($M = 40.58$) performed significantly better than did both the children in the StrI-condition ($M = 30.30$) and children in the SI-condition ($M = 25.00$). Differently put, for critical information, children in the ECI-condition produced 34% more correct information than did the children in the StrI-condition and 62% more correct information than did the children in the SI-condition. In terms of performance for critical information, we found no significant differences between the children in the StrI- and the SI-condition.

DISCUSSION

The aim of the present study was to further investigate the completeness and reliability of children's eyewitness testimony; more specifically, to contrast three different memory techniques (the Enhanced Cognitive Interview, the Structured Interview, and the Standard Interview).

The first prediction, children in the ECI-condition will recall more correct information compared to children in the StrI- and the SI-condition, was confirmed. We obtained a clear cut result showing that the children in the ECI-condition recalled 56% more correct information than children in the StrI-condition, and no less than 133% more correct information than the children in the SI-condition. This finding is in line with previous work within the domain (see, for example, Hayes & Delamothe, 1997; McCauley & Fisher, 1996; Memon et al., 1997). However, no previous study has been able to show such impressive differences as the current one. To explain this, we believe it is important to consider that we used a large set of components previously suggested as having potential for establishing a favorable communicative milieu. We think it is reasonable to believe that the combined effect of all these components gave a powerful contribution to the ECI.

The second prediction, children in the StrI-condition will recall more information compared to children in the SI-condition, was also confirmed. The third prediction, that there would be no differences between the three techniques in terms of incorrect information and confabulations, was confirmed as well. This result is also in line with previous findings (see, for example, Chapman & Perry, 1995; Memon et al., 1993; Memon et al., 1997). Furthermore, our results underline those of previous studies showing that children's recall, in comparison to adults', is not necessarily less reliable. It is also important to note that the proportions of both incorrect information and confabulations were very low in the current study.

We also set out to try to trace potential differences in terms of which of the two different question-phases (the Free-recall-phase and the Specific-question-phase) contributed most to the total memory performance. Our results showed that both phases were affected by the interview technique used. For the Free-recall-phase, we found that both the ECI- and the StrI-techniques were more efficient, compared to the SI-condition, at producing correct information. We believe that these results are due to different reasons, for example, that the children in both the ECI- and the SI-condition had a short training session before the actual interview started. It could be that this component served two different functions; (a) that the children became more comfortable with the interview setting, and; (b) that they, in a positive way, were primed to talk about the to-be-remembered event on a detailed level.

For the Specific-question-phase, we found that children in the ECI-condition recalled more correct information compared with children in the StrI-condition. A reasonable explanation for this is that the children in the ECI-condition were asked to form a "mental reinstatement" of both the external and internal conditions present as they watched the fakir's performance. It is reasonable to believe that one effect of this instruction could be that the children had the scenario more accessible in their memory as they were asked about it. Furthermore, we found that the children in the ECI-condition recalled more Object- and Action-related information than did children in the StrI- and the SI-condition. In line with Memon et al. (1997), we found no differences between the techniques for Person-related information.

The total number of questions put in the Specific-question-phase did not differ among the three conditions. This result contradicts findings of previous studies that have shown that interviewers in the ECI/CI-condition often ask more questions than do the interviewers in a StrI- or SI-condition (see, for example, Hayes & Delamothe, 1997; Memon, 1998). However, in line with previous research, we found that it took a longer time to carry out the ECI compared to both the StrI and the SI (e.g., Hayes & Delamothe, 1997; Saywitz et al., 1992).

The Free-recall-phase took a significantly longer time to carry out in the ECI-condition and the StrI-condition compared to the SI-condition. The Specific-question-phase also took a significantly longer time to carry out in the ECI-condition compared to both the StrI- and the SI-condition. It may seem contradictory that the Specific-question-phase in the ECI-condition took a longer time to carry out in spite of the fact that the number of questions put in that phase did not differ between the conditions. A reasonable explanation for this is that the interviewers in the ECI-condition tended to use more open questions (e.g. "You said that the fakir played with fire, can you tell me more about that part?") compared to the interviewers in the two other conditions who tended to use more closed questions (e.g., "What did he put on fire?"). That the specific questions put in the ECI-condition really were effective was further underscored by the fact that we found a significant positive correlation between the number of questions put in this phase and memory performance for the same phase (the same correlation was not significant for the other two conditions).

A sub-analysis showed that the overall result pattern also held for the most critical information in performance. That is, the children in the ECI-condition recalled more correct critical information than did the children in the other two conditions. However, the children in the StrI-condition did not outperform the children in the SI-condition in terms of critical information.

CONCLUSIONS

The current study showed that the children interviewed according to the guidelines of the Enhanced Cognitive Interview outperformed both children who were interviewed according to a Structured Interview and children who were interviewed according to a Standard Interview. Importantly, we did not find any differences between the three interview techniques in terms of incorrect information and confabulations. In conclusion, the most important findings were (i) that the type of interview technique used is crucial when it comes to the completeness of children's testimony; (ii) both the communicatively-inspired components (used in the ECI-condition and the StrI-condition) and the cognitive components (used in the ECI-condition only) were positively related to memory performance; (iii) that children who were interviewed according to the Enhanced Cognitive Interview not only recalled more information, but also more relevant (critical) information. In sum, it stands clear that the current study lends strong evidence to those advocating the Enhanced Cognitive Interview. However, a host of questions awaits to be addressed. For example, our contention is that future work would profit from merging the Cognitive Interview paradigm and the source/reality-monitoring paradigm. Furthermore, and in line with what has been requested by Köhnken et al. (1998), we believe that it is important to gain more knowledge about the consequences that might follow as the interval between the to-be-remembered-event and the interview increases.

REFERENCES

Bower, G. H. (1967). A multicomponent view of a memeory trace. In K. W. Spence & J. T. Spence (Eds.), *The psychology of learning and motivation. Vol 1.* New York: Academic Press.

Ceci, S. J., & Bruck, M. (1993). Suggestibility of the child witness: a historical review and synthesis. *Psychological Bulletin, 113*, 403–439.

Ceci, S. J., & Bruck, M. (1995). *Jeopardy in the courtroom: A scientific analysis of children's testimony.* Washington: American Psychological Association.

Chapman, A. J., & Perry, D. J. (1995). Applying the cognitive interview procedure to child and adult eyewitnesses of road accidents. *Applied Psychology: An International Review, 44*, 283–294.

Fisher, R. P., & Geiselman, R. E. (1992). *Memory-enhancing techniques for investigative interviewing: The cognitive interview.* Springfield: Thomas.

Geiselman, R. E., Fisher, R. P., MacKinnon, D. P., & Holland, H. L. (1986). Enhancement of eyewitness memory with the cognitive interview. *American Journal of Psychology, 99*, 385–401.

Geiselman, R. E., & Padilla, J. (1988). Cognitive interviewing with child witnesses. *Journal of Police Science and Administration, 16*, 236–242.

Hayes, B. K., & Delamothe, K. (1997). Cognitive interviewing procedures and suggestibility in children's recall. *Journal of Applied Psychology, 82*, 562–577.

Kebbell, M., & Milne, R. (1998). Police officers' perception of eyewitness factors in forensic investigation. *Journal of Social Psychology, 138*, 323–330.

Köhnken, G., Milne, R., Memon, A., & Bull, R. (1998). The cognitive interview: A meta-analysis. *Psychology, Crime, and Law, 5*, 3–28.

McCauley, M. R., & Fisher, R. P. (1995). Facilitating children's eyewitness recall with the revised cognitive interview. *Journal of Applied Psychology, 80*, 510–516.

McCauley, M. R., & Fisher, R. P. (1996). Enhancing children's eyewitness testimony with the cognitive interview. In G. Davies, S. Lloyd-Bostock, M. McMurran, & C. Wilson (Eds), *Psychology and criminal justice: International developments in research and practice* (pp. 127–134). Berlin: Walter de Gruyter.

Memon, A. (1998). Telling it all: the cognitive interview. In A. Memon, A. Vrij, & R. Bull, (Eds), *Psychology and law: Truthfulness accuracy and credibility* (pp. 170–187). Berkshire: McGraw-Hill Publishing Company.

Memon, A., Cronin, O., Eaves, R., & Bull, R. (1993). The cognitive interview and child witnesses. *Issues in Criminological & Legal Psychology, 20*, 3–9.

Memon, A., Wark, L., Bull, R., & Koehnken, G. (1997). Isolating the effects of the cognitive interview techniques. *British Journal of Psychology, 88*, 179–197.

Poole, D. A., & Lamb, M. E. (1998). *Investigative interviews of children. A guide for helping professionals*. Washington: American Psychological Association.

Saywitz, K. J., Geiselman, R. E., & Bornstein, G. K. (1992). Effects of cognitive interviewing and practice on children's recall performance. *Journal of Applied Psychology*, *77*, 3–15.

Tulving, E., & Thomson, D. M. (1973). Encoding specificity and retrieval processes in episodic memeory. *Psychological Review*, *77*, 1–15.

Author Note

This research was supported by a grant from the *Swedish Crime Victim Compensation and Support Authority*. Correspondence concerning this article should be addressed to P. A. Granhag, Department of Psychology, Göteborg University, Box 500, SE 405 30 Göteborg, Sweden. Electronic mail may be sent via Internet to pag@psy.gu.se

Chapter 15

COURTROOM PRESSURES CAN ALTER EYEWITNESS CONFIDENCE

John S. Shaw, III, Keith A. Woythaler, and Tana K. Zerr

Much of the research on the relationship between eyewitness accuracy and eyewitness confidence has concentrated on the circumstances surrounding the first two stages of the eyewitness experience: (a) the initial witnessed event and (b) the collection of evidence between the witnessed event and trial. Examples of studies involving the witnessed event, during which the encoding of the to-be-remembered information occurs, include research on the distinctiveness of the culprit (Brigham, 1990; Mueller, Thompson, & Vogel, 1988), exposure duration (Bothwell, Deffenbacher, & Brigham, 1987; Read, 1995), arousal of the witness (Brigham, Maass, Martinez, & Whittenberger, 1983; Hosch & Bothwell, 1990), and more generally, the optimality of the witnessing conditions (Bothwell, et al., 1987; Lindsay, Read, & Sharma, 1998). As to the numerous studies examining the evidence-collection stage of the witness experience, research foci have included the timing of the confidence testing (see Cutler & Penrod, 1989, for a review), providing feedback about a witness's lineup choice (Luus & Wells, 1994; Wells & Bradfield, 1998), the effects of self-focused attention (Kassin, 1985), comparing choosers—witnesses who make a choice from a lineup—with non-choosers (see Sporer, Penrod, Read, & Cutler, 1995), and repeated postevent questioning of the witness (Shaw, 1996; Shaw & McClure, 1996).

In contrast, researchers have paid little attention to the final stage of the witnessing experience—testimony in a courtroom during a criminal or civil trial. Although a few studies have included testifying simulations as part of the experimental procedures (e.g., Wells, Ferguson, & Lindsay, 1981), none has focused specifically on how the courtroom experience can affect the relationship between eyewitness confidence and accuracy. The present research was designed to study how eyewitness confidence might be affected by three particular characteristics of courtroom testimony: (a) courtroom testimony is often very important and carries great weight, (b) courtroom testimony is given in the most public of forums, and (c) courtroom testimony is given in situations that limit witnesses' available processing resources.

Importance of the testimony

Research has clearly demonstrated that jurors accord a great deal of weight to eyewitness testimony (Cutler, Penrod, & Dexter, 1990; Cutler, Penrod, & Stuve, 1988; Wells, Lindsay, & Ferguson, 1979). Even in this age of scientific evidence such as DNA fingerprinting, nothing is more powerful in a courtroom than when a witness points at the defendant and declares that she or he is the one who committed the crime. Given the high stakes in many courtroom cases, eyewitnesses themselves surely appreciate the importance of their testimony.

In such critical situations, one would think that eyewitnesses would be very cautious in making their courtroom identifications. Might this caution result in lower—that is, more cautious—confidence ratings? Although that is certainly a possibility, self-perception theory suggests that the opposite might occur. Self-perception theory (Bem, 1967, 1972) holds that when internal cues are ambiguous, people may infer their attitudes by observing their own behavior. As applied to the importance of courtroom testimony, witnesses could make several observations that would lead them to produce inflated confidence ratings. For example, a testifying witness might think, "This testimony is really important, so I must be trying really hard to get it right. Since I'm trying so hard, I'm more likely to actually get it right." Similarly, a witness could reason, "Since this testimony is so important, I wouldn't be testifying if I wasn't certain that I've got it right." Under self-perception theory, these sorts of thoughts could result in confidence ratings that are higher for important than unimportant matters, independent of any changes in witness accuracy.

Public nature of courtroom testimony

Another aspect of witness testimony that sets it apart from daily life is the very public nature of courtrooms. Not only are there judges, jurors, and attorneys, but friends and family members of the parties and witnesses, as well as other members of the public, may also be in the courtroom. In high visibility cases, even members of the press may attend the trial proceedings. One might expect witnesses to be cautious and provide more conservative confidence ratings in such situations, but several theoretical perspectives suggest otherwise. Self-perception theory (Bem, 1967, 1972) is again relevant, for witnesses who testify in a public setting might think something along the lines of "If I'm willing to testify in public, I must be right," which could result in overly optimistic confidence ratings.

Researchers have also found that people employ self-presentation strategies in order to present themselves in the most favorable light (Arkin, 1981;

Jones & Pittman, 1982). As judges (Neil v. Biggers, 1972), attorneys (Brigham & WolfsKeil, 1983; Rahaim & Brodsky, 1982), and lay people (Brigham & Bothwell, 1983) all believe that witness confidence is a good predictor of witness accuracy, there may be pressures on witnesses in a public courtroom to present themselves as more confident than they really are. That is, in order to be perceived as accurate, an eyewitness may assert that she or he "is absolutely certain" when identifying the defendant in the courtroom. This might be more likely to happen in a crowded, public courtroom, where the witness seeks the approval of many people, than in a private setting such as a police detective's office.

Finally, people have a desire to appear consistent to others as an impression management technique (Fiske & Taylor, 1991; Tedeschi, Schlenker, & Bonoma, 1971). Thus, once a witness has identified a suspect in a lineup or other pretrial proceeding, the witness may feel that there is "no turning back" and that she or he must identify that person in public (with a high degree of confidence) in order to appear consistent.

Limited processing resources

On the stand, witnesses must answer questioning that can be rapid-fire, confusing, and even hostile, and they also have to attend to complicated legal maneuvering and frequent interruptions, which can include objections from counsel and rulings from the judge. Combined with the impression management issues described previously, these high cognitive demands leave witnesses little time to engage in controlled processing concerning their confidence judgments. That is, testifying witnesses often do not have time in the courtroom to engage in the sort of reflective thought that often accompanies important decisions (e.g., "I wonder if that really is the robber. Maybe the robber was a little taller and had lighter hair...").

When a witness is unable to engage in controlled processing, the influence of automatic types of processing may become relatively more important. Shaw and his colleagues (Shaw, 1996; Shaw & McClure, 1996; Shaw, McClure, & Wilkens, in press) argue that witnesses may rely on the speed with which a memory trace is accessed (i.e., response fluency) in arriving at their judgments of confidence. If, as seems likely, this process occurs at an automatic level, then response fluency will be relatively more important with respect to confidence judgments in situations in which limitations on processing resources prevent the witness from engaging in controlled processing such as reflective thought.

Whether limiting processing resources results in higher or lower confidence ratings depends on the direction of the influence of the automatic and controlled processes. For example, in a situation where controlled processing (such as reflective thought) would cause a witness to second-guess her or himself and thus lower her or his confidence level, limiting processing resources could prevent this decrease in confidence. Conversely, if reflective thought would yield confirming evidence that would cause a witness to increase her or his confidence, limiting that witness's processing resources could prevent that witness's confidence from rising.

Overview of the present research

The goal of the present study was to test whether simple laboratory analogues of these three characteristics of courtroom testimony would have the expected effects on witness confidence (without affecting witness accuracy). Two experiments were conducted, each involving three phases. In the initial study phase, participants viewed two sets of faces of college-age males, and they were told that the first set of faces depicted Chemistry majors while the second set depicted English majors. After a five-minute retention phase, there was a surprise memory test in which the participants were asked to remember whether each face belonged to a Chemistry or English major and to indicate how confident they were in their memory.

Three independent variables—Importance, Response Privacy, and Speed—were incorporated in the two experiments. In both experiments, Importance was manipulated through an instruction during the final memory test which stated that some of the slides actually counted in the experiment (count condition), while others were simply "practice slides" that were being used to pilot materials for a future experiment (don't-count condition). Consistent with self-perception theory (Bem, 1967, 1972), we expected that the confidence ratings for the slides that counted would be higher than the ratings for the slides that didn't count.

We manipulated Response Privacy in Experiment 1 by creating a situation in which half of the participants' responses were shared with the other participants (public condition), while the other half remained private and confidential (private condition). Because of the effects of self-perception, self-presentation strategies, and consistency pressures, we expected that the confidence ratings would be higher in the public condition than in the private condition. Finally, in Experiment 2, the availability of processing resources was manipulated through the speed in which the slides were presented during the final test phase. Half of the slides were presented at the rate of one every 3 s (fast condition), and the other half were shown one every 8 s (slow condition), with the expectation that the fast condition would limit the processing resources available to the participant witnesses. Given that it was impossible to make a firm prediction concerning the effect of limiting processing resources without knowing the direction of the contribution to confidence of any controlled processing that might occur, the inclusion of the Speed factor was exploratory in nature.

EXPERIMENT 1

METHOD

Participants

Forty undergraduates at a small liberal arts college participated in Experiment 1 in return for partial fulfillment of a requirement of an introductory psychology class. Participants included 29 females and 11 males, and the participants' ages ranged from 18 to 21 years, with a mean of 18.7.

Materials and procedures

Participants attended in groups of 3 or 4 and sat around a central table in a small laboratory with a 1.5 m by 1.5 m screen. All participants were within 4 m of the screen and within 2 m of each other. The experiment was titled "Impression Formation," and the experimenter informed the participants that the main purpose of the experiment was to "see how people classify students according to their field of study."

Study phase. In the study phase, the participants viewed 40 slides of male college students. The slides were projected with a Kodak slide projector one at a time on the screen at the front of the laboratory, and each slide remained on the screen for five seconds. The slides were shown in two blocks of 20. The participants were told that the pictures were taken about 30 years ago at a mid-size university and that the students in the first 20 slides were Chemistry majors at that university while the second 20 were English majors; the actual majors of the students were unknown. The experimenter instructed the participants to "examine each student's face carefully and think about that student's major." No mention was made of any future memory test.

Each of the 40 black and white slides pictured a male college student. These slides were randomly selected from a pool of 48 slides.[1] Only the face and shoulders of each student were visible, and all of the students wore identical white t-shirts. None of the students wore eyeglasses or jewelry. Although all of the students were white males, the faces were heterogeneous on other dimensions, including hairstyle, facial hair, feature sizes, etc. The assignment of the slides to the first group (Chemistry majors) or second group (English majors), as well as to positions within each group, was randomly determined. All participants viewed the same two groups of slides in the same order.

Retention phase. In the retention phase, participants were asked to write two very brief stories—one about a Chemistry major and one about an English major. They were to be given two minutes to write each "story," and they were led to believe that this portion of the experiment was relevant to the experimenter's interest in impression formation. They were told that the stories were to be about hypothetical Chemistry and English majors, and they were encouraged to be as creative as possible. Including instructions, the retention phase lasted five minutes. The stories were not examined or scored.

Test phase. Finally, the participants were given a surprise memory test. In keeping with the stated purpose of the experiment, the participants were asked to view the faces from the study phase and to try to remember whether each face belonged to a Chemistry major or an English major. Exact copies of the slides from the study phase were projected on the screen one at a time for five seconds each. The participants recorded their answers on response sheets on which they had to circle either CHEMISTRY or ENGLISH for each face and then indicate how confident they were in their choice by circling one number on an 11-point scale that ranged from 0% confident to 100% confident. This particular confidence scale was chosen in order to enhance the realism of the public condi-tion. That is, whereas testifying witnesses might say that they are 80% certain that the robber was wearing a blue cap, generally they would not claim that their confidence is about a "4" on a 5-point scale. Confidential code numbers were used throughout the experiment to ensure the anonymity and confidentiality of the participants' *written* responses.

Four groups of 10 slides were shown in the test phase. The slides from the study phase were randomly assigned to the four groups with the constraint that there were an equal number of "Chemistry" and "English" majors in each group of 10 test slides. Two independent variables—Importance (count v. don't count) and Response Privacy (private v. public)—were embedded in the instructions given to the participants prior to and during the final memory test, and both of these factors were manipulated within participants. The response privacy manipulation was introduced through the following instruction, which was read to the participants at the beginning of the final test phase.

> We are going to use two different methods of collecting the data in this final phase. For some of the slides you are just going to fill out your response sheets, and your answers will remain completely private. When you're done with those, you will hand them in to me. For other slides, though, I am going to ask you to share your responses out loud with everyone in the group here. After each one of these slides, you will read your answer and confidence rating aloud. We're doing this because we want to look at answers that are shared out loud and compare them to answers that remain private and confidential. So for all of the slides you're first going to fill out your response sheet by recording your choice and your confidence rating. But for half of the slides you will then read your answer and your confidence rating out loud. When we do this, you will take turns going first.

Then the participants were instructed about the importance manipulation.

> Some of the slides won't actually count toward the data in this experiment. That is, half of the slides that you saw in the first phase of the experiment, and which you will see again in a few minutes, are being tested for use in a future experiment. This is sort of what the SAT testing people do. Each year, they have several sections of the SAT that consist of new, untested questions. Unlike the SAT, though, as we go along I will tell you which slides count toward this study and which ones don't. The reason I'm doing this is because it is very important to me that you do your very best on the 20 slides that do count.

Thus, the participants were led to believe that only half of the slides "counted" in the study (when in fact they all were included in the results). Just prior to each group of 10 slides in the final test phase, the participants were instructed as to whether their answers for those slides "counted" and whether their answers would remain private or be shared with the other participants.

All participants were tested on the same four groups of slides in the same order, but the assignment of the groups to the levels of the Importance and Response Privacy factors was counterbalanced across participants to control for specific-item and testing-order effects. Thus, for one-fourth of the participants the Private/Count instructions were given for the first group of 10 slides, for one-fourth the Private/Count instructions were given for the second group, and so on. The four testing instruction orders yielded four counterbalanced versions of the experimental procedures ($N = 10$ for each version).

RESULTS

As to the accuracy of the participants' responses, a two-way within-participants analysis of variance (ANOVA) revealed that there was no main effect of Importance, $F(1,39) = 1.47$, $MSE = .03$, *ns*, no main effect of Response Privacy, $F(1,39) = 2.04$, $MSE = .02$, *ns*, nor an Importance by Response Privacy interaction, $F(1,39) = 1.24$, $MSE = .03$, *ns*. The mean response accuracy was similar in all four cells of the design ($M = 55.5\%$ correct in the Private/Count condition; $M = 55.0\%$ correct in the Private/Don't-Count condition; $M = 55.7\%$ correct in the Public/ Count condition; and $M = 61.8\%$ correct in the Public/Don't-Count condition).

Figure 1 displays the confidence ratings in Experiment 1 as a function of Importance and Response Privacy. Contrary to expectations, there was no significant main effect of Importance, $F < 1$. However, there was a significant Importance by Response Privacy interaction,

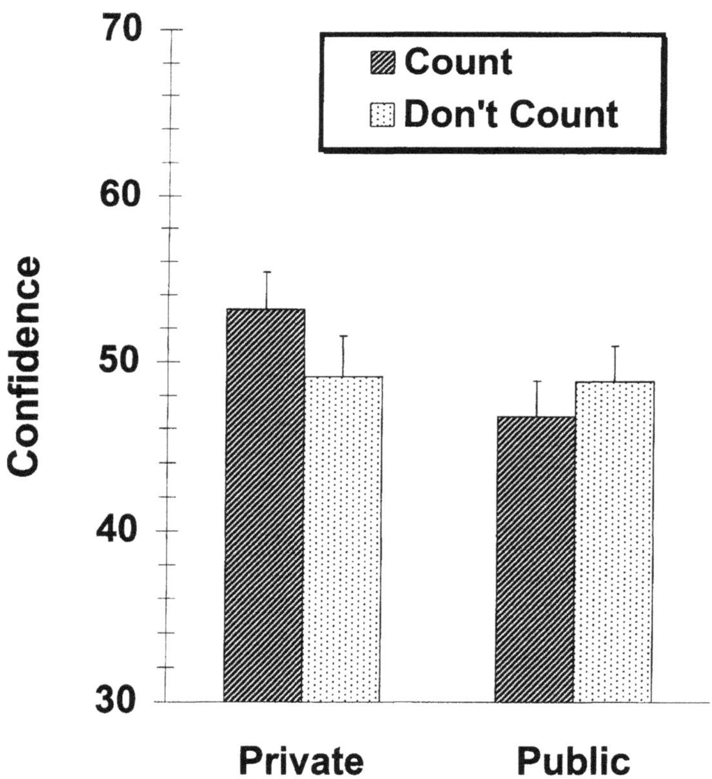

FIGURE 1: CONFIDENCE RATINGS FOR EXPERIMENT 1 AS A FUNCTION OF IMPORTANCE (COUNT V. DON'T COUNT) AND RESPONSE PRIVACY (PRIVATE V. PUBLIC). CONFIDENCE RATINGS WERE PROVIDED ON AN 11-POINT SCALE THAT RANGED FROM 0% CONFIDENT TO 100% CONFIDENT.

$F(1,39) = 5.86$, $MSE = 61.92$, $p < .05$. A further examination of the data reveals that the mean confidence for the count condition was significantly higher than for the don't-count condition for the responses that remained private ($M = 53.1$ versus $M = 49.1$, $t(39) = 2.32$, $p < .05$), but there was no significant difference between the confidence ratings for the count and don't-count conditions for the responses that were shared publicly ($M = 46.7$ versus $M = 48.8$, $t(39) = 1.34$, *ns*). There was also a main effect of Response Privacy, with the mean confidence for the private responses ($M = 51.1$) significantly higher than for the public responses ($M = 47.7$), $F(1,39) = 4.49$, $MSE = 99.16$, $p < .05$.

EXPERIMENT 2

In Experiment 1, the expected effect of Importance only occurred for the items that remained private. Because a central goal of the study was to test the hypothesis that witnesses will give higher confidence ratings for important memory reports than for unimportant ones, Experiment 2 was designed, in part, to replicate the effect of Importance for the private condition in Experiment 1. In place of the response privacy manipulation, the speed of the slide presentation in the test phase was varied in Experiment 2. In addition, Experiment 2 included impossible questions, which consisted of new faces interspersed in the test phase (for which there could be no right answer to the question concerning the student's major). The impossible questions allowed us to examine confidence ratings for responses that, by their very nature, had to be guesses, and it afforded us the opportunity to alter confidence completely independent of an original memory trace.

METHOD

Participants

Seventy-two undergraduate students participated in Experiment 2 in return for partial fulfillment of a requirement of an introductory psychology class. There were 50 women and 22 men, and the participants' ages ranged from 18 to 22 years ($M = 19.9$).

Materials and procedures

The materials and procedures in Experiment 2 were similar to those in Experiment 1, except as noted below.

Study and retention phases. To allow for the creation of the impossible questions during the final test phase in Experiment 2, two study lists of 36 slides (Study Lists A and B) were created from the pool of 48 slides.

Twelve of the 48 slides were randomly chosen to be in both study lists. These slides would appear again as possible questions in the final test phase of the experiment. A second set of 12 slides was randomly assigned to be in Study List A. In the final test phase, these 12 slides would be possible questions for the participants who had viewed Study List A and impossible questions for participants who had viewed Study List B. A third set of 12 slides was randomly assigned to Study List B, and these slides would later appear as possible questions for participants who had viewed List B and impossible questions for participants who had studied List A. A final set of 12 slides, which served as filler items and did not appear at all during the final test, appeared in both study lists. The purpose of the filler items was to equate the number of slides in the study phase and test phase so that the participants would be less likely to notice that there were impossible questions.

From each set of 12 slides, six were randomly assigned to the first group of 18 slides (the Chemistry majors), and six were randomly assigned to the second set (the English majors). Other than the set of 12 filler slides, which were assigned to the first three and last three positions in each of the two blocks of 18 slides, the positions of the slides within each group (Chemistry and English) were randomly determined. Each participant viewed either Study List A or Study List B. The general viewing procedures and instructions in the study phase, as well as the filler task in the retention phase, were identical to those in the first experiment.

Test phase. The procedures in the test phase were similar to those in Experiment 1. Again, the participants viewed faces from the study phase, tried to remember whether each face was a Chemistry or English major, and recorded their answers and confidence ratings on anonymous confidential response sheets. In Experiment 2, confidence ratings were provided on a 7-point Likert scale that ranged from 1 (*Totally Guessing*) to 7 (*Absolutely Certain*). Although the scale in the first experiment had more ecological validity, it also presented measurement problems. Despite the fact that the participants were told that 0% corresponded to guessing, some participants, understanding the nature of a two-alternative multiple choice question, may have used 50% as their confidence level for guessing. The 7-point scale used in Experiment 2 eliminated this interpretation problem.

The test phase was conducted in four groups of nine slides each, with each group consisting of three slides that had appeared only in Study List A, three slides that had appeared only in Study List B, and three slides that had appeared in both study lists. Thus, for each participant, six of the nine slides in each group were exact duplicates of ones that she or he had viewed in the study phase, and three were new faces that had not been seen before. While the six slides from the study phase had correct answers (i.e., the face either appeared in the Chemistry group or English group), there were no possible correct responses for the three new slides. Thus, these new slides presented "impossible" questions. The participants were not informed about the existence of the impossible slides, but they were told that "you may find some of the slides to be easy and some to be hard, but please answer every question, even if you have to guess."

The test phase incorporated three independent variables, all manipulated within participants. One was Question Type, which had two levels—possible questions and impossible questions—as just described. Importance was manipulated in the same way as in Experiment 1, both through the introductory instructions at the beginning of the test phase, and by informing participants during the test phase as to which slides "counted" and which did not. Finally, Speed (fast versus slow) was also manipulated through instructions given to the participants:

> In order to continue to develop procedures for future studies, I am going to show the slides in this final phase at two different speeds. Some of the slides will be shown at the rate of one every 3 seconds, and the others will be shown at the rate of one every 8 seconds.

Prior to each group of nine slides, the participants were told whether or not the slides counted and whether they would be shown every three or eight seconds. The assignment of the slides to the four groups was random, except for the constraint that each group had to contain three slides that had appeared only in Study List A, three slides that had appeared only in Study List B, and three slides that had appeared in both lists. All participants were tested on the same four groups of slides in the same order, but assignment of the groups to the levels of the Importance and Speed variables was counterbalanced across participants to control for specific-item and testing-order effects. Thus, for one-fourth of the participants the Fast/Count instructions were given for the first group of nine slides, for one-fourth the Fast/Count instructions were given for the second group, and so on. Combining the four testing instruction orders with the two study-list groups resulted in eight counterbalanced versions of the experimental procedures ($N = 9$ for each version).

RESULTS

The mean response accuracy for the possible questions was virtually identical in all four cells of the Importance by Speed within-participants design (M = 60.2% correct in the Slow/Count condition; M = 60.4% correct in the Slow/Don't-Count condition; M = 57.6% correct in the Fast/Count condition; and M = 59.3% correct in the Fast/Don't-Count condition). A two-way within-participants ANOVA confirmed that there were no main effects of Importance or Speed nor an Importance by Speed interaction (all $Fs < 1$).

As to the confidence ratings, a three-way ANOVA was conducted to examine the effects of Importance, Speed, and Question Type. There was no significant three-way interaction, nor any Importance by Question Type or Importance by Speed two-way interactions (all $Fs < 1$). The Speed by Question Type interaction was statistically reliable, though, $F(1,71) = 14.10$, $MSE = 0.42$, $p < .001$, so the confidence data were examined separately for the possible and impossible questions.

Figures 2 and 3 display the confidence ratings for the possible and impossible questions, respectively. As is evident in Figure 2, the mean confidence ratings for possible questions in the count condition ($M = 4.40$) were significantly higher than for possible questions in the don't-count condition ($M = 4.15$), $F(1,71) = 7.56$, $MSE = 0.56$, $p < .01$. Although the confidence ratings in the slow condition ($M = 4.34$) tended to be higher than in the fast condition ($M = 4.21$), that difference did not reach statistical significance, $F(1,71) = 3.60$, $MSE = 0.37$, $p = .06$. There was no Importance by Speed interaction for the possible questions, $F(1,71) = 1.50$, $MSE = 0.35$, *ns*.

The pattern of results for the impossible questions (see Figure 3) was different than for the possible questions. Although the confidence ratings for the impossible questions appeared to be higher for the count condition ($M = 3.63$) than for the don't-count condition ($M = 3.48$), the difference was not statistically reliable, $F(1,71) = 2.18$, $MSE = 0.79$, $p > .10$. In contrast to the trend for the possible items, the mean confidence ratings for the impossible items in the slow condition ($M = 3.42$) were significantly lower than for items in the fast condition ($M = 3.69$), $F(1,71) = 7.54$, $MSE = 0.70$, $p < .01$. Again, there was no Importance by Speed interaction, $F < 1$.

GENERAL DISCUSSION

Effect of importance

The importance manipulation had no significant effect on response accuracy in either experiment. As to the participants' confidence, the results were generally consistent with our expectations. When answers were given in private, the confidence ratings for the items that "counted"

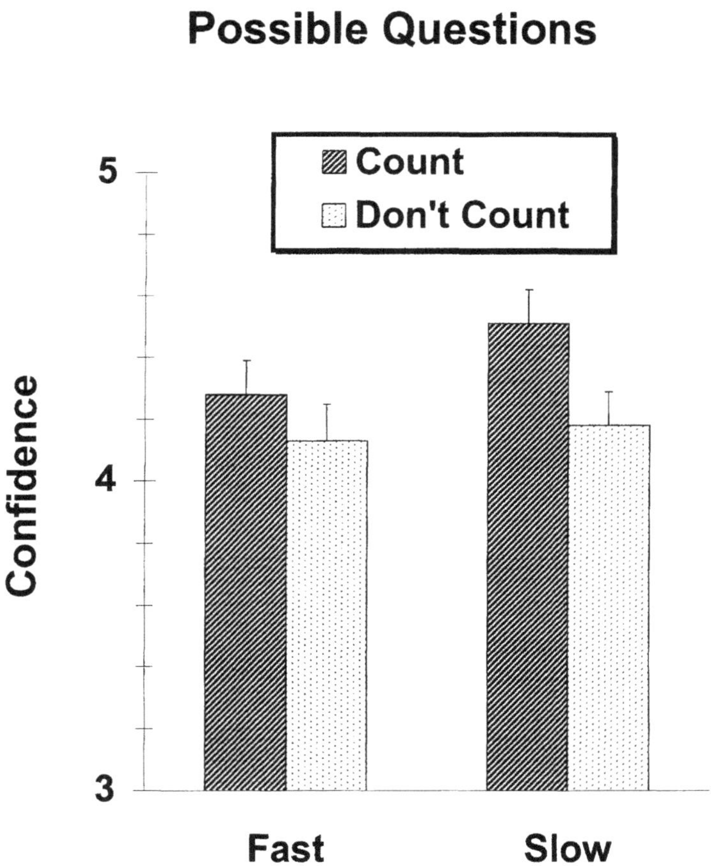

FIGURE 2: CONFIDENCE RATINGS FOR THE POSSIBLE QUESTIONS IN EXPERIMENT 2 AS A FUNCTION OF IMPORTANCE (COUNT V. DON'T COUNT) AND SPEED (FAST V. SLOW). CONFIDENCE RATINGS WERE PROVIDED ON A 7-POINT SCALE THAT RANGED FROM 1 (*TOTALLY GUESSING*) TO 7 (*ABSOLUTELY CERTAIN*).

were higher than for the items that did not count, both in Experiment 1 and for the possible questions in Experiment 2. Although the confidence ratings for the impossible questions in Experiment 2 also appeared to be higher for the items that counted, the difference was not statistically significant.

When the answers were given in public in Experiment 1, however, the difference between confidence ratings for items that counted and items that did not count disappeared. In retrospect, it seems likely that the importance manipulation was ineffective in the public condition. That is, when the answers were shared with the other participants, from the participants' point of view, all of the items were important, so it

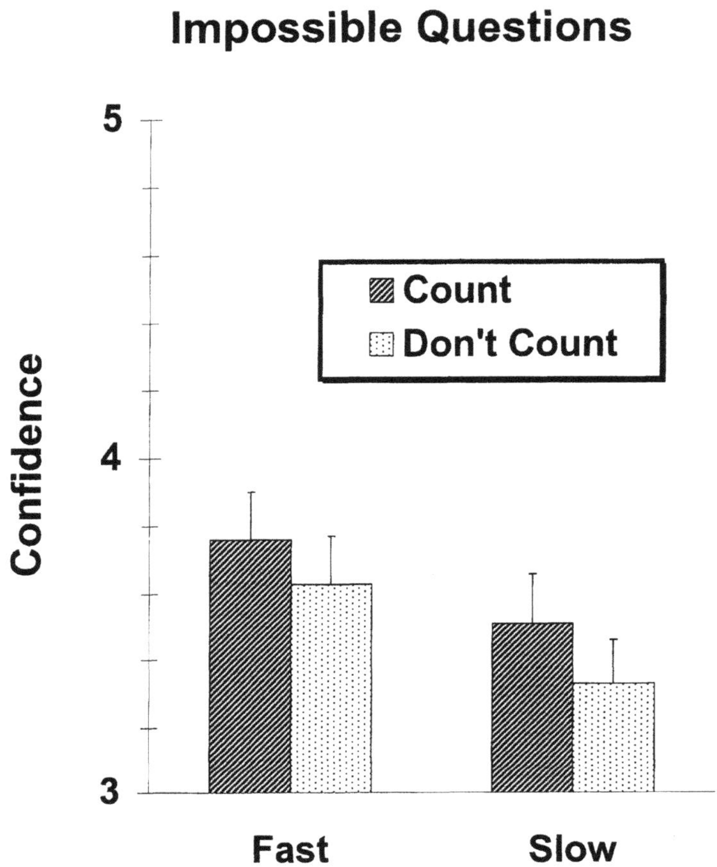

FIGURE 3: CONFIDENCE RATINGS FOR THE IMPOSSIBLE QUESTIONS IN EXPERIMENT 2 AS A FUNCTION OF IMPORTANCE (COUNT V. DON'T COUNT) AND SPEED (FAST V. SLOW) FACTORS. CONFIDENCE RATINGS WERE PROVIDED ON A 7-POINT SCALE THAT RANGED FROM 1 (*TOTALLY GUESSING*) TO 7 (*ABSOLUTELY CERTAIN*).

probably didn't matter whether or not they were told that certain items "counted."

Although the present results are somewhat limited by the weak nature of the importance manipulation, the finding that confidence for items that counted was higher than for items that did not count has important implications for the legal system. If replicated in more realistic situations, this result implies that eyewitnesses may be chronically overconfident during their courtroom testimony simply because courtroom testimony carries so much weight.

Effect of response privacy

Contrary to our expectations, the confidence ratings for the private responses in Experiment 1 were significantly higher than for those shared publicly. There are several possible explanations for this finding. One is that the nature of the experimental procedures may have encouraged the participants to be cautious when they gave their answers out loud. In the public condition, the participants shared responses to the same questions answered by their fellow participants. In such a setting, one would expect that there would be strong normative pressures to be conservative in public pronouncements of confidence in case the other participants "knew" that you were wrong. This contrasts with the situation typically faced by eyewitnesses in the courtroom, when they are the only ones who saw what happened, and they can provide inflated confidence levels with little or no fear of being contradicted.

Second, it may be that we only manipulated whether the participants' answers were *anonymous* or *shared*, rather than whether they were given in public or private. In both the private and public conditions, the participants answered their questions in the same setting, surrounded by several other participants. Because of the relatively small size of the college at which the data collection took place, many of the participants knew each other (as well as the experimenter) by sight or name, and the participants may have felt that they were always "in public," even when they were keeping their answers to themselves.

Finally, of course, it may be that confidence ratings given in public are generally lower than those given in private. Clearly, further research is needed to examine which, if any, of these explanations can account for the present results.

Effect of speed

Whereas the confidence ratings for the impossible items were significantly lower in the slow condition than in the fast condition in Experiment 2, there was no reliable difference between the slow and fast conditions for the possible items. For the impossible questions, reflective thought in the slow condition may have allowed participants to confirm that they didn't remember seeing the face at all, which might have led to lower confidence ratings than in the fast condition. Reflective thought would have had no such effect for the possible questions, since these faces actually did appear in the study phase. Given the exploratory nature of this manipulation, our interpretation of this finding is necessarily post hoc and somewhat speculative, but it is consistent with the explanation that when the test slides were presented quickly, the participants were unable to engage in extensive controlled processing before producing their confidence ratings.

Concluding comment

Despite admittedly low ecological validity, these results demonstrate that even rudimentary laboratory analogs of courtroom pressures can affect eyewitness confidence without altering eyewitness accuracy. Not only does this study add further support to the proposition that eyewitness confidence is malleable, but it also highlights the need to focus more attention on how the unique pressures of courtroom testimony may moderate the eyewitness confidence-accuracy relationship.

REFERENCES

Arkin, R. M. (1981). Self-presentation styles. In J. T. Tedeschi (Ed.), *Impression management theory and social psychological research* (pp. 311–333). New York: Academic Press.

Bem, D. J. (1967). Self-perception: An alternative interpretation of cognitive dissonance phenomena. *Psychological Review*, *74*, 183–200.

Bem, D. J. (1972). Self-perception theory. In L. Berkowitz (Ed.), *Advances in experimental social psychology* (Vol. 6, pp. 1–62). New York: Academic Press.

Bothwell, R. K., Deffenbacher, K. A., & Brigham, J. C. (1987). Correlation of eyewitness accuracy and confidence: Optimality hypothesis revisited. *Journal of Applied Psychology*, *72*, 691–695.

Brigham, J. C. (1990). Target person distinctiveness and attractiveness as moderator variables in the confidence-accuracy relationship in eyewitness identifications. *Basic and Applied Social Psychology*, *11*, 101–115.

Brigham, J. C., & Bothwell R. K. (1983). The ability of prospective jurors to estimate the accuracy of eyewitness identifications. *Law and Human Behavior*, *7*, 19–30.

Brigham, J. C., Maass, A., Martinez, D., & Whittenberger, G. (1983). The effect of arousal on facial recognition. *Basic and Applied Social Psychology*, *4*, 279–293.

Brigham, J. C., & WolfsKeil, M. P. (1983). Opinions of attorneys and law enforcement personnel on the accuracy of eyewitness identification. *Law and Human Behavior*, *7*, 337–349.

Cutler, B. L., & Penrod, S. D. (1989). Forensically relevant moderators of the relation between eyewitness identification accuracy and confidence. *Journal of Applied Psychology*, *74*, 650–652.

Cutler, B. L., Penrod, S. D., & Dexter, H. R. (1990). Juror sensitivity to eyewitness identification evidence. *Law and Human Behavior*, *14*, 185–191.

Cutler, B. L., Penrod, S. D., & Stuve, T. E. (1988). Juror decision making in eyewitness identification cases. *Law and Human Behavior*, *12*, 41–55.

Fiske, S. T., & Taylor, S. E. (1991). *Social cognition*. New York: McGraw-Hill.

Hosch, H. M., & Bothwell, R. K. (1990). Arousal, description and identification accuracy of victims and bystanders. *Journal of Social Behavior and Personality*, *5*, 481–488.

Jones, E. E., & Pittman, T. (1982). Toward a general theory of strategic self-presentation. In J. Suls (Ed.), *Psychological perspectives on the self* (Vol. 1, pp. 231–262). Hillsdale, NJ: Erlbaum.

Kassin, S. M. (1985). Eyewitness identification: Retrospective self-awareness and the accuracy-confidence correlation. *Journal of Personality and Social Psychology*, *49*, 878–893.

Lindsay, D. S., Read, J. D., & Sharma, K. (1998). Accuracy and confidence in person identification: The relationship is strong when witnessing conditions vary widely. *Psychological Science*, *9*, 215–218.

Luus, C. A. E., & Wells, G. L. (1994). The malleability of eyewitness confidence: Co-witness and perseverance effects. *Journal of Applied Psychology*, *79*, 714–723.

Malpass, R. S., & Kravitz, J. (1969). Recognition for faces of own and other "race". *Journal of Personality and Social Psychology, 13*, 330–334.

Malpass, R. S., Lavigueur, H., & Weldon, D. E. (1973). Verbal and visual training in face recognition. *Perception and Psychophysics, 14*, 285–292.

Mueller, J. H., Thompson, W. B., & Vogel, J. M. (1988). Perceived honesty and face memory. *Personality and Social Psychology Bulletin, 14*, 114–124.

Neil v. Biggers, 409 U.S. 188, 34 L.Ed.2d 401 (1972), *cert. denied*, 444 U.S. 909, 100 S.Ct. 221, 62 L.Ed.2d 144 (1979).

Rahaim, G. L., & Brodsky, S. L. (1982). Empirical evidence versus common sense: Juror and lawyer knowledge of eyewitness accuracy. *Law and Psychology Review, 7*, 1–15.

Read, J. D. (1995). The availability heuristic in person identification: The sometimes misleading consequences of enhanced contextual information. *Applied Cognitive Psychology, 9*, 91–121.

Shaw, J. S., III (1996). Increases in eyewitness confidence resulting from postevent questioning. *Journal of Experimental Psychology: Applied, 2*, 126–146.

Shaw, J. S., III, & McClure, K. A. (1996). Repeated postevent questioning can lead to elevated levels of eyewitness confidence. *Law and Human Behavior, 20*, 629–653.

Shaw, J. S., III, McClure, K. A., & Wilkens, C. (in press). Recognition instructions and recognition practice can alter the confidence-response time relationship. *Journal of Applied Psychology.*

Sporer, S. L., Penrod, S., Read, D., & Cutler, B. (1995). Choosing, confidence, and accuracy: A meta-analysis of the confidence-accuracy relationship in eyewitness identification studies. *Psychological Bulletin, 118*, 315–327.

Tedeschi, J. T., Schlenker, B. R., & Bonoma, T. V. (1971). Cognitive dissonance: Private ratiocination or public spectacle? *American Psychologist, 26*, 685–695.

Wells, G. L., & Bradfield, A. L. (1998). "Good, you identified the suspect": Feedback to eyewitnesses distorts their reports of the witnessing experience. *Journal of Applied Psychology, 83*, 360–376.

Wells, G. L., Ferguson, T. J., & Lindsay, R. C. L. (1981). The tractability of eyewitness confidence and its implications for triers of fact. *Journal of Applied Psychology, 66*, 688–696.

Wells, G. L., Lindsay, R. C. L., & Ferguson, T. J. (1979). Accuracy, confidence, and juror perceptions in eyewitness identification. *Journal of Applied Psychology, 64*, 440–448.

Authors Note

This research was supported in part by faculty research funds provided to the first author by Lafayette College and by EXCEL scholar funding provided by Lafayette College to the second and third authors. Correspondence should be addressed to: John S. Shaw, III, Department of Psychology, Lafayette College, Easton, PA 18042 (e-mail: shawj@lafayette.edu).

Notes

1. The slides used as stimulus materials were created by Roy Malpass (Malpass & Kravitz, 1969; Malpass, Lavigueur, & Weldon, 1973), and we are grateful to him for giving us permission to use them in this study.

Chapter 16

CREATING CONFUSION: UNCONSCIOUS TRANSFERENCE IN MEDIA CRIME REPORTING

Peter B. Ainsworth

Psychologists both in Europe and North America have for some time been investigating how and why eyewitnesses make mistaken identifications (Ainsworth, 1998a; Cutler & Penrod, 1995; Loftus, 1979; Ross, Read, & Toglia, 1994; Shepherd, Ellis, & Davies, 1982; Wagenaar, 1988; Wells & Loftus, 1984). A large number of possible reasons for such errors have been identified. These include factors such as witness expectations, prompts, time delays, interference, and incorrect procedures. However there are some cases where mistaken identifications appear to have resulted from the process of *unconscious transference* (Ainsworth, 1998a, p. 72.) This is the phenomenon in which a face is remembered as being familiar, but is incorrectly identified as being that of a suspect. Unconscious transference can for example result in an innocent bystander at the scene of a crime being incorrectly identified as the perpetrator. In such a case, a witness remembers (correctly) that the face is familiar, perhaps associates it with the scene of the crime, but incorrectly recalls the face as being that of the perpetrator.

The process was illustrated in a case cited by Houts (1963). In this example, a railway booking clerk was robbed at gunpoint and was later asked to attend an identification (I.D.) parade. The clerk picked out the suspect from the parade, but the accused was able to provide an alibi that was accepted by the police. When interviewed later, the booking clerk claimed that the suspect's face was the only one on the parade that looked familiar, and that this was why he had picked him out. It later emerged that the suspect (who was a sailor from a local camp) had in fact purchased tickets from the clerk on a number of occasions during the previous year. The clerk had thus recognized the person as being familiar, associated him with the location of the robbery, but had misclassified the face as being that of the robber. Other examples have been provided by Brown, Deffenbacher, and Sturgill (1977), Gudjonsson (1992), and Loftus (1976).

In the Brown et al. study (1977) subjects first viewed a number of target "suspects" live and were then asked to study a photo array. This array contained photographs of the targets seen live earlier, plus a number of other faces not encountered previously. After a gap of between four and seven days subjects viewed another live line up and were asked to say whether each person in that line up had been in the original live parade. In reality this second live parade contained three different types of person, i.e. some who had been on the original live parade, some whose photographs had been seen earlier (but who had not been on the original parade) and some foils whose faces had not been previously presented. Brown et al found that although subjects could generally differentiate between those faces which had and those which had not been encountered previously, they were incapable of discriminating between those seen in the original live parade and those shown later in the photo array. Thus in this study, subjects had little difficulty in recognising familiar faces, but had much more difficulty in correctly stating where and when the face had been encountered previously.

This is not unlike some everyday memory lapses in which a person recognizes a face as being familiar, yet has difficulty (at least initially) in deciding where he/she knows the person from, or even who the person is. This problem is likely to arise in particular when a person encounters a face outside of the usual context. Thus a television presenter may be recognized instantly when occupying his/her usual prime-time slot, but may be more difficult to place if encountered shopping at the local supermarket. In some such instances it is quite possible that a person will reach the wrong conclusion as regards where he/she knows the person from and unconscious transference will occur with the person being wrongly labeled.

Despite the evidence cited above, Ross et al. (1994) note that the small number of studies carried out to date have not always proved that unconscious transference does occur with any great frequency. These authors note that "To date there are only a handful of studies on unconscious transference and the findings are mixed, providing weak and inconsistent support for the existence of unconscious transference" (p. 81).

While examples of unconscious transference may only occasionally come to light, it is difficult to establish the number of cases in which the phenomenon may have occurred. Some suspects who have been wrongly convicted may have been unsuccessful in persuading the legal authorities that there has been a miscarriage of justice (Cutler & Penrod, 1995). Such people may at this moment be in prison, still protesting their innocence. It is not every wrongly accused suspect who will be able to provide an alibi or to otherwise prove his/her innocence. Indeed in the case cited by Houts above, it is quite possible that the accused would have been convicted if he had not been fortunate enough to be able to provide an alibi.

Part of the problem of misidentifications stems from the fact that there is some pressure on a witness to pick out someone from an identity parade. Indeed Thomson (1995) has likened the process to that of a multiple choice test—the witness may see his/her task as simply to find "the right answer" by picking out someone from the parade. Despite the introduction of a caution warning witnesses that the "person who you saw may or may not be on the parade" witnesses may understandably believe that the police would not have asked them to attend the parade unless they thought that they had detained the real perpetrator. If the witness is particularly nervous, this may also interfere with memory retrieval processes and lead the witness to pick out the most likely candidate (see Ainsworth & King, 1988). Thus if the witness views the parade and sees nine unfamiliar faces and one which appears familiar, he/she may well pick out the one face which has been seen before. In some cases this will be the face of the perpetrator, but in other cases it may simply be a face that has been encountered on some other occasion, or is associated with the crime scene.

One instance in which unconscious transference may occur is when the media show photofits of suspects, or when crime reconstructions are staged using actors. The purpose of such reconstructions is said to be to jog people's memories and to provide new leads for the police to pursue. One potential problem with such reconstructions is that viewers may well remember the face of the actor who played the suspect, but may not remember the photofit picture of the real suspect. Alternatively features of the "new" face (i.e. that of the actor) may well interfere with the original memory or lead to a new memory which blends together some features of the old face with some features of the new one (Ross, Ceci, Dunning, & Toglia, 1994).

There may be similar problems of interference or unconscious transference when newspapers carry portraits or photofits of suspects alongside or near to pictures of innocent parties. This is the subject examined here. It stems from a report in the *Manchester Metro News* of 12th March 1993. The story was entitled "Sex fiends hunted" and described a number of sex attacks in Manchester. In addition to the narrative, the story contained two pictures. The first of these was a photofit of a suspect (labelled "Sex monster: Face of a fiend"). The second was an actual photograph of a local man who rescued one female who was being attacked, and who may well have prevented serious injury to the victim. This photograph is labelled with the name of the man and the caption " Foiled attacker". This caption may in itself be interesting, as it could have been interpreted in one of two different ways; either the man was an attacker who was himself foiled or he was someone who foiled an attack by someone else. It was the latter that was intended, and this was made abundantly clear in the text.

METHOD

Two experiments using this stimulus material have now been carried out. The results of the first study have been reported elsewhere (Ainsworth, 1998b) but will be reviewed here so as to make clear the reasoning behind the second study.

STUDY 1

A total of 63 British students were recruited to take part in this study (59 were Undergraduates and four Postgraduates). Over 90% of the subjects were non-psychology specialists. All subjects were told that they were to take part in a simple memory test. When subjects entered the experiment they were asked to read the article from the *Manchester Metro News*, and were told that they would later be asked a number of questions about the contents of the article. Each subject was given 5 minutes in which to study the material. At this stage, subjects were *not* informed that they would later be asked to try to identify the suspect whose face was shown in the article. At the end of the 5-minute learning period, subjects were given a distracter task for 1 minute and were then given a simple 10-part questionnaire asking about factual information that had appeared in the article. Subjects were not at this stage asked any questions about the facial appearance of either the suspect or the intervener (hereinafter referred to as The Good Samaritan). One week later subjects were asked to view a photospread of 6 pictures and to say whether the suspect whose face had appeared in the original article was present. As would be the case with real-life identification attempts, subjects were warned that "The person who you saw earlier may or may not be in the array and you should only make an identification if you are certain."

Subjects in the experiment were in fact randomly assigned to one of three groups: Group A was shown an array of six photographs which had been cut from the *Manchester Metro News* but which did not contain the original suspect's picture nor that of the Good Samaritan. Group B was shown an array of six pictures that contained the real suspect's picture along with five foils. Group C was shown an array of six pictures that contained five foils and the picture of the Good Samaritan that had appeared in the original article. However the array did **not** contain the picture of the actual suspect.

RESULTS

The results are summarized in the following tables.

Table 1: Numbers in Each Group who Failed to Identify/Identified Suspect, Foils and "Good Samaritan"

	Failed to Pick out Anyone	Picked out Suspect	Picked out Foil	Picked out Good Samaritan
Group A (Foils only) $N = 21$	14	n/a	7	n/a
Group B (Suspect + 5 foils) $N = 21$	8	8	5	n/a
Group C (Good Samaritan + 5 foils) $N = 21$		n/a	4	10

As can be seen from this table, seven subjects in Group A (who were shown an array which contained neither the suspect nor the Good Samaritan) picked out a foil and believed this to be the face of the suspect. Only eight people from Group B were able to correctly identify the suspect, while a further five picked out one of the foils. However, in Group C, 10 subjects picked out the face of the Good Samaritan and incorrectly identified this as being the face of the suspect. These findings will be discussed further below.

Table 2: Number of Subjects who Picked From Array X Familiar/Unfamiliar Face Presentation

	Unknown Faces only Presented (Group A) ($N = 21$)	Familiar Face Presented (Groups B + C) ($N = 42$)
Pick made	7	27
No pick made	14	15

The results in Table 2 show that the probability of a face being picked is significantly higher when subjects are presented with an array which contains one familiar face (i.e., target/familiar face present) as opposed to an array which contains no familiar faces (i.e., a "target absent" condition). A chi square test showed that this difference was statistically significant ($p < .05$).

The results presented in Table 3 show that the probability of picking out a familiar face as being that of the suspect are no greater when

Table 3: Number of Subjects who Picked/Failed to Pick When Presented with Suspect V. Good Samaritan

	Good Samaritan Presented	Real Suspect Presented
Pick made	10	8
No pick made	11	13

subjects are presented with the real suspect as opposed to the Good Samaritan. A chi square test showed that there was no statistically significant difference ($p > .05$) between the two groups despite the fact that one group was shown an array containing the actual suspect, whilst the other was shown an array containing the Good Samaritan.

STUDY 2

While the results of this first study provided some interesting results, commentators pointed out that subjects were given arrays that contained at most only one of the faces seen previously. For this reason a second study was carried out in which all subjects were shown an array that contained both the photofit picture of the real suspect and the photograph of the Good Samaritan.

Some 60 subjects were recruited for the purposes of this second study. All were undergraduate students, though none were majoring in psychology. The initial procedure was identical to the first study in that subjects were asked to read the newspaper article and to then answer a number of questions about the material within. At this stage, the subjects' attention was not drawn specifically to the photographs, and no questions were asked about the appearance of the two people shown.

One week later, and without warning, subjects were asked to view a photospread containing ten pictures and to try to identify the suspect whose face had appeared in the article. (Six of the original subjects were not present at this time, resulting in a final sample of 54 subjects.) Unlike in Study 1, the photospread contained both the picture of the suspect and that of the Good Samaritan. Subjects were given the standard warning to the effect that "The person who you saw earlier may or may not be in the array and you should only make an identification if you are certain".

RESULTS

The results shown in Table 4 confirm one of the findings from the first study in that subjects who are presented with an array which contains at least one familiar face are likely to pick out one of those faces as opposed

Table 4: Numbers who Picked Out Suspect/Good Samaritan/Foil

	Picked Suspect	Picked Good Samaritan	Picked Foil	No Pick Made
Numbers (%) $N = 54$	20 (37)	16 (30)	7 (13)	11 (20)

to picking out a foil or failing to pick out anyone. A chi square test showed that this difference was statistically significant ($p < .05$).

However, Table 4 also shows that subjects who were shown an array containing both the real suspect and the Good Samaritan were no more likely to pick out the former than the latter. A chi square test showed that the slight difference in the number who picked out the suspect rather than the Good Samaritan (20 v. 16) was not statistically significant ($p > .05$).

DISCUSSION

As can be seen from the results above, Study 1 provided a number of interesting findings. Firstly one third of Group A (who were shown an array which contained neither the suspect nor the Good Samaritan) picked out a foil as the suspect. Although numbers were small, there did not appear to be a tendency to pick out any one particular foil. It is possible that some who acted in this way felt that they should try to make a selection despite the fact that none of the faces presented was familiar. Others may simply have had an inaccurate memory of the suspect's appearance and selected a face which best matched their (false) memory. Future research may wish to consider questioning those subjects who do make incorrect identifications in an effort to establish why such errors occurred.

Within Group B (who were shown an array that contained the suspect plus five foils, but not the Good Samaritan) only eight subjects (38%) correctly identified the real suspect. A further eight failed to pick out anyone while five (24%) picked out one of the foils in the array. The fact that only just over one third of subjects were able to correctly identify the suspect perhaps points to the difficulty of this task given that subjects were given no prior warning of the fact that they would be asked to identify someone whose photograph had appeared within the article. It is also possible that remembering and later identifying a face presented as a black and white photofit image is perhaps more difficult than remembering a face seen "live". Thus direct comparisons between rates of identification in this study and rates in "real world" cases may not be appropriate. There are a large number of factors that will affect identification rates, including the stress associated with the crime, and the motivation of the witness/victim (Ainsworth, 1998a, chapter six).

Within Group C (which contained the Good Samaritan and five foils, but not the real suspect) of most interest was the fact that almost half the subjects (48%) picked out the Good Samaritan and identified him as the suspect in the case. This finding appears to offer some support for the existence of unconscious transference in this particular case. Subjects appeared to have recognized the face as familiar, associated it with the original story, but then mislabeled it as being the face of the suspect.

As can be seen in Table 2, the probability of a face being picked is much higher when one of the faces is familiar as opposed to when there is no familiar face. Furthermore the probability of detecting a familiar face as belonging to the suspect is no higher whether the familiar face is that of the actual suspect or is that of the Good Samaritan. Statistical analysis showed that there was no statistically significant difference between these two groups. In other words, and crucially, familiar faces tended to be chosen, but the familiar face of the real suspect was chosen no more often than was the face of the previously presented Good Samaritan in this study.

In the case of Study 2, the results confirm one of the findings of Study 1, i.e., that subjects were significantly more likely to pick out a familiar face than they were to pick out a foil or to fail to pick out anyone. In fact two thirds picked out one of the faces seen a week earlier, compared to one third who either picked a foil, or failed to pick anyone. However those subjects who did choose one of the two faces seen a week earlier, were no more likely to pick out the real suspect than they were to pick out the Good Samaritan. Although the suspect was slightly more likely to be picked (37% v. 30%) analysis showed that this difference was not statistically significant. This thus suggests that even when subjects are given an array containing both the suspect and the Good Samaritan, they are no more likely to correctly identify the former than they are to incorrectly identify the latter as being the suspect. Thus presenting subjects with an array that contains both the suspect and an innocent bystander does not appear to reduce the chances of unconscious transference occurring. Both studies suggest that in cases such as this almost a third of subject witnesses are likely to show evidence of unconscious transference having occurred.

The results of these two studies thus give some cause for concern. In the case of study 1, a man whose actions saved a victim from injury, was incorrectly identified as a suspect by almost 50% of subjects who were shown his photograph. However the results of study 2 suggest that even when subject witnesses are given an array containing both the real suspect and an innocent bystander they are just as likely to pick out the former as the latter. This appears to provide some evidence for the existence of unconscious transference in this instance. In the absence of the real suspect (Study 1), almost half of the subjects appeared to be picking out the person whose photograph was familiar, and incorrectly thinking of it as the picture of the suspect.

While this research was based on a newspaper article, the results may have implications for other media. If the police arrest, and put on an I.D. parade, a suspect whose face is in some way familiar to a witness he or she may be likely to be picked out even if he or she is genuinely innocent. If the results of this research are generalizable, then there is an increased chance that the (innocent) suspect would be picked out simply because of the familiarity of his/her face. There may well be cases in which the police issue a photofit picture of a suspect that results in a witness subsequently coming forward with information. If the same witness then attends an identification parade, it is likely that he/she will pick out the person who best matches the photofit picture, but that this person may not be the individual who actually committed the crime.

The somewhat worrying results emanating from this research may in part be due to the particular conditions of the study. The fact that subjects were not warned in advance that they would be asked to identify someone, and that identification was attempted one week after viewing, may have been partly responsible for some subjects' tendency to pick out the wrong person. However, such conditions are not dissimilar from many real-life cases where witnesses and victims are not warned in advance that they will be asked to identify a suspect, and are called to an I.D. parade a week or more later. Unlike many laboratory-based studies, subjects in this study were not told in advance that their identification skills would be tested. Thus comparison with "real life" cases may be more appropriate than would be the case with some previous research.

There are certain other factors in this case, which may have contributed to the high level of incorrect identifications. The fact that the article was headlined "Sex Fiends hunted" and then contained two pictures, may have contributed to the confusion. As was noted earlier, the caption below one of the photographs ("Foiled attacker") may have added further to the confusion. However newspapers should perhaps be made aware of the possible consequences of such reporting. In this case the paper's desire to portray the bystander as a hero may paradoxically have branded him as a suspect in this case, at least in the minds of some readers. Having identified that there are some unique conditions in these studies the findings are very much in line with the more traditional laboratory based research described by Ross et al. (1994).

Future research in this area is needed in order to establish other circumstances in which unconscious transference may occur, and perhaps to consider whether other media, especially television, may unwittingly label innocent people as suspects. It might be hypothesized that unconscious transference might be more likely to occur in the case of television than was the case in the present study that used a newspaper article. The number of television programs that use reconstructions of crime incidents in an effort to solve cases appears to be increasing. If such programs lead inadvertently to confusion in the minds of witnesses and ultimately to a possible miscarriage of justice then concerns should be voiced. Although we have some information on the interaction between crime, the media and the law (Howitt, 1998) information about the media's role in possible misidentifications is lacking.

There are a number of ways in which such matters might be investigated further. For example, one interesting piece of research that might usefully be carried out in the future would be to examine the number of occasions on which actors who play the part of suspects on programs such as *Crimewatch U.K.* are later "identified" as the suspect by members of the public. There is at least one reported case in which a viewer contacted the Crimewatch U.K. team to say that she recognized the "suspect" shown in a reconstruction (Ainsworth, 1998a, p. 75). However, on this occasion the viewer actually provided (correctly) the name of the actor who had played the part of the suspect, rather than information that might have helped the police to identify the real suspect in the case. Psychologists who are asked to appear on such programs should perhaps be made aware of such possible confusions (and unconscious transference) in the minds of some viewers.

Even if unconscious transference does not in itself occur, reconstructions can lead to some confusion in the minds of witnesses and to possible alterations in memory. For example, Hall, Loftus, and Tousignant (1984) showed that any new information about a suspect's appearance can lead to an alteration in a witness's original memory. Thus even if a full unconscious transference affect does not occur, media portrayals of crime information might lead to further confusion and possibly to miscarriages of justice.

REFERENCES

Ainsworth, P. B., & King, E. (1988). Witnesses' perceptions of identification parades. In M. M. Gruneberg, P. E. Morris, & R. N. Sykes (Eds.), *Practical aspects of memory:Current research and issues* (pp. 66–70). Chichester: Wiley

Ainsworth, P. B. (1998a). *Psychology, law and eyewitness testimony*. Chichester: Wiley.

Ainsworth, P. B. (1998b). Turning heroes into villains: The role of unconscious transference in media crime reporting. In J. Baros, I. Munnich, & M. Szegedi (Eds.), *Psychology and criminal justice: International review of theory and practice* (pp. 399–406). Berlin: De Gruyter.

Brown, E., Deffenbacher, K., & Sturgill, W. (1977). Memory for faces and the circumstances of encounter. *Journal of Applied Psychology*, *62*, 311–318.

Cutler, B. L., & Penrod, S. D. (1995). *Mistaken identification: The eyewitness, psychology and the law*. Cambridge: Cambridge U.P.

Gudjonsson, G. (1992). *The psychology of interrogations, confessions and testimony*. Chichester: Wiley.

Hall, D. F., Loftus, E. F., & Tousignant, J. P. (1984). Postevent information and changes in recollection for a natural event. In G. L. Wells & E. F. Loftus (Eds.), *Eyewitness testimony: Psychological perspectives*. New York: Cambridge University Press.

Houts, M. (1963). *From evidence to guilt*. Springfield IL: Thomas.

Howitt, D. (1998). *Crime, the media and the law*. Chichester: Wiley.

Loftus, E. F. (1976). Unconscious transference. *Law & Psychology Review*, *2*, 93–98

Loftus, E. F. (1979). *Eyewitness testimony*. Cambridge MA: Harvard University Press.

Ross, D. F., Ceci, S. J., Dunning, D., & Toglia, M. P. (1994). Unconscious transference and lineup identification: Toward a memory blending approach. In D. F. Ross, J. D. Read, & M. P. Toglia, (Eds.), *Adult eyewitness testimony: Current trends and developments* (pp. 80–97). Cambridge: Cambridge University Press.

Ross, D. F., Read, J. D., & Toglia, M. P. (1994). *Adult eyewitness testimony: Current trends and developments*. Cambridge: Cambridge University Press.

Shepherd, J. W., Ellis, H. D., & Davies, G. M. (1982). *Identification evidence: A psychological evaluation*. Aberdeen: Aberdeen University Press.

Thomson, D. M. (1995). Eyewitness testimony and identification tests. In N. Brewer & C. Wilson (Eds.), *Psychology and policing* (pp. 119–154). Hillsdale, NJ: Erlbaum.

Wagenaar, W. (1988). *Identifying Ivan*. Hemel Hempstead: Harvester Wheatsheaf.

Wells, G. L., & Loftus, E. F. (1984). *Eyewitness testimony: Psychological perspectives*. Cambridge: Cambridge University Press.

Chapter 17

THE DISCRIMINATION OF DECEPTIVE, MISTAKEN, AND TRUTHFUL WITNESS TESTIMONY

Stephen Porter, John C. Yuille and Angela R. Birt

If and when convincing evidence is produced that reasonably reliable scientific methods of exposing falsehoods either in or out of the courtroom are available, these methods should be promptly utilized by the legal profession.

William Wicker (1953)

As legal scholar William Wicker observed four decades ago, an important agenda in the criminal justice system is to decide whether a witness is telling the truth about a crime. In most criminal trials within an adversarial justice system, there are contradictions between the testimonials of different witnesses, especially reports given by complainants and defendants. Deception is very difficult to identify, however, even for law enforcement professionals with considerable investigative experience (e.g., Ekman & O'Sullivan, 1991). Although intentional lying on the stand is a salient concern with witnesses, it is not the only one. Courts have long recognized that witnesses sometimes relate a sincere but mistaken recollection of an alleged crime. For nearly a century, research has demonstrated that aspects of memory can be susceptible to the effects of misleading information (Bartol & Bartol, 1999; Yuille, Daylen, Porter, & Marxsen, 1995). Since the early 1970s, the post-event misinformation paradigm has been used to establish beyond a doubt that eyewitness memory is malleable (e.g., Schacter, 1996, 1999). Recent research has shown that some individuals can even come to hold confident memories for entire events that never occurred (see Loftus, 1997a, 1997b, 1997c). Thus, legal decisions often come down to the question of a witness' credibility: is the testimony based on deceit, mistaken recollection, or truth? This chapter describes recent work by Canadian researchers that illuminates the nature of deceptive and mistaken testimony and has created a novel approach with which to discriminate them from accurate witness accounts.

The detection of deception

Deception plays an important role in the social interactions of most animal species (Trivers, 1985) and humans are no exception, employing deceit on a daily basis (e.g., DePaulo & Kashy, 1998; Ekman, 1992). Deceit is particularly prevalent and consequential in forensic contexts (e.g., Ekman, 1992; Porter & Yuille, 1995, 1996). Offenders, complainants, and other witnesses all have occasion to lie about alleged criminal incidents. Certain types of criminal offenders, such as psychopaths, habitually employ manipulation, lying, and malingering, arguably to a pathological degree (e.g., Hare, 1998; Hare, Forth, & Hart, 1989; Hare & Hervé, 1999; Porter, Birt, Hervé, & Yuille, in press). In addition, it is clear that complainants have fabricated a criminal victimization in many cases (e.g., Yuille, Tymofievich, & Marxsen, 1995). For example, in Nova Scotia, Canada, nearly two hundred individuals are currently under investigation for fabricating child abuse incidents and defrauding millions of dollars from government programs.

In addition to deception being a common occurrence in legal settings, its detection is notoriously difficult. Previous research indicates that, on the whole, neither laypersons nor professionals in forensic settings are able to identify deceptive reports at levels greater than chance. Ekman and O'Sullivan (1991) showed that customs officials, policemen, trial court judges, FBI agents, CIA agents, forensic psychiatrists, and other professional groups were no better than chance at judging the truthfulness of videotaped deceptive statements. Their poor performance in these judgments may have resulted from focusing on the wrong cues or failing to notice cues that are indicative of deception. Poor performance may also have been due to decision-making based on inaccurate myths or training in deception detection. Kassin and Fong (1999) found that participants trained in traditional police detection methods made less accurate judgments of videotaped deceptive speakers than those with no training. Thus, most people, even those who require the skill in investigative settings, cannot detect lies accurately. Further, popular techniques for identifying deception such as the polygraph have serious shortcomings that limit their utility (e.g., Iacono & Patrick, 1999). Recently, it has been argued that verbal clues to deception have been under-researched (Porter & Yuille, 1995, 1996; Porter, Yuille, & Lehman, 1999), despite their promising validity (e.g., Zuckerman & Driver, 1985). Accumulating anecdotal and empirical evidence suggests that attention to verbal cues may contribute to the identification of deceit. In a study of lying in an interrogation context (Porter & Yuille, 1996), we found that deceptive testimonials could be identified based on their level of detail, coherence, and how often the speaker admitted to not recalling something about the incident in question. In our present research, a primary objective was to investigate the validity of a novel approach using verbal clues to deception when participants were lying about fabricated emotional events.

The identification of implanted memories

False memories are by no means rare occurrences in most of us.

William James (1890).

Occasionally, a witness or complainant reports that he/she "recovered" memories for a crime after a long period of forgetting or "repression" (e.g., Loftus, 1993). The judicial response to reports of recovered memories has been inconsistent (Porter et al., 1999; Porter et al., in press). In some cases, reports of recovered memories have been viewed as unreliable (e.g., *Jane Doe et al. v. Joseph Maskell*, 1996), whereas many courts have accepted such evidence in convicting defendants (e.g., *R. v. Francois*, 1994). Beginning in the late 1980s, social scientists have engaged in a heated debate over the validity of recovered memories (e.g., Lindsay & Read, 1994; Read, 1999). A key issue in the recovered memory debate has been whether people can mistakenly remember entire traumatic experiences. Some researchers have argued that at least some "recovered" memories may actually be false memories implanted during a police investigation or psychotherapy (e.g., Loftus, 1997a). It is clear that the use of leading and misleading questioning during police interviews has resulted in inaccurate reports (e.g., Ceci & Bruck, 1993; Marxsen, Yuille, & Nisbet, 1995). Similarly, suggestive methods used in psychotherapy (e.g., guided imagery, hypnosis) are associated with elevated suggestibility and memory distortion. Poole, Lindsay, Memon, and Bull (1995) surveyed North American and British clinicians and found that 25% of respondents reported using practices focusing on memory recovery; some also reported high rates of memory recovery. Loftus and Pickrell (1995) provided the first empirical demonstration of mistaken "recovered" memories. They successfully misled a quarter of twenty-four adults into believing that they had been lost and rescued at age five. In a study by Hyman, Husband, and Billings (1995), participants were presented with brief descriptions of childhood events outlined by their parents plus two false events contrived by experimenters. In the first experiment, 20% of participants came to remember information about the false events over two interviews. With an additional interview, the number of participants who incorporated false information into their memories increased to 25%. Still, many researchers and clinicians remained unconvinced about the validity of implanted memories for more emotional childhood events. Addressing this issue, Pezdek and Roe (1997) found that they were unable to implant memories in children for an intrusive event more akin to sexual abuse—a rectal enema. Pezdek, Finger, and Hodge (1997) attempted to implant a memory for a Catholic ceremony or a Jewish ceremony in both Catholic and Jewish high school students. As predicted, they were successful in implanting memories only for plausible events. In sum, although a small number of studies have demonstrated that false memories can occur, there is much controversy over the types of events that can be implanted (e.g., Porter & Marxsen, 1998). In particular, the generalizability of existing implanted memory studies is unclear (e.g., Berliner & McDougall, 1997). The possibility of false memories for emotional incidents, a central concern in the memory debate, has yet to be addressed.

If implanted memories for emotional incidents can occur, an important issue to pursue would be whether they could be discriminated from real memories (e.g., Payne, Neuschatz, Lampinen, & Lynn, 1997; Pezdek & Taylor, in press). Professional organizations contend that the identification of implanted memories is a difficult task in the absence of corroboration (American Psychological Association, 1996; Canadian Psychological Association, 1996). There is some empirical evidence to support this position. When Ceci, Crotteau-Huffman, Smith, and Loftus (1994) provided videotapes of children relating either implanted or real memories to psychologists who specialized in interviewing children, the participants were unable to discriminate them. They concluded that, "repeatedly thinking about a fictitious event can lead some preschool children to produce vivid, detailed reports that professionals are unable to discern from their reports of actual events" (p. 103). Next, Leichtman and Ceci (1995) showed such videos to more than a thousand researchers and clinicians who worked with children. Again, participants failed to detect when real experiences were being described, although many expressed high confidence in their judgments (Ceci, 1995). Although this has not been replicated with adult reports, implanted memories may be equally difficult to identify. However, content analyses of real and mistaken memories in adults have revealed a number of unique phenomenological and qualitative features of implanted memories for non-emotional events (Lampinen, Neuschatz, & Payne, 1998). These differences could serve as useful cues to identifying distortion in testimony. In fact, two lines of research, reality monitoring and Statement Validity Analysis, indicate that the content of accounts for events not experienced may differ from the content of real memories (see Memon, Vrij, & Bull, 1998). Johnson and colleagues proposed the model of reality monitoring to investigate subjective differences in memories and imagined experiences (e.g., Johnson & Raye, 1981). Research investigating this model indicates that actual memories are associated with a higher degree of external sensory information whereas imagined experiences are associated with more internally-generated subjective and cognitive details (e.g., Schooler, Gerhard, & Loftus, 1986). Statement Analysis was devised for the assessment of potentially deceptive reports by children (e.g., Horowitz, 1991; Porter & Yuille, 1995). Research on this approach suggests that reports of fabricated experiences differ qualitatively and systematically from reports based on real experiences (e.g., Ruby & Brigham, 1997), but its utility has not been examined with implanted memories.

In our research, criteria derived from these two approaches were examined and selected as potential discriminators of deceitful, implanted, and real memories. Other novel criteria were selected and, collectively, the approach was called the *Memory Assessment Procedure* or MAP (Porter et al., 1999; Porter & Birt, in press). Based on a thorough literature review (Porter, 1998), the assessment technique included the most promising criteria for discriminating reports of true and false experiences. The MAP provided an examination of both phenomenological and content characteristics of the witness reports. Phenomenological criteria concerned subjective, personally experienced features of the memories that required participants to think about their memories and judge them according to specific qualities, including vividness/clarity, stress, and confidence. By contrast, content criteria were concerned with more objective, presentation-specific, features of the memories such as amount of detail and coherence of the memory account (see Porter et al., 1999 for a detailed description of the MAP).

In sum, the continuing controversy over recovered memories compelled us to conduct a large-scale investigation of whether highly emotional incidents could be implanted in memory and whether lies, implanted memories, and truthful reports could be differentiated based on their qualitative features.

In our recent research (Porter et al., 1999; Porter, Birt, Yuille, & Lehman, 2000), we employed a misleading interview approach to encourage participants to "recover" a memory for an emotional event which had not actually occurred. A within-subjects design was used to examine whether there would be different verbal patterns and phenomenological features when a person is lying, relating a mistaken event, or telling the truth.

METHOD

Participants

Undergraduate participants were recruited to take part in research "examining how well people can recall emotional childhood events," in exchange for monetary payment. Following the application of exclusionary criteria, 77 participants were eligible for continuing participation. Parents were initially contacted with a detailed questionnaire inquiring about the participants' childhood experiences and were asked about six emotional events that their child may have experienced between the ages of four and 10 years. The event categories were selected to be of a negative emotional tone (highly stressful to a child, but non-criminal) and required that the participant was the central "victim" in the event. The events were: *a serious medical procedure*, *getting lost*, *getting seriously harmed by another child*, *a serious animal attack*, *a serious indoor accident*, and *a serious outdoor accident*. Three events were then selected for use in the interviews, one of which had actually occurred. From the remaining non-experienced events, an event was randomly selected to be the subject of an implanted memory and another was for a fabricated witness report. The ages, locations, and a plausible set of information clues were contrived from the information provided on the parental questionnaires. All participants and their parents were asked to refrain from discussing any childhood events until the end of the study.

Procedure

The recovered memory interviews. The interview format included a *free narrative phase*, a *general questions phase* to clarify details offered in the free narrative, and a *specific-questions phase* inquiring specifically about degree of stress at the time of the event, level of confidence that the event occurred, memory perspective, and other subjective aspects of the memory image. The interviews were conducted by eight research assistants who had been extensively trained in the highly scripted interview procedure. In the first interview, the titles of one real and one false event were presented to the participant. The participant was informed that each event had occurred according to his/her parents, and had been randomly selected from the parental questionnaire. The interviewer then introduced the first event and asked the participant to explain what had happened. For each event, the interviewer provided four details: age, location, time of year, and people present—information supposedly provided by the parents. The purpose of the first interview was to give the participants an opportunity to make an initial attempt to remember the real and false events. Failure to recall the false event (as expected) resulted in encouragement by the interviewer to take time and focus on recovering it. Next, the participant was informed that one purpose of the study was to test the effectiveness of various memory retrieval techniques. The interviewer slowly repeated the event information to bring the participant "mentally back to the scene of the event." Guided imagery instructions were used to help participants generate images for the false event. At the end of this interview, the participant was encouraged to take a few minutes each night to try to recover the memory and write down any thoughts pertaining to it. The main purpose of the second and third interviews, one and two weeks later, was to further facilitate the creation of a false memory by repeating the memory retrieval process. The second purpose of the final interview was to have participants lie about an event. Following the final discussion of the false event, the interviewer exited the room for fifteen minutes after asking the participant to read a note of written instructions. In the note, participants were instructed to fabricate a believable account of an emotional childhood incident that had not occurred. Again, participants were provided with the event category and the four details. They were told that the interviewer would be unaware that they would be lying and were offered a monetary incentive for successfully convincing a judge that the report was truthful. Upon returning, the interviewer proceeded with an interview about the event.

Following the last interview, the interviewer recorded whether the participant experienced an implanted memory. Then, for each participant, either two or three memories (depending on whether a memory had been successfully implanted) were transcribed from audio tapes. Three volunteer coders, kept blind to the purpose of the experiment, were carefully trained in the coding and scoring procedures for the MAP criteria.

RESULTS

Proportions of participants who recalled the truthful and false childhood events

Most participants (88.3%) immediately recalled the real event. Overall, 26% of participants "recovered" a complete memory for the false event and another 30% exhibited a partial false memory. Thus, while 44.2% participants did not "recover" any false information, more than half experienced memory distortion, either partly or completely. For the implanted memories, the frequencies with which the different emotional events were falsely remembered were as follows: serious animal attack (35%), getting seriously hurt by another child (25%), serious indoor accident (20%), getting lost (15%), and serious medical procedure (5%). In 35% of the implanted memories, the memory distortion first appeared in the initial interview. In half the cases, distortion first emerged in the second interview, and in 15% of the cases memory distortion was not evident until the third interview. There was no significant difference in likelihood of distortion occurring in any particular interview, $\chi^2(2) = 3.70$, $p > .05$. Looking at the implanted memory cases only, it is important to note that the real event had been presented first in 70% of the cases. The real event had been presented first in 52.2% of the partial memory cases but in only 46.9% of the cases of no memory distortion. Therefore, although not statistically significant, there was a trend for susceptibility to implanted memories to increase if the real event had been discussed first, $\chi^2 (1) = 3.20$, $p = .073$.

Content analysis comparing real, implanted, and fabricated memories

A multivariate analysis of variance (MANOVA) examined whether there were phenomenological/subjective or content differences in real, implanted, and fabricated memories (in participants who reported all three types of memories). The MANOVA was significant, Hotelling's $T^2 = 1.69$; $F(20,56) = 2.36$, $p = .006$. Table 1 shows the mean scores and standard deviations for the various dependent measures. Univariate tests were significant on five criteria: Stress, $F(2,38) = 6.75$, $p = .003$; Vividness/Clarity, $F(2,38) = 14.46$, $p < .0001$; Confidence, $F(2,38) = 9.11$, $p = .001$; Coherence, $F(2,38) = 4.05$, $p = .025$; and Amount of Detail, $F(2,38) = 4.50$, $p = .018$.

Table 1: Comparison of True, Implanted, and Fabricated Reports ($N = 20$)

MAP Criteria	True Memories (*M* and *SD*)	Implanted Memories (*M* and *SD*)	Fabricated Memories (*M* and *SD*)
Vividness/ Clarity****	4.85 (1.42)	3.20 (1.32)	4.85 (1.35)
Stress Rating***	4.65 (1.73)	4.30 (1.75)	5.80 (1.01)
Sensory Components	2.30 (.92)	2.10 (1.02)	2.40 (1.23)
Confidence***	6.40 (1.14)	4.80 (1.99)	5.90 (1.17)
Re-experiencing Mental Experience	3.85 (4.75)	2.30 (2.45)	3.10 (3.39)
Admitting Lack of Memory	4.45 (4.80)	5.65 (3.83)	3.20 (3.24)
Number of Details*	78.05 (59.46)	61.63 (44.32)	96.23 (61.39)
Relevancy	5.15 (1.42)	4.50 (1.24)	4.95 (.94)
Repeated Details	15.25 (16.31)	12.50 (12.74)	19.65 (24.20)
Reasons for Lack of Memory	.20 (.52)	.60 (1.79)	.30 (.66)
Coherence*	4.85 (1.31)	3.90 (1.12)	4.75 (1.48)

****$p < .0001$ ***$p < .005$ **$p < .01$ *$p < .05$.

Note. Table 1 has been reproduced from Porter, Yuille, & Lehman (1999) with permission from Plenum Publishing.

Stress ratings. Each participant was asked to rate how stressful the event in question was for each of the real, created (if experienced), and fabricated memories according to a 7-point Likert scale. As shown in Table 1, participants gave significantly higher mean stress ratings when fabricating a memory for an emotional childhood event than when relating either a real memory (p = .04) or an implanted memory (p = .003). However, the latter two memory accounts did not differ (p > .05).

Vividness/Clarity ratings. Each participant was asked to indicate, on a 7-point scale, how vivid and clear his/her memory was for each of the childhood events. As depicted in Table 1, participants gave higher mean ratings on vividness for fabricated memories than for implanted memories (p = .0004). They also gave higher vividness ratings for real than implanted memories (p = .0001), but the ratings did not differ for real and fabricated memories (p > .05). Thus, memories for both fabricated and real events were rated similarly, but were rated as more vivid than implanted memories.

Confidence ratings. Participants were asked to indicate on a 7-point scale how confident they were that each event reported actually occurred. As can be seen in Table 1, participants gave significantly higher mean confidence ratings for real than implanted memories (p = .002). They also gave significantly higher mean confidence ratings for fabricated than implanted memories (p = .01), but did not differ in their confidence ratings for real and fabricated memories (p > .05).

Coherence. Coherence refers to how well a memory report hangs together and follows a logical sequence with a beginning, middle, and end, reported in that order. That is, it reflects how logical and sensible the memory report is to the listener or coder. Coders rated real memories as significantly more coherent than implanted memories (p = .024). Further, they rated fabricated memories as more coherent than implanted memories (p = .026), but did not rate real and fabricated memories differently (p > .05) (see Table 1).

Amount of Detail. The total number of details was calculated for each memory report. As shown in Table 1, fabricated memories contained significantly more details than implanted memories (p = .019) and marginally more details than real memories (p = .07). Real and implanted memories did not differ in their number of details (p > .05), despite a trend for real memories to be more detailed.

*Real and fabricated memories across the total sample (*N = 75). A MANOVA comparing the content of the real and fabricated memory reports was significant, Hotelling's T^2 = 0.88; $F(11,64)$ = 5.14, p < .0001.

Follow-up univariate tests were conducted, and as Table 2 indicates, when relating a real experience, participants admitted lacking memory for the event more often than when fabricating, $F(1,74) = 4.69$, $p = 0.34$. When fabricating, participants rated the vividness level of the memory as higher than when relating a real event, $F(1,74) = 10.21$, $p = .002$. As in the original analysis, fabricated events were rated as more stressful than real experiences, $F(1,74) = 11.35$, $p = .001$. Finally, fabricated memories contained more repeated details than truthful memories, $F(1,74) = 7.56$, $p = .007$, even though there was no difference in the overall number of details. When fabricating an experience, participants rated their memories as 11.9% more vivid, 14.0% more stressful, and repeated details 24.4% more frequently than when relating a real experience. When relating a real experience, participants reported lacking memory 20.3% more often than when fabricating (see Table 2).

Memory perspective

Participants were asked which perspective/vantage point characterized each memory image. A "*participant*" perspective meant that participants re-experienced the event from their own eyes and could not see themselves in the memory, whereas an "*observer*" perspective indicated that they re-experienced the event like "watching a video" and could see themselves in the memory. Chi-square analyses indicated that neither memory type was significantly more likely to be experienced from either a participant or an observer perspective, with $\chi^2(1,20)$ ranging from .80 to 1.80. However, there was a pattern differentiating real memories from the other two types

Table 2: Comparison of True and Fabricated Memories Across the Entire Sample ($N = 75$)

MAP Criteria	True Memories (*M* and *SD*)	Fabricated Memories (*M* and *SD*)
Vividness/ Clarity***	4.68 (1.46)	5.31 (1.11)
Stress Rating***	4.84 (1.68)	5.63 (1.32)
Sensory Components	2.13 (1.11)	2.20 (.97)
Confidence	6.37 (1.15)	6.35 (.89)
Re-experiencing Mental Experience	3.64 (4.17)	3.07 (3.07)
Experiencing Lack of Memory*	4.87 (3.80)	3.88 (3.25)
Number of Details	83.18 (60.51)	92.29 (56.07)
Relevancy	5.04 (1.29)	4.68 (1.29)
Repeated Details**	14.07 (15.19)	18.60 (20.40)
Reasons for Lack of Memory	.21 (.47)	.19 (.46)
Coherence	4.57 (1.37)	4.63 (1.29)

Note. Table 2 has been reproduced from Porter, Yuille, & Lehman (1999) with permission from Plenum Publishing.
*$p < .05$. **$p < .01$. ***$p < .005$. ****$p < .0001$.

of memories. For real memories, 40% and 60% of participants recalled the event from a participant and observer perspective, respectively. For fabricated memories, 65% of participants recalled the event from a participant perspective. For implanted memories, 60% of participants recalled the event through a participant perspective.

Confidence and vividness

Although, overall, implanted memories had lower confidence ratings than real or fabricated memories, 75% of implanted memories had confidence ratings greater than 4 (moderate) and 20% gave a rating of 7 (absolutely certain). However, 75% and 70.7% of real memories were rated a 7 in the implanted memory sub-sample and entire sample, respectively. Forty percent and 57.3% of fabricated memories were rated a 7 in the implanted memory sub-sample and across the entire sample, respectively. For implanted memories, confidence was related to vividness ($r[20] = .70$, $p < .05$).

Overall, 85.3% participants indicated that they would be willing to wager money that the real event had occurred. However, only 30.7% would wager that the false event had occurred. Of the participants who had not experienced memory distortion, 87.5% would wager that the real event occurred. Eighty-seven percent of participants who had a partial false memory and 80% of those who had a complete false memory were willing to do so. Participants also were informed that one of two events (real or false) had not actually occurred and were asked to guess which. Overall, 92% guessed correctly that the false event was the event which had not occurred. The other 8% were unable to guess.

Individual differences in false memories

An important question that has arisen from the recovered memory debate is whether individual differences contribute to susceptibility to memory distortion. Research has consistently shown that under controlled laboratory conditions, many participants experience false memories while others are not susceptible to misinformation effects (e.g., Loftus, 1997a, 1997c). What differentiates those people who are susceptible to implanted memories and those who are not? We hypothesized that memory distortion would be influenced by characteristics of both interviewers and rememberers (Porter et al., 2000).

To examine the relationship between susceptibility to memory distortion with both dissociation and personality, we administered the Dissociative Experiences Scale (DES; Bernstein & Putnam, 1986) and the NEO-Five

Factor Inventory (NEO-FFI; Costa & McCrae, 1992) to the participants. Given that there were a number of different interviewers in this study, the impact of interviewer personality features (as measured by the NEO-FFI) was investigated also. Results demonstrated that participants who had experienced memory distortion were much more dissociative (according to DES scores) than their counterparts. The mean DES score of the memory distortion group (M = 20.53, SD = 10.77) was approximately twice as high as the no memory distortion group (M = 10.44, SD = 7.54), $t(45) = -3.19$, $p = .01$. Interestingly, neither age, gender, nor education influenced degree of susceptibility to false memories. However, susceptibility to memory distortion was related to extraversion, $F(2, 36) = 3.85$, $p < .05$. Participants who experienced a complete mistaken memory had significantly lower extraversion scores (M = 49.08, SD = 13.46) than those who experienced minor distortion (M = 60.71, SD = 8.91). There also was a trend for conscientiousness scores to differ, $F(2,35) = 3.27$), p = .051, with the no distortion group scoring the highest on this measure (M = 53.25, SD = 12.01). Further, participants' susceptibility level was higher ($F(2,43) = 3.08$, $p < .05$) with interviewers who scored high (M = 2.10, SD = 0.55) on extraversion than interviewers who scored low (M = 1.40, SD = 0.70). Overall, this pattern of findings indicates that a suggestive interaction between an extraverted interviewer and a more introverted, less conscientious, dissociative rememberer may be a recipe for memory distortion. These results support the view that memory distortion result from a social *negotiation* between interviewers and interviewees and that particular personality characteristics and interpersonal/situational dynamics contribute to their creation.

DISCUSSION

Deception and memory distortion are important concerns in the legal system. Our research sought to answer a critical question: can we tell whether a person is lying, mistaken, or truthful? First, we demonstrated that different types of incidents, which would have been highly emotional or traumatic had they occurred, can be mistakenly "recovered" as memories (Porter et al., 1999). Over repeated interviews, more than half of participants came to report that they experienced a stressful incident that actually had been contrived by the researchers. Some of these "recovered" memories were quite dramatic; for example, one participant experienced a false memory for falling on his head, getting a painful wound, and being sent to an emergency room. The high degree of memory distortion that resulted in this research was likely due to the multiple suggestive techniques employed by the well-trained interviewers. As well, participants were asked to repeatedly think about the false event each evening and make notes about any "recovered" information. Despite the fact that a large number of participants experienced memory distortion, it should be kept in mind that nearly half of them thoroughly resisted the misinformation. This indicates that memory distortion is not an inevitable consequence of misinformation provision.

After establishing that implanted memories for emotional incidents can occur, it was next shown that features of the false memories differed from those of real and fabricated memories. Implanted memories were less vivid and clear than real or fabricated memories. In turn, fabricated memories were more vivid than real memories. Second, although some implanted memories were recalled with a high degree of confidence, overall, participants were generally less confident in their false memories than in their real or fabricated memories. Confidence was high, and did not differ, for the real and fabricated memories. Third, fabricated events were rated as more stressful than both real and implanted events, which did not differ on this dimension. Fourth, the implanted memory reports were rated as less coherent than both the real and fabricated memories. The latter two memory types did not differ from each other on this measure, unlike previous findings (e.g., Porter & Yuille, 1996). Fifth, fabricated memories were rich in detail relative to the real and implanted memories. There was also a trend for real memories to contain more details than implanted memories. Interestingly, for most of the real memories, participants reported that they could see themselves in the memory image (i.e., observer perspective) whereas in both implanted and fabricated memories, a participant perspective dominated. Additional content differences were discovered in the real and fabricated memories over the whole sample. Fabricated memories had fewer admissions of lack of memory (see also Porter & Yuille, 1996) but more *repeated* details than real memories.

Overall, when discussing their memories for real experiences, the subjective ratings and memory content were generally of high quality, perhaps not surprisingly, given the emotional significance of the events being reported. These memories, usually based on events from ten to twenty years ago, had stood the test of time. On the other hand, compared to real memories, implanted memories had some good (e.g., relevance) and some poor content features (e.g., coherence), and generally poor subjective features, including lower vividness and confidence in the memories. (However, some of the implanted memories were rated with high confidence and vividness). Fabricated memories had high subjective ratings of vividness, stress, and confidence. However, they also contained some poor qualities. Overall, the fabricated memories had an exaggerated, unrealistic, "over-the-top" quality.

Individual differences contributed to susceptibility to memory distortion (Porter et al., 2000). Susceptible individuals were far more dissociative and tended to score lower on measures of extraversion and conscientiousness than their counterparts. Interviewers who were more "successful" at implanting the memories were generally more extraverted than those who were less successful. These individual difference factors may be useful in clarifying the social nature of memory distortion. They might also be used in applied forensic settings to identify particularly suggestible individuals and suggestible social interactions/ dynamics.

The implications of the current findings are considerable. Investigators and psychotherapists can benefit from the knowledge that even confidently held mistaken memories can be produced from suggestive interviewing. It is recommended that suggestive techniques such as guided imagery be avoided in practice (e.g., Courtois, 1997; Knapp & Vandecreek, 1997). In assessing the credibility of emotional memories, professionals may keep in mind the content criteria and individual differences identified here. We think that an important remaining empirical issue for psychology and law researchers to address is whether professionals in legal contexts be trained to use empirically-based clues to deception and implanted memories. Our ongoing program of research offers some promising findings relevant to this issue. For example, we recently found that the ability of a sample of Canadian federal parole officers to detect videotaped deceit increased substantially with two days of intensive training, from chance levels to a rate of accuracy over 70% (e.g., Porter, Woodworth, & Birt, in press). This indicates that research findings on deception can indeed facilitate investigative practice in forensic settings. Next, we plan to extend this type of research to the effect of training on the identification of implanted memories.

REFERENCES

American Psychological Association. (1996). *Working group on investigation of memories of childhood abuse final report.* Washington: American Psychological Association.

Bartol, C. R., & Bartol, A. M. (1999). History of forensic psychology. In A. K. Hess & I. Weiner (Eds.), *The handbook of forensic psychology, 2nd*. ed. (pp. 24–47). NY: Wiley.

Berliner, L., & McDougall, J. (1997). Agenda for research: Clinical approaches to recollections of trauma. In J. D. Read & D. S. Lindsay (Eds.), *Recollections of trauma: Scientific evidence and clinical practice* (pp. 523–530). NY: Plenum.

Bernstein, E. M., & Putnam, F. W. (1986). Development, reliability, and validity of a dissociation scale. *Journal of Nervous and Mental Disease, 174*, 727–735.

Canadian Psychological Association (1996). *Guidelines for psychologists addressing recovered memories.* Ottawa: Author.

Ceci, S. J. (1995). False beliefs: Some developmental and clinical considerations. In D. L. Schacter (Ed.), *Memory distortion: How minds, brains, and societies reconstruct the past* (pp. 91–125). Cambridge: Harvard University Press.

Ceci, S. J., & Bruck, M. (1993). Suggestibility of the child witness: A historical review and synthesis. *Psychological Bulletin, 113*, 403–439.

Ceci, S. J., Crotteau-Huffman, M. L., Smith, E., & Loftus, E. F. (1994). Repeatedly thinking about non-events. *Consciousness and Cognition, 3*, 388–407.

Costa, P. T., Jr., & McCrae, R. R. (1992). *NEO PI-R: Professional Manual.* Odessa, FL: Psychological Assessment Resources.

Courtois, C. A. (1997). Informed clinical practice and the standard of care: Proposed guidelines for the treatment of adults who report delayed memories of childhood trauma. In J. D. Read & D. S. Lindsay (Eds.), *Recollections of trauma: Scientific evidence and clinical practice* (pp. 337–370). NY: Plenum.

DePaulo, B. M., & Kashy, D. A. (1998). Everyday lies in close and casual relationships. *Journal of Personality and Social Psychology, 74*, 63–79.

Ekman, P. (1992). *Telling lies* (2nd ed.). NY: Norton.

Ekman, P., & O'Sullivan, M. (1991). Who can catch a liar? *American Psychologist, 46*, 913–920.

Hare, R. D. (1998). Psychopathy, affect, and behavior. In D. Cooke, A. Forth, & R. Hare (Eds.), *Psychopathy: Theory, research, and implications for society* (pp. 105–137). The Netherlands: Kluwer.

Hare, R. D., & Hervé, H. F. (July, 1999). *The psychopath as clinical prototype for pathological laying and deception.* Paper presented at the Psychology and Law International Conference. Dublin, Ireland.

Hare, R. D., Forth, A. E., & Hart, S. D. (1989). The psychopath as prototype for pathological lying and deception. In J. C. Yuille (Ed.), *Credibility assessment* (pp. 24–49). Dordrecht, The Netherlands: Kluwer.

Horowitz, S. W. (1991). Empirical support for Statement Validity Analysis. *Behavioral Assessment, 13*, 293–313.

Hyman, I. E., Husband, T. H., & Billings, J. F. (1995). False memories of childhood experiences. *Applied Cognitive Psychology, 9*, 181–197.

Iacono, W. G., & Patrick, C. J. (1999). Polygraph ("Lie Detector") testing: The state of the art. In A. K. Hess, & I. B. Weiner (Eds.), *The handbook of forensic psychology* (2nd ed.) (pp. 440–473). NY: Wiley.

James, W. (1890). *The principles of psychology* (Vol. 1). NY: Dover.

Jane Doe et al. *v. Joseph Maskell* et al. (1996). No. 102 Court of Appeals (Maryland 29).

Johnson, M. K., & Raye, C. L. (1981). Reality monitoring. *Psychological Bulletin, 88*, 67–85.

Kassin, S. M., & Fong, C. T. (1999). "I'm innocent!": Effects of training on judgments of truth and deception in the interrogation room. *Law and Human Behavior, 23*, 499–516.

Knapp, S. J., & Vandecreek, L. (1997). *Treating patients with memories of abuse: Legal risk management.* Washington, DC: American Psychological Association.

Lampinen, J. M., Neuschatz, J. S., & Payne, D. G. (1998). Memory illusions and consciousness: Examining the phenomenology of true and false memories. *Current Psychology: Developmental, Learning, Personality, & Personality, 16*, 181–224.

Leichtman, M. D., & Ceci, S. J. (1995). The effects of stereotypes and suggestions on preschoolers' reports. *Developmental Psychology, 31*, 568–578.

Lindsay, D. S., & Read, J. D. (1994). Psychotherapy and memories of childhood sexual abuse: A cognitive perspective. *Applied Cognitive Psychology, 8*, 281–338.

Loftus, E. F. (1993). The reality of repressed memories. *American Psychologist, 48*, 518–537.

Loftus, E. F. (1997a). Creating false memories. *Scientific American, 277*, 70–75.

Loftus, E. F. (1997b). Dispatch from the (un)civil memory wars. In J. D. Read & D. S. Lindsay (Eds.), *Recollections of trauma: Scientific evidence and clinical practice* (pp. 171–198). NY: Plenum.

Loftus, E. F. (1997c). Memory for a past that never was. *Current Directions in Psychological Science, 6*, 60–65.

Loftus, E. F., & Pickrell, J. E. (1995). The formation of false memories. *Psychiatric Annals, 25*, 720–725.

Marxsen, D., Yuille, J. C., & Nisbet, M. (1995). The complexities of eliciting and assessing children's statements. *Psychology, Public Policy, and Law, 1*, 450–460.

Memon, A. Vrij, A., & Bull, R. (1998). *Credibility assessment: Psychology and the law*. NY: McGraw-Hill.

Payne, D. G., Neuschatz, J. S., Lampinen, J. M., & Lynn, S. J. (1997). Compelling memory illusions: The qualitative characteristics of false memories. *Current Directions in Psychological Science, 6*, 56–60.

Pezdek, K., Finger, K., & Hodge, D. (1997). Planting false childhood memories: The role of event plausibility. *Psychological Science, 8*, 437–441.

Pezdek, K., & Roe, C. (1997). The suggestibility of children's memory for being touched: Planting, erasing, and changing memories. *Law and Human Behavior, 21*, 95–106.

Pezdek, K., & Taylor, J. (in press). Discriminating between accounts of true and false events. In D. F. Bjorklund (Ed.), *Research and theory in false-memory creation in children and adults*. Mahwah, NJ: Erlbaum.

Poole, D. A., Lindsay, D. S., Memon, A., & Bull, R. (1995). Psychotherapy and the recovery of memories of childhood sexual abuse: U.S. and British practitioners' opinions, practices, and experiences. *Journal of Consulting and Clinical Psychology, 63*, 426–437.

Porter, S. (1998). *An architectural mind: The nature of real, created, and fabricated memories of emotional childhood events*. Unpublished doctoral dissertation, University of British Columbia, Vancouver, Canada.

Porter, S., & Birt, A. (in press). Is traumatic memory special? An investigation of the qualities of traumatic memories. *Applied Cognitive Psychology*.

Porter, S., Birt, A. R., Yuille, J. C., & Lehman, D. R. (2000). The negotiation of false memories: Influence of interviewer and rememberer characteristics on memory distortion. *Psychological Science. 11*, 513–516.

Porter, S., Woodworth, M. & Birt, A. R., (in press). The effect of training on deception detection by federal parole officers. *Law & Human Behavior.*

Porter, S., Birt, A. R., Hervé, H., & Yuille, J. C. (in press). Memory for murder: A psychological perspective on dissociative amnesia in legal contexts. *International Journal of Law and Psychiatry.*

Porter, S., & Marxsen, D. (1998). Challenging the eyewitness expert: An update considering memory for trauma and false memories. In J. Ziskin (Ed.), *1997 Supplement to: Coping with psychiatric and psychological testimony, 5th ed.* (pp. 112–129). Law and Psychology Press: Los Angeles.

Porter, S., & Yuille, J. C. (1995). Credibility assessment of criminal suspects through statement analysis. *Psychology, Crime, and Law, 1*, 319–331.

Porter, S., & Yuille, J. C. (1996). The language of deceit: An investigation of the verbal clues to deception in the interrogation context. *Law and Human Behavior, 20*, 443–458.

Porter, S., Yuille, J. C., & Lehman, D. (1999). The nature of real, implanted, and fabricated memories for emotional childhood events: Implications for the recovered memory debate. *Law and Human Behavior, 23*, 517–537.

R. v. Francois [1994]. 2 S.C.R. 827.

Read, J. D. (1999). The recovered/false memory debate: Three steps forward, two steps back? *Expert Evidence*.

Ruby, C. L., & Brigham, J. C. (1997). The usefulness of the criteria-based content analysis technique in distinguishing between truthful and fabricated allegations: A critical review. *Psychology, Public Policy, and Law, 3*, 705–737.

Schacter, D. L. (1996). *Searching for memory: The brain, the mind, and the past*. NY: Basic Books.

Schacter, D. L. (1999). The seven sins of memory: Insights from psychology and cognitive neuroscience. *American Psychologist, 54*, 182–203.

Schooler, J. W., Gerhard, D., & Loftus, E. F. (1986). Qualities of the unreal. *Journal of Experimental Psychology: Learning, Memory, and Cognition, 12*, 171–181.

Trivers, R. (1985). *Social evolution*. Menlo Park, CA: Benjamin/Cummings.

Wicker, W. (1953). The polygraph truth test and the law of evidence. *Tennessee Law Review*, *22*, 32–39.

Yuille, J. C., Daylen, J., Porter, S., & Marxsen, D. (1995). Challenging the eyewitness expert. In J. Ziskin (Ed.), *Coping with psychiatric and psychological testimony* (5th ed., Vol. 2) (pp. 1266–1298). Los Angeles, CA: Law and Psychology Press.

Yuille, J. C., Tymofievich, M., & Marxsen, D. (1995). The nature of allegations of child sexual abuse. In T. Ney (Ed.), *Allegations of child sexual abuse: Assessment and case management.* NY: Brunner/Mazel.

Zuckerman, M., & Driver, R. E. (1985). Telling lies: Verbal and nonverbal correlates of deception. In A. W. Seigman, & S. Feldstein (Eds.), *Multichannel integrations of nonverbal behaviors* (pp. 129–147). Hillsdale, NJ: Lawrence Erlbaum.

Author Notes

Correspondence regarding this article should be made to Dr. Stephen Porter at the Department of Psychology, Dalhousie University, Halifax, N.S., B3H 4J1, or by electronic mail: sbporter@is.dal.ca.
Appreciation is extended to the Social Sciences and Humanities Research Council of Canada (SSHRC) and the American Psychology and Law Society (Division 41) of the American Psychological Association for supporting this research.

Chapter 18

PREVIOUS EXPOSURE TO THE SENDER'S BEHAVIOR AND ACCURACY AT JUDGING CREDIBILITY

Eugenio Garrido and Jaume Masip

The idea that familiarity among sender and receiver will facilitate the latter's credibility judgments (i.e., his/her judgments as to whether the sender is lying or telling the truth) is intrinsically appealing. It constitutes the basis behind Ekman's Brokaw hazard (e.g., Ekman, 1992; Ekman & Frank, 1993), which suggests that misjudgments of credibility may be made by looking at certain cues associated with deception, which are nevertheless displayed by the particular sender, even when she or her is truthful. According to Ekman (1992), "lie catchers are vulnerable to the Brokaw hazard when they are unacquainted with the suspect, not familiar with idiosyncrasies in the suspect's typical behavior" (p. 91), and "the only way to reduce mistakes due to the Brokaw hazard is to *base judgments on a change in the suspect's behavior* ... People are likely to be misled in first meetings because there is no base for comparison, no opportunity to note changes in behavior" (pp. 166–167, emphasis in the original). It is therefore not surprising that some scholars have explored the effects of familiarity on accuracy at detecting deception and truthfulness. However, there seems to be a lack of agreement concerning the definition and operationalization of familiarity, which may account for some of the inconsistent findings in this area of research, as Feeley, deTurck, and Young (1995) have noted. Thus, some have looked at how *relational familiarity* or *relational development* influences detection accuracy or deception cues (e.g., Bauchner, 1978; Buller & Aune, 1987; Buller, Burgoon, White, & Ebesu, 1994; Buller, Strzyzewsky, & Comstock, 1991; Burgoon, Buller, Ebesu, & Rockwell, 1994; Comadena, 1982; Levine & McCornack, 1992; McCornack & Levine, 1990; McCornack & Parks, 1986, 1990; Stiff, Kim, & Ramesh, 1992). That kind of familiarity refers to "the presence of an emotional bond between partners based on a prior interaction" (Buller et al., 1994, p. 370) or "overall increases in emotional attachment, intimacy and caring and an overall decrease in the level of global uncertainty" (McCornack & Parks, 1990, p. 110). Thus, in the typical experiment, comparisons are made between the accuracy of strangers, friends, and intimates at judging the sender's truthfulness.

Familiarity can also be conceptualized as the number of previous exposures to the truthful behavior of the target. Buller and Burgoon (1996) label background information about the interactant as *informational familiarity*. In general, research on informational familiarity (e.g., Becerra, Sánchez & Carrera, 1989; Brandt, Miller & Hocking, 1980a,b, 1982; Ekman & Friesen, 1974; Feeley et al., 1995; O'Sullivan, Ekman & Friesen, 1988; Zuckerman, Koestner, & Alton, 1984; Zuckerman, Koestner, & Colella, 1985) tends to support the notion that knowledge of the baseline, truthful behavior of the sender increases deception accuracy by receivers. In line with this, Becerra et al. (1989) advanced the idea that perhaps there are no specific cues signaling deception. Instead, they propose that deception judgments depend upon a general expressive pattern that is displayed by the sender and cannot be easily analyzed into concrete and isolatable behavioral units. When the sender lies, such a pattern, given its departure from the usual, truthful behavior, is perceived by the receiver as altered. This allows the receiver to correctly infer that the sender is being deceptive.

Finally, a third way of conceptualizing familiarity is as professional expertise or *behavioral familiarity*: "knowledge about prototypical cues gained through training or experience" (Buller & Burgoon, 1996). Research has checked whether on-the-job experience increases detection accuracy. Results show that neither oil company executives (Druckman, Rozelle & Baxter, 1982), nor barristers (Jackson & Granhag, 1997), nor members of a military human intelligence school (Burgoon et al., 1994), nor police officers (DePaulo & Pfeiffer, 1986; Ekman & O'Sullivan, 1991; Garrido, Masip, Herrero, & Tabernero, 1997; Henderson & Hess, 1982; Köhnken, 1987; Kraut & Poe, 1980; Sanderson, 1978; Vrij, 1992; see reviews by Bull, 1989, and Garrido & Masip, 1999) are more skilled than lay people at judging credibility. Instead, there is some evidence that police officers may even be worse than lay persons, due to a lie bias they may display when making their judgments (Garrido et al., 1997; Sanderson, 1978).

In this study, we performed some further analyses on Garrido et al.'s (1997) data in order to explore the following issues: first, the role of informational familiarity on credibility judgments. According to existing research, our first hypothesis predicts that previous exposure to the sender's honest behavior will increase accuracy rates among receivers judging credibility.

The second issue pertains to whether observers perceive a general expressive pattern as predicted by Becerra et al. (1989). In our opinion, there are some problematic issues in Becerra et al.'s paper. First, there is a confounding of the real truth value of statements and observers' perceptions of them (as truthful or deceptive). Based on their findings that the frequency of correct judgments of false statements is higher when observers have previously seen a truthful performance by the same sender than if they have not seen such a performance, Becerra et al. concluded that there is a general pattern that receivers perceive as altered when senders lie. However, to conclude that they perceive a change in sender's expressive pattern, we should pay attention not to the *real* quality of the previous performance (truthful), but to how it is *perceived* by the observers. For instance, if they judge the first, truthful statement as false and then they judge the second, false statement also as false, they do not show that they have perceived any behavioral change in the sender's performance.

Second, Becerra et al. (1989) concluded that there are differences between truthful and deceptive performances, but they do not measure them directly. Instead, they based such conclusion on observers' judgments. We think it is not advisable to infer senders' deceptive behaviors by looking at observers' perceptions. The existing discrepancies between real and perceived deception cues (e.g., Akehurst, Köhnken, Vrij, & Bull, 1996; Vrij & Semin, 1996; Zuckerman, Koestner, & Driver, 1981; see also reviews by DePaulo, Stone, & Lassiter, 1985; Vrij, 1998; Zuckerman, DePaulo, & Rosenthal, 1981) support our argument. Third, Becerra et al. hold that the general behavioral pattern they seem to find is idiosyncratic to each sender. However, there is no evidence for such an assertion: they used only two senders, who differed in gender and, as stated previously, they did not measure their behavior. To conclude that a behavioral pattern is idiosyncratic, the behavior of a number of people should be coded, avoiding confoundings between factors such as sender and gender. If differences do emerge between truthful and deceptive performances on most senders, and if such differences are not the same across senders, then we may conclude there is an idiosyncratic change in the behavior people display when they deceive as compared to their behavior when being truthful.

In this study, our emphasis was upon checking whether observers *perceive* any unspecific difference between truthful and deceptive performances. We did not explore whether that change is idiosyncratic or not. Unlike Becerra et al. (1989), we did not measure the correct classifications of false statements as such, but rather whether there was a shift in observers' judgments from the first to the second presentation when the real quality (truth value) of the first and second statements change. Given the great amount of research showing that there may be some isolatable behavioral cues to deceit (reviewed by Buller & Burgoon, 1994; DePaulo et al., 1985; DePaulo, DePaulo, Tang, & Swaim, 1989; Ekman, 1992; Ekman & O'Sullivan, 1989; Ford, 1996; Kalbfleisch, 1992; Kapardis, 1997; Kraut, 1980; Miller & Burgoon, 1982; Miller & Stiff, 1993; Vrij, 1998; Zuckerman et al., 1981), we are unsure as to whether we can expect to find the general pattern described by Becerra and his colleagues or not. However, we hypothesized that we would. Therefore, our second hypothesis stands that if the two stimuli (i.e., the sender's performances) observers watched were both truthful or both deceptive, the raters' judgments would also be both truthful or both deceptive, regardless of whether such judgments are accurate or not, because observers will perceive no general change in the sender's pattern of behavior. Conversely, if one of the stimuli is deceptive and the other is truthful, the raters will judge one as deceptive and the other as truthful, regardless of whether these judgments are accurate or not, because they will perceive the sender's expressive pattern as altered in the second performance as compared to the first.

Finally, in addition to the role of informational familiarity and whether observers perceive a general expressive pattern, we also explored the influence of behavioral familiarity (on-the-job experience) on the perception of that pattern. For instance, it could be argued that differences between police officers and undergraduate students found by Garrido et al. (1997) could be due to the fact that the former, given the relevance of deception detection for their job and their more frequent involvement in what Robinson (1996) calls competitive interactions (as opposed to cooperative ones), hold an initial generalized communication suspicion (Burgoon et al., 1994; Levine & McCornack, 1991), which will prevent them from scrutinizing the sender's behavioral displays, thus not perceiving his or her general expressive pattern. If this is the case, then perhaps police officers made only a biased "guess" based on their initial suspicion. Alternatively, police officers' generalized suspicion may have given rise to a confirmation bias, making them attentive to only those behaviors supporting their view that the sender was lying. In either case, police officers would be unable to perceive the general pattern described by Becerra et al. (1989). Thus, our third hypothesis is that non-officers (undergraduate students) will be better able to perceive the pattern predicted in hypothesis two than police officers.

METHOD

Participants

The sender was one female undergraduate student of psychology at the University of Salamanca (Spain) in her 20s. Observers were 121 police officers (21 females and 100 males) studying to become police inspectors at the Police Academy of Ávila (Spain), and 147 undergraduate students of psychology (122 females and 24 males) at the University of Salamanca.

Measures

The independent measures were: (a) truth value of the first videotaped statement by the sender (truthful/deceptive), (b) nature—same (if both statements are truthful or both are deceptive) or different (if one statement is truthful and the other is deceptive)—of the pair of statements observers watched, and (c) occupation of the observers (i.e., police officers vs. undergraduate students). The dependent measures were: (a) observers' accuracy at judging the credibility of the second statement by the sender, and (b) the degree of similarity between observers' judgments of the first statement and those of the second.

Procedure

In order to increase the ecological validity of this study, we addressed some of the concerns expressed by various authors in this area (e.g., Köhnken, 1987, 1989) by (a) motivating our senders to be convincing, (b) making the content of the statements relevant to police interrogation settings: the topic was the reporting of criminal actions (factual deception), (c) by giving senders a few minutes to prepare their line before giving their statements, (d) by having observers make a dichotomous decision ("true" or "false") instead of rating the degree of truthfulness or deceptiveness, and (e) by showing observers only two statements of some length (no less than two minutes). Normally, in laboratory research on nonverbal detection of deception, a large number of small behavioral samples are shown to observers. However, in the real world police officers rarely have to judge the credibility of dozens of statements which are only a few seconds long. We addressed this issue by showing observers only two statements of some length, although this prevented us from using a large sample of senders.

In order to motivate our sender, we offered all psychology students at the University of Salamanca who were taking a social psychology module a substantial academic reward if they participated as senders in a lie detection study and were the most convincing of all senders. Four females volunteered. Each of them was shown two film sequences depicting criminal actions. After watching each of these sequences, senders were instructed to work out a deceptive version (D) and a truthful one (T) of the sequence. They were left ten minutes to create each version, and were video recorded as they made their statements—a free narrative account no less than two minutes long. A pilot study was conducted with a few participants (undergraduates) in order to choose the most convincing liar for the main study[1]. All four candidates received the advertised reward for their participation.

The four performances of the sender who was chosen were edited and shown to 121 police officers and 147 psychology students. The statements in each group, and number of participants from each occupation per group are shown in Table 1.

After watching each performance of the sender, observers were given a few minutes to complete a questionnaire. One of the items was whether they thought the sender had lied or told the truth.

Coding Procedures

Data were subjected to two different coding procedures.

Accuracy coding. Each observer answer to the second stimulus was coded as 1 if it was correct (e.g., if the observer said the sender lied when in fact she did lie), and it was coded as 0 if it was wrong (e.g., if the observer said the sender lied when in fact she told the truth). This coding procedure enabled us to check hypothesis one.

Similarity coding. As shown in Table 1, TT and DD are those cases in which both performances by the sender are either truthful or deceptive. According to our second hypothesis, observers in those conditions are expected to give the same kind of answer in the face of each stimulus (i.e., to judge both statements as truthful or both as deceptive). On the other hand, TD and DT are those cases in which one of the sender's performances is truthful and the other is deceptive. Observers in those conditions are expected to judge one stimulus as truthful and the other as deceptive. In order to measure the degree of similarity between both of observer's answers, we coded for each observer truth responses (i.e., the observer said

Table 1: Group Composition (Stimulus Pairs) and Number of Observers from Each Occupation Within Each Group

Group	Sequence 1[a]	Sequence 2[a]	Number of Police Officers	Number of Students
1	D	D	28	41
2	D	T	30	32
3	T	T	31	38
4	T	D	31	36

Note.[a] D: deceptive account of the sequence; T: truthful account of the sequence.

the sender told the truth) as 1, and lie responses (the observer said the sender lied) as –1. Then, each observer's coded answer to the first statement was multiplied by his/her coded judgment for the second statement. As shown in Table 2, we expected that for TT and DD stimuli the mean value of that product would tend to be 1, whereas for TD and DT stimuli the mean value of that multiplication would tend to be –1. Thus, this coding procedure will allow us to check hypotheses two and three.

RESULTS

Hypothesis One: Informational Familiarity

Means of observers' responses to the second statement coded as described in the accuracy coding section were .68 for TT, .69 for TD, .42 for DT, and .69 for DD. We performed a 2 (truth value of the first statement: truthful/ deceptive) X 2 (truth value of the second statement: truthful/ deceptive) ANOVA, with accuracy at judging the second statement coded as described above as the dependent measure. Consistent with hypothesis one, we found that accuracy at judging the truthfulness of a second statement was higher among observers who first saw a truthful baseline (M = .68) than among those who first saw a deceptive performance (M = .56), $F(1,261) = 4.67$, $p = .032$. Also, accuracy at judging the truthful version of the second statement (M = .55) was poorer than accuracy at judging its deceptive version (M = .69), $F(1,261) = 5.82$, $p = .017$. The interaction between both factors was also significant, $F(1,261) = 5.02$, $p = .026$, indicating that, as shown in Figure 1, accuracy for the truthful version of the second statement was poorer if the first exposure had been deceptive, but not if it had been truthful. In short, detection accuracy at judging a second statement after having watched a truthful performance of the same sender was significantly higher than accuracy at judging a second statement after watching a previous

Table 2: Stimulus Pairs, Expected Answers from Observers (According to Hypothesis Two) and Coding Procedure for Those Answers (Similarity Coding)

Video Sequences		Expected Answers	Coding of Answers		Coded Expected Answers
Seq. 1	Seq. 2				
D	D	DD	(–1) × (–1)	=	1
		TT	1 × 1		
D	T	DT	(–1) × 1	=	–1
		TD	1 × (–1)		
T	T	DD	(–1) × (–1)	=	1
		TT	1 × 1		
T	D	DT	(–1) × 1	=	–1
		TD	1 × (–1)		

deceptive performance by the same sender, but only when that second statement was *truthful*. There was no improvement in the detection of *deception* in a second videotaped sample of a person's behavior by merely having previously watched another tape showing that person behaving honestly. This is reflected in our finding that there was no significant difference between accuracy for DD (M = .69) and accuracy for TD (M = .69). This difference was significant in Becerra et al.'s (1989) experiment.

Perhaps only watching a sample of the sender's honest behavior does not improve deception accuracy unless observers know that that sample is an honest one. In order to check for this possibility, we took observers who had seen the honest version of the first statement, and looked at differences in accuracy at judging the false second statement between those who had judged it correctly as truthful, and those who misjudged it as deceptive. Means for the second statement were, respectively, .65 and .70. Although this difference is clearly nonsignificant, t (65) = –72, p = .679,

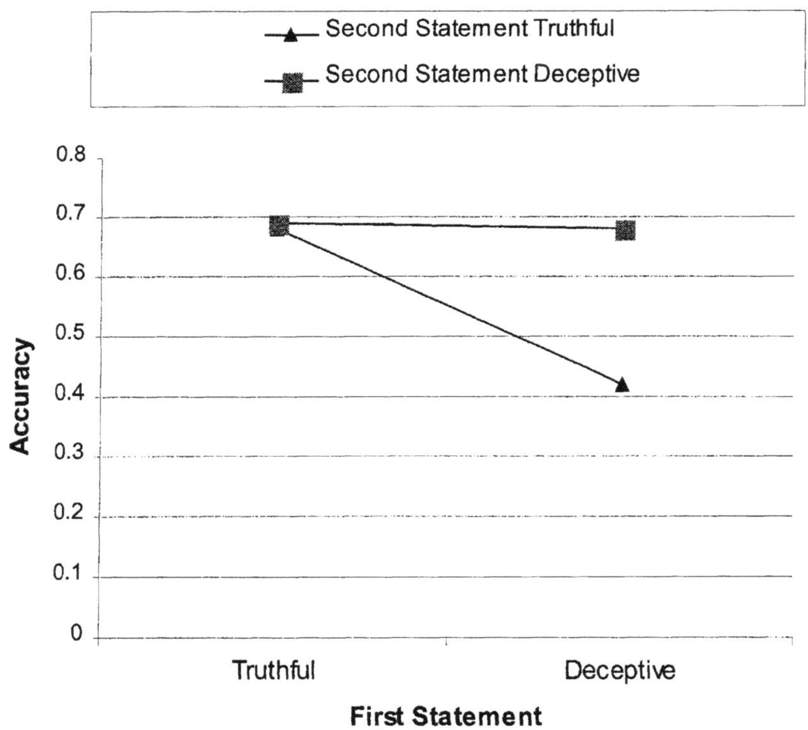

FIGURE 1. ACCURACY AT JUDGING A TRUTHFUL OR A DECEPTIVE SECOND STATEMENT AFTER HAVING SEEN A TRUTHFUL OR DECEPTIVE FIRST STATEMENT BY THE SAME SENDER.

the tendency is contrary to what was expected[2]. Thus, observers' wrong beliefs about the truth value of the previous exposure do not account for the lack of significance between deception accuracy of observers in DD and TD conditions.

In summary, hypothesis one is generally supported, but only for truthful statements, where accuracy among observers who first saw a deceptive performance is particularly poor.

Hypotheses Two and Three: General Expressive Pattern and Behavioral Familiarity

We performed several analyses to check these hypotheses.

Differences between single pairs of statements (TT, TD, DT, and DD). Table 3 shows the number (n) and proportion (p) of observers whose answers, coded according to the similarity coding procedure, were 1 and –1, as well as mean values for each occupation (police officers, students, overall) in every stimulus pair (DD, DT, TD, and TT). A 2 (occupation: officers/students) X 4 (stimulus pair: DD/DT/TD/TT) ANOVA was performed, with observers' answers, coded according to the similarity coding procedure and multiplied as described above, as the dependent variable. The occupation factor had no significant effect, $F(1,257) = 1.84$, $p = .180$. The stimulus pair variable yielded a significant main effect, $F(3,257) = 5.26$, $p = .002$). The interaction was not significant, $F(3,257) = .22$, $p = .880$.

We dismissed, therefore, the occupation variable and performed an ANOVA taking the stimulus pair as the only factor. There was a significant difference among the stimulus pairs, $F(3,261) = 5.16$ and $p = .002$. Fisher's PLSD showed that the TT pair differed significantly from DT ($p \leq .05$), DD ($p \leq .01$), and TD ($p \leq .0005$).

Table 3: Frequencies and Proportions of Observers Whose Coded Responses Yield Values of 1 and –1, and Mean Values for Each Occupation Group in Each Stimulus Pair

Occupation	Stimulus Pair	n[1]	p[1]	n[–1]	p[–1]	n	Mean
Police Officers	DD	17	60.71	11	39.29	28	0.21
	DT	16	53.33	14	46.66	30	0.07
	TT	9	30.00	21	70.00	30	–0.40
	TD	21	67.74	10	32.26	31	0.35
Students	DD	19	47.50	21	52.50	40	–0.05
	DT	15	46.88	17	53.13	32	–0.06
	TT	11	28.95	27	71.05	38	–0.42
	TD	20	55.56	16	44.44	36	0.11
Overall	DD	36	52.94	32	47.06	68	0.06
	DT	31	50.00	31	50.00	62	0.00
	TT	20	29.41	48	70.59	68	–0.41
	TD	41	61.20	26	38.80	67	0.22

Differences between pairs of statements grouped as "same" (TT and DD) or "different" (TD, DT). Observers' coded and multiplied responses for TT and DD conditions were grouped as the "same" category, and those for DT and TD as the "different" category. Their mean values are shown in Table 4.

As we can see in this table, differences between those conditions in which statements are both truthful or both deceptive ("same" category) and those in which one statement is truthful and the other deceptive ("different" category) are not significant either among police officers, $t\ (117) = -1.74$, $p = .085$, or among psychology students, $t\ (144) = -1.58$, $p = .116$.

Differences from 1, −1, and 0. Finally, in order to properly check our hypotheses, we performed t-tests for the means for TT, TD, DD and DT, as well as for those of the "same" category (for police officers, psychology students and overall) and the "different" category (also for police officers, psychology students and overall), setting μ at 1, −1 and 0. Some possibilities were: (a) the means for DD, TT and the "same" category would tend to 1, while those for DT, TD and the "different" category would tend to −1; if so, our prediction of a perceived general expressive pattern would be supported; (b) the means for DD, TT and the "same" category would tend to −1, while those for DT, TD and the "different" category would tend to 1; if so, the opposite pattern would be supported: participants shown two stimuli which were both truthful or both deceptive would tend to judge them as different (i.e., one statement as truthful and the other as deceptive); subjects shown one truthful stimulus and a deceptive one, would tend to judge them as being both truthful or both deceptive; (c) the means for DD, TT, the "same" category, DT, TD and the "different" category would differ significantly from 1 and −1; if so, there would be no pattern at all. Furthermore, if all the means not only differed significantly from 1 and −1 but also did not differ significantly from 0, the non-existence of any pattern would further be supported.

Table 4: Mean Values for Each Occupation Group with Stimulus Pair Grouped as "Same" and "Different" Categories

	Mean Values			
	Same	Different	t	p
Officers	−0.1	0.21	−1.74	0.0851
Students	−0.23	0.03	−1.58	0.1162

As shown in Table 5, in fact: (a) the means for DD, DT, TT and TD all differed significantly from both 1 and –1, (b) except for TT, these means did not differ significantly from 0, (c) the means for the "same" category were, for all groups, different from both 1 and –1; however, they differed significantly from 0 for the student group and the whole sample (psychology group plus police group), (d) all the means for the "different" category differed significantly from 1 and –1, and are not significantly different from 0.

Thus, our second and third hypothesis received no support: there were no differences between police officers and students of psychology, and observers did not perceive a pattern in the sender's behavior.

Additional analysis. Despite our findings that observers perceived no pattern at all, it can be seen that the stimulus pair TT introduces certain "distortion". If we look at Table 3, we will see that both for police officers and psychology students, means for TT were negative, mean values for the "same" category in Table 4 were slightly negative too, and Table 5 shows that the mean value for TT departed significantly from 0 as did the "same" category (which comprises the TT group) for the psychology students. More noteworthy, as described above, the TT pair differed significantly from DT, DD, and TD, with these differences responsible for the main effect of the stimulus pair variable in our ANOVAs. One possible reason for this result is the tendency found by Garrido et al. (1997) for both police officers and undergraduates to judge the truthful version of the first sequence as false. This tendency may make the mean accuracy for TT artificially negative (i.e., below 0), and that for TD very positive (notice that the mean for TD is .22, it does not differ significantly from 0, see Table 5). In order to explore this possiblity, we repeated our second

Table 5: Mean Values for Each Occupation Group Taking Stimulus Pairs Individually or Grouped

				$\mu = 1$		$\mu = 0$		$\mu = -1$	
Statements			Mean	t	p	t	p	t	p
Single pairs		DD	.06	8.61	≤ .0001	0.48	.6311	–7.72	≤ .0001
		DT	.00	7.81	≤ .0001	0.00	—	–7.81	< .0001
		TT	–.41	5.28	≤ .0001	–3.70	.0004	–12.70	≤ .0001
		TD	.22	1.20	≤ .0001	1.87	.0665	–6.47	≤ .0001
Grouped pairs	Same	Officers	–.10	6.81	≤ .0001	–.79	.4356	–8.38	≤ .0001
		Students	–.23	6.94	≤ .0001	–2.08	.0407	–11.10	< .0001
		Overall	–.19	9.60	≤ .0001	–2.18	.0309	–14.00	≤ .0001
	Different	Officers	.21	9.62	≤ .0001	1.69	.0963	–6.24	≤ .0001
		Students	.03	8.43	≤ .0001	.24	.8104	–7.95	≤ .0001
		Overall	.12	12.70	≤ .0001	1.32	.1877	–1.10	≤ .0001

ANOVA excluding from our sample those observers who misjudged the truthful version of the first statement as false. In that case, none of the effect of occupation (officers/students) nor that of stimulus pair (DD/DT/TD/TT), nor their interaction proved to be significant: F and p values were, respectively, $F(1,154) = .7$, $p = .415$; $F(3,154) = 1.27$, $p = .287$; $F(3,154) = .94$, $p = .423$.

DISCUSSION

We found support for our first hypothesis that informational familiarity improves observers' ability to judge credibility. In this experiment, observers' accuracy at judging a second statement was higher if they had previously seen a truthful performance from the same sender than if they had seen a deceptive one, but only when the second statement was truthful; where accuracy among observers who first saw a deceptive performance was particularly poor. No differences emerged when the second statement was false. This lack of significance for deceptive statements cannot be accounted for by the knowledge observers had about the quality of the first statement they saw: observers who correctly judged the first statement as truthful were no more acurate at judging a deceptive second statement than those who misjudged the first statement as false. This is at odds with Zuckerman et al.'s (1984, 1985) findings showing that knowledge about the truth value of previous exposures was beneficial for later credibility judgments. Perhaps the inconsistency between our results and Zuckerman et al.'s is due to the nature of that knowledge: Zuckerman et al. (1984, 1985) gave feedback to observers about the truthfulness of the previous exposures, therefore their observers could be completely sure about the real truth value of those exposures, and therefore, could use them confidently as a comparison baseline. We did not provide feedback to our observers, but took into account, in our analyses, whether they judged the previous performance as truthful or deceptive. However, even in those cases in which those judgments were right, observers could not be absolutely sure about the real truth value of the first statement, so that they probably could not use it confidently as a comparison baseline.

Turning back to the finding that viewing a truthful first statement did not result in improved accuracy in judging a second, deceptive statement, we cannot dismiss the interesting possiblity that these results may be dependent upon our experimental setting. As said above, we manipulated some features in order to make them similar to real situations in which police officers have to judge witnesses' credibility. Certainly, research on informational familiarity conducted in other experimental settings yielded other results. Thus, for instance, Becerra et al. (1989) found that watching a truthful performance improved the accuracy at classifying a second, deceptive statement of the same sender, regardless of whether observers knew or not that the first performance was honest. Feeley et al. (1995) suggested that increased informational familiarity increases accuracy at judging truthful accounts to a higher degree than accuracy at judging false accounts. However, Ekman and Friesen (1974) found that, in a sample who previously saw an honest sample of behavior, means for the deceptive interview were higher than those for the truthful, although it is unclear whether those differences were significant. Researchers exploring the role of informational familiarity should report not only overall accuracy at judging both truthful and deceptive performances ("detection accuracy" according to Miller and Stiff, 1993), but also the separate accuracy for deceptive (deception detection) and truthful (truth detection) performances. In addition, conditions under which one or the other increases or remains constant should be studied.

It is important to note that to test hypothesis one, we did not compare the accuracy of observers having first seen no baseline sample with that of observers having seen one baseline exposure (or several). Instead, we compared the accuracy of observers who first saw an honest statement with that of those who first saw a deceptive one. We think that both kinds of comparison can be of interest. However, the fact that our observers always saw statements about the first sequence first and statements about the second sequence second (see Table 1), prevented us from comparing accuracy after watching one previous sample with accuracy obtained with no comparison baseline.

Our second hypothesis—that if the two performances observers watch are both truthful or both deceptive, the raters' judgments will also tend to be both truthful or both deceptive, while if one of the stimuli is deceptive and the other is truthful, the raters will judge one as deceptive and the other as truthful—received no support. In all conditions the means for the similarity ratings differed significantly from both 1 and –1. Additionally, in most cases they did not differ significantly from 0; in those cases in which they did differ from 0, the trend was contrary to what was expected, and can be accounted for by a tendency, which was detected by Garrido et al. (1997), for both officers and students to rate the truthful version of the first sequence as deceptive.

Similarly, our third hypothesis—that non officers would be better able to perceive the pattern predicted in hypothesis two than police officers—was not supported. Our ANOVAs and t tests showed that both police officers and undergraduate students were similarly incapable of perceiving the pattern predicted in hypothesis two.

In summary, our conclusions are that, at least in the experimental setting we used: (a) whether there is a general expressive pattern in the behavior of honest and deceptive witnesses or not, this pattern is not detected by observers, neither by undergraduate psychology students nor by police officers (no effect of behavioral familiarity); (b) accuracy level at detecting *deception* in a second videotape is not higher among participants who saw the sender behaving truthfully in a previous tape than among those who saw her behaving in a deceptive manner; previous exposure, however, is beneficial if the second statement is *truthful*, since it prevents accuracy from dropping considerably (informational familiarity has an effect when the second statement is truthful, but not when it is deceptive).

The value of our findings for real cases rests upon our effort to increase the ecological validity of this experiment. Still, more effort must be made in that pursuit: unlike real-life criminals, our sender did not chose by herself to lie (unsanctioned deception), but lied instructed by the experimenter (sanctioned deception), Feeley and deTurck (1998) showed that there are differences between cues to sanctioned deception and cues to unsanctioned deception; this may have an effect on observers' accuracy. Also, our sender did not speak to a uniformed officer in a police station, but to a psychology lecturer; she was not probed by any question, but gave just a free narrative account; and she did not witness any live criminal action, but two movie sequences. In our future research, we plan to address these issues. However, if other highly ecological studies confirm the results reported here, we will have gained some insight into the detection of deception and truthfulness in real criminal situations.

REFERENCES

Akehurst, L., Köhnken, G., Vrij, A., & Bull, R. (1996). Lay persons' and police officers' beliefs regarding deceptive behaviour. *Applied Cognitive Psychology*, *10*, 461–471.

Bauchner, J. E. (1978). *Accuracy in detecting deception as a function of level of relationship and communication history*. Unpublished Doctoral Dissertation. Florida State University, Florida.

Becerra, A., Sánchez, F., & Carrera, P. (1989). Indicadores aislados versus patrón general expresivo en la detección de la mentira. *Estudios de Psicología*, *38*, 21–29.

Brandt, D. R., Miller, G. R., & Hocking, J. E. (1980a). Effects of self-monitoring and familiarity on deception detection. *Communication Quarterly*, *28*, 3–10.

Brandt, D. R., Miller, G. R., & Hocking, J. E. (1980b). The truth deception attribution: Effects of familiarity on the ability of observers to detect deception. *Human Communication Research*, *6*, 99–110.

Brandt, D. R., Miller, G. R., & Hocking, J. E. (1982). Familiarity and lie detection: A replication and extension. *Western Journal of Speech Communication*, *46*, 276–290.

Bull, R. (1989). Can training enhance the detection of deception? In J. C. Yuille (Ed.), *Credibility assessment* (pp. 83–99). Dordrecht: Kluwer Academic.

Buller, D. B., & Aune, R. K. (1987). Nonverbal cues to deception among intimates, friends, and strangers. *Journal of Nonverbal Behavior, 11*, 269–290.

Buller, D. B., & Burgoon, J. K. (1994). Deception: strategic and nonstrategic communication. In J. A. Daly, & J. M. Wiemann (Eds.), *Strategic interpersonal communication* (pp. 191–223). Hillsdale, NJ: Erlbaum.

Buller, D. B., & Burgoon, J. K. (1996). Interpersonal deception theory. *Communication Theory, 6*, 203–242.

Buller, D. B., Burgoon, J. K., White, C. H., & Ebesu, A. S. (1994). Interpersonal deception: VII. Behavioral profiles of falsification, equivocation and concealment. *Journal of Language and Social Psychology, 13*, 366–395.

Buller, D. B., Strzyzewsky, K. D., & Comstock, J. (1991). Interpersonal deception: I. Deceivers' reactions to receivers' suspicions and probing. *Communication Monographs, 58*, 1–24.

Burgoon, J. K., Buller, D. B., Ebesu, A. S., & Rockwell, P. (1994). Interpersonal deception: V. Accuracy in deception detection. *Communication Monographs, 61*, 303–325.

Comadena, M. E. (1982). Accuracy in detecting deception: Intimate and friendship relationships. In M. Burgoon (Ed.), *Communication yearbook* (pp. 446–472). Beverly Hills: Sage.

DePaulo, P. J., DePaulo, B. M., Tang, J., & Swaim, G. W. (1989). Lying and detecting lies in organizations. In R. A. Giacalone, & P. Rosenfeld (Eds.), *Impression management in the organization* (pp. 377–393.). Hillsdale, NJ: Lawrence Erlbaum.

DePaulo, B. M., & Pfeiffer, R. L. (1986). On-the-job experience and skill at detecting deception. *Journal of Applied Social Psychology, 16*, 249–267.

DePaulo, B. M., Stone, J. I., & Lassiter, G. D. (1985). Deceiving and detecting deceit. In B. R. Schlenker (Ed.), *The self and social life* (pp. 323–370). New York: McGraw–Hill.

Druckman, D., Rozelle, R. M., & Baxter, J. C. (1982). *Nonverbal communication: Survey, theory and research*. Beverly Hills: Sage.

Ekman, P. (1992). *Telling lies. Clues to deceit in the marketplace, politics, and marriage.* (2nd. edition). New York.: Norton.

Ekman, P., & Frank, M. G. (1993). Lies that fail. In M. Lewis, & C. Saarni (Eds.), *Lying and deception in everyday life.* (pp. 184–200). London: Guilford Press.

Ekman, P., & Friesen, W. V. (1974). Detecting deception from the body or face. *Journal of Personality and Social Psychology, 29*, 288–298.

Ekman, P., & O'Sullivan, M. (1989). Hazards in lie detection. In D. C. Raskin (Ed.), *Psychological methods in criminal investigation and evidence* (pp. 253–280). New York: Springer.

Ekman, P., & O'Sullivan, M. (1991). Who can catch a liar? *American Psychologist, 46*, 913–920.

Feeley, T. H., & deTurck, M. A. (1998). The behavioral correlates of sanctioned and unsanctioned deceptive communication. *Journal of Nonverbal Behavior, 22*, 189–204.

Feeley, T. H., deTurck, M. A., & Young, M. J. (1995). Baseline familiarity in lie detection. *Communication Research Reports, 12*, 160–169.

Ford, C. V. (1996). *Lies! Lies!! Lies!!! The psychology of deceit.* Washington, DC: American Psychiatric Press.

Garrido, E., & Masip, J. (1999). How good are police officers at spotting lies? A review of nonverbal research. *Forensic Update, 58*, 14–21.

Garrido, E., Masip, J., Herrero, C., & Tabernero, C. (1997). *Policemen's ability to discern truth from deception of testimony.* Paper presented at the 7th European Conference on Psychology and Law, Stockholm, Sweden, September 3–6, 1997.

Henderson, J., & Hess, A. K. (1982). *Detecting deception: The effects of training and socialization levels on verbal and nonverbal cue utilization and detection accuracy.* Unpublished manuscript. Auburn University, Auburn, AL.

Jackson, J. L., & Granhag, P. A. (1997). The truth or fantasy: The ability of barristers and laypersons to detect deception in children's testimony. In J. F. Nijboer, & Reijntjes (Eds.), *Proceedings of the First World Conference on New Trends in Criminal Investigation and Evidence* (pp. 213–220). The Hague: Kononklijke Vermande bv/Open University of the Netherlands.

Kalbfleisch, P. J. (1992). Deceit, distrust and the social milieu: Application of deception research in a troubled world. *Journal of Applied Communication Research, 20*, 308–334.

Kapardis, A. (1997). *Psychology and law. A critical introduction.* Cambridge: Cambridge University Press.

Köhnken, G. (1987). Training police officers to detect deceptive eyewitness statements: Does it work? *Social Behaviour*, *2*, 1–17.

Köhnken, G. (1989). Behavioral correlates of statement credibility: Theories, paradigms, and results. In H. Wegener, F. Lösel, & J. Haisch (Eds.), *Criminal behavior and the justice system* (pp. 271–289). London: Springer–Verlag.

Kraut, R. (1980). Humans as lie detectors. *Journal of Communication*, *30*, 209–216.

Kraut, R., & Poe, D. (1980). Behavioral roots of person perception: The deception judgments of customs inspectors and laymen. *Journal of Personality and Social Psychology*, *39*, 784–798.

Levine, T. R., & McCornack, S. A. (1991). The dark side of trust: Conceptualizing and measuring types of communicative suspicion. *Communication Quarterly*, *39*, 325–339.

Levine, T. R., & McCornack, S. A. (1992). Linking love and lies: A formal test of the McCornack and Parks model of deception detection. *Journal of Social and Personal Relationships*, *9*, 143–154.

McCornack, S. A., & Levine, T. R. (1990). When lovers become leary: The relationship between suspicion and accuracy in detecting deception. *Communication Monographs*, *57*, 219–230.

McCornack, S. A., & Parks, M. R. (1986). Deception detection and relational development: The other side of trust. In M. L. McLaughin (Ed.), *Communication Yearbook*, *9*. Beverly Hills, CA: Sage.

McCornack, S. A., & Parks, M. R. (1990). What women know that men don't: Sex differences in determining the truth behind deceptive messages. *Journal of Social and Personal Relationships*, *7*, 107–118.

Miller, G. R., & Burgoon, J. K. (1982). Factors affecting assessments of witness credibility. In N. Kerr, & R. Bray (Eds.), *The psychology of the courtroom* (pp. 169–194). New York: Academic Press.

Miller, G. R., & Stiff, J. B. (1993). *Deceptive communication.* Newbury Park: Sage.

O'Sullivan, M., Ekman, P., & Friesen, W. V. (1988). The effect of comparisons on detecting deceit. *Journal of Nonverbal Behavior*, *12*, 203–215.

Robinson, W. P. (1996). *Deceit, delusion, and detection.* Thousand Oaks, CA: Sage.

Sanderson, J. B. (1978). *The detection of deception by non-verbal signals.* Unpublished Bachelor's thesis. University of Lancaster.

Stiff, J. B., Kim, H. J., & Ramesh, C. N. (1992). Truth biases and aroused suspicion in relational deception. *Communication Research*, *19*, 326–345.

Vrij, A. (1992). Credibility judgments of detectives: The impact of nonverbal behavior, social skills, and physical characteristics on impression formation. *Journal of Social Psychology*, *133*, 601–610.

Vrij, A. (1998). Nonverbal communication and credibility. In A. Memon, A. Vrij, & R. Bull. (Eds.), *Psychology and law. Truthfulness, accuracy and credibility* (pp. 32–58). New York: McGraw–Hill.

Vrij, A., & Semin, G. R. (1996). Lie experts' beliefs about nonverbal indicators of deception. *Journal of Nonverbal Behavior*, *20*, 65–80.

Zuckerman, M., DePaulo, B. M., & Rosenthal, R. (1981). Verbal and nonverbal communication of deception. *Advances in Experimental Social Psychology*, *14*, 1–59.

Zuckerman, M., Koestner, R., & Alton, A. O. (1984). Learning to detect deception. *Journal of Personality and Social Psychology*, *46*, 519–528.

Zuckerman, M., Koestner, R., & Colella, M. J. (1985). Learning to detect deception from three communication channels. *Journal of Nonverbal Behavior*, *9*, 188–194.

Zuckerman, M., Koestner, R., & Driver, R. (1981). Beliefs about cues associated with deception. *Journal of Nonverbal Behavior*, *6*, 105–114.

Author Note

The research reported here has been funded by the *Junta de Castilla y León, Programa de Apoyo a Proyectos de Investigación*, Ref. 30/98.

1. The main study, reported by Garrido, Masip, Herrero and Tabernero (1997), compared police officers and lay people's ability to detect truthful and deceptive statements. In order to ensure

that credibility judgments were not obvious, so that differences between more skilled and less skilled groups could emerge, a liar was chosen who, according to the ratings by the participants in the pilot study, was relatively good at deceiving.

2. Differences were, however, significant for truthful statements: observers who correctly judged the previous truthful exposure were significantly worse at judging a second, truthful statement than those who misjudged the previous exposure as false (means were .42 and .73 respectively, t (66) = −2.16, p = .0343. Overall detection accuracy of the second statement among those who had correctly identified the truthful previous performance (M = .56) was not significantly different from that obtained by those observers who misjudged that previous performance (M = .72), t (133) = −1.66, p = .0996; there is, however, a negative trend.

Chapter 19

THE INFLUENCE OF PERSONAL CHARACTERISTICS, STAKES AND LIE COMPLEXITY ON THE ACCURACY AND CONFIDENCE TO DETECT DECEIT[1]

Aldert Vrij, Fiona Harden, Jo Terry Katherine Edward and Ray Bull

Research has convincingly demonstrated that people are not good at detecting lies. In studies concerning the detection of deception, observers (mostly college students) are typically given videotapes or audiotapes and asked to judge whether each of a number of people is lying or telling the truth. The alternatives to choose from in these studies are "the person is lying" or "the person is not lying", resulting in a 50% chance of a correct answer by just guessing. In a review of 39 recent detection of deception studies (all published after 1981), Vrij (2000) found that the percentages of lie detection (the "accuracy rate") in most of these studies ranged from 45% to 60%, with only five studies exceeding the 60% accuracy level. The mean accuracy rate was 56.6%. It sounds plausible that several factors, such as the circumstances under which the lie takes place, and the personal characteristics of the lie detector will have an impact on the ability to detect lies. Such factors, that are widely disregarded in the detection of deception research so far, will be addressed in the present studies.

Circumstances under which the lie takes place: stakes and lie complexity
The consequences for the liar of lies being detected (the stakes) are not always the same. They are more serious for a murderer when, during a police interview, he denies having committed the crime, than for a girl who exaggerates the number of CD's she has in a conversation with friends. And the consequences are bigger for smugglers when customs officers discover that they tried to smuggle heroin, than when they were in possession of too much alcohol.

Lies might also differ in complexity. Some lies are more difficult to tell than others. For example, lying is more difficult when the other person has some form of evidence that a person may well be lying. Suppose a twelve-year-old boy smokes cigarettes despite his parents forbidding him to do so. When his parents ask him straight out whether he smokes, it is more difficult for him to deny this when they have found an empty cigarette packet in his room, than when they do not have any evidence to prove his smoking habits. Lying is also more difficult when the other person is suspicious (Ekman, 1992). The adulterous wife will have more difficulties in hiding her affair when her husband is suspicious than when he is not. Finally, a lie is easier to tell when the liar has the opportunity to prepare the lie. It is easier for the girl to lie about why she does not want to go out with a particular boy, when she already expected his request for a date, and had therefore prepared an excuse, than when his request took her by surprise and she had to lie spontaneously. It is important to take stakes and lie complexity into consideration when discussing lies, as they may influence people's behavior when lying.

Typical deceptive behavior does not exist (DePaulo, Stone, & Lassiter, 1985; Vrij, 2000). That is, there is no unique pattern of specific behaviors people show when they are lying, or in other words, there is nothing like Pinocchio's nose. Liars, however, may experience each of three different processes during deception, namely emotion, content complexity, and control, and each of these may influence liars' behavior in similar or dissimilar ways (DePaulo et al., 1985; Edinger & Patterson, 1983; Ekman, 1992; Köhnken, 1989; Vrij, 1991, 2000; Zuckerman, DePaulo, & Rosenthal, 1981).

Deception can result in a variety of emotions. The three most common types of emotion associated with deceit are guilt, fear, and excitement (Ekman, 1989, 1992). Suppose that a politician has secretly accepted a large sum of money from a company in exchange for lobbying. A journalist becomes suspicious and asks the politician about his links with the company. While denying any wrongdoing, the politician might feel *guilty*. He might feel guilty because of the fact that he inappropriately accepted money, or he might feel guilty because he realizes that it is wrong to deceive the journalist. He also might be *afraid*, because he might be worried that the journalist will find out that he is lying, which could result in the end of his political career. Or he might become very *excited* because he enjoys the opportunity of fooling the journalist. Guilt might result in gaze aversion because the liar does not dare to look the target straight in the eye while telling a lie. Fear and excitement might result in signs of stress, such as an increase in movements, an increase in speech hesitations (e.g., mm's and er's) and speech errors (stutters, repetition of words, omission of words), or a higher pitched voice. These emotions may also result in brief facial expressions. For example, eyebrows which are raised and pulled together and a raised upper eyelid and tensed lower eyelid typically mark fear (Ekman, 1992).

Lying can be a cognitively complex task. Liars have to think of plausible answers, should not contradict themselves, should tell a lie that is consistent with everything the observer knows or might find out, and should avoid making slips of the tongue. Moreover, they have to remember what they have said, so that they can say the same things when asked to repeat their story. It is therefore much easier for a suspect to present an alibi when the alibi is real than when it is fabricated. Evidence has suggested that people engaged in cognitively complex tasks make more speech hesitations and speech errors, speak slower, pause more, and wait longer before giving an answer (Goldman-Eiser, 1968). Cognitive complexity also leads to fewer hand and arm movements and to more gaze aversion (Ekman, 1997; Ekman & Friesen, 1972). The decrease in hand and arm movements is due to the fact that a greater cognitive load results in a neglect of body language, reducing overall animation. Gaze aversion (usually to a motionless point) occurs because looking at the conversation partner distracts thinking.

So far, the predictions of how liars behave are straightforward. A liar may experience emotions or may find it difficult to lie, and this will result in behavioral signs of emotion and content complexity. The situation, however, is more complicated. Liars may be afraid that signs of emotions or content complexity will give their lies away and therefore will try to suppress such signs in order to avoid getting caught. They should suppress their nerves effectively, should mask evidence that they have to think hard, should know how they normally behave, and should be able to show the behavior they want to show, that is, be good actors. Many liars will not manage to show, when lying, the behavior they normally show when telling the truth. Consequently, some behaviors will give the lie away despite liars' efforts, most likely those behaviors which are the most difficult to control (Ekman & Friesen, 1974).

People are better at controlling their facial behavior (smiling and gaze behavior) than body movements (movements of arms, hands, legs and feet) and vocal characteristics, such as speech rate and stutters. Facial behavior is more important in the exchange of information than body movements and vocal characteristics. For example, via gaze behavior people can make clear whether they are interested in someone's conversation, whether they feel happy or sad, whether they understand what somebody is saying and whether they want to say something (Ekman, 1992; Vrij, 2000). The great communicative potential of the face means that people are practiced at using, and therefore controlling it. The body is a channel that may not be so salient in communication and is less often attended to and reacted to by others. We are therefore less practiced in making body movements and less good at controlling them. It may well be the case that, when controlling their behavior, liars exhibit a pattern of behaving that will appear planned, rehearsed, and lacking in spontaneity. For example, liars may believe that body movements will give their lies away, and will therefore move very deliberately and tend to avoid those movements that are not strictly essential. This will result in an unusual degree of rigidity and inhibition, because people normally make movements that are not essential, such as movements of the hands, arms, and fingers, movements of the legs and feet.

Like most movements, vocal characteristics such as speech hesitations, speech errors, and pauses between sentences and words are usually made unintentionally and are not usually important in the exchange of information (Vrij, 2000). We therefore may assume that people do not often practice controlling these behaviors, and are not very good at controlling them. It is likely that liars will think that the use of speech hesitations, errors and pauses will make them sound suspect. Therefore they will try to avoid making such hesitations and errors. This, however, may result in a speech pattern that sounds unusually smooth, as it is normal for most people to make some errors in speech. Research has indicated that the more liars try to control their behavior, the more behavioral rigidity will occur. This is called the motivational impairment effect (DePaulo & Kirkendol, 1989; DePaulo, Kirkendol, Tang, & O'Brien, 1988; DePaulo, Lanier, & Davis, 1983). In their efforts to avoid displaying any behavioral cues to deception, the highly motivated liar often seems to think that the best strategy to achieve this is to refrain from showing any (suspicious signs of) body language at all, resulting in an unusual absence of body movements and in speech which is unusually smooth and fluent.

The forgoing makes clear that different behaviors can be expected when stakes and lie complexity are manipulated. High stakes may result in more behavioral cues to deception than low stakes. They may result in more nervous behaviors or in more rigid behaviors caused by the motivational impairment effect. Obviously, the more behavioral clues a liar reveals, the better the opportunity for the lie detector to detect a lie. In study 1, observers were exposed to video fragments of a number of people who either told the truth, a low stake lie or a high stake lie. It was predicted that observers would be better at detecting high stakes lies than low stakes lies (Hypothesis 1).

Similarly, complicated lies may result in more behavioral clues than do easy lies, as they may reveal signs of hard thinking or unsuccessful attempts to suppress the signs believed to be indicators of deceit. In study 2, observers were exposed to video fragments of a number of people who either told the truth, an easy lie or a difficult lie. It was predicted that observers would be better at detecting difficult lies than easy ones (Hypothesis 2).

Personal characteristics

Deception is an interaction process between the liar and the lie detector in which liars often "act"; they deliberately try to fool the lie detector by hiding their true feelings and thoughts. It might be possible that people good at acting are better lie detectors than people poor at acting because they may be better at distinguishing between "natural" behavior (displayed by truth tellers) and "acting" (displayed by liars).

People high in public self-consciousness tend to accommodate themselves to other people in social interactions (Kashy & DePaulo, 1996). Knowing well how to interpret someone's nonverbal behavior may be very valuable to achieve this. Their experience in interpreting someone's behavior may be a benefit in detecting lies. It was therefore predicted that positive correlations would be found between detecting truths and lies, and someone's ability to act (Hypothesis 3a) and public self-consciousness (Hypothesis 3b).

Apart from people's ability to detect lies, people's confidence in their ability to detect lies is investigated in the present studies. In their review of 18 studies concerning the accuracy—confidence relationship, DePaulo, Charlton, Cooper, Lindsay, and Muhlenbruck (1997) found a correlation close to zero, namely .04. In other words, there seems to be no relationship between people's ability to detect lies and their confidence in detecting lies. We had no reason to believe that our studies would be an exception to this, and we therefore predicted that the accuracy—confidence correlation would not differ significantly from zero (Hypothesis 4). We did, however, expect individual differences in lie detectors' confidence to detect lies. Some people are typically reserved in social contexts (Kashy & DePaulo, 1996; Vrij, 2000). This is either because they prefer their own company and prefer to focus themselves on thoughts and reflections that deal solely with the self (people who are introverted), or because they are socially anxious (feel discomfort in the presence of others), or shy (feel awkward and tense when with others). It sounds plausible that being reserved and insecure in social interactions will make people insecure in judging social interactions as well. It was therefore predicted that negative correlations would be found between being introverted, shy or socially anxious, and being confident about the ability to detect deceit (Hypothesis 5).

STUDY 1: THE IMPACT OF STAKES AND PERSONAL CHARACTERISTICS

METHOD

Participants

A total of 61 university students participated in this experiment, 36 males and 25 females. Their average age was 21 years (*SD* = 2.1 years).

Stimulus material

In our ongoing research (Vrij, Edward, & Bull, 1999b), 39 nursing students were shown a videofilm about a (staged) theft in a hospital and were asked the following three questions about this film: "What did the nurse do?",: What did the patient do?" and "What did the visitor do?". One-third of the nurses were asked to answer the questions honestly, whereas the remaining two-thirds were asked to lie. The interviews were videotaped with a camera that was clearly visible to the nursing students. In order to make the task not too difficult for the liars, they were given 15 seconds to think about an answer. Half of the liars were randomly allocated to the low stakes lie condition, the other half to the high stakes lie condition. Participants in the low stakes lie condition received the following instructions before the interview started: "Before you start, I should assure you that this is a very easy task, because it is very difficult for other people to tell when you are lying, so relax." The instructions for the participants in the high stakes lie condition were as follows: "This study is examining your ability to lie, because research has suggested that nursing ability is related to ability to lie effectively. So try and be as convincing as possible. The raters next door will be coding you as to how well you lie." In order to show the participants how the coding took place, they were then brought to an adjacent room where four raters were sitting in front of a TV screen that was connected to the camera in the interview room and on which was visible what was happening in the interview room.

For the present study, a videotape was compiled with fragments of 30 different interviews (the fragments were about 15 seconds in length and randomly selected), and consisted of ten truths, ten low stake lies and ten high stake lies. The truths, low stake lies and high stake lies were put onto the videotape in a random order.

Procedure

Students visiting the Students' Union of the University of Portsmouth were asked to participate in a short study testing the ability to detect lies. Only a small minority of students who were approached (less than 10%) refused to participate. Participants were brought to a room in the

Students' Union and exposed to the videotape of 30 fragments. They were given the following instructions: "You will see 30 videoclips of 30 different people who are either lying or telling the truth about a film they just saw. Please indicate after each clip (1) whether or not the person is lying and (2) how confident you are in the decision you made." In order to do this, the participants were given a questionnaire which clearly showed headings (fragment 1, fragment 2, fragment 3 and so on) and two questions under each heading: (1) Is this person lying? (yes or no) and (2) How confident are you in this decision? The answer to this latter question could be given on a 7-point Likert scale ranging from (1) not confident at all to (7) very confident. Accuracy rates (the percentage of correct answers) for truths, low stake lies and high stake lies and the mean confidence scores for truths, low stake lies and high stake lies were calculated.

Prior to the lie detection task, participants were requested to fill in a questionnaire related to their personality. The three subscales of Fenigstein, Scheier and Buss' (1975) Self-Consciousness Scale were used to measure *Introversion* (10 items, Cronbach's alpha = .67), *Public Self-Consciousness* (7 items, Cronbach's alpha = .80) and *Social Anxiety* (6 items, Cronbach's alpha = .83). The *Ability to Act* was measured with eight questions, derived from Briggs, Cheek, and Buss' (1980) acting scale (items 1 to 5) and Riggio's (1986) emotional control scale (Cronbach's alpha = .77); *shyness* was measured with nine items (Cheek & Buss, 1981) (Cronbach's alpha = .84). Answers could be given on 7-point Likert scales ranging from (1) untrue to (7) true.

RESULTS

The accuracy rates and confidence scores for truths, low stake lies and high stake lies are depicted in Table 1.

Table 1 reveals that the observers were better at detecting high stakes lies (58%) than low stakes lies (48%), $F(1,60) = 4.24$, $p < .05$, which supports Hypothesis 1. When a comparison is made with the accuracy rate for detecting truths (57%), it can be seen that observers were

Table 1: Accuracy and Confidence Scores as a Function of Stakes

	Condition			
	Truth	Low	High	F(2,120)
Accuracy	$.57^{b}$	$.48^{a}$	$.58^{b}$	3.25*
Confidence	5.20^{c}	4.85^{a}	5.03^{b}	9.93**

Note. Only means with a different superscript differ significantly from each other ($p < .05$).
$^{*}p < .05$ $^{**}p < .01$.

relatively poor at detecting low stake lies (rather than particularly good at detecting high stake lies). Table 1 further reveals that observers were most confident in their ability to detect truths and least confident in their ability to detect low stakes lies.

Table 2 shows the relationship between the ability to detect truths and lies and personal characteristics.

Table 2: Correlations between Personal Characteristics and Accuracy or Confidence

			Personal Characertistics		
	Acting	PSC	Introversion	Anxiety	Shyness
Accuracy					
Truth	–.14	–.06	.02	–.11	–.10
Low	.01	–.02	.04	–.00	–.08
High	–.04	–.12	–.13	–.12	–.14
Confidence					
Truth	.32*	.10	–.33**	–.39**	.27*
Low	.41**	.20	–.32*	–.36**	–.24*
High	.41**	.10	–.32*	–.34**	–.23*

*$p < .05$ **$p < .01$.

All correlations between accuracy rates and personal characteristics were low and none of them was significant. Hypothesis 3 is therefore not supported.

Table 3 provides the relationship between accuracy and confidence for the three conditions (truths, low stake lies and high stake lies).

Table 3: Accuracy—Confidence Relationship

		Accuracy	
Confidence	Truth	Low	High
Truth	–.07		
Low		.20	
High			.18

None of the correlations were significant, which is in line with previous deception research and supports Hypothesis 4.

Table 2 shows the correlations between confidence scores and personal characteristics. Confidence was negatively correlated with introversion, social anxiety and shyness, indicating that the more introverted, socially anxious and/or shy the participants were, the less confident they were in their ability to detect truths and deceit. These findings support Hypothesis 5. Unpredicted positive correlations were found between confidence scores and the self ratings of the ability to act: The better the observers rated themselves at acting, the more confident they were in their ability to detect truths and deceit.

STUDY 2: THE IMPACT OF LIE COMPLEXITY AND PERSONAL CHARACTERISTICS

METHOD

Participants

A total of 61 university students participated in this study, 26 males (43%) and 34 females (57%). Their average age was 21 years (SD = 1.9).

Stimulus material

In our ongoing research (Vrij, Edward, & Bull, 1999a), 90 nursing students were shown the video and were asked the three questions described in Study 1. One-third of the nursing students were requested to answer the questions truthfully, the remaining 60 nursing students were asked to lie about what they had seen. In order to motivate the liars to lie the following instructions were given: "This study is examining your ability to lie, because research has suggested that nursing ability is related to ability to lie effectively, so try and be as convincing as possible." Half of the liars were randomly allocated to the easy lie condition, and the other half to the difficult lie condition. The participants in the easy lie condition were told prior to the actual interview which three questions would be asked and were given time to prepare their answers. They could take as much preparation time as they wanted. Participants in the difficult lie condition had to lie spontaneously: They were unaware of the questions asked and were not given any time to prepare themselves. In order to prepare the stimulus material for Study 2, a random sample of 30 interviews were selected and fragments of those 30 interviews were copied onto another videotape. This tape consisted of ten truths, ten easy lies and ten difficult lies. The truths, easy and difficult lies were put on the videotape in a random order.

Procedure

The procedure of this study was identical to the procedure of Study 1. The following reliability coefficients were obtained: introversion (Cronbach's alpha = .79); public self-consciousness (Cronbach's alpha = .84); social anxiety (Cronbach's alpha = .89); ability to act (Cronbach's alpha = .81) and shyness (Cronbach's alpha = .91).

RESULTS

The accuracy scores and confidence scores for the three conditions (truths, easy lies and difficult lies) are given in Table 4.

Table 4: Accuracy and Confidence Scores as a Function of Lie Complexity

	Condition			
	Truth	Easy	Difficult	F(2, 118)
Accuracy	.53[a]	.59[b]	.51[a]	4.29*
Confidence	4.76[b]	4.53[a]	4.48[a]	6.06**

Note: Only means with a different superscript differ significantly from each other ($p < .05$).
*$p < .05$ **$p < .01$.

Table 4 reveals that observers were better at detecting easy lies (59%) than difficult lies (51%), $F(1,59) = 5.86$, $p < .05$, which was not predicted. Hypothesis 2 should therefore be rejected. A comparison with the accuracy rates for truths (53%) shows that the observers were relatively good at detecting easy lies. The confidence scores show that the observers were most confident in detecting truths.

Table 5 displays the correlations between accuracy rates and personal characteristics.

Table 5: Correlations between Personal Characteristics and Accuracy or Confidence

	Personal Characteristics				
	Acting	PSC	Introversion	Anxiety	Shyness
Accuracy					
Truth	.29*	–.07	–.23	–.17	–.10
Easy	.36**	.03	–.29*	–.15	–.17
Difficult	.07	–.08	.08	.07	.03
Confidence					
Truth	.33**	–.08	–.34**	–.28*	.39**
Easy	.22	–.04	–.26*	–.31*	–.40**
Difficult	.08	.05	–.22	–.15	–.29*

*$p < .05$; **$p < .01$.

Table 5 shows significant positive correlations between the self-rated ability to act and detecting truths and easy lies, indicating that the better the observers rated themselves in acting, the better they were at detecting truths and easy lies. These findings support Hypothesis 3a. The predicted positive correlations between accuracy rates and public self-consciousness were not found. Hypothesis 3b is therefore rejected.

Table 6 gives the correlations between accuracy rates and confidence scores.

Table 6 shows a significant positive correlation between the ability to detect easy lies and being confident about this ability. This significant relationship was not predicted.

Table 6: Accuracy—Confidence Relationship

Confidence	Truth	Accuracy Low	High
Truth	.21		
Easy		.37**	
Difficult			.09

*$p < .05$; **$p < .01$.

Table 5 shows the correlations between confidence and personal characteristics. Similar to the findings of Study 1, significant negative correlations were found between confidence and introversion, social anxiety and shyness, indicating that the more introvert, socially anxious and/or shy the participants were, the less confident they were in their ability to detect truths and easy lies. These findings support Hypothesis 5. Finally, Table 5 reveals an unpredicted significant correlation between the self-rated ability to act and confidence in detecting truths. Such a correlation was also found in Study 1.

DISCUSSION

The present experiments investigated differences in people's ability to detect high and low stakes lies (Study 1), and easy and difficult lies (Study 2). It was predicted that high stakes lies would be easier to detect than low stakes lies, which indeed was the case. A closer examination of the accuracy scores showed that observers were relatively poor at detecting low stakes lies, and relatively insecure in their ability to detect such lies. Perhaps the liars in the low stake lies condition did not experience much emotion while lying, and therefore gave no evident behavioral cues away.

It was also predicted that it would be easier to detect difficult lies than easy lies. This, however, was not the case. On the contrary, observers were better at detecting easy lies than difficult lies. It might be that liars in the easy lies condition were particularly prone to the motivational impairment effect, the tendency of motivated liars to control themselves too hard. All liars in the lie complexity study were told about the possible connection between being a good liar and being a good nurse. It is therefore reasonable to assume that all liars in this study were motivated to perform well. Liars in the easy lie condition were facing an easy lie task, and could therefore fully concentrate themselves on making an honest impression, which apparently went wrong. It might well be possible that easy lies would be more difficult to detect if the motivation message would not have been given prior to the lie task. This, however, would have made the difficult lie situation probably unrealistic. Without any motivation to perform well, liars in that condition would not have faced any consequences of getting caught and could therefore have shown clear signs of hard thinking while lying without bothering about it. Obviously, this would have been a situation rarely seen in real life.

It was further predicted that the ability to detect lies would be positively correlated with self ratings of the ability to act and with public self-consciousness. There was some support for the predicted relationship between the rated ability to act and the actual ability to detect lies, but only in Study 2. Unfortunately, we do not have a plausible explanation as to why the predicted correlations did not emerge in the first study. There was no support at all for the predicted positive correlation between public self-consciousness and the ability to detect deceit. We expected such a relationship because high public self-conscious people are probably experienced in interpreting someone's nonverbal behavior. They tend to adapt themselves to other people and interpreting someone's nonverbal behavior may be beneficial to achieve this aim. Perhaps high public self-conscious people were not successful in interpreting liars' behavior due to the specific characteristics of deception. In most situations, people convey their true feelings and thoughts, and people high in public self-consciousness may be good at decoding this information while paying attention to nonverbal cues. While lying, however, people attempt to hide their true feelings and thoughts (DePaulo, Epstein, & Wyer, 1993), and observers should not focus on what people want to convey but should focus on what they want to conceal. Perhaps, public self-conscious people are not better trained than others in doing this.

Apart from observers' ability to detect lies, their confidence in the ability to detect lies was also investigated. Three important findings emerged from the analyses. First, the accuracy-confidence relationship was, most of the time, not significant. This means that inaccurate lie detectors are as confident as accurate lie detectors, and that someone's confidence about his or her ability to detect lies cannot be used to predict that person's accuracy in detecting lies. Second, when the judges were confident of their belief as to whether the person was lying or telling the truth, the person tended to be telling the truth. This finding replicates that of DePaulo et al. (1997), in their meta-analysis of accuracy-confidence relationships in deception studies. They highlight the importance of this finding by suggesting that feelings of confidence might function as a measure of deception detection. In that case, judges should take their own confidence levels into account when determining whether someone is lying or not, and should judge a statement as truthful when they feel confident (even when they actually think that the person is lying). Third, as predicted, the more introverted, socially anxious, and/or shy the judges were, the less confident they were about their ability to detect deceit. This finding may have important implications. One way of improving people's ability to detect deceit is to teach observers the skills to do this, although, as we have argued elsewhere (Bull, 1989; Vrij, 2000), a suitable training program has not yet been developed. One might argue that the less confident people are, the more keen they will be on learning new ways to detect deceit, which implies that training programs will be especially beneficial to introverted, socially anxious, and shy people. A positive correlation was found between confidence and the self-rated ability to act. Following the same reasoning, this suggests that it will be difficult to teach new methods to detect lies to those who rate themselves good at acting. However, there may be less need for them to improve their skills, since Study 2 revealed positive correlations between self-rated ability to act and actual ability to detect lies.

REFERENCES

Briggs, S. R., Cheek, J. M., & Buss, A. H. (1980). An analysis of the Self-Monitoring Scale. *Journal of Personality and Social Psychology*, *38*, 679–686.

Bull, R. (1989). Can training enhance the detection of deception? In J. C. Yuille (Ed.), *Credibility assessment* (pp. 83–97). Dordrecht, the Netherlands: Kluwer.

Cheek, J. M., & Buss, A. H. (1981). Shyness and sociability. *Journal of Personality and Social Psychology*, *41*, 330–339.

DePaulo, B. M., Charlton, K., Cooper, H., Lindsay, J. L., & Muhlenbruck, L. (1997). The accuracy—confidence correlation in the detection of deception. *Personality and Social Psychology Review*, *1*, 346–357.

DePaulo, B. M., Epstein, J. A., & Wyer, M. M. (1993). Sex differences in lying: How women and men deal with the dilemma of deceit. In M. Lewis & C. Saarni (Eds.), *Lying and deception in everyday life* (pp. 126–147). New York, NJ: The Guildford Press.

DePaulo, B. M., & Kirkendol, S. E. (1989). The motivational impairment effect in the communication of deception. In J. C. Yuille (Ed.), *Credibility assessment* (pp. 51–70). Dordrecht, the Netherlands: Kluwer.

DePaulo, B. M., Kirkendol, S. E., Tang, J., & O'Brien, T. P. (1988). The motivational impairment effect in the communication of deception: Replications and extensions. *Journal of Nonverbal Behavior*, *12*, 177–201.

DePaulo, B. M., Lanier, K., & Davis, T. (1983). Detecting the deceit of the motivated liar. *Journal of Personality and Social Psychology*, *45*, 1096–1103.

DePaulo, B. M., Stone, J. L., & Lassiter, G. D. (1985). Deceiving and detecting deceit. In B. R. Schenkler (Ed.), *The self and social life* (pp. 323–370). New York, NJ: McGraw–Hill.

Edinger, J. A., & Patterson, M. L. (1983). Nonverbal involvement and social control. *Psychological Bulletin*, *93*, 30–56.

Ekman, P. (1989). Why lies fail and what behaviors betray a lie. In J. C. Yuille (Ed.), *Credibility assessment* (pp. 71–82). Dordrecht, the Netherlands: Kluwer.

Ekman, P. (1992). *Telling lies: Clues to deceit in the marketplace, politics and marriage*. New York, NJ: W. W. Norton.
Ekman, P. (1997). Deception, lying, and demeanor. In D. F. Halpern & A. E. Voiskounsky (Eds.), *States of mind: American and post-soviet perspectives on contemporary issues in psychology* (pp. 93–105). New York, NJ: Oxford University Press.
Ekman, P., & Friesen, W. V. (1972). Hand movements. *Journal of Communication*, *22*, 353–374.
Ekman, P., & Friesen, W. V. (1974). Detecting deception from the body or face. *Journal of Personality and Social Psychology*, *29*, 288–298.
Fenigstein, A., Scheier, M. F., & Buss, A. H. (1975). Public and private self-consciousness: Assessment and theory. *Journal of Consulting and Clinical Psychology*, *43*, 522–527.
Goldman-Eisler, F. (1968). *Psycholinguistics: Experiments in spontaneous speech*. New York, NJ: Doubleday.
Kashy, D. A., & DePaulo, B. M. (1996). Who lies? *Journal of Personality and Social Psychology*, *70*, 1037–1051.
Köhnken, G. (1989). Behavioral correlates of statement credibility: Theories, paradigms and results. In H. Wegener, F. Lösel, & J. Haisch (Eds.), *Criminal behavior and the justice system: psychological perspectives* (pp. 271–289). New York, NJ: Springer-Verlag.
Riggio, R. E. (1986). Assessment of basic social skills. *Journal of Personality and Social Psychology*, *51*, 649–660.
Vrij, A. (1991). *Misverstanden tussen politie en allochtonen: Sociaal psychologische aspecten van verdacht zijn*. Amsterdam, The Netherlands: VU Uitgeverij.
Vrij, A. (2000). *Detecting lies and deceit: Psychology of lying and its implications for professional practice*. Chichester: Wiley.
Vrij, A., Edward, K., & Bull, R. (1999a). *Lying as a function of lie complexity*. Unpublished data.
Vrij, A., Edward, K., & Bull, R. (1999b). *Lying as a function of stakes*. Unpublished data.
Zuckerman, M., DePaulo, B. M., & Rosenthal, R. (1981). Verbal and nonverbal communication of deception. In L. Berkowitz (Ed.), *Advances in experimental social psychology, volume 14* (1–57). New York, NJ: Academic Press.

Note

1. This project is sponsored by a grant from The Leverhulme Trust.

PART 5

VICTIMS OF CRIME

Chapter 20

THE ROLE OF SOCIAL INFLUENCE IN CRIME VICTIM'S DECISION TO NOTIFY THE POLICE

Martin S. Greenberg and Scott R. Beach

Criminal justice systems are typically viewed as representing a sequential series of stages of decision making. As such, the decisions of those who make the earliest decisions carry the greatest weight since these decisions determine which individuals will be subject to the discretionary power of later decision makers. Whereas the police have traditionally been thought of as the system's gatekeepers, victimization surveys conducted in the United States show that 60% of crimes that come to the attention of the police result from notification by the victim, while just 37% are reported by others, including bystanders (Bureau of Justice Statistics, 1985). It is for this reason that Hindelang and Gottfredson (1976) labeled the victim "the gatekeeper of the criminal justice system." That victims exercise their discretion to report or not report crimes has been well documented by victimization surveys in many nations. Surveys conducted in the United States (Rennison, 1999), the Netherlands (Van Dijk & Steinmetz, 1979), and Australia (Clifford, 1983) show that less than half of the alleged victimizations are reported to the police.

Efforts to account for victims' reporting decision have focused on characteristics of the situation and of the victim. This research shows that reporting is more strongly related to situational variables, such as the nature of the crime, than to characteristics of the individual, such as the victim's age, sex, and race. According to results from the ongoing National Crime Victimization Survey conducted in the United States (Rennison, 1999), the rate of reporting is highest for completed motor vehicle theft and lowest for household theft. In addition, reporting is higher for more serious than less serious crimes. This appears to be true regardless of how seriousness is measured. Thus, completed crimes are more likely to be reported than attempted crimes. Reporting is more likely for crimes of violence (e.g. robbery) than for property crimes (e.g. theft). Among violent crimes, those involving injury to the victim are more likely to be reported than those not involving injury. In the case of property crime, reporting is positively correlated with the value of the stolen property (Bureau of Justice Statistics, 1985; Maguire & Pastore, 1998). When victim characteristics are related to reporting, they interact with features of the situation. For example, higher reporting rates are observed for women than for men, but only for crimes of violence (Bureau of Justice Statistics, 1997; Rennison, 1999).

One variable that has received little attention from victimization surveys is the role of social influence in victim decision making. There is a strong intuitive and theoretical basis for assuming that social influence plays an important role in crime victim decision making. As Bard and Sangrey (1979) insightfully noted, "A crime victim's entire structure of defenses becomes weakened under the stress of violation, leaving him or her unusually accessible to the influence of others. This characteristic response makes the behavior of other people unusually powerful in the period right after the crime" (pp. 37–38). Indeed, as Asch (1952), Festinger (1954), and Schachter (1959) have shown, individuals are particularly likely to rely on others when confused and upset. In contrast to the enormous volume of research on the role of social influence on bystander decision making, occasioned by the 1964 murder of Kitty Genovese in New York (e.g., Latane & Darley, 1970), few studies have investigated the impact of social influence on victim decision making (Ruback, Greenberg, & Westcott, 1984). This is particularly surprising since, as we have noted, victims, and not bystanders, are the major activators of the criminal justice system. One of the few studies that examined the impact of others on victim reporting involved interviews with victims and others who had reported crimes (Van Kirk, 1978). Results from this study showed that almost half of crime victims delayed reporting their victimization as a result of talking with another person. Similar results were obtained in a multi-city interview study by Spelman and Brown (1981). However, both studies examined the influence of talking with others on delays in reporting, not on the decision to report the crime.

In this chapter, we briefly summarize findings from a multimethod research program conducted by Greenberg and Ruback (1992) on the role that social influence plays in a crime victim's decision to report a crime to the police. We then outline a model of victim decision making that emerged from this earlier work. The model provides a theoretical framework for viewing the impact of social influence on victim decision making. Following the presentation of the model, we discuss some recent findings from a community sample of crime victims.

Field-laboratory experiments

Our initial efforts to investigate the role of social influence in victim decision making took place in an off-campus laboratory. This setting allowed us to create victims of theft and to manipulate social influence factors. Participants consisted of over 1200 paid volunteers ranging in age from 17 to 66. They consisted of men and women, African–Americans and whites, and all were either professional or blue-collar workers from the greater Pittsburgh area. They were solicited via newspaper advertisements to participate in a study of "clerical efficiency" being conducted by a local business consulting firm—"Industrial Research Associates of Pittsburgh." The bogus organization was housed in a suite of offices located in a middle class retail section of Pittsburgh. In the course of their participation, participants earned $11 for their work on a clerical task. The money was subsequently "stolen" from them by one of our assistants posing as a participant. Another confederate, posing as either a bystander or a co-victim, subsequently attempted to influence them to call the police. (No calls were ever completed as the phone was not connected.) Six studies were conducted using this experimental paradigm. The results, which are described in Greenberg and Ruback (1992), clearly show that under appropriate conditions, a stranger can influence victims of a small theft to notify the police. The actions of a co-victim exerted a particularly strong influence on victims' decision making, causing them to all but ignore the advice of a bystander. However, when a co-victim was not present, bystanders exercised considerable influence over victims' decisions to call the police. Victims were most likely to follow the bystander's advice when the advice was specific (e.g., "call the police" as opposed to "do something"), when the bystander remained at the victim's side while the victim was deciding what to do, and when the bystander offered to support the victim in his or her future dealings with the police and criminal justice system.

Limitations of the experimental paradigm

There are several limitations of this paradigm. First, this paradigm dealt with only a single type of crime, and a very minor one at that. Second, since the money stolen from the participants was not in their possession when they entered the laboratory, their reactions might differ from victims who have something stolen from their purse or wallet. Finally, while the paradigm is informative about victims' susceptibility to influence, it tells us nothing about the frequency with which crime victims are typically exposed to social influence attempts in everyday life. How often do victims of real crimes seek out and receive advice from others about what to do, and does this vary with the type of victimization? In order to answer these questions, four studies were conducted. We asked actual victims of burglary, theft, robbery, and rape to provide information about their victimization experience.

Self-reports from real crime victims

The first study involved phone interviews with 364 female sexual assault victims who had reported their victimization to Pittsburgh Action Against Rape (PAAR), a rape crisis center in Pittsburgh. As shown in Table 1, 78% said that they had talked with others (family and friends) before making their decision to report the crime (72% reported it to the police). Of those who talked with others, 76% said that they received advice about what to do. Of those who received advice, 84% followed the advice given them.

Study 2 involved 58 burglary, theft, and robbery victims who had reported their victimization to the police. All were volunteers whose cooperation was solicited by the local police. They were paid $10 for a one-hour interview. As can be seen, while the majority of respondents talked with others and received advice about reporting the crime, the percentage of those who talked with others and received advice was somewhat less than that obtained in the first study. Participants in Studies 3 and 4 consisted of college students who had identified themselves as having been a victim of either a burglary or a theft in the preceding 12 months. Unlike respondents in Study 2, respondents in Studies 3 and 4 included Nonreporters (59% in Study 3 and 75% in Study 4). The major difference between Studies 3 and 4 is that the first involved written questionnaires and the second involved telephone interviews. The results of the two studies are generally consistent, with the one exception being that less than half the respondents in Study 4 (43%) said that they received advice from others. However, the results across all four studies present a fairly consistent picture of social involvement by crime victims immediately following their victimization. Most respondents talked with others before deciding what to do and received advice during these interactions. And, consistent with our theorizing, the vast majority of those who received advice followed the advice given to them. One problem with the four studies is that the participants may not be representative of those

Table 1: Results from Four Studies of Crime Victims Employing Self-Reports

	Study 1	Study 2	Study 3	Study 4
Type of Victim	Rape Theft	Burglary Theft Robbery	Burglary Theft	Burglary
Sample Source	Rape Crisis Centre	Police Records	College Students	College Students
Sample Size	364	58	97	98
Talked with Others	78%	62%	77%	85%
Received Advice	76%	58%	81%	43%
Followed Advice	84%	95%	90%	77%

Adapted from *After the Crime: Victim decision making.* by M. S. Greenberg and R. Ruback who are victimized. That is, each of the groups studied represented a special population of victims. The rape victims in Study 1 consisted of sexual assault victims who sought help from a rape crisis center. The burglary, theft, and robbery victims in Study 2 consisted solely of those who chose to report their victimization to the police. And, participants in Studies 3 and 4 were college students enrolled in introductory psychology classes. In order to test the generalizability of the findings to a wider population of crime victims, we investigated the importance of social influence in a community sample of crime victims. Before describing this study, we would first like to summarize the model of crime victim decision making developed by Greenberg and Ruback (1992) that emerged from this earlier phase of the research and that served as a guide for the study presented on the following pages.

A model of crime victim decision making

The model of victim decision making accords special importance to the role of social influence. As shown in Figure 1, there are three stages to the model, with social influence playing a role at each stage. First, victims label a suspicious event as a crime, second, they determine its seriousness, and third, they decide what to do. In order for a suspicious event to be labeled a crime, it must first be discovered. As can be seen, the mere discovery of a suspicious event is likely to trigger arousal and distress. Whether or not a suspicious event is labeled a crime depends on the individual's personal definition of what constitutes a crime (which may or may not agree with the legal definition) and the degree to which the event fits or matches that definition. If the event is not labeled a crime, there will be little incentive to notify the police. Others may provide information that will help the victim define the event as a crime or they may exert normative pressure to define the event in accordance with group norms. If victims label the event a crime, the level of distress is likely to increase, and they will move to the second stage of the model: determining the seriousness of the crime.

The more serious the event is perceived to be, the greater the ensuing level of arousal and distress. However, the model allows for a reverse possibility. In other words, the level of arousal and distress may influence how serious the crime is considered. Victims make this judgment of seriousness based on how "wronged" or unfairly treated they perceive themselves to be and how vulnerable they feel they are to subsequent victimization. The affective counterpart to these judgments are feelings of anger and fear. As can be seen, the sense of being wronged and feeling vulnerable is a function of (1) the unexpectedness of the crime, (2) the

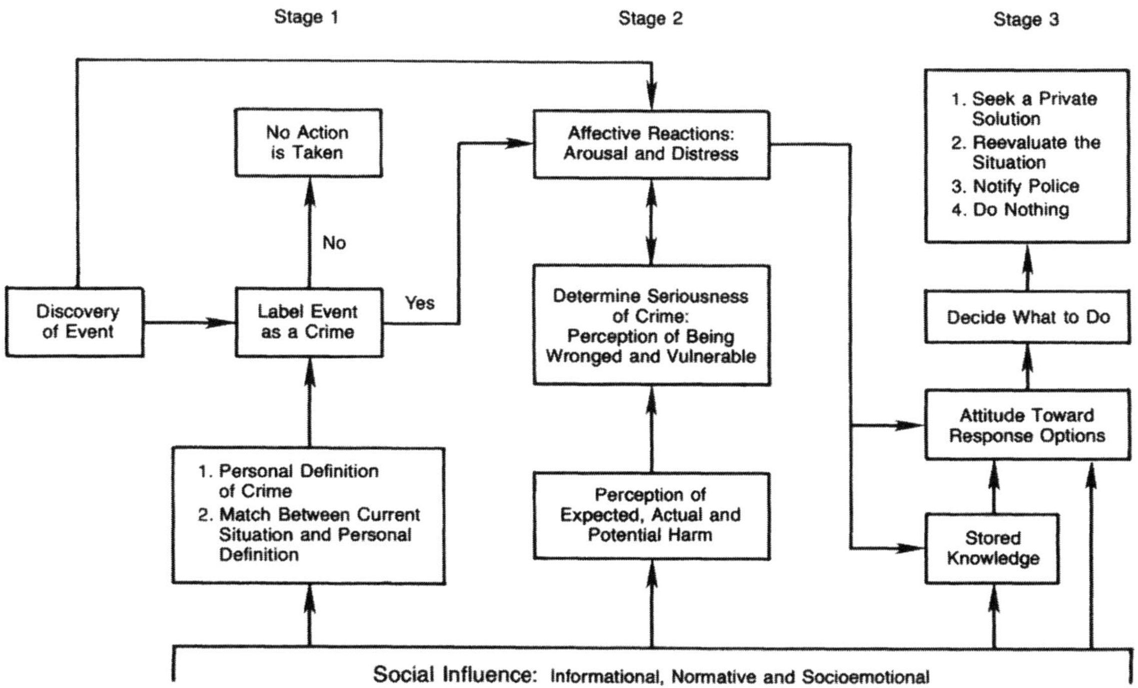

FIGURE 1. MODEL OF CRIME VICTIM DECISION MAKING. FROM AFTER THE CRIME: VICTIM *DECISION MAKING* BY M. S. GREENBERG AND R. B. RUBACK. COPYRIGHT 1992 BY PLENUM PRESS. REPRINTED BY PERMISSION.

perceived magnitude of actual harm (physical, material, financial, psychological), and (3) the perceived magnitude of potential or possible harm that could have occurred. Social influence could occur at this stage in the form of informational influence, normative influence, and socio-emotional influence that can either reduce or enhance the victim's sense of being wronged and vulnerable to future harm. Having determined the seriousness of the crime, victims then move to the third stage which focuses on deciding what to do from a set of options that may include (1) seeking a private solution, (2) cognitively reevaluating the situation, (3) notifying the police, or (4) doing nothing. The choice of option(s) will depend on the relative subjective utility of each option (i.e., expected benefits versus expected costs). Here too, others may exert influence in the form of advice, the application of normative pressure, and socio-emotional influence.

We are not proposing that the model is applicable to all victims or that victims must experience all stages. For some victims, the decision process may involve minimal mediating cognitive activity. Their decisions may be more reflexive than reflective. In such cases, no effort would be made to assess the seriousness of the crime or the utility of the various perceived alternatives. Once the incident has been labeled, the decision would be automatic or governed by simple heuristics, such as "when a crime occurs, the police should be called."

Interviews with a community sample of crime victims

Now, having described the model that guided our thinking, we will describe the study of social influence that employed a community sample of burglary and theft victims. The study was part of a two-wave panel study involving four groups: 1) victims of burglary, 2) victims of theft, 3) those with whom victims consulted immediately after the crime, and 4) a sample of nonvictims. The data reported derives from a subset of respondents who identified themselves as victims at wave 1.

METHOD

A computer-assisted random digit dialing procedure was used to identify victims of burglary or theft in the greater Pittsburgh metropolitan area for the preceding 12-months. At the time of the initial screening, respondents were asked a series of questions designed to determine the number and type of criminal victimizations experienced during the past 12 months. To qualify for inclusion, respondents had to meet the following criteria: (1) be at least 18 years old, (2) been a victim of either a burglary or a theft in the past 12 months (and not any other crime), and (3) been the person who made the decision to report or not to report the incident to the police. Those who qualified were offered $10 for a 30–40 minute computer-assisted telephone interview at a time that was convenient for them. This procedure yielded a sample of 422 victims of burglary and theft. The characteristics of the sample are presented in Table 2.

Table 2: Description of Sample of Respondents to Random-Digit Dial Survey

Type of Victim	Burglary: 31%	Theft: 69%
Report Status	Reporter: 46%	Nonreporter: 54%
Sex	Female: 65%	Male: 35%
Marital Status	Married: 52%	
Ethnicity	White: 85%	African-American: 13%
Age	Mean = 37.7	Median = 35
Family Income	Median = $30,000	
Education	Some College: 56%	

RESULTS

From our sample of respondents, 60% said that they had talked with others before deciding whether or not to call the police. These "others" tended to be a family member (60%) or a friend (24%). In 61% of the cases, the other person was present when the victim discovered the crime. Of those who talked with others, 47% received advice about what to do. In the vast majority of instances (84%), victims were advised to call the police. These findings mirror the findings from our earlier studies, and thus extend their generalizability.

In order to explore the role of social influence in victims' decisions to report the crime, we conducted a logistic regression analysis using variables derived from our model of victim decision making. We entered as predictors seven variables presumed to be operative at Stage 2 and one Stage 3 variable—Type of Advice. For purposes of economy, the seven Stage 2 variables were subjected to a principal components analysis with varimax rotation. Five of the variables loaded on a single factor that we labeled "Generalized Arousal." The five variables and their loadings can be seen in Table 3. The regression analysis included 11 variables.

They included (1) the generalized arousal measure, the two model variables that did not load on this factor: (2) how expected the crime was, (3) the amount of actual harm measured in terms of dollar loss, (4) type of advice, which was measured on a 2-point scale: advised to call the police (scored 1), received no advice or advised not to call the police (scored 0). And, for purposes of control, we also entered (5) participants' age, (6) sex, (7) race,

Table 3: Generalized Arousal Factor

Variable	Loading
Vulnerability	.80
Seriousness	.67
Wronged	.62
Potential Harm	.61
Upset	.60

Note: Alpha = .67.

(8) income, (9) education level, (10) marital status (3 dummy variables), and (11) type of crime. Since the measure of reporting was a dichotomous variable (report-not report), we analyzed the data using logistic regression. Participants with missing data on any of the variables were excluded from the analysis resulting in a final n of 391. The results of this analysis are presented in Table 4.

These data show that with all variables controlled, type of advice was the best predictor, with amount of actual harm, generalized arousal, and type of crime also significant predictors of reporting. Respondents were more than twelve and a half times as likely to report when they were advised to do so than when they received no advice or were advised not to report the crime, OR = 12.61, $p < .001$. They were over three and a half times as likely to report a burglary than they were to report a theft, OR = 3.65, $p < .001$; and they were more likely to report when the dollar loss was greater, OR = 1.37, $p < .001$, and when they were highly aroused, OR = 1.19, $p < .001$. The overall model chi square was highly significant, X^2 (13) = 170, $p < .001$.

These results show that advice from others was by far the best predictor of whether or not victims reported their victimization to the police. The data

Table 4: Logistic Regression Analysis on Reporting (n = 391)

Predictor	Odds Ratio
Type of Advice	12.61***
Actual Harm ($ loss)	1.37***
Generalized Arousal	1.19***
Type of Crime	3.65***
Expected Harm	1.10

Note. Demographic variables (i.e., age, sex, race, marital status, education, and income) were controlled for.
Coding for Type of Advice
0 = No Advice Received, Do Not Call Police.
1 = Call Police.
***$p < .001$.

further reveal that even when controlling for social influence (i.e., type of advice), other variables, such as the type of crime, the amount of the victim's losses, and the level of the victim's emotional arousal, independently affected the reporting decision. This finding suggests that in addition to social influence, there may be several alternative routes to reporting crimes to the police, such as the level of emotional arousal.

DISCUSSION

The findings from the community sample of crime victims attest to the importance of social influence in a crime victim's decision making. Results show that a substantial proportion of victims consulted with others when deciding whether or not to report the crime and that the advice received from others appears to have exerted a significant influence on their decision making. In effect, if one wants to know whether or not victims will notify the police, it may be useful to find out what advice they were given and who gave them the advice. The data are consistent with the proposed model of victim decision making in showing that type of advice, the only Stage 3 model variable entered in the equation, was the best predictor of reporting.

The results call attention to the need for more research on the decision process of those who advise victims in the immediate aftermath of the crime and what factors determine the type of advice offered to victims. In addition, future research should examine how victims choose who they will seek advice from, how much weight they give to others' accessibility and credibility (e.g., expertise, trustworthiness), and their belief that others are likely to reinforce a preliminary decision already made by them.

These results also have important policy implications for efforts to influence the level of reporting by crime victims. As Greenberg and Ruback (1992) noted, in order to make public policy recommendations, one has to choose from among three conflicting goals: (1) crime control, (2) victim welfare, and (3) system efficiency. If the primary goal is to control crime, then victims should be encouraged to report all crimes. However, if the goal is to improve the victim's welfare, then victims should be encouraged to be selective in their reporting. That is, they should be encouraged to report only those victimizations where there is a high likelihood of positive personal outcomes, such as retrieval of the stolen property. However, if the goal is to increase the efficiency of the criminal justice system, then we might want to encourage victims to report only the more serious victimizations. Since most nonreported crimes are of lesser seriousness (Rennison, 1999), increased reporting of all types of crime would inundate the system with paper work.

One possible outcome of this situation might be to reduce the system's efficiency in dealing with serious crime.

Of the three goals, we would place priority on public policy efforts to improve victims' welfare. One way to accomplish this is to help victims become more rational decision-makers in the period immediately following their victimization. Since, as our research has shown, victims are highly susceptible to the influence of others, efforts to improve victim decision making might be more effective if they are directed at those to whom victims turn to for advice. We would therefore favor educational campaigns that are directed at individuals in their role as advice givers rather than as victims. As such, our recommendation is similar to educational campaigns to reduce drunk driving. These campaigns are directed not at the drunk driver, but at those who are in a position to influence the drunk driver.

CONCLUSIONS

The present research adds to a growing body of evidence showing that social influence is an important determinant of crime victims' decision to notify the police. As such, the results are consistent with previous research on the role of social influence in bystander decision making. Our multimethod approach to victim decision making shows that a substantial number of victims, of different types of crime, consult with others immediately after the crime, and that the advice received from these others is the best predictor of whether or not the police will be notified. In addressing the public policy implications of these findings, we stressed the importance of first prioritizing among three often conflicting policy goals: crime control, victim welfare, and system efficiency. The present findings suggest that educational campaigns designed to improve the welfare of victims might be more effective if they were directed at those to whom victims turn to for advice and assistance.

REFERENCES

Asch, S. E. (1952). *Social psychology*. Englewood Cliffs, NJ: Prentice-Hall.

Bard, M., & Sangrey, D. (1979). *The crime victim's book*. New York: Basic Books.

Bureau of Justice Statistics. (1985). *Reporting crimes to the police*. Washington, DC: U. S. Department of Justice.

Bureau of Justice Statistics (1997). *Criminal victimization in the United States, 1994*. Washington, DC: U. S. Department of Justice.

Clifford, W. (1983). Victimology in Australia. *Victimology: An International Journal*, *8*, 35–44.

Festinger, L. (1954). A theory of social comparison processes. *Human Relation*, 7, 117–140.

Greenberg, M. S., & Ruback, R. B. (1992). *After the crime: Victim decision making*. New York: Plenum.

Hindelang, M. J., & Gottfredson, M. (1976). The victim's decision not to invoke the criminal justice process. In W. F. McDonald (Ed.), *Criminal justice and the victim* (pp. 57–78). Beverly Hills, CA: Sage.

Latane, B., & Darley, J. M. (1970). *The unresponsive bystander: Why doesn't he help?* New York: Appleton-Century-Crofts.

Maguire, K., & Pastore, A. L. (Eds.). (1998). *Sourcebook of criminal justice statistics 1997*. Washington, DC: Bureau of Justice Statistics.

Rennison, C. M. (1999). *Criminal victimization in 1998: Changes 1997–98 with trends 1993–98*. Washington, DC: U. S. Department of Justice.

Ruback, R. B., Greenberg, M. S., & Westcott, D. R. (1984). Social influence and crime victim decision making. *Journal of Social Issues, 40*(1), 51–76.

Schachter, S. (1959). *The psychology of affiliation*. Palo Alto, CA: Stanford University Press.

Spelman, W., & Brown, D. K. (1981). *Calling the police: Citizen reporting of serious crime*. Washington, DC: Police Executive Forum.

Van Dijk, J. J. M., & Steinmetz, C. H. D. (1979). *The RDC Victim Surveys 1974–1979*. The Hague: Research and Documentation Centre, Ministry of Justice.

Van Kirk, M. (1978). *Response time analysis: Executive summary*. Washington, DC: Law Enforcement Assistance Administration.

ACKNOWLEDGEMENTS

This research was supported by grants from the National Institute of Mental Health's Center for Studies of Crime and Delinquency (ROI MH 27526) and the center for the Studies of Antisocial and Violant Behavior (ROI MH 4336).

Chapter 21

STRUCTURED TRAUMA WRITING (*STW*) AS A VICTIM-SUPPORTIVE INTERVENTION: EXAMINING THE EFFICACY OF EMOTIONAL VENTILATION AND DOWNWARD WRITING[1]

Frans Willem Winkel and Eric Blaauw

The notion that the provision of psychological support to crime victims and to victims involved in traffic accidents constitutes an integral part of the criminal justice mandate is currently broadly adhered to, unlike some 20 years ago (Smith, 1985). Emotional support is mainly offered by individuals lacking extensive psychological expertise, such as police officers and volunteers engaged in victim support organizations (e.g., the National Association of Victim Support Schemes (NAVSS) in the UK, the Netherlands Victim Support (NVS), the National Organization for Victim Support (NOVA) in the US, and Association Plaidoyer-Victimes (APV) in Canada). However, early studies on the quality of police-based victim support revealed rather disappointing results (Skogan, 1984; Winkel, 1987). Programs proved to be either ineffective or even counterproductive. Similarly, more recent studies on volunteer provided victim support highlight the risk of backlash effects on victims' psychological re-adjustment (Fattah, 1999; Winkel & Renssen, 1998). Many volunteers and professionals, more or less explicitly, tend to foster the impression in clients that victims are helpless, and cannot cope on their own without the assistance of external supporters. Victims are easily labeled with the "Mark of Abel" (Fattah, 1999). In his discussion of potential "nocebo effects" and potential dangers of victim therapy, Fattah (1999, p. 201) suggests that many of the dangers of questionable and potentially harmful practices, such as overzealous therapists implanting false memories of sexual abuse during childhood or practices involving individuals who have adequate social support and do not suffer from specific vulnerability factors in psychological debriefing programs (Bisson & Deahl, 1994), can be traced to the fact that the methods and the techniques used are not based on solid empirical evidence or hard scientific facts. Instead, these practices stem from the popular tendency to pathologize natural symptoms and perfectly normal reactions and to fit these displays under new illness categories. Moreover, analyses done by Winkel and Renssen (1998) reveal a highly prevalent "upward bias" among victim assistance workers. This misperception refers to an incorrect expectation on the part of support workers regarding the direction of victims' social comparison processes: helpers tend to expect victims to engage in upward comparisons, on a comparison-dimension the victim is saying "I'm worse off" than the comparison target, while these victims actually engaged in downward comparison processes, such as "I'm better off". Three recent studies reported by Winkel, Blaauw, and Wisman (1999) not only underscored the high prevalence of downward comparison processes among crime victims, but also revealed that these victims profit psychologically from engagement in these processes. In other words, downward comparisons were vital in controlling fear of crime responses, and they were associated with more successful adjustment and with lower levels of reported trauma symptoms. Effective victim support in their view entails methods in which "downward signals" emitted by victims are reinforced by the support worker. A lack of sensitivity for such signals, such as an upward bias, may then seriously undermine the therapeutic value of current interventions.

In order to enhance the quality of victim support a series of field experiments, financially supported by the *Achmea Foundation Victim and Society*, were recently conducted in cooperation with NVS, including an exploration of the potential efficacy of Structured Trauma Writing (*STW*) in facilitating the process of coping with traumatic memory. For various reasons, *STW*, for example in the form of home work assignments to victims, in addition to face-to-face contacts with the support provider, may be an interesting supportive option as it explicitly calls upon the victim's own responsibility for coping outcomes, while it does not require extensive psychological skills and expertise from the support worker. Moreover, the written material produced by victims may give direction regarding the needed number, course, and nature of follow up victim-helper contacts.

Theoretically, the potential efficacy of *STW* in reducing trauma-symptomatology is underscored in that it provides the victim with an opportunity for (a) self confrontation, (b) for self-disclosure and emotional disinhibition, and (c) for "narrativation".

As to self-confrontation, the basic assumption underlying prolonged, in vivo or imaginal, exposure trauma-focused therapies is that explicit confrontation with the distressing episode will eventually result in extinction of the emotional response due to habituation (Foa & Meadows, 1997). Georges (1995, p. 11) recently concluded that "the disclosure of deeply personal topics as a therapeutic technique is an entrenched and long-standing feature of Western culture. Cross-culturally, as well, (self) confession-as-therapy is found in a widely diverse array of societies". Similarly, Borkovec, Roemer, and Kinyon (1995, p. 47) noted: "that verbal disclosure of traumatic events would lead to beneficial results, is an assumption upon which the majority of verbal psychotherapy rests". Non-disclosure, for example in the form of keeping one's negative thoughts or worries secret for others, is known to have deleterious effects on well being. Wegner and Lane's (1995, p. 31) empirically validated pre-occupation model suggests that nondisclosure sets into motion certain cognitive processes that can create an obsessive pre-occupation with a negative life experience. Their model comprises three steps: (a) secrecy causes thought suppression, (b) thought suppression causes intrusive thought, (c) intrusive thought causes renewed efforts at thought suppression, and (d) steps b and c continue in cyclic repetition, as each occurs in response to the other.

Constructing a narrative around the distressing episode (narrativation) appears to have a healing effect. Van der Kolk, Burbridge, and Suzuki (1997) examined the sensory modalities in which traumatic memories were experienced, like as a story, as an image, in sounds, as a smell, as bodily feelings, or as emotions. Most of their subjects initially remember the distressing episode in the form of somato-sensory flashback experiences, as "visual, affective, auditory, or kinesthetic imprints. As the trauma came into consciousness with greater clarity, more sensory modalities were activated, and a capacity to tell what actually had happened emerged over time" (p. 102). Most of their subjects reported that they initially had no narrative memory of the episode, in that they could not tell a story about what had happened. Initial storage is thus mainly in terms of sensory fragments that have few or no linguistic components. These outcomes lead Van der Kolk et al. (1997) to suggest that the incapacity to weave a coherent narrative out of these disparate sensory imprints and a failure to express the episode in communicable language lies at the very core of the pathology of Post Traumatic Stress Disorder (PTSD).

The popularity of *STW*, also as a trauma-focused type of intervention, is mainly due to the work of Pennebaker. Procedures in which clients write about their stressors were labeled as "Pennebaker's exercises" by Dominguez et al. (1995). Like Van der Kolk et al. (1997), Pennebaker's (1995) guiding idea was that a translation of upsetting experiences into words can promote physical and mental health. He recently noted that:

> A growing number of researchers from several disciplines have begun investigating why talking or writing about emotional upheavals can influence mental and physical health. For example, investigators have now found that writing about traumatic experiences produces improvements in immune function, drops in physi-

> cian visits for illness, and better performance at school and work. Similarly, other studies indicate that the failure to talk or acknowledge significant experiences is associated with increased health problems, autonomic activity, and ruminations (1995, p. 4).

Although *STW* has received some initial support as a potentially effective method to treat type C trauma memories (Winkel, 1998),[2] several studies (Schoutrop & Lange, 1997; Smyth, 1998) suggest that its beneficial impact is mediated by the type of writing instruction utilized. Writing about thoughts, deepest feelings, and emotions regarding the incident appear to work better than writing about the stressor per se. Curiously enough, however, almost none of the instructions used so far (Donnelly & Murray, 1991) resulted in a short term impact. If a beneficial effect emerged, it only did so after a substantial period of time. To explain this "sleeper effect", it was hypothesized that clients take advantage of this extra time period to arrive at new, more positive insights regarding the distressing episode.

To further test the potential short-term efficacy of *STW* on more common measures of trauma symptomatology, we exposed clients to two experimental instructions that aim to stimulate the formation of new insights more directly. In the emotional expression condition, clients were requested to write along the lines suggested by Pennebaker's combined instruction. The request to list the major insights the client had arrived at the end of each writing session was here added as a new element. In the downward writing condition, that also used an insight-listing procedure, clients were directly requested to write about their emotional upheaval from a more optimistic perspective. This downward writing task elaborated on the suggestions advanced by Winkel and Renssen (1998) and Winkel et al. (1999).

Individual difference variables may moderate the beneficial impact of *STW* (Cameron & Nicholls, 1998). In writing down their emotions, it may be more easy for an optimist to distance oneself psychologically from the written material, known as the distancing hypothesis, while for pessimists such writing may enhance the salience and vividness of the pertinent negative emotion, referred to as the salience hypothesis. Thus, emotional ventilation may be more beneficial for victims exhibiting dispositional optimism than for victims exhibiting dispositional pessimism. Similarly, writing from a more optimistic perspective, as is done in a downward writing task, is probably easier for optimists than for pessimists. Thus, the beneficial impact due to downward writing is expected to be bigger for optimists than for pessimists.

METHOD

STW OUTCOME STUDY

Participants

Participants were recruited via advertisements in two university newspapers: Ad Valvas of Vrije Universiteit Amsterdam, and Folia Civitatis of the University of Amsterdam. The sample consisted of 27 subjects, 23 females and 4 males (with a mean age of 24 years, $SD = 3.20$) who presented with various problems, such as the involvement in a violent criminal victimization, personal involvement in a serious accident, or the involvement of significant others in such an accident, and the unexpected, suicidal death of a loved one.

Participants were randomly assigned to two experimental writing tasks, which either focused on emotional expression or on writing from a downward perspective. Each writing session was preceded by a specific instruction. The primary instructions had a length of about 3/4 of a page in both conditions. Follow-up instructions were shorter and consisted of a summary of the main points. Elements of the emotional expression-condition included: "Please imagine the distressing episode and start writing, continuously for about 30 to 45 minutes, about your deepest fears, pain, and emotions regarding the episode. It is essential not to be critical about what you are writing. You may write whatever you like, and there is no need to spare anyone. You are writing for Yourself.[...]. Again, the intention is to write about your deepest thoughts and feelings regarding the incident. Let your deepest fear, pain, or emotions guide you while writing. Nothing is wrong, everything is allowed".

The downward writing instruction inter alia suggested that every victim is coping in his or her own way. Some victims cope relatively well, other victims cope less successfully. "The questionnaire you filled out for us actually suggests that you are coping 'well' (the other alternatives provided, namely 'on average', and 'less well' were crossed out by hand) in comparison to others, in particular given the circumstances. Please try to bear this in mind when you start writing about the episode. Please remind yourself that in comparison to other people you are dealing 'well' (other alternatives crossed out) with the present situation. Please try to imagine that it could have been worse, and that things took a relatively favorable turn".

Participants who engaged in four sessions of trivial writing, such as writing about their plans for tomorrow, served as controls. The control group consisted of 22 subjects,[3] who participated for course credit. A majority were female ($N = 16$). The mean age was 19 years ($SD = 1.5$).

Measures

Trauma-symptomatology was assessed via the Impact of Event Scale (IES; Intrusion and Avoidance Sub-scale; Horowitz, Wilner, & Alvarez, 1979), and the Anxiety and Depression Sub-scales of the Symptom Checklist 90 (SCL 90; Arrindell & Ettema, 1986; Derogatis, 1998). In addition, the Profile of Mood States (POMS; Wald & Mellenbergh, 1990) was administered both before and after completion of the writing task. Optimism was measured using a single item, rated on a 7-point scale ranging from optimistic to pessimistic.

Among the numerous self-report measures used to assess psychopathology, the SCL 90 is one that has received extensive clinical use, and has been the focus of much research interest (Carpenter & Hittner, 1995). SCL 90 was used in about 33% of the studies on PTSD diagnostic evaluations reviewed by De Girolamo and McFarlane (1996). Moreover, Derogatis (1998) noted that the instrument "is very well researched with more than 940 research studies demonstrating its reliability, validity, and utility". In the present study, ratings were requested for two symptom dimensions. Sample items illustrating anxiety included "suddenly scared for no reason, feeling fearful, and feeling tense or keyed up". Depression items included "thoughts of ending your life, feeling of being trapped or caught, and feeling no interest in things".

The second measure used to assess trauma-symptomatology was a Dutch version of the Impact of Event Scale (IES). The focus of this scale is on the classic trauma symptoms "Intrusions" and "Avoidance". Sample items illustrating intrusions include: "I thought about it when I didn't mean to", "I had trouble falling asleep or staying asleep because of pictures or thoughts about it that came into my mind", "I had waves of strong feelings about it", "Pictures about it popped into my mind", and "Other things kept making me think about it". Sample items illustrating avoidance include: "I avoided letting myself get upset when I thought about it or was reminded of it", "I tried to remove it from memory", "I stayed away from reminders of it", "I tried not to talk about it", and "I tried not to think about it".

Although some commentators suggest that IES and SCL 90 provide genuine and reliable indicators of chronic PTSD (see Rothbaum, 1997), other commentators voiced reservations. De Girolamo and McFarlane explicitly note that:

> The IES and the SCL 90 R have been used extensively, probably because of the ease of administration. Strictly speaking, they are not diagnostic instruments, but rather measures that document only some of the phenomena of PTSD and

> provide thresholds above which the probability of being diagnosed with PTSD can be defined. Thus, these instruments have shown good psychometric properties in a number of studies, but the extent to which they are able to generate reliable PTSD diagnoses is questionable. Rather, they are useful to screen subjects likely to be suffering from the disorder who should then be evaluated with a structured interview (1996, p. 55).

The present focus obviously was on initial screening and testing STW efficacy, and not on precise diagnosing per se. Moreover, both instruments were characterized as sensitive to therapeutic change (Rothbaum, 1997).

RESULTS

MANOVA's were conducted on the basis of a time (pre/post test) representing a within-subjects factor by instruction type (emotional expression versus downward writing) by client type (optimism/pessimism) design, in which the latter two variables represented between subject factors. Analyses revealed a multivariate main effect due to time, $Fm(9,216) = 62.81$; $p < .001$, and a time by optimism interaction, $Fm(11,253) = 2.55$; $p < .01$. No main effects due to instruction or interactions with instruction emerged. The major outcomes are summarized in Tables 1 and 2

Univariate analyses revealed the multivariate main effect to be due to significant effects of time on Intrusions, $F(1,25) = 25.87$; $p < .001$, on Avoidance, $F(1,25) = 16.17$; $p < .001$, and on the Anxiety Sub-scale of the SCL 90, $F(1,25) = 6.73$; $p < .05$. Table 1 reveals that clients' post-test scores on these dimensions were more favorable than their pre-test scores, suggesting that writing had a beneficial impact on general trauma symptomatology. In view of their pre-test scores, clients in both conditions met the criteria for PTSD, as IES scores were substantially higher than the cut-off-point of 38 as suggested by Rothbaum (1997). Post-test scores on IES clearly fell outside the critical PTSD-region.

Table 1: Trauma Symptomatology: Pre-test and Post-test Means (and Standard Deviations) by Experimental Condition (Emotional Expression versus Downward Writing)

Trauma Writing Condition:	Emotional Expression		Downward Writing	
	Pre-Trauma Writing	Post-Trauma Writing	Pre-Trauma Writing	Post-Trauma Writing
Symptomatology	M (SD)	M (SD)	M (SD)	M (SD)
Intrusion	26.36 (8.35)	15.50 (9.04)	24.69 (7.42)	18.00 (8.15)
Avoidance	22.71 (11.91)	14.08 (12.37)	19.31 (10.28)	12.00 (6.76)
Anxiety/Arousal	23.14 (7.04)	21.07 (8.87)	23.77 (7.97)	19.46 (8.04)
Depression	37.21 (14.79)	35.86 (11.61)	38.15 (13.20)	36.08 (10.41)
Profile of Mood States	46.20 (14.74)	40.73 (16.58)	59.75 (25.81)	62.08 (24.02)

Table 2: Trauma Symptomatology: Pre-test and Post-test Means (and Standard deviations) by Dispositional Optimism/Pessimism

Individual Differences: Trauma Writing (Combined):	Optimists		Pessimists	
	Pre-Trauma Writing	Post-Trauma Writing	Pre-Trauma Writing	Post-Trauma Writing
Symptomatology	M (SD)	M (SD)	M (SD)	M (SD)
Intrusion	24.72 (8.64)	14.67 (8.03)	27.00 (5.51)	20.00 (9.59)
Avoidance	21.00 (10.48)	10.94 (7.81)	18.29 (13.24)	15.86 (12.79)
Anxiety/Arousal	23.06 (6.86)	17.72 (5.41)	23.43 (9.81)	26.29 (12.09)
Depression	34.00 (9.86)	32.72 (10.05)	40.86 (18.28)	40.71 (10.52
Profile of Mood States	46.39 (16.38)	41.67 (16.85)	55.00 (23.57)	63.71 (18.45)

An inspection of Table 2 suggests that effect sizes were generally bigger for optimists than for pessimists. The multivariate time by optimism-interaction particularly consisted of significant interactions on Anxiety, $F(1,23) = 9.52$; $p < .01$, and on the Profile of Mood States, $F(1,23) = 4.63$; $p < .05$. Table 2 reveals slight increases in arousal and in negative mood for pessimists, while such side effects did not emerge in optimists.

Instruction type appears not to have resulted in differential effects. However, the analyses conducted so far typically involved group-based comparisons, which did not take individual improvement, or no change or even deterioration, into consideration. In general, treatment effects due to therapy are typically inferred on the basis of statistical comparisons between mean changes resulting from the treatments under study. This use of statistical significance tests to evaluate treatment efficacy is limited in various ways. Jacobson and Truax suggest that:

> The existence of a treatment effect has no bearing on its clinical significance. Questions regarding the *efficacy* of psychotherapy refer to the benefits derived from it, its potency, its impact on clients, or its ability to make a difference in people's lives. Conventional statistical comparisons between groups tell us very little about the efficacy of psychotherapy (1991, p. 12).

Jacobson, Folette, and Revenstorf (1984, 1986) proposed various methods for defining clinically significant change in psychotherapy research. One of these methods was a reliable change index (RC), which was later amended by Christensen and Mendoza (1986), entailing that RC $= x_1 - x_2/S_{diff}$, where x_1 represents a subject's pre-test score, x_2 represents that same person's post-test score, and S_{diff} is the standard error of difference between the two test scores. When RC is greater than 1.96, it is unlikely that the post-test score is not reflecting real change. RC tells us whether change reflects more than the fluctuations of an imprecise measuring instrument. The major outcomes of a RC-analysis per case are summarized in Table 3.

In half of the subjects who were engaged in downward writing, significant improvements emerged on intrusive symptoms. On these symptoms, downward writing was 10 times more likely to result in clinically significant improvements compared to controls, and was more than twice as likely to have a beneficial impact in comparison to emotional expression. Moreover, the odds of improvement in subjects who were engaged in emotional ventilation relative to controls were 4 to 1. Relative to controls, downward writing appeared to be ineffective in accomplishing reliable changes in avoidance symptoms. On this dimension, emotional writing clearly outperformed both relative to controls, and to subjects engaged in downward writing.

From a clinical perspective, Table 3 suggests that emotional writing has a general, although more modest, impact on both types of symptoms, while downward writing has a more specific and substantial beneficial impact on intrusions. The RC analyses suggest that instruction type does have a differential impact that did not emerge in the more conventional type of analyses. As intrusions appear to be more critical, in terms of coping with a traumatic memory, downward writing clearly deserves further research attention.

DISCUSSION

The rapid worldwide proliferation of victim support organizations working in close cooperation with the criminal justice system is a remarkable development in terms of therapeutic jurisprudence (Wexler & Schopp, 1992). The ultimate criterion then, to evaluate its social significance, is the actual therapeutic impact and quality of these services on victims. As to support quality, the above outcomes further validate the notion that STW may facilitate trauma-resolution. Moreover, they offer some suggestive evidence for speeding up the recovery process. The current writing-paradigm, unlike

Table 3: Proportions of Clients Exhibiting Clinically Significant Improvements on Intrusion—and Avoidance Symptoms by Type of Writing Task (Emotional Expression, Downward Writing, and Trivial/Control Writing)

	Reliable Improvement ($RC_{>1.96}$)	
Symptoms:	Intrusions	Avoidance
Trivial Writing/ Controls	.05	.09
Emotional Expression	.21	.35
Downward Writing	.50	.08

previous procedures, at least resulted in short-term effects. The design used, however, does not permit to isolate the specific contribution due to the insight-listing utilized as a new element in both instructions, while longer-term stability was not assessed. The RC-analyses, although partly based on a quasi-experimental setup through the inclusion of a non-randomized control group, in combination with the more conventional analyses, point to potentially different pathways underlying the instructions' impact on intrusive symptomatology. Downward writing appears to have a direct effect on intrusions, while emotional expression appears to have an indirect effect on intrusions via a reduction of avoidance responses. Emotional writing thus appears to break the intrusion-avoidance cycle, which for some clients tends to perpetuate traumatic memory. The direct effect of downward writing might be mediated by a more direct priming of new, more positive insights relating to the episode. To validate this hypothesis, a further analysis of the actual narratives produced by clients is required. Future studies might profit from integrating the current instructions, for instance by starting with two emotional writing sessions, followed by two or more sessions of downward writing. To enhance ecological validity, the impact of various "integrated" *STW*-tasks should be assessed against a random sample of crime victims or victims involved in a traffic accident receiving more traditional types of NVS-victim support. In view of its relative ease of implementation, *STW*—procedures appear to offer fertile vehicles for reinforcing the quality of victim support.

A basic formula underlying effective victim support is that (1) the right type of client, such as victims who actually need external support, receives (2) the right type of treatment from (3) the right type of support provider. For most victims, after a crime occurs, police officers are their first official contact. Thus, the police are a frontline organization for selective referral of "needy victims" to victim support agencies. Effective referral assumes the implementation of objective, instead of subjective or self-referral systems, which are common in most countries, referral rules (Winkel & Vrij, 1998), such as the RISK4—decision rule, recently developed by Wohlfarth and Winkel (1999).[4]

A major impediment to effective treatment, noted in the introduction, is the high prevalence of "upward biases" among support providers. Particularly susceptible to such biases appear to be support workers with heavy caseloads, those who exhibit burn out, and workers exhibiting a professional "Mark of Abel" orientation, who expect almost every victimization to constitute a psychological catastrophe for victims (Fattah, 1999). These outcomes underscore the necessity to implement training programs focusing on downward comparison theory in victim support circles, and to design admission procedures, that carefully screen for the therapeutic quality of volunteers who wish to participate in support organizations as support providers. A nice additional feature of implementing *STW*-procedures, as forms of "programmed self-instruction", is that they provide an autonomous buffer against the potential negative influence of upward biases on victims' coping potential.

REFERENCES

Arrindell, W. A., & Ettema, J. H. M. (1986). *SCL 90: Handleiding bij een multidimensionele psychpathologie-indicator*. Lisse: Swets Test Services.

Bisson, J, I., & Deahl, M. P. (1994). Psychological debriefing and prevention of posttraumatic stress: more research is needed. *British Journal of Psychiatry*, *165*, 717–720.

Borkovec, T. D., Roemer, L., & Kinyon, J. (1995). Disclosure and worry: Opposite sides of the emotional processing coin. In J. W. Pennebaker (Ed.), *Emotion, disclosure, and health* (pp. 47–71). Washington, D. C.: American Psychological Association

Cameron, L. D., & Nicholls, G. (1998). Expression of stressful experiences through writing: effects of a self-regulation manipulation for pessimists and optimists. *Health Psychology*, *17*, 84–92.

Carpenter, K. M., & Hittner, J. B. (1995). Dimensional characteristics of the SCL-90-R: evaluation of gender differences in dually diagnosed inpatients. *Journal of Clinical Psychology*, *51*, 383–391.

Christensen, L., & Mendoza, J. L. (1986). A method of assessing change in a single subject: An alteration of the RC index. *Behavior Therapy*, *17*, 305–308.

De Girolamo, G., & McFarlane, A. C. (1996). The epidemiology of PTSD: a comprehensive review of the international literature. In A. J. Marsella, M. J. Friedman, E. T. Gerrity, & R. M. Scurfield (Eds.), *Ethnocultural aspects of posttraumatic stress disorder: Issues, research, and clinical applications* (pp. 33–87). Washington, DC: American Psychological Association.

Derogatis, L. R. (1998). *Symptom Checklist-90-R*. http://assessments.ncs.com/assessments/tests/scl90r.htm.

Dominguez, B., Valderrama, P., De Los Angeles Meza, M., Perez, S. L., Silva, A., Martinez, G., Mendez, V. M., & Olvera, Y. (1995). The roles of disclosure and emotional reversal in clinical practice. In J. W. Pennebaker (Ed.), *Emotion, disclosure, and health* (pp. 255–271). Washington, D. C.: American Psychological Association.

Donnelly, D. A., & Murray, E. J. (1991). Cognitive and emotional changes in written essays and therapy interviews. *Journal of Social and Clinical Psychology*, *10*, 334–350.

Fattah, E. A. (1999). From a handful of dollars to tea and sympathy: the sad history of victim assistance. In J. J. M. van Dijk, R. G. H. van Kaam, & J. Wemmers (Eds.), *Caring for Crime Victims* (pp. 187–207). Monsey, New York: Criminal Justice Press.

Foa, E. B., & Meadows, E. A. (1997). Psychosocial treatments for posttraumatic stress disorder: a critical review. *Annual Review of Psychology*, *48*, 449–480.

Georges, E. (1995). A cultural and historical perspective on confession. In J. W. Pennebaker (Ed.), *Emotion, disclosure, and health* (pp. 11–25). Washington, D. C.: American Psychological Association.

Horowitz, M. J., Wilner, N., & Alvarez, W. (1979). Impact of Event scale: A measure of subjective stress. *Psychosomatic Medicine*, *41*, 209–218.

Jacobson, N. S., Follette, W. C., & Revenstorf, D. (1984). Psychotherapy outcome research: methods for reporting variability and evaluating clinical significance. *Behavior Therapy*, *15*, 336–352.

Jacobson, N. S., Follette, W. C., & Revenstorf, D. (1986). Toward a standard definition of clinically significant change. *Behavior Therapy*, *17*, 308–311

Jacobson, N. S., & Truax, P. (1991). Clinical significance: A statistical approach to defining meaningful change in psychotherapy research. *Journal of Consulting and Clinical Psychology*, *59*, 12–19.

Pennebaker, J. W., (Ed.), (1995). *Emotion, disclosure, and health*. Washington, D. C.: American Psychological Association.

Rothbaum, B. O. (1997). A controlled study of EMDR in the treatment of posttraumatic stress disordered sexual assault victims. *Bulletin of the Menninger Clinic*, *61*, 317–334.

Schoutrop, M., & Lange, A. (1997). Gestructureerd schrijven over schokkende ervaringen: resultaten en werkzame mechanismen. *Directieve Therapie*, *17*, 77–97.

Smyth, J. M. (1998). Written emotional expression: Effect sizes, outcome types, and moderating variables. *Journal of Consulting and Clinical Psychology*, *66*, 174–184.

Skogan, W. G. (1984). *Recent experiments in fear reduction. A summary of research conducted by the Police Foundation 1983–1984*. RDC: The Hague.

Smith, C. B. (1985). Response to victims: are the institutional mandates of police and medicine sufficient. *Victimology*, *10*, 560–573.

Van der Kolk, B. A., Burbridge, J. A., & Suzuki, J. (1997). The psychobiology of traumatic memory: clinical implications of neuro-imaging studies. In R. Yehuda, & A. C. McFarlane (Eds.), *Annals of the New York Academy of Sciences* (Vol. 821, pp. 99–114). Psychobiology of Posttraumatic Stress Disorder. New York: New York Academy of Sciences.

Wald, F. D. M., & Mellenbergh, G. J. (1990). De verkorte versie van de Nederlandse vertaling van de Profile of Mood States (POMS). *Nederlands Tijdschrift voor de Psychologie*, *45*, 86–90.

Wegner, D. M., & Lane, J. D. (1995). From secrecy to psychopathology. In J. W. Pennebaker (Ed.), *Emotion, disclosure, and health* (pp. 25–47). Washington, D. C.: American Psychological Association

Wexler, D. B., & Schopp, R. F. (1992). Therapeutic jurisprudence: a new approach to mental health law. In D. K. Kagehiro & W. S. Laufer (Eds.), *Handbook of psychology and law* (pp. 361–383). New York: Springer.

Winkel, F. W. (1987). *Politie en voorkoming misdrijven: Effecten en neven-effecten van voorlichting*. Amsterdam: Mens en Recht Foundation Press.

Winkel, F. W., & Vrij, A. (1993). Facilitating problem- and emotion focused coping in victims of burglary: evaluating a police crisis intervention programme, *Journal of Community Psychology*, *21*, 97–113.

Winkel, F. W., Denkers, A., & Vrij, A. (1994). The Effects of Attributions on Crime Victims' Psychological Re-adjustment. *Genetic, Social and General Psychology Monographs*, *120*, 147–169.

Winkel, F. W. (1998). Verkeersongevallen en geestelijke schade: het Achmea-model van trauma-verwerking. *Handboek Personenschade*, Supplement 2, 5–9.

Winkel, F. W. (1998a). Fear of crime and criminal victimization: testing a theory of psychological incapacitation of the "stressor" based on downward comparison processes. *British Journal of Criminology*, *38*, 473–485.

Winkel, F. W., & Renssen, M. (1998). A pessimistic outlook on victims and an "upward bias" in social comparison expectations of victim support workers regarding their clients: Uncovering a potential threat to the quality of victim-supportive interactions. *International Review of Victimology*, *5*, 203–220.

Winkel, F. W., & Vrij, A. (1998). Who is in need of victim support: the issue of accountable, empirically validated selection and victim referral. *Expert Evidence*, *6*, 23–41.

Winkel, F. W. (1999). Repeat victimization and trauma-susceptibility: Prospective and longitudinal analyses. In: J. J. M. van Dijk, R. G. H van Kaam, & J. Wemmers (Eds.), *Caring for crime victims* (pp. 207–221). Criminal Justice Press: Monsey, New York.

Winkel, F. W., Blaauw, E., & Wisman, F. (1999). Dissociation-focused victim support and coping with traumatic memory: An empirical search for evidence sustaining the effectiveness of downward comparison based interventions. *International Review of Victimology*, *6*, 179–201.

Wohlfarth, T., & Winkel, F. W. (1999). *Improving the quality of referral to victim support: A study on the identification of victims in need of psychological support*. Stichting Achmea Voortgangs-Rapport. Vrije Universiteit Amsterdam: Dept. of Social and Clinical Psychology.

Notes

1. Preparation of this chapter was facilitated by a grant from the Achmea Foundation Victim and Society (*Stichting Achmea Slachtoffer en Samenleving*). We are indebted to Dr. Sanne Douwes for data-gathering and analyses.
2. STW—impact on more common measures of trauma symptomatology was seldom studied (see also Schoutrop & Lange, 1997).
3. Raw scores on Intrusions and Avoidance were made available by A. Lange and M. Schoutrop. For more detailed information we refer to Schoutrop and Lange (1997).
4. RISK4 entails 4 simply worded questions with a dichotomous response format. Referrals based on a cutoff-point of 2 (e.g., two affirmative answers by the victim) result in acceptable hit- and false alarm rates with regard to the prediction of future psychological problems, in particular the emergence of PTSD symptoms 1 and 3 months after reporting to the police (sensitivity = .75; specificity = .83). Questions relate to the perceived seriousness of the episode (Winkel & Vrij, 1993), downward expectancies (Winkel, 1998a), character attributions (Winkel, Denkers, & Vrij, 1994), and to prior victimizations (Winkel, 1999).

Index

For Product Safety Concerns and Information please contact our EU
representative GPSR@taylorandfrancis.com
Taylor & Francis Verlag GmbH, Kaufingerstraße 24, 80331 München, Germany

www.ingramcontent.com/pod-product-compliance
Ingram Content Group UK Ltd.
Pitfield, Milton Keynes, MK11 3LW, UK
UKHW022115190926
475702UK00013B/1455

* 9 7 8 0 4 1 5 6 5 4 0 0 5 *